The View from the Fortieth Floor

THE
VIEW
FROM
THE
FORTIETH
FLOOR

by

Theodore
H.
White

WILLIAM SLOANE
ASSOCIATES
NEW YORK

to Gladys R. White

In my time of reporting, I have witnessed, from within, the collapse of three great publishing enterprises and have observed, from the close fringes of friendship, at least as many other such disasters. Almost any American reporter of this generation can claim similar experience. It would be preposterous, therefore, to insist that such disasters have not furnished my imagination with various suggestions for this story. But it would be even more preposterous for the reader to assume that any character in this tale ever existed in actual life, or that the situation, the problems, the events here chronicled ever transpired in reality. The characters are entirely imaginary, and bear no relation to any person, living or dead.

T.H.W.

PART ONE

1. Monday in November

Warren closed the door of the car deliberately behind him, controlling the impulse to hurry. He motioned the chauffeur off, then entered the marbled lobby of the building.

The impulse to hurry had been swelling for weeks now—faster, faster, to rip faster into the accumulation on his desk, somehow to tear from the mound of papers the problem they hid. But he knew that any conspicuous haste, as any motion, any gesture, any frown, any smile he showed would be translated by office gossip into meaning and significance. Warren saw the little knot of people at the foot of the elevators opening before his coming as at an invisible force and was aware that their eyes were on him—friendly, yet wary. The elevator door was opening and Warren quickened his step. But the starter, seeing him, had thrown out his arm to block the way to all but him. "Good morning, Mr. Warren," he called.

Warren stepped in, the starter stepped back, the doors flicked shut and up the elevator shot, expressing Warren to the fortieth, the top, the executive floor of General American Publishing Company.

Habit had carried him within minutes down the corridor, through the anteroom, into his great square corner office, to the closet where he hung his coat, back to his desk. His hand was almost on the buzzer to summon Laura, his secretary, when he saw the proof sheets on his desk.

It was already ten of this Monday morning; he was late; work pressed—but there was his own face, smiling up from the picture on the proof-page. It was a muddy reproduction, as all proofs are, and Warren catalogued the type-face instantly as being that of a news-weekly. Someone of his own staff must have acquired an advance page-proof of an issue that would not be on public sale until the weekend.

Warren's hand drew back from the buzzer. His feet slowly came up on the desk, and he lifted the page to look at the picture more closely. It was a good picture.

He was shaking hands with Eisenhower and he noted again the particular buoyancy of the Eisenhower smile—but when was it? It must have been in Paris, before Eisenhower went home to be President. And Eisenhower was not in uniform. Now he remembered—it was the Sunday afternoon, when they had brought him around to Eisenhower's villa at Marnes-la-Coquette, to be introduced formally as a new ECA Ambassador.

Six years ago.

Warren studied the picture again. Have I aged as much as he since then? Or does a man ever know when he begins to age? Warren touched his temples where the black hair was just beginning to fleck with the first touch of silver—it did not show yet. It was the smile that was different. The touch of the boy in the face of the man standing smiling beside Eisenhower was no longer there. It was probably a better face then than now—the dark eyes twinkling, as if half-amused by the pomp of the ceremony, the black hair neat yet somehow slightly ruffled too, the broad mouth suppressing a grin.

Warren was smiling now, but differently.

Under the bold black head, the story ran for more than two columns:

WAKING GIANT

Last week a sleeping giant stirred and was heard once more in the land.

Trumpet, the once-great, long-ailing, loss-leader of General American Publishing Company's stable of magazines (*Trumpet*, *Gentlewoman*, half-a-dozen small specialty weeklies) announced that next spring it would guarantee marketers an audience of six million readers on its way to an eventual seven million, to reclaim supremacy among general weekly magazines.

One Man Plus The Truth

In the magazine world, this was like a blast from the dead—cause for rejoicing to friends, for consternation to rivals. Founded in 1890 by iconoclast Abbott Shalom Pepper (his warcry: One Man Plus The Truth Makes A Majority), *Trumpet* for half a century blasted Pepper's truths and prejudices into American ears. It blew the horn for such once unpopular causes as free silver, women's votes, income taxes, Al Smith. It blasted away savagely at trusts, railways, municipal corruption, crooked sports. Each year Pepper launched a new crusade, with each issue inflamed American nerve ends, lost many a flamboyant battle, won many another now established in the law and custom of the land. With unerring instinct, *Trumpet* also touched the simpler, homely concerns of the American heart, for Ab Pepper was as single-minded about fine foods, cats, smoking (he was against it), speeding (he demanded that all speeders be flogged), as he was about wars, politics, elections. By spring of 1940 when Ab Pepper dropped dead (of stroke, said his magazines, of overeating, said his friends), his magazines had become a

national institution thronged with American memories of muckraking, ging-
ham dresses, five-cent cigars, booms, depressions, wars and happy yesterdays.

It took ten years for the world to recognize that buried with Pepper's roaring voice was the voice of his magazines. Left in custody of a Board of
Directors named by the family estate, uncertain *Trumpet* floundered from
editor to editor (six in fourteen years). From an ad-fat profit-maker (average
issue at peak: 186 pages), weekly *Trumpet* dwindled to a starving ghost
(average issue this year: 92 pages). Monthly *Gentlewoman*, whose feminine
flare Pepper had left to softer hands, suffered less from his death, nonetheless
hobbled slowly downhill. But so powerful was the echo of Pepper's voice
that *Trumpet's* audience still climbed after his death (though slowly), did
not begin to dip until two years ago (postwar low: 4,500,000).

The Giant's New Jockey

The voice that last week boasted of the change in fortune of the giant was
as different from Ab Pepper's as the shrill of a jet from the crack of a bull-
whip. It came from tall, smooth, Roman-nosed John Ridgely Warren, 47,
the giant's newest jockey, a newcomer to New York and big-time publishing
two years ago. When some-time-devout-New Dealer, one-time-Marshall-Plan-
Ambassador, later slick-Washington-operator Warren was appointed President of General American Publishing two years ago, he was regarded as the
magazines' liquidator. Warren's total experience in journalism had been two
years as an agency reporter in Washington twenty years before, his reputation
since that of a colorful, yet cold, executive. But hustler Warren, whose ad-
ventures in World War II earned him two medals, a wound, a near court-
martial, meant business.

First to feel his muscle were the aging family custodians of the Board who
had invited him to the Presidency. Warren quickly trimmed their number
from twelve to a tight seven, emerged as Chairman. For two of the seven
places, he recruited tight-fisted financier Walter J. Morrissey and a Morrissey
henchman (their credentials: $4,500,000 of new financing). Next he turned
his guns on *Trumpet's* staff, firing its last embattled editor, pensioning off
its ulcerated advertising chief. With new staff blood in their places and on
Gentlewoman, with new equipment in his Massachusetts plant (a risky
$2,000,000 investment in new color and other presses), Warren quietly
nursed the giant back into the race.

The Engineer

Last week, Jockey Warren flexed the giant's muscle in public. *Trumpet's*
circulation, he claimed, had chalked up a net gain of almost three quarters
of a million this year, since this fall has been scoring consistently but ex-
pensively over its new five-million guarantee. Its target in the next twelve

months: six million; by the mid-sixties, seven or eight million. Also bouncing with vitality, said he, was *Gentlewoman*—a plump five-million plus.

Cynics, noting Warren's claims, noted also that advertising to feed the giant had failed to follow circulation up, wondered how long the giant could stand the costly pace. Said Warren cockily last week: "Times change. These days we engineer our majorities. If we engineer our share of the attention, we'll get our share of the market."

That was all. The story was good, the space it occupied magnificent. Warren tossed the magazine aside with a deep sense of relief. He had been afraid for weeks that one such story might assemble the fragments of gossip into the explosive truth. So might the anonymous writer of this story have done had he been able to perceive reality beneath the impeccable facts and figures he quoted; but he had not.

This, then, was still the public picture. It was going to be all right.

Warren swung his feet to the floor, rose, stretched, went to the window. The world beneath glittered. The city that he could see, falling away in the stern geometry of its splendor, wore an entirely different air today. Last week, under the clouds and the rain, while the fear swelled in him, the city had scowled, and danger crouched in its hidden ambuscades. Today, the sun flooded the spectacle of Manhattan below, bouncing its brilliance from a hundred thousand mirroring windows, trilling its sparkle off the delicate tracery of frost that edged his pane, sweeping the glass-blue skies of autumn clean.

New Monday. New week. New deck. New chance.

Briskly, he turned back to the desk, pressed the buzzer for Laura, and drummed his fingers impatiently on the desk as he waited for her to enter. Today, he knew, was going to be good. His mind still on the story and the circulation figures, he watched Laura enter, sit down, and adjust her pad and folders. Then, smiling to apologize for his brusqueness, he said, "Hi, I'm late. Have to catch up. Let me have the outside calls first."

She flipped her pad with its list of telephone calls.

"Mr. Campbell of Intertone Ink, wanting to speak to you."

"That's for Austin to deal with," said Warren. Austin was the Treasurer. It was up to Austin to pay—or to postpone—the routine traffic of bill payment. They both knew what Mr. Campbell wanted. He wanted money.

"I know," said Laura, "but he said he specifically wanted to speak to you."

"Tell Austin to call him," he replied firmly. Campbell could wait a few weeks more.

"Silverman of East Coast Paper," she read next from her pad.

"Silverman, too?" repeated Warren, an involuntary grin puckering. "Both of them before ten on Monday morning? Silverman himself?"

"Yes. I managed to pass Silverman to Austin. But he sounded nasty."

"Good girl," said Warren. He did not want to think of Silverman. He listened to the other outside messages, disposing of each with a sentence, then asked, "What's the inside traffic like?"

She shook her head as she flipped the page, and brought a memorandum out from beneath it.

"The usual crazy Monday, only worse. Everyone wants to see you— advertising, editorial, finance, production— Well, anyway," she continued, handing over the memorandum she had brought out, "Russell brought this up himself about ten minutes ago. He wanted to make sure you read it early today, and then asked me, please, to slip him in to you as soon as possible."

"What's it about?" he asked, taking the paper.

"About advertising. Not good. You read it. Hopkins wants to see you, too. He's in town today from Anderbury, says he has a problem."

She waited. Russell was Chief of Advertising Sales, new on the job. Still it was not like Russell to hand-carry a message from his own twenty-seventh floor all the way to the fortieth floor. Warren liked Russell, his own new choice. And he liked Hopkins, too. Hopkins had been with the firm, time out of mind, up from press man at the Anderbury plant where they rolled out the magazines to chief of all production there. Both with problems.

"Who else?" asked Warren.

"Purcell called. And Foley called. They both want you to come downstairs to the story conference on the Christmas issue this afternoon, only Purcell calls it a 'Creative Push.' Foley was furious when I said Purcell had already invited you. Then he said he wanted to see you too. So does Purcell. So does Austin."

She paused.

"Come on," he smiled, "there must be somebody else, too."

"Eliot. Eliot says he wants to see you. Personally. Personally but importantly. That's his word, 'importantly,' not mine."

She had plucked at the nerve endings of the organization, and it would take him a minute to sort out the quivering interconnections fogged in this blur of names. But each name was a fragment of a problem. Foley—

Managing Editor of *Trumpet*. Old Team, Managing Editor for twelve years. Purcell—New Team, Warren's own choice, brought in as editorial director of all publications last year. But no editor between them. Ever since Warren had fired the last editor of *Trumpet* a year ago, he had avoided hiring a responsible new editor, hoping that between them Foley and Purcell could work out *Trumpet's* problems to his satisfaction. But they were fighting. He could not see them both this morning, and to see one and not the other would aggravate matters.

"All right," he said finally. "I take it I ought to see Russell first. Then . . . what about my lunch with old man Bronstein, is that set up?"

"Yes. Your usual table at the Skyline Club. Russell will meet you in the lobby and go on with you to that."

"That leaves Purcell, Foley, Eliot and Hopkins—all between Russell and quarter to twelve. I tell you what," he said, grinning again, "let's ask them all up here at eleven o'clock, along with Silverman and Campbell, and they can all talk to each other. Then you and I could go into the other room and get some work done."

He rose from his chair again, began to pace, then turned.

"Who sounds the most excited?" he asked.

"Well," she replied, "Eliot screams the least. But he sounded as if he meant it. Shall I put him after Russell?"

The telephone's ring cut them short.

"I'll get it," said Laura. He nodded, then heard her voice.

". . . Oh, good morning, Mr. Morrissey . . . yes . . . yes . . . he's in conference now . . . I'll see if I can."

Her eyes turned to him a question.

Warren hesitated. He had dodged Morrissey's calls twice last week. Ever since Morrissey had come on the Board of Directors last year, a call from him meant trouble.

"I'll take it," he said to Laura, "but get Russell up here fast. Then the others—let's see, I'll talk to Eliot. Baby the rest along until this afternoon."

He waited until Laura had left, then, turning to the telephone he had barely said "Hello" when the familiar, harsh, grit-lined voice was in his ear.

"Warren, it's me, Morrissey."

"Yes, Walt," said Warren.

"Warren," said the voice abruptly, "I don't like this whole goddamned situation. It stinks. I want to talk to you."

"Go ahead, Walt—that's why Alexander Graham Bell invented the telephone."

"Goddamnit, I don't mean talking on the telephone. I want to talk to you across a table. We got an idea."

"Yes, Walt."

"What I'm calling for is this . . . say, you listening there, Warren?"

"Of course, Walt."

"O.K. My crowd feels we ought to get together before next month's Board meeting. Can't do any real work at a big meeting full of lawyers and hired hands. Ought to get set for action, you know what I mean? You listening there, Warren?"

Warren was listening. The voice with its chopped sentences, its easy swing between vulgarity and charm, between coarseness and subtlety had fascinated Warren for a full year. When Morrissey wanted to charm, the voice could achieve a silken elegance. But Morrissey had not been charming to Warren for months. Now, his voice was hard.

"I'm listening, Walt," said Warren, "but I don't follow. Spell it out for me."

"Board meetings don't do a goddamned bit of good, Warren. You know that. Particularly this Board. It stinks. Jerks. Can't do anything at next month's meeting unless we're set before then, unless we decide what's got to be done, and then we tell them. See?"

"Just what are you getting at, Walt?" asked Warren. "There's no emergency, no reason—"

"What the hell do you mean, no emergency?" snarled Morrissey. "First of the year coming up. Bills got to be paid. Bank wants to be paid. Creditors want to be paid. If the bills don't get paid, we're bust. You listening, Warren? Bust! Do you want to wait for the marshal to come with a subpoena? You listening, Warren? Can you pay the year-end bills with what's in the till, can you raise it?"

"Take it easy, Walt," said Warren, his voice trying to mollify the growling telephone. "You ought to see this week's circulation figures. We've outsold everyone in the field at newsstands for the third week running, we're delivering more circulation than ever before in history, the All-America issue going on press now has a print order of five million eight—"

"Oh the hell with that," rasped Morrissey's voice, "I don't give a damn about those figures. That's the crazy end of the magazine business. All I know is you price a copy at fifteen cents, you get back nine cents, and the goddamn book costs us twenty, twenty-five, thirty cents to manufacture. So you lose fifteen, twenty cents every time you sell a copy. So you sell two hundred thousand more copies, we've lost another thirty, forty thousand bucks. Unless you get more advertising to pay the freight. And you ain't getting it. Balance-sheet figures are all that counts. Either we're solvent or we're not. Worth more than we owe, or we ain't. No two ways about it. Warren—you listening there?"

"I'm listening," said Warren, furious.

"You following me, Warren? I don't want to wait until the Board meeting next month, then decide we've got to decide to fold the magazines. I want a couple of us to decide now—you and me, we're responsible. You got me into this thing—"

"Walt, I'm responsible to you for your money and no more. Those debentures of yours are fully covered. But while I sit at this desk I'm responsible for running these magazines and I share that with nobody else—"

"You're responsible for a hell of a lot more, Warren," said Morrissey. "That corporation has three other divisions, and when you gamble those other divisions on the goddamn magazines you're gambling with property I bet my money on. Those magazines are a couple of toys. I didn't put up four and a half million dollars just to earn five per cent on debentures. I want to convert those debentures into a stock that's going to double my money, and if those magazines—"

"Walt," broke in Warren, "those magazines have been in business for sixty years, and I didn't come here to liquidate them. Anytime you can talk the Board into liquidating them, you can also talk the Board into firing me—"

There was a pause, and then Morrissey's voice had changed. It was softer, sly.

"Nobody's talking about firing you, Ridge. But you've got to be careful yourself, too. You're President of this corporation. Chairman of the Board. Chief Executive Officer. Not only of the magazines but all the rest of the properties. You've got personal responsibility. You know they have laws about bankruptcy. You keep on spending the corporation's money when the books tell you you're broke, and then you're spending money that already belongs to creditors. Not your own money to spend any more. Legal situation on that makes you responsible. Civil responsibility, though. Not criminal responsibility unless they can prove— You listening there, Warren?"

Warren could see the man's thin face on the screen of his mind, could see Morrissey's thin, pointed tongue flick out, slick over his lips, then suck in again, ready to stab—

"Walt," snapped Warren, "is that all you have to say? You broke in on a conference saying it was urgent!"

"From where I sit, Warren," came the cold voice, "everything's goddamned urgent. There's a pot of money to be made in this. End of the year coming up, all sorts of tax angles to be thought of, bank-line of credit coming up for renewal— You think over what I said. Didn't expect you to say yes or no on the telephone. Just think it over, then call me back and we'll talk turkey."

The phone clicked silent with no good-by. For a moment, Warren held the dead phone, then put it down with exaggerated control, reflecting that he really did not hate Morrissey. He did not hate Morrissey any more than he hated tigers, eagles, sharks, or other beasts of prey. It was Morrissey's nature to behave as he did. There had been a clean razor-edged logic about Morrissey from the very beginning—the logic of money, the logic of arithmetic. If the figures did not balance, then Morrissey would pounce. That was the nature of the animal.

But he must not sit here, waiting for Morrissey to pounce.

He must—

The buzzer on his desk rang. He answered it, and Laura spoke.

"Russell is here," she said.

He had forgotten Russell. He ought to read that memorandum first. "Give me a minute," he said, "I'll buzz when I'm ready."

Warren picked up Russell's memorandum and began to read.

RIDGE—it said, in capitals—

THEY KISSED US FIRST.

THEN WHEN I WAS ENJOYING IT, I FELT THE SNICK OF THE BLADE AND MY THROAT WAS CUT.

YOU'LL SEE BY THE MAKEUP SCHEDULES THAT WE'VE LOST THE CRANBERRY ACCOUNT IN TRUMPET.

LENOX HIMSELF CALLED WITH THE NEWS. THE CHARMBIT FOR FIVE FULL MINUTES. HOW IMPRESSED HE AND ALL OTHER AGENCIES WERE BY JUMP IN OUR CIRCULATION. EVERYONE WATCHING AND ROOTING FOR US. GREAT JOB WE'RE DOING.

THEN THE HARD WORD. HE HATED TO SAY IT. HE WASN'T SPEAKING FOR HIMSELF. ALL ADVERTISING AGENCIES JUST SERVANTS OF THEIR CLIENTS HE SAID. CRANBERRY GROWERS FELT SOMETHING HAD TO BE CUT OFF ADVERTISING APPROPRIATIONS FOR THIS YEAR'S HOLIDAY SEASON AND HAD TO BE MAGAZINE

COMMITMENTS—BECAUSE THEY CONCENTRATING HEAVY ON LAST MINUTE TV PROMOTION. THUS HAVE TO PARE DOWN MAG ADVERTISING. THUS HAVE TO CANCEL FOUR PAGES SCHEDULED TRUMPET IN PRECHRISTMAS ADS. SORRY SO CLOSE TO OUR DEADLINE. ALSO HAVE TO THIN OUT GENTLEWOMAN CONTRACTS FOR NEXT YEAR. DOWN FROM TWELVE PAGES TO FOUR. BUT NO CRITICISM IMPLIED SAID HE.

CRAP.

EYE SAID: SIX MONTHS AGO ALL YOU BASTARDS YELLING FOR NUMBERS. NOW WE GIVING YOU NUMBERS, GUARANTEEING FIVE MILLION CIRCULATION FOR TRUMPET, FIVE MILLION FOR GENTLEWOMAN. WHAT ELSE DO YOU WANT?

HE SAID: NOT MINIMIZING OUR ACHIEVEMENT. BUT TOO EARLY TO JUDGE TEXTURE OF NEW AUDIENCE COMING INTO OUR READERSHIP FIGURES. WHO ARE THEY? HE ASKED. NEED TIME OVER THERE TO EVALUATE IDENTITY OF OUR AUDIENCE. JUST KEEP ON DOING WAY WE'RE DOING THOUGH, HE SAID, EVERYONE COMMENTING ON OUR CIRCULATION GAINS. SO SORRY TO BREAK CRANBERRY COMMITMENT THIS LATE DATE.

COULD SUE THEM IF YOU WANT. BUT NO PERCENTAGE DOING SO, I THINK. ANY TIME AGENCY AS BIG AS LENOX, FORD & MADIGAN WANT TO BREAK CONTRACT FOR SPACE THEY CAN GET AWAY WITH IT. IF WE SUE THEM, MAYBE CAN MAKE THEM PAY, MAYBE NOT. BUT THEN THEY BLACKLIST US FOR ALL OTHER ACCOUNTS THEY HANDLING. WHICH MEANS WE LOSE A HELL OF A LOT MORE DOUGH THAN THIS.

FRANK.

P.S. MUST TALK. SITUATION SERIOUS.

Reading the memorandum, Warren's mind automatically translated the blow into money. Four pages of *Trumpet,* for which advertisers paid 25,000 dollars a page made a total of 100,000 dollars which had been canceled; eight pages of *Gentlewoman* at 26,000 dollars was another 208,000 dollars—altogether 300,000 dollars of gross that could not be expected in next year's figures. But it was not the lost gross that made him wince. It was the way the wind blew.

Russell's memorandum, taken with the circulation reports, did not make sense. It mocked all the planning, despised his gamble.

It had seemed so simple two years ago on first coming here, when it seemed everything could be engineered. First, and above all things, you needed audience numbers. Therefore you engineered attention, which brought audience numbers to circulation, which brought advertisers, which brought profit.

And then, after that, you were free and in the clear—free to perform magic, free with a rhythm and purpose that was more than money, free as Abbott Pepper had been free to stand astride a nation and make it listen to his truths.

But first the numbers. That had been the gamble—that the numbers and audience came first, then the money—then the magic and the truths could come later. Win or lose, everything had been staked on it. Now he had numbers. But no advertisers. Hence no money. And he was out so far, for so long, that if the gamble did not work, he could not turn back. It was too late to change course—to change course needed time and money. With Morrissey breathing down his neck.

With an angry jab Warren pressed the button to summon Russell, then took the memorandum in his large square hands to study it again.

When he lifted his eyes, Russell was in the room, standing, waiting to sit down. Lithe and graceful, Russell normally bubbled. Given a silk hat and cane, a white scarf and white gloves, Russell, usually, appeared ready to swing into a tap dance. But not this morning. His smile was serious.

"I was hoping you'd read that," said Russell.

"Sit down," said Warren, "let me look it over once more and see if it reads the same way the second time as it did the first. The only way the rest of the week can go from here is up."

"It reads the same way," said Russell. "Believe me, under this polished exterior, I'm bleeding, Ridge, bleeding. Been bleeding all morning, hemorrhaging. Bind my wounds."

Warren ignored Russell's remark and dropped his eyes again to the memorandum. It was from Russell's desk that rose the combat reports of the front where the magazines must thrive or perish. It was he who commanded the ninety-six salesmen of the two magazines, the huntsmen who were supposed to bring back the contracts for pages of advertising in the two magazines which would swell the magazines with wealth. But who did not.

"I still don't get it," said Warren to Russell.

"It's all there in the memo," said Russell, "and I can understand Lenox canceling the pages in *Trumpet*. It's a general magazine. TV hits harder, quicker than we do and if the cranberry people want to heat up impulse buying just before Thanksgiving and Christmas, maybe TV is better for them. But canceling *Gentlewoman* is different, that hurts. They want to make cranberries a year-round item, they say, and we're one of the two or three media that really blanket the kitchen—"

"I wish they'd make cranberries taste better while they're at it," broke in Warren, not meaning to be irrelevant, but now they were on cranberries he knew he did not like the way cranberries tasted.

"What?" asked Russell, puzzled.

"Nothing," said Warren, "go on."

But Warren was not listening now, he was thinking about cranberries and why cranberries no longer tasted like cranberries. He had not seen cranberries since he had come home from Europe—real, live cranberries, that is, that pop their tender skins and squirt their pink-white pulp into a boy's mouth, making his face pucker with the acid-sweet. Now cranberries came in cans, and the labels on the cans changed every year as the packagers retooled words, colors and taste as market surveys indicated. Ever since the end of the war Warren could remember eating only the jellied cranberry pulp in which, under the too-sweet taste of sugar and syrup, was buried the faint memory of boyhood and going with Mother to Mr. Jackson's store and ladling the glowing berries, live and fresh, from the barrel into the brown paper bag, and bringing them home and watching Mother in the kitchen jelly them herself, not too sweet, not too sour, but just right. The smell of the cranberries simmering on the old iron stove was the first fragrance of the holiday season. But now cranberries happened all year round, slung out of cans at restaurants, hotels, dinner parties, drugstore counters, at once more common and more elegant, because Lenox, Ford & Madigan had designed a new image for the country. Just the way everything got redesigned from the back of a steer's rump to the breastbone of a turkey, to the taste of mustard and pickles so that the greatest absorption of the redesigned product in the over-all market could be engineered right into product quality. They claimed they could engineer anything for a broader market by knocking the highs and lows off the taste spectrum. But when it came right down to cranberries, what they really meant was just adding more sugar. Warren wondered how many consumer surveys had gone into redesigning cranberries into this pulp that moved along the supermarket shelves—and what survey over there in Lenox's shop had engineered his magazines off their list of advertising media?

Not wanting Russell to know his attention had wandered, Warren decided to take over the conversation by questioning.

"Well, *why*, Frank—what's their real reason?"

"Why?" repeated Russell. "That's why I came to see you. Not just about cranberries. About all the accounts. Ridge, look, my salesmen have got to have some ammunition to shoot with. We need—"

Warren cut across him. "Frank, when you joined us in January, you were yelling for an audience to peddle to the advertisers. You were yelling for readership. For numbers. It's cost us a fortune to engineer the kind of circulation you said you needed to sell. Now you've got two packages of five million each—solid, audited, guaranteed circulation! Why can't you sell them to the advertisers?"

"Ridge," said Russell earnestly, "have you ever been out selling space on the Avenue? When what you're selling is nothing more than a flick of attention in the readers' minds, and you can't prove whether the flick is there or not, and they can't either? When you know the competition's been in there twice this week, cutting your throat?"

"But those numbers—" began Warren, only this time Russell was cutting him off, with an odd intensity Warren had never noticed in his debonair advertising chief before.

"It's not numbers alone that count, Ridge. That was only the beginning; if circulation had been falling, we'd be dead. They know the numbers over there. They count them as carefully as we do. But they buy by hunch. They need the numbers only to justify their hunch. It's what *kind* of numbers, that's what matters. Or what we can make them believe about our numbers. Like that oil-mouth Lenox. 'Identify the audience,' he says to me. That's what they all want. Ever since TV began to bite the meat off our bones. Identity."

Russell was speaking very rapidly, as if not wanting Warren to break in. "That's the change, Ridge, you've got to see it, you've got to be out there to see it. TV, what it's doing to us. Any advertiser who wants balloon figures, then TV gives it to him— Sock! One big sock! And there are thirty million bluejays every night, any night you want, just people with no identity and no personality who lie there on the couch, with their belts unbuckled after dinner, waiting to see if the sheriff will really plug the bad guy. And while they lie there with their minds turned over in the dark to the idiot-box, they're nothing but appetites. You can sell green toothpaste to people who never even brushed their teeth ten years ago, or Slippy-Glo to their wives, promising it'll wave their hair and clean the sink at the same time— Ever since 'fifty-four, Ridge, we've been facing it. The ad-men have to present magazines to their clients now on a basis of numbers plus. Numbers plus identity, Ridge, we got to—"

But Warren stopped him again. "Frank," he said, getting up from behind his desk, walking out, circling the desk to the couch where he sat down so that Russell had to swivel in his seat to follow him, "hey, Frank —take it easy, you don't talk that way downstairs, do you?"

Russell lifted his eyebrows in astonishment. Then he smiled, rose, made a dapper bow and his mien changed. He pulled a gold cigarette-case out of his pocket, lit a match, lit the cigarette, which he cocked jauntily in his mouth, then held the match out for inspection.

"Look, cousin," said Russell, "no shakes, not a quiver! Downstairs, on my floor, they almost believe I *threw* the cranberry account out of the book on your personal instructions."

Then he sat down abruptly and the smile vanished; he spoke again, somberly. "Ridge, if I can't let go on you, where can I? When you suckered me into this job and told me it was going to be tough, I had no idea how tough. Do you know what I'm up against on the advertising floors? I have ninety-six salesmen here and in the branch offices. And they're *demoralized*. Do you know what demoralized means? It means Merrill who sells space to food accounts for *Trumpet*. Merrill comes in from Larchmont every morning on the nine-oh-five and heads straight for the nearest bar and two quick shots of whiskey. Not on the way home—on the way *in*. What he takes on the way home, I don't know, and it's none of my business. But what he takes on the way in *is* my business and it means he can't face it. I have three or four guys like that, all of them infecting the rest."

"Fire him!" broke in Warren. "Fire Merrill."

"No," said Russell, "I can't. Because I have at least thirty people down there on the advertising floor who've been giving their living guts to this firm for twenty or twenty-five years. I arrived in January. I'm still an outsider. These people have kids who were born on paychecks from this firm. They expect to send those kids to college on paychecks from this firm. If I fire an old-timer like Merrill because he's cracked under strain, I shake the morale of all the rest who think this place is home. I'll bet I could name five people right now who are putting in as much time scouting for new jobs as selling space for us. I know for sure that Page has been leaking every secret we have to *Spectacle*, hoping he can switch to their payroll—"

"Fire Page," said Warren. "Fire him now, don't wait."

"I'm going to fire Page right after Christmas," said Russell, "but I've been waiting for a big new account so I can fire on the upbeat, not the downbeat. Only the big new account hasn't come in, and I spend more of my time putting heart into that shop than I do engineering a new sales approach."

"All right, Frank," said Warren, "say it clearly, you came upstairs looking for something, for an answer from me. What do you want? What do you need?"

"I need . . ." said Russell, groping for words ". . . Ridge, this may sound like YMCA stuff to you, but I need, we need a point of view. The magazines have to stand *for* something or *against* something, and I don't care what it is. TV can assemble blank appetites, but we can't any more—we can love or hate or denounce or cheer, I don't care what, just so long as people feel it's important what we do and reach for the next issue because they want to see how we do it. We either have to guarantee seven or eight or nine million circulation to advertisers to compete with TV—or else we have to offer a personality, a point of view that makes people need to listen to us. Otherwise all we're selling is two magazines offering five million certified copies of each page through the mails and on one hundred thousand newsstands, and it isn't enough. My salesmen have got to be able to explain who we are, what we are—"

Warren was glad Russell had paused as he did. It saved the exertion of cutting him off so that this mood of despair could be sealed up here, on the Executive Floor. With an apparent unconcern, which he did not feel, Warren now leaned back on the couch, and sprawled full length.

"Frank," he said finally, "let's relax. Some day we'll both sit here and laugh about the cranberry account. Some day we'll take Lenox's favorite account and toss it out of our pages. We'll blacklist him, the oil-mouth. Some day we'll both lie on our yachts, no, you'll bring your yacht up alongside mine, and we'll both lie on the sundeck of my yacht in the sun and we'll laugh."

"I can't wait," said Russell. "When do I pack? Can I bring my wife?"

"Bring your mother-in-law, too," said Warren, "it's going to be a big yacht. But let me tell you first how we got there. Eighteen months ago I took a calculated risk. I gambled that every nickel of cash I could nurse away from the other divisions of the corporation, every nickel I could borrow, would go into building audience for the magazines. Then I decided to get the best advertising man in New York to retrain the sales staff to be ready for the circulation jump when it came, when we had them listening—that was you."

"Who?" said Russell, his voice now light again. "Who—me?"

"Then we had to reorganize production and editorial and circulation to get more numbers. Then finally when the magazines began to pull— that was the strategy—they'd beat their knuckles raw to get advertising into our pages."

"What happened to that strategy?" asked Russell calmly, as if he were examining Warren's problems, not Warren his.

"Things got out of phase," said Warren, still making himself relaxed, "partly money, a lot of my time wasted just getting money. Partly person-ality problems taking over an old organization. But we *have* the fastest-growing audience in the industry now. Now the problem is editorial—Meaning. Identity. And I'm moving on it. I know what you need. I've ordered a survey from Carnahan Associates on the pattern of our reader-ship, who they are, what they want to read, the bounce-back we get from them. Five thousand depth interviews with our readers around the coun-try, seventy-five thousand dollars to establish an identity we can promote. It'll be on the desk in January."

"Nice, if you can do it," said Russell. "Seventy-five thousand dollars is cheap enough if you can buy a personality with it. But what do I do until January? I'd like to put my staff in an icebox until I can send them out with a new pitch."

"I'll tell you what we do," said Warren, now that he had Russell in a good mood.

Warren rose, walked slowly to his desk, leaned over with his two hands pressed on the glass top and said in a voice he meticulously restrained, "I'll tell you what *you* do. You *sell*. When I brought you over here, I jumped your salary from thirty thousand to forty thousand dollars. That's as much as I make myself. That extra ten thousand is ulcer money. Any guy with an order book can take advertising when a magazine is strong. But you have to make bricks, for the time being, without straw. You've got to sell, and your staff has got to sell whether they have to strip naked on Madison Avenue in midwinter or seduce the media-buyers' secretaries. You have to pass your ulcer on to every salesman on your staff. And what's worse, do you know what's worse?"

"What?" said Russell.

"You've got to laugh while you're doing it, and they've got to laugh. I don't care if I have to subsidize a joke clinic over here, you've got to laugh. Because when you're afraid in this town, they smell it on you. They smell it on you the way a dog smells meat. And when they smell you're afraid, you're through. I chose you on your record as the best advertising man in New York. You can't leave here whipped and I can't either; neither one of us can hire out to someone else. You're part of my gamble, Frank," continued Warren, still standing. "If you've got to bleed, do it up here with me in this office, nowhere else. I know you have troubles. Leave the editorial end of it to me, the whole identity thing. Leave the thing lie until we have this survey in, and we'll see how we can doctor it."

Russell rose now, the normal jaunty Russell, and turned to the door.

At the door, he stopped, stuck two fingers in the corners of his mouth and turned them up. When he pulled the fingers out, he was still smiling, and Warren laughed in spite of himself.

"How's that?" asked Russell. "Better? You're a hell of a guy, Ridge. I never thought a man who came into this industry only two years ago could learn so much so fast. Just one thing—"

"What?" asked Warren.

"That Carnahan survey. You can't buy what I need for seventy-five thousand bucks. It's the one thing we can't engineer. You've got to give it to the editorial floor yourself. From down here, from the gut, Ridge, from the gut."

Russell placed both his hands on his abdomen beneath the belt, and heaved. Then he smiled. And Warren smiled back.

"Meet you in the lobby at ten of twelve for the lunch with Bronstein," said Warren.

"A pleasure, sir," said Russell, bowing out. "No trouble with Bronstein," and the door closed.

Warren shook his head as soon as Russell had closed the door, shut his eyes as he tried to recollect who and what was next, then, when he opened his eyes, Laura was standing before him, grave.

"There's a call for you," she said.

It could not be good. He could tell by the tone in her voice. She went on, "Silverman called again. Really nasty. He said he didn't want to speak to Austin, he wanted to speak to you. He said to tell you either he would speak to you himself or his lawyers would speak to our lawyers. He preferred to speak to you himself."

Warren sensed the first foretaste of a headache now. It stabbed. Stabbed with a branded figure, $3,000,000, and the figure meant paper. You could not produce a magazine without paper, thousands of acres of trees pulped and ground and machined into thousands and thousands of tons of paper. Month by month, Warren had whittled down on buying paper, feeding the magazines from inventory, until now, using fifteen hundred tons of new paper a week, only a two-week store of paper remained at the warehouse in the plant. And even that was unpaid for. All in all, with paper costing 250 dollars a ton, he was behind by two months in his paper bills, or an unbearable three million dollars. It was the biggest of the debts, overdue now for more than two months. It was more than the entire liquid cash of the corporation at the moment. He could not dodge this call.

"Get him back," he said to Laura, "dial from my phone here if Eliot's out there."

She bent over the telephone to dial the number and in a moment he heard her saying, "Just a moment, sir, here he is," and Warren held the phone, leaping in to strike the first note because he knew Silverman was angry.

"Mr. Silverman, this is Ridge Warren. I'm dreadfully sorry about the trouble you've had making contact with me. I was deep in conference. My apologies," and not giving Silverman a chance to break in, Warren hurried on. "Actually, I was about to call you in a day or so to let you know that we were acting on your account. I know what's on your mind and that you must be disturbed—"

"You're godda—" Silverman's angry voice broke in the middle of the expletive and began again in key with Warren's courtesy, but still stiff, "You're right we're worried, Mr. Warren. Do you know what our books show?"

"Of course. We're in your debt for three million dollars. Is that right?"

"Right. And I have to know what you plan to do about it. We're in the paper business, not the banking business. We can't carry any customer for that much credit, no matter how big he is."

"Exactly," said Warren, smiling at Laura, knowing that the smile would sound in his voice, too, and that he had to keep this conversation gentlemanly, "exactly. If I were in your position, I'd be furious."

"Well, I am furious"—the edge was off Mr. Silverman's voice—"and I can't get a straight answer from Will Austin. What's the score over at your place?"

"In brief, Mr. Silverman," said Warren, knowing that current cash on hand was less than a million and a half, and thinking rapidly as he talked, "we're refunding some of our major obligations. So we find ourselves in a temporary cash-bind which should last roughly into January, say January fifteenth, when we come out in the clear again. Now since East Coast Paper is our oldest supplier, and I think we're your biggest customer—"

"Mr. Warren," said Silverman, breaking in, "if you're asking me whether we want to lose your business, the answer is no. We want your business. But you're into us for three million dollars right now. I'm responsible to my Board for a year-end balance sheet, and I have to know what you can do to get me off this hook."

"I'm coming to that, Mr. Silverman. We've been discussing it over here. How would this do? I'll get a check out to you for a million this morning, and we'll chew up the rest of it at five hundred thousand a month, starting January first, if that's agreeable to you."

"Well—let's do this. You get that million in the mail today. I don't want to back you against the wall. But I still have to face my Board. We ship paper from our plant to yours on Wednesday of each week. Starting this week we ship only on a C.O.D. basis. Every Monday from now on I want a check for that week's shipment, or no paper that week. That's it. Starting now. I don't want any lawyers in this, not yet. Not if I can work it out with you—"

There was no way of arguing with the voice. Without Silverman's paper there would be no magazines. Silverman had him cornered. Instantly recalculating all his figures in his mind, wincing as he realized how vulnerable he was letting himself get, Warren replied, "Well . . . that squeezes . . . but I suppose you have a problem in your shop, too. This week's check will go out of here this afternoon. And we'll cut this week's shipment down to one thousand tons and keep it at that level until just before Christmas when we'll stock up again."

That was 250,000 dollars more.

He did not want to show Laura how he felt as he hung up.

"Live dangerously, it says here," he said.

She smiled weakly. "Did he growl, or did he bark?"

"He growled. But a check for one and a quarter million dollars will cheer him up."

She lifted her eyebrows and asked softly, "Do we have that much money?"

"As of this morning we had about one million four in our cash account. As of now, we'll have about one hundred fifty thousand dollars. In a few days, the money due us comes in from the advertisers who owe us for last month, and there'll be cash from the other divisions. But for the next forty-eight hours I just don't want to think about it. So hold your breath and smile when you walk out that door."

"I'm smiling but it hurts," she said, retreating. "Shall I send Eliot in when he comes?"

"Send him in."

He pulled out his personal memo pad and began to scrawl a note to Austin. He did not want to tell his Treasurer, aloud, what he had just promised Silverman and see the thin frown of disapproval on Austin's face. As he scrawled the figures for Austin, and underlined them, and added a word of explanation, it occurred to him that Silverman had been considerate. If Silverman had pushed with a lawyer—there would simply have been no money to meet his full claim. It was thinner than ever before. Morrissey had said bankruptcy. Silverman had said lawyers.

Warren pushed the pad away and shook his head as if trying to shake away the thought that had just tangled there. Silverman had said lawyers. Morrissey had said bankruptcy. Warren tried to shake away the thought, but it remained; it had brushed him, then caught.

Bankruptcy? Just what did the laws say about bankruptcy? It was so long ago, as far back as before the war in Washington, in his early years in government with the SEC, since Warren had been familiar with the words of the acts. How did they go? He was trying to pull the phrases back from the misted past ". . . by his fraud, embezzlement, misappropriation, or defalcation while acting as an officer or director in any fiduciary capacity . . ." and beyond that a special definition of fraud which could catch the most innocent, so that every innocent act or transfer honestly made now could be reviewed later by new and harsher standards. . . .

He ought to talk to someone about this. He needed lawyers himself. Meade & Crane, that was it—what was their number?

No. Not Meade & Crane. They were the corporate lawyers downtown, they were not his, they belonged to the Board—white-faced, well-tailored, interchangeable men, legal servants for a generation of this organism called General American Publishing. Who else? Who else to whom he could speak privately—Schlafman & Mulcahy? Schlafman & Mulcahy were the libel lawyers used whenever the magazines had a libel suit. They were uptown lawyers, real people, with names and faces. Yes, Schlafman. Call Schlafman.

Or should he?

Warren rose, pacing, stopped at the window and looked down. It was the season of the year, that was it, the judgment of the calendar which now in fall was pressing Silverman to think of next year's balance sheet, forcing Morrissey to think of this year's results. All of them down there that he could see, hurtling and hurrying through the streets, were pressed by the same private purposes and private urgencies as the season of harvest drew close. He could see the little man-and-woman figures weaving and interweaving through the stream of traffic like serpentines of ants, and, as the red-lights warned, slow to a trickle at the crossings, then stop. As he watched, he saw a tiny man-figure beetle back across the street and jerk to a halt, naked with fear, in the arena of the crossing, as the lights at the intersection changed from red to green and the column of traffic surged forward. The man had dropped something which lay flat in mid-street as he hesitated whether to retrieve it or not.

"Go it," said Warren aloud, his attention diverted by the man's fright. "Go it, man!"

The figure far below burst forward in a scramble, then stopped again.

"Goddamnit, go!" yelled Warren, pounding on the windowsill. "You're halfway there, man, grab it and go!"

The tiny figure darted spastically forward once more, snatched the flat package in a sweeping movement—an automobile stopped short in front of the tiny figure as traffic clotted behind the first car, its screech and honking silenced by distance. But the man was safe, back on the curb, with his precious package, disappearing into the drift of the crowd, and Warren felt better.

Then he whirled. There was someone in the room listening to him.

Embarrassed, he flushed. It was David Eliot who had quietly entered. But Warren was relieved. If anyone else had found him talking to himself in this office they would have thought him ready for the man with the net. But it was only Eliot, and Eliot was a friend, and Warren smiled as Eliot asked, "Am I interrupting you?"

"No," said Warren, "I was just considering the city."

"And talking to it," continued Eliot quizzically.

"No, to myself," said Warren, as Eliot approached and stood beside him, gazing down, too, on the city in its wonders. It was a companionable silence, the first friendly sound of the day, and Warren reflected that it had been too long since he had seen Eliot. Much too long.

"Different from the view in Paris, isn't it?" said Eliot after a while, as if following Warren's thoughts.

"Yup," said Warren, trying to push away the memories. It was Paris that had made them friends. Long before Warren had ever dreamed he would come to this desk, when he and Mary had finally reached Paris with the Marshall Plan, they had known Eliot as *Trumpet's* Paris correspondent, reporting the Plan. The intimate link that grows between a correspondent and an official when both trust each other had flourished in a friendship that overspread their working hours. It had brought Eliot, finally, as a friend of the family, to their fireplace—and there came back to Warren now the memory of himself and Mary, and Mary's affection for this correspondent who made their house his home. But it was different now. With Mary gone. And he President of the corporation that published *Trumpet* for which Eliot was political correspondent and staff talent. Every now and then, Eliot, returning from one of his trips to

Chicago, or the Coast, or Washington, would call Warren, if the news were particularly exciting, and then they would lunch and gossip of politics in the land, as once they had talked of Europe in Paris, when the Americans were changing it. But it was not the same.

"How far can you see from here, Ridge?" said Eliot quietly.

Warren could see the uneven turreted skyline of buildings outlined against the silver breadth of the Hudson, and beyond that the hummocks of New Jersey. Beyond that again, in the far blue haze, rose the gentle barrier of a mountain wall, soft against the far horizon, beyond which lay the land.

"On a clear day, without this haze," answered Warren, "you can see the far ridge there just as crisp as if it were across the river. But it's thirty miles deep in New Jersey. And beyond that, if you could see over it, is Pennsylvania—almost close enough to touch—"

"I didn't mean that," said Eliot quietly, "I meant—"

Then Eliot stopped, and Warren realized that Eliot had come to talk about something.

"Sit down, Dave," said Warren, hoping it would be gossip, or friendship, or politics.

Eliot sat down gracefully, hooking a leg over the arm of his chair. In anyone else, the position of feet and body would have annoyed Warren. Yet Eliot never made a gesture without style. When Eliot eventually rose, his gray, loose-hanging suit would not be rumpled; it never was. It would hang flawlessly. It always did.

"I was just wondering," said Eliot, "as I came up here—should I make conversation first, or should I come to the point?"

"Shoot," said Warren. "If there's a point, let's have it first."

"I had a disturbing call this morning," said Eliot. "That, and a lot of other things, brought me upstairs to you."

"Yes?" said Warren. "I've had a lot of disturbing calls, too—what was yours?"

"From a friend downtown, a Wall Street friend," said Eliot, "who called to say that the word is strong in the Street that both magazines will be folded by Christmas of this year."

Warren froze.

"Just who in hell told you that?" he said, trying to conceal the stab's effect.

"Tom Lipsett told me," said Eliot. "Lipsett runs one of the better investment advisory letters downtown. We trade information. When he calls, I listen. He was doing me a favor, I guess. He says the magazines are going to fold."

"I don't give a damn who he is," said Warren, "this is the kind of talk the competition has been putting out for months just to wreck our advertising sales, it's the oldest rumor—" He stopped, rose, began to pace. This was not a midtown rumor fed by competition; this was a downtown rumor where men measured properties. Talk down in the Street was the worst talk. Who could be spawning the story there? How far had it gone?

He turned on Eliot hard.

"Have you repeated this to anyone?" he asked, his anger transferring to Eliot now, his voice cold. "Is this men's room gossip on your floor already?"

"The word sped from the telephone to my ear, and from my lips only to you," replied Eliot. "That's why I wanted to see you fast. Down on our floor? About half an hour ago someone posted the first flash of our newsstand sales last week by the water cooler. Up seven and two-tenths per cent this week, topping all competition, third successive week. Downstairs all is euphoria, happiness and jubilation. Except for one or two cynics like me who notice that advertising in the makeup schedule for the Christmas issue is down to sixteen pages when it should be over forty. How about it, Ridge, what's happening?"

"We're in a cash-bind, David," said Warren, wishing he could be honest with his friend. "We have to pay bills now with cash that won't be on hand for another three months or a year. That's all. As soon as advertising responds to the lift in circulation, our own cash will flow in, and we'll be clear. But it's absolutely vital to squash the rumors while I turn the corner."

"How tight is the squeeze, Ridge?"

"What difference does it make?" said Warren, conscious of irritation beginning to simmer over the interrogation. "We'll get through it."

"And if we get through it this time, what then?"

"What do you mean, what then?"

"If the magazines are in trouble, Ridge, then I'm in trouble, too, we all are—"

"Supposing," interrupted Warren frigidly, "you let me do the worrying and you do your reporting. I'm the one responsible. I'm responsible for meeting the notes at the bank. I'm responsible for meeting the paper bills. I'm responsible to the Board of this firm, to the stockholders, to the law. Let's say it's my problem, not yours."

Eliot made no move to go. Instead, he raised his eyebrows and said, as if to himself, "You know, Ridge, somehow you make it all sound like a widget factory in a sales slump. Except we're not in the widget business."

"Now what does that mean?"

Eliot walked across the room, picked up a copy of the shining new issue of *Trumpet* from the display table, rippled its pages with his fingers, and laid it gently, almost reverently, face up on Warren's desk.

"That's not a widget, Ridge," he said quietly, "that's *Trumpet*. That magazine used to talk and the White House would listen. That magazine used to thunder and the rafters would shake. Hitler denounced that magazine from Berchtesgaden because he didn't like what it said. That magazine is woven into the dreams and memories of this country. It means something. But it won't mean much for a lot longer the way things are going downstairs."

"That magazine," said Warren coldly, "is selling more copies today than ever before in sixty years. That magazine gets read by one out of ten people in this country; that magazine is selling more copies at newsstands than any other magazine in—"

"That magazine," broke in Eliot, sharply, "is in a jam, Ridge. That magazine was a voice. A man called Pepper made it, and I came in after old man Pepper died, but you could still hear him roaring and ranting through the corridors. He started out with this magazine busting trusts, and he wound up busting unions. He damn near seceded from the flag because we fought the Germans in the first war—and he damn near seceded again because we didn't fight the Germans fast enough to suit him the second time. He thought he was responsible to the country. Anybody who runs these magazines is responsible to a lot more than the Board of Directors, or the stockholders, or the bill collectors. He's responsible for the kind of truth people hear, and how they make up their minds—"

But Warren had had enough.

"Can it!" he bellowed, surprised by the sudden fury in his voice, knowing that temper was venting only because temper vents most easily in the climate of affection. "Can it! Shall I tell you what I'm responsible for?"

"What?" said Eliot.

"I'm responsible for keeping the magazines alive. For survival, goddamnit! That's first—and that takes money. To get that money I have to make an audience and sell the audience to the advertisers. Truth and dreams get paid for these days by breakfast foods, by patent medicines, by cranberries, by under-armpit deodorants. And advertisers want an audience first, not the truth. I've got to make money first, then after that you can come in here and make speeches to me about truth or dreams or anything else you want. That's my gamble—"

"And it isn't working, is it, Ridge?"

"Is that what you came up here to tell me?"

"As a matter of fact, yes—Lipsett doesn't bother me, except that you should know. What bothers me is what's happening to *Trumpet*. Sooner or later, you have to come down to the editorial floor and straighten out the mess. No one knows who's boss, or who's responsible, or—"

"Foley is boss. That's his title. Managing Editor. He's been at that desk for twelve years. He ought to know what's going on; why don't you take up your problem with him?"

"Because he isn't boss, and his nerve is shot. He sees you once every two or three weeks. Purcell is in and out of your office every day. He's the one who passes your word to Foley."

"Purcell is a consultant to me on editorial and circulation matters. We need an audience. Purcell is engineering the audience—"

"Ridge, that's the trouble—you can't engineer away what's wrong downstairs. Why don't you come down to our floor and see what's happening? There's a conference on the Christmas issue this afternoon—come on down, smell the air, see how the Foley-Purcell thing smells from close up."

Warren was simmering down now, part of his tension spent in the outburst, more of it quieted by the soft yet urgent concern in Eliot's plea.

"That's the third invitation I've got to that conference today. What time is the meeting?"

"At three. They run about an hour."

Eliot rose from his chair, lifted the magazine from Warren's desk, hefted it, walked back to the coffee table where he had found it and neatly squared it in place.

"Ridge," he said, turning to the door, "this talk didn't work out the way I had in mind. We don't see each other any more. All I came to say was—if there is trouble, count on me and several others downstairs. We've been here a long time—"

"Thanks," said Warren, and then, as Eliot sauntered to the door, "and for God's sake get back to that man Lipsett and tell him the rumor is garbage. Tell him our circulation gains are phenomenal, our financing problems are purely technical. And ask him to kill the talk."

"I already have, Ridge," said Eliot, and then turning, "Oh, one thing, I forgot—Lipsett said he heard it from a friend of Morrissey's. Does that mean anything?"

Warren's face froze.

"No," he said curtly, "not a goddamn thing, I'm the man responsible here. Tell Lipsett that."

The door closed on Eliot, but Warren was already dialing Schlafman. He could not talk to the Meade & Crane lawyers. They would leak to Morrissey. It must be Schlafman. What did the law say about his responsibilities?

"Nat," he was saying to Schlafman over the telephone shortly, his voice controlled, "Nat, I need a little personal counsel; can you come over here this afternoon?"

"I guess so," said Schlafman easily. "What do you need? Tell me so I can impress you with my learning when I come. Advice on what?"

"The responsibility of a corporate officer in a Chapter Ten proceeding."

"Did you say Chapter Ten?" said Schlafman unbelieving. "Do you mean Chapter Ten in bankruptcy?"

"You heard me," said Warren, "but there's nothing urgent. Someone just made a grab at my short hairs this morning, and I want to find out what the rules are."

"How about two thirty? I could cancel a date and get over after lunch," Schlafman's voice was quick, "or now if it's serious."

"Hey, Nat," Warren laughed, "calm down. There isn't a sheriff within miles of the door. And there isn't going to be. I just want some advice."

"All right," said Schlafman, "if you mean that I'll put it down at four. Let's have your Treasurer on hand with some simple figures I can understand easily if we're talking bankruptcy. You're sure it's not serious? You don't want to monkey with a bankruptcy situation. I can break this date and get there at two thirty if you want."

"No," said Warren easily, "thanks. See you at four."

In a moment he had replaced the phone and pressed the buzzer for Laura. In an instant she was there. He gave her his memorandum to Austin on the commitment to Silverman, told her to ask Austin to be ready with the November first balance sheets for a four o'clock conference, told her he was going to make the three o'clock story conference, rose, walked to the closet where he kept his coat and as he walked, she said, "Oh, Mr. Warren, there are several messages for you—"

"Too late now," he said. "Tell them I went out to lunch before you could grab me. I want to be at the restaurant when Bronstein gets there. Bruno Liquors is the biggest solid account we have. Nothing is so important as keeping old man Bronstein happy. Besides, I hate to keep an old man waiting."

He had said all this while getting into his coat, and was now swiftly wrapping the silk scarf about his throat when Laura said again, "A Mrs. Warren called."

His fingers on the scarf stopped and he could feel his hands pull it rigid.

"She said she was your wife," continued Laura. "I didn't know what to do. I said I'd put her right through to you even though you were in conference, but she said not to disturb you."

Laura stopped, her whole bearing a question. Warren had never mentioned Mary to Laura, nor that he had ever been married.

"She *was* my wife," he said.

"I gathered that. She said she only wanted to leave word with you that she was passing through New York from Paris."

"Where is she staying?" he said, trying to keep his voice flat, concealing from himself the confusion at the knowledge that Mary was in New York.

"At the New Weston Hotel. I have the telephone number here."

He looked at his watch. He would be late for lunch with Bronstein, but . . .

"Will you get her back, please?" he said.

"She said she was going out to shop this morning and she'll be back in late afternoon. She said there was nothing important, just that she wanted you to know she's going to be back in the States for a few weeks."

"Oh," said Warren blankly.

He adjusted the scarf about his neck.

"How did she sound?" he asked finally.

"I don't know," replied Laura, flustered. "I don't know; that is, I've never heard her voice before, I—"

"I don't mean that. How does she sound to you?"

"She . . . she has a beautiful voice. Throaty, and well, strong—what should I say?"

"Yes," he said, remembering, "she has a beautiful voice. Send her some flowers, will you? I'll make a card out for them."

"What kind?"

"You choose them—no, make it roses, two dozen yellow roses."

"All right. Do you want the other messages? Purcell and—"

"No. Not now. I have to rush. I'm already late."

I'll be damned, I'll be damned, repeated Warren to himself as he hurried down the corridor to the elevator. I'll be damned. Mary. In from Paris, this week of all weeks. She never did ask to have her calls put through to me when I was at an office. So I have to call her. If I want to. It's up to me to make the first call. He knew he would have been glad had it been any other day but this. But today, seeing her, trying to conceal this. . . . He could not conceal from Mary. She always knew.

2. Lunch with Mr. Bronstein

Warren and Russell arrived at the Skyline Club only minutes before Mr. Bronstein, with barely enough time to be out of their coats, then turn and greet their guests.

Louis J. Bronstein was a short man, whose bald, round head came to the level of Warren's chest. At first, as Warren bent to help him off with his coat, he resented being trapped in this lunch. It was absolutely unnecessary on a day of such urgencies—yet very important at the same time.

Every level of Bruno Liquors had already agreed on next year's advertising contract; the contract was all but signed. Yet old Mr. Bronstein, who had built Bruno Liquors from nothing to this commanding empire of alcohols still liked to feel his hand on the throb of business; his annual review of Bruno's advertising in *Trumpet*, his favorite magazine, was important to him even though it had become only a detail in the immensity of Bruno Liquors' present affairs. Now, as the old man withdrew his arms stiffly, slowly, from the sleeves of his coat, Warren observed the glistening head with its neatly barbered crown of thin hair fringing the neck, noticed the tufts of ear-hair, gray and wire-like, and realized that Mr. Bronstein was very old indeed.

The voice, when Mr. Bronstein finally spoke, was old, too, with the half-tones of vigor muted in its vibrations.

"I want you fellows to meet Mr. Martin, of Stippler-Leventritt, our advertising agency," announced Mr. Bronstein, waving to a lean, young man who had entered with him. His old eyes twinkled, as he continued, "My sons think I'm too old to do business with slick young fellows like you, Warren, so they send Mr. Martin along to watch me. Martin—this is Mr. Warren of General American Publishing. Russell you know already. Now let's sit down and talk."

The voice was gentle, but nonetheless authoritative. It did not suggest; it directed. And the three younger men found themselves following the old one to the table beside the huge glass windows from which all New York, the Hudson, the avenues, the lesser towers, and the estuary all fell away as unreal scenery below. A waiter hovered over them.

"Something to drink, gentlemen?"

"Mr. Bronstein?" Warren turned to his guest.

"No," replied the old man. "It's funny, a man in my business and I can't drink any more. One a day, the doctor says, and I wait for it all day until dinner, one drink. You fellows go ahead, have something, don't mind me."

They ordered two Martinis, a Bloody Mary, tea and lemon for Mr. Bronstein and waited.

"So what should we talk about?" asked Mr. Bronstein, smiling his gentle smile; then, answering himself, his pudgy hands coming up to spread flat on the table, "If we talk about our business now, we can finish it before you finish your drink. Then, after that, you can tell me how business is with you."

He waited and when no one spoke, he ambled on.

"About the business between us—there isn't much to say. Bruno Liquors is advertising in *Trumpet*, same program we've had every year since nineteen thirty-three, maybe a little more this year than last. All decided. I said to my boys when I was coming here—even before Prohibition I was advertising in *Trumpet*. What we owe to Ab Pepper and his *Trumpet* we owe more than to anyone except President Roosevelt who repealed it. There was a man!"

"Mr. Roosevelt?" asked Warren.

"No, Ab Pepper!" said Mr. Bronstein. "His magazines licked Prohibition. He was the first one who wasn't afraid. He used to say, 'I like to drink, I'm going to keep on drinking, nobody's going to make a criminal out of me for a little drink.' You know, in the end everybody agreed with him. It saved us. So we advertise in *Trumpet* this year, next year, so long as I have anything to say—and I still have a lot to say."

"Of course," said Martin, talking swiftly, for the first time, "all of us at Stippler-Leventritt feel the same way. We advised placing fifty-two weeks of full-page four-color ads in *Trumpet* just as we have every year since the war."

"Now you say it clear, Martin," said Mr. Bronstein, an edge of hardness crusting his soft voice, "but the figures and recommendations you fellows sent over to us, you could read them either way. I couldn't make out what they said. Bruno Liquors does two hundred million dollars' worth of business a year these days, so we get so much information we have to buy machines to tell us what it means. Otherwise, they'd think we're old-fashioned. You know, I said to my sons, 'you fellows are getting so tied up in this scientific market stuff, you're forgetting what business is like.' This year it cost us fifty thousand dollars to have some fancy survey on the shape of the new holiday bottles; should it have a pinch in the middle or square shoulders?"

The old man was growing red-faced, and the ring of vitality in his voice made Warren realize that here was someone who once, years ago, must have been a force.

"And colors, colors, colors!" Bronstein was now saying in disgust. "You ought to hear these color consultants talk about colors. Color? A good whiskey is brown, bourbon browner than Scotch. And a good brandy should be pale, pale, pale, the paler the better. So what do these motivation fellows tell us—for Americans, a good brandy should be 'Robust Brown.'"

The old man spat out the two words again. "Robust Brown! Now I ask you, what does that mean? They tell me after they make these research surveys, Americans think brandy is a rich man's drink, too effete, that's the word they use, too effete. So to get over the prejudice, the brandy should be Robust Brown. Why? Because it's more manly! You imagine that—me going to Bordeaux, talking to DuVallier and Cie, telling them that from now on motivation research says cognac got to be Robust Brown because it's more manly."

With an abrupt silence the old man was quiet, as if one surge of energy had been spent and he was waiting for another. The waiter was near, menus in hand.

"I want scrambled eggs, no butter," said Mr. Bronstein, "that's all I can eat. But you boys go ahead and order a good meal."

The food was already on the table when Warren noticed that Mr. Bronstein was still looking at his menu.

"I enjoy just looking at a good menu," Bronstein was saying, "I can't eat any of this stuff any more but, my God, how I used to love to eat—and drink, too. Me and Ab Pepper. He used to love to eat even more than I did. Twenty years older than me he was, but we were friends. The day I took out my very first page of national advertising—that was before the first war—Pepper had me to lunch in his office. What a cook! What a lunch! Did you ever meet Pepper, Mr. Warren?"

"No," said Warren, "but I've been fascinated by the stories about him. I saw him once. I really don't know too much about him."

Warren really did not. All he knew, Warren reflected, was little more than what was contained in the brochure handed out to new employees at the company, the brochure that capsulized the history of the firm in two pages before it went on to explain about sick benefits, Social Security, and how to find the men's room.

Aloud, hoping to urge Bronstein to reminisce, Warren continued,

"The old-timers at the shop still tell stories about him. They say he knew more about press work and printing equipment than any other man in the country. He could look at a piece of equipment—"

But a grunting noise deep in Mr. Bronstein's throat cut Warren off. It was a grunt of disapproval. Solemnly, the old man held up his little hand signaling that he wanted to speak, and finished munching his mouthful of muffin and eggs before clearing his throat.

"You got it wrong, you got it wrong," he expostulated. "Sure he knew about machinery and he knew his figures. But what he did with the machinery, the kind of words he put on paper—that was the secret. He touched paper and all of a sudden, it was more than paper—"

Mr. Bronstein stopped abruptly, forked up another mouthful of eggs and muffin without relish, swallowed and said, "I'm not supposed to get excited, but I like talking with young fellows; my sons don't give me a chance."

His voice mellowed as he resumed the interrupted thought. "Once Ab Pepper took me along to his office for an editorial conference. He always liked to bring in strangers. So at this conference they were talking about what kind of a picture to put on the cover. It was springtime. I understand in your business in springtime they always put a picture of a woman on the cover, nowadays mostly in bathing suits. This was, mind you, twenty-five years ago, but even then it was fashionable to have pictures of these dames with dark eyes, their chin stuck up in the air, their cheeks sunk in like they have tuberculosis, like they haven't eaten a good meal in five months. So they had a picture like that, and Pepper looks at it when they shove it up the table to him and you can see his face begin to get mad.

"He turns to me and says, 'Lou'—he always used to call me Lou— 'Lou, what do you think of that one?' I look but I don't want to mix in their business, all these high-paid editors of his, it's their business to pick pictures for covers. So all I say is, 'Well, Ab, I don't know, she looks thin to me.' And he yells at all of them, 'It stinks.' Then he takes this picture, tears it apart, throws the pieces on the floor and says, 'What else have you got?' So they show him a lot more pictures and he goes through them as if he was fanning out a deck of cards and suddenly he says, just like that, 'I want this one.' A nice pretty girl, round, you understand, with one of those dirndl skirts they used to wear in those days, a clean girl, fresh, who uses soap and water, not perfume. The kind, if you kiss her just once, right away she hears the piano playing, 'Here comes the bride.' That was all there was to it. He knew what he wanted."

Warren started to speak but Mr. Bronstein was holding up his hand, like a traffic-director, sternly, the quality of his vigor still building.

"Cats!" he suddenly ejaculated. "Cats! You take cats. Every year in the wintertime on the cover of *Gentlewoman*, there used to be a picture of a cat. Once I said to him, 'Ab—why cats? Why a cat every winter, why not a dog?' And he says to me, 'Sister'—that's what he called his wife—'likes cats, that's why.' So I said to him, 'Ab, you mean that? Is this a reason in your business? If I pushed what Mrs. Bronstein liked, I'd be selling nothing but kosher wine, so sweet you could use it to stick paper together.' So he said, 'That's why my business is more fun than yours. But there's another reason, too, Lou—if you put a cat on the cover of a magazine, newsstand sales go way up. If you put a dog on the cover, newsstand sales stay exactly the same. Nobody knows why except that cat-lovers, when they pass, stop at a newsstand and buy a magazine with something about cats. Dog-lovers don't.' You see, Mr. Warren, this was a man who knew his business and he didn't have a motivation-research fellow to tell him why he should do things."

Warren was silent. He remembered the cats well. Somehow, all through his boyhood that oddly recurrent cat—the cat with the red ribbon bowed at the throat, the black cat on the fawn-yellow pillow, the angora cat with its almost-smile—had appeared and reappeared on his mother's sewing table. He had grown up with *Gentlewoman* in his house, it was part of his mother's reading and mind; thus something of Abbott Shalom Pepper's personality had been pressed on him through his mother.

"How about *Gentlewoman*?" asked Warren. "Did he run that directly, too?"

"I keep telling you," replied Bronstein, "everything Pepper owned, he ran. In *Gentlewoman*, he didn't meddle so much, only when it was important to him, like breast-feeding and cigarettes. He kept saying that women should feed their babies from the breast, nurse them, not stick a piece of rubber in their mouth. And the other thing—Pepper felt women shouldn't smoke in public."

"That could cut into advertising," said Russell, "but it's nice to run two magazines that way if you can afford it."

"Not that he was crazy," continued Mr. Bronstein, "but the magazines were his circus. If he liked you, he'd let you open your stall under his tent and advertise—if he didn't, out you went."

Bronstein paused, and Warren noticed he seemed to be sinking into other thoughts. All three younger men now began to speak at once to fill the gap. They talked of business, of research, of how no operation could be run any longer by instinct. They had finished their meals when Bronstein rejoined the conversation as if there had been no interruption between his last reminiscence of Pepper and the next.

"I suppose I make him seem like a funny man now when I talk about him," said Bronstein, with a touch of melancholy, "but he wasn't, he was important. That was it. He made the magazines important. He talked in those magazines, how shall I say, like America belonged to him, he was taking care of it—"

Mr. Bronstein trailed into silence and Warren could hear Martin agreeing as Bronstein paused, "Great advertising media they were, too: clean circulation, good merchandising, readership loyalty, all of it, we used to top-list them in every package we proposed. . . ."

The two words "were" and "used to" made Warren wince. But Russell, quicker than Warren, pounced on Martin's phrasing.

"'Were' did you say, Martin?" he asked, "I guess you haven't seen our latest figures. Rest easy, friend, our newsstand sales over the past six months beat anything in the entire field; we've added six hundred thousand readers, we've—" Russell was talking with a whispering intensity as if hoping not to call Mr. Bronstein's attention to his in-punching, but Bronstein had heard and was saying, "Yes, they *were* great magazines. You know what happened to them?"

"What?" asked Martin.

"I'll tell you what," Bronstein replied, "it was daughters."

Bronstein maintained his position firmly in the face of their surprise. "Yes. I'm telling you. Bad luck, that's all. I had boys, Pepper had two girls. Girls? I think of them as girls, old ladies they were when they died. Ellie, she died only three years ago."

Warren knew well when Eleanor Pepper Kendall had died. That was when the estate had been reorganized for perhaps the fifth time since Pepper's death and it had been out of that reshuffle that the invitation to enter had been brought him. Warren had never known Mrs. Kendall or the other Pepper daughter. Pepper had sired his children young and they had all died in their sixties, being less rugged than the old stock.

"So long as he lived, he ran the magazines," Mr. Bronstein rambled on, "and they meant something then. Then he dies. The money, the stock, the magazines, everything was tied up in this estate of his, all to the girls. But they didn't know business. Breast-feeding wasn't enough. Well, you know what estates are like—lawyers run estates. And what do lawyers know about business either? Lawyers are experts, so they only trust other experts. So the estate lawyers hired experts to run the company, mind you, not from people on the inside, but the upstairs kind of experts, the tax experts, the consultant boys, these financial geniuses they got nowadays who they just rub on a nickel and it shines like a quarter. First the lawyers advise the girls to make it a public company, put the stock on the market, take a capital gain.

"But when you sell shares to the public, naturally, you got to pay dividends. So in the war this is easy, you could run any business with an adding machine. But all of a sudden when the war is over, people have other things to do on weekends besides read. The advertisers get choosy because now a buck means a buck again. But the firm keeps on paying dividends. The stock keeps going higher. The girls and the estate keep selling out their shares, all of it clean capital gains. Gradually thousands of people own the stock, but the lawyers for the family, the trustees, they sit on the Board. And they're losing money. So they call in other experts, consultants, young editors, old editors. Every new consultant, he's got a new gimmick, the magazines change every year like a Dr. Jekyll-Mr. Hyde. Gradually nobody cares, only to make the balance sheet look good, only to keep paying dividends."

Abruptly, surprisingly, Mr. Bronstein's voice, which had been building to indignation, modulated. He turned to Warren, kindly and gentle again.

"Warren, mind you, this has nothing to do with you. It's just that Pepper had girls, that was the trouble; they didn't know they had a living thing in this business, they thought it was a property, so it went downhill. I was lucky. I had boys. My Phil, my Leo, my Jack. I taught them everything myself. Only you wouldn't think so when you hear them talk to me. They keep telling me it's a big business we've got now, big business needs engineering, administration, research. They tell me *I* don't understand America any more."

Mr. Bronstein was off on another track and Warren was glad they had left General American Publishing for the problems of Bruno Liquors.

"*I* don't understand America any more?" said Mr. Bronstein in private astonishment. "It's *you* who don't understand America, I say to them. You come into business behind desks, so you don't know what people want, you have to hire experts and specialists to tell you. With organization charts. It's a bureaucracy they got there, not a business. It's *you* who got to run your own business, I keep telling them, you either got a feeling for this country, or you don't, but you can't buy it from experts."

Martin deftly leaped in, and as Martin spoke, Warren recognized that

Stippler-Leventritt would not entrust the handling of the Bruno Liquor account and Mr. Bronstein to just anybody. Martin was smart.

"You're so right, Mr. Bronstein," Martin was saying. "The greatest problem our agency has lies in dealing with firms that can't make strong executive decisions. We're specialists. We know something about consumer tastes and impulses. We try to tell our clients what we know. But that's where we stop—we give them the maps and the road information. Then it's up to the client to decide whether he's going, say, from New York to Chicago, it's up to him whether he wants to go via Buffalo or via Cincinnati, after we've supplied him with the road information. We're map-makers and chauffeurs; the client is the master. Our worst trouble, as I said, Mr. Bronstein, is a client who doesn't know where he wants to go. And I must say that's one problem we don't have at Bruno Liquors. The Bronstein men make damned good, hard decisions on their own and it's a pleasure to work with them."

Martin had brilliantly soothed the old man, yet praised his sons and defended Stippler-Leventritt all at the same time. It was a good performance and when Mr. Bronstein resumed talking, he had been mollified.

"Yes," he said, "I didn't mean to criticize my boys. I suppose I gave them a bad time. You know I think they feel better every time I go off to Florida. As soon as it gets cold, like now, off I go back to Palm Beach. Always, before Christmas, I go down to Florida. It's a good life now. The only thing is I miss doing a little business, like this today with Mr. Warren. I've had a good time, gentlemen, I hope I didn't talk too much."

The restaurant was crowding now, and Warren knew it was time to go. Summoning the check and the coffee at the same time, he tried to stretch the conversation. But in the wait, Mr. Bronstein found voice again. "Just one thing," he resumed, "so you shouldn't get me wrong. There's all kinds of businesses, and some businesses, they need this scientific market survey stuff. You take electricity. People got to have it—or gas for the house, or food. When you're selling people something they got to have, you run the business with statistics, the tricks are all in financing and distribution, the way you measure how much they need and what it's going to cost you.

"Now, my business," he went on, "is selling something they don't need, but something they want. You can even measure that, if you've got the right touch."

"But your business, Warren—people don't know they need ideas and dreams. They don't even necessarily want it. They don't know what they want until you show it to them. How can you measure that? Your magazine business, this Hollywood business, this new TV business—any business where you're selling ideas, news, stuff like that for their minds and hearts—believe me that's a real crazy business, it takes a crazy man like Ab Pepper to do it. You got to know where you're going yourself, then maybe the people follow you, maybe they don't. But you got to know first where you're going, see what I mean?"

The check came. Warren signed for it. They rose to go.

Briskly, Mr. Bronstein, their leader, turned and marched at the head of the file to the checkroom. Martin and Russell were negotiating the return of the coats from the checkroom girl, and in the brief moment of their busy-ness, Mr. Bronstein turned to Warren, his eyes clear and strong.

"Warren," he asked, "are you in trouble?"

"In trouble?" Warren repeated as though he were puzzled. "We have some serious problems, but I wouldn't call it trouble. Why do you ask?"

"Because I like you, Warren. Maybe because you're *Trumpet* now. If you're in trouble, let me know if I can help you."

"I don't know how you can, Mr. Bronstein, I wish—"

"I'm not a blabbermouth, Warren. I don't leave for Palm Beach for another month. You think. You figure out where you're going. Then call me at the house. Tell me if I can help you. I'm in the phone book, the only Louis J. Bronstein—Trafalgar four-one-oh-nine-eight."

Martin and Russell were back with the coats and they were leaving. Warren looked at his watch. It was only one twenty. It was still Monday, the beginning of the week. Somehow, lunch with Mr. Bronstein had made him feel better. Louis J. Bronstein, he noted, the only one in the phone book. It might be useful to remember.

3. A Short Winter's Nap

As Warren closed the door of his office behind him, he glanced at his watch.

It was only one thirty, still the mid-lunch hour. For a brief while, no one would bother him; here, in the hammering of the day, was a moment of peace.

He could sense the lift of the two lunch Martinis ebbing now, and the couch invited him. There was the desk. But there was the stretch of the couch. His fingers began to loosen his necktie; then his shoes came off, then his jacket—and he lay down. It had been a long time since he had done this; but sleep in midday, the nap after lunch, had always seemed to him the ultimate nose-thumbing at a hostile world; and today had been hostile.

There was a time, he remembered, when he could drowse easily, peeling the husk of the day's problems from his mind by an effort of will. But now, the moiling of the morning's emotions clung, and as he tried to invite sleep, all the jagged fragments of the day grated. There was Mary in mind, and almost in sight, here in New York. But he did not want to think of her in midday, not of her, not of her, or he would never sleep; she had left him. There was Mr. Silverman and the money. No. Not that, not that. There were other voices, too, and he knew he must single out some sound of comfort and let the mind coast after it to sleep.

There was the contract with Bruno Liquors, safe, solid, signed and he lingered on that hoping it would lead to quiet and sleep, but Bruno Liquors had a voice, too, and Mr. Bronstein's voice now soft, then loud, now kind, then firm, was saying, "Are you in trouble, Warren? You got to figure out where you're going first, Warren. Are you in trouble?"

His body turned and twisted to find a cradle in the yielding leather, an escape down which he could slip away to sleep. But escape to where? Back to where he had been? Yet this was where he had always wanted to be—at the top. Here he should, at last, be free. But he was not.

It had not seemed this way when he first saw the top from below. When—

When?

When you first started feeding the news into the great flow from the bottom, as a reporter, at eighteen dollars a week, in Washington, during the depression, legging it for the wire agencies—it all had looked so different. You fed news as it happened into the trunk wires, and then you saw it come back in print hours, or days, or weeks later, each fact appearing in print again under the lens each publisher used for retracting truth. The facts were not as important as the pattern that could be made of them. You had to be at the top before you could arrange them in your own pattern—before you could be free to make a truth of them.

With an easy roll of the mind, Warren was back in Washington with the joy and frustration of change around him. You could not explain to anyone now what it had been like in those days, in those long evenings in Georgetown, as the young men sat talking half the night, considering the change of the nation as if it were theirs to change. And whether it was because those were his own years of the twenties, that decade of life when, for every man, the horizons explode with opportunity, or because it was Washington when the New Deal was young—he did not know. He had pondered long whether it was more exciting to act, or to report of action, and then had come the invitation of the Munitions Investigating Committee to become a Congressional investigator. He had joined the Committee because it seemed only another way of finding out what was happening, temporarily, he thought, as an interlude in the minute-to-minute deadlines of the news agency. He had told himself that he would be back describing the news and the changes again some day—only at the top, when he would be free to describe it his own way. But he had never gone back to reporting for, as special investigator, he had discovered the thrill of government, the excitement of stirring things.

It was even more exciting when he had joined the SEC. That had been a gamble. But the SEC in those days was power. And, after that, shifting from one government agency to another, always one notch higher up on the zig-zag, he discovered that each shift was a gamble. But if you had luck, as he had luck, a whole new world opened each time you moved. Warren had gone from the SEC to the Maritime Commission; and thence to the War Shipping Administration. And, gradually, as the war drew on, as shipping became important, he discovered he was shaping things. A little bit. He was advising the men at the top. He could see the top where decisions were made.

Now it was easier. He was relaxing. He could feel the muscles of strain relaxing. The Washington memories were soothing him. They had been good years. Even the war. It made him uncomfortable to think that he had really enjoyed the war. But there it was.

The War Shipping Administration had wanted to ask a deferment for him, but Warren had said no. At thirty-two, he wanted to be in it—the war was an excitement he did not want to miss. He had entered the Air Force thus, as a major in Intelligence, and the work had fascinated him. He had been assigned to target analysis and selection. Planning, analyzing, dealing with other intelligence agencies, probing how to twang the nerves of Germany from the air with the big bombers, he felt he dealt with masses of force. The awkward stumbling mass of Americans gave men to the war, who performed either stupidly, or cowardly, or heroically over the awkward stumbling masses of the Germans. But they were all caught blindly in the decisions of the leaders who enchanted them. It was the temper of enchantment as much as the quality of decision that made one mass superior to the other. The enchantment and dreams of Americans were better than those of the Germans, more solid. Yet he would never have understood how the dreams were linked to decision, how leadership really worked, or won his colonel's eagles, had it not been for that raid over Düsseldorf. When they noticed him.

He had not done it to be noticed. It had just happened. And he had learned so much from it. He should not have gone on that raid. Intelligence officers were forbidden any flights over German soil for, if shot down, they knew too much. But having flown to London for a conference to mesh Washington's scheme of post-D-day-bombardment with British strategy and Eighth Air Force strategy, Warren had visited one of the forward fields where the bombers which executed the strategy were based. On impulse, he persuaded one of the pilots into letting him hitchhike on a raid. He wanted to see Germany from high up, not from the charts and statistics and photos, but to see it burning at night.

No one would have known of the flight had the flak not cut the Plexiglass turret. Warren had been in the nose with the gunner, watching, and the cone of light the German searchlights made had caught and held them for minutes as they came in on the run, illuminating the inside of the nose, where he crouched in the glare that made ribs, panels, rivets all clearer than day. Then suddenly the gunner had fallen away from the gun and in the stark white light of the searchlights, before the plane heeled sharply off target, he had seen in the glare a jet of scarlet blood coming from the throat of the gunner, beneath the goblin's oxygen mask, spilling over the black leather of the gunner's flight jacket. He had then, almost by reflex, himself slipped over to the twin handles of the fifty-caliber—he remembered how very difficult it was to pull the lever back to charge it, the great exertion, then how easy it was to fire with the gun in hand, and the sound of the machinegun going, and the empty brass cartridge cases rattling out of the breech on the floor like popcorn from a popper. He fired until they were out of it and, looking back, he could see the red and streaking tracers in the sky behind him as the beast clawed back in agony in the night. Only then did he realize that the gunner was dead, that what hurt in his arm was the slash of a shell fragment, and that the ache of the wound in his side was greater.

What he had learned out of the raid, came later. They blistered him when he returned to Washington from the hospital, threatened him with a court-martial after the wound healed, called him a military tourist. But they had noticed him, and the notice brought him to the attention of the regulars. Not because he was wiser now. But the Air Force generals still considered target analysts-in-uniform a long hair bloat burdening men who risked their lives pounding Germany to death. Warren had flown over Düsseldorf on a night when eight planes were lost, and not chickened; even the lowly Purple Heart made a difference. They accepted him.

It was the new attitude of the regulars that instructed him. You had to be one of the in-group. And when once you were part of the in-group, you learned how they used technicians, experts, analysts, pilots, mechanics. It was the beginning of Warren's feeling, in government and business, that there was always an in-group. Once you were "in," you need only find the right men, who knew how to do the technical things—and you could make almost any kind of policy you wanted to with them. The wound, and being part of the in-group, had undoubtedly helped to make him lieutenant colonel two months later, after the court-martial was dropped. And later colonel. And it probably helped with Mary, too.

The weight of his tumbled emotions were pulling him down to Mary, and not Mary in the bitterness of parting, but Mary as he first remembered her, in Washington.

How old could she have been when he first saw her? Twenty-three? Twenty-four?

He remembered her for the first time across the conference table when his target-selection group in the Air Force met with an O.S.S. group of French specialists in early 1943 to talk about targets in France. At first he had thought she was a secretary, but then as he saw her take only an occasional note he knew that she must be one of the O.S.S. Research-

and-Analysis girls. She sat at the end of the table, her body camouflaged by a gray tailored suit, her black hair wound in a glistening bun above a face whose deep black eyes were almost too round for the look of complete attention with which she followed the talk. She spoke only once, in a low even voice, giving a quick summary of what the O.S.S. had learned about the output of the Ford plant that worked for the Germans outside Paris. He had been surprised by how clearly, almost masculine-fashion, her ideas flowed. But she had left the conference before he could speak to her or learn her name.

He had not seen her again until ten days later when, at an after-dinner party, he had entered a room, and, sweeping it with his eyes, had seen her sitting cross-legged on the floor, her legs tucked beneath her, and they were good legs. His glance caught hers for a moment, and then she turned away. She was talking to two men in the uniform of the Free French, and her face, which he had remembered as being striking in its dark, high-boned features, yet not beautiful, was now animated. There was a quality of gaiety about the conversation he could not over-hear.

Very late that evening, people had begun to sing, and as his own voice rolled out, harmonizing over and under the tune, he found another voice winding with it, and it was hers. He had moved over to sit beside her on the floor, and as their voices wound one within the other, he discovered that she liked to sing as much as he. Other people hushed to listen to them. He remembered studying her then, as their voices married, and they half-smiled into each other's eyes in the harmony of the songs. Searching her wide eyes, seeing the round of her cheeks, seeing the swelling of her body, following the curve of her firm hips, he had begun to want her.

In Washington at war, when companionship-of-the-bed came so easily, her firm reluctance came as a surprise. She was so difficult that when finally it happened to them, it happened with importance. It was after his arm had healed from the slash of the Düsseldorf raid. He had been given a three-day weekend leave and had suggested she spend it with him in New York. She had thought about it for quite a while, and finally said yes.

They had stayed at the Old Lancaster Hotel in the early heat of New York's summer, the weekend before D-Day, both of them glowing in the marvelous discovery of each other's body. He had sent yellow roses up to her each day, for no reason at all.

One evening, their flesh warm and spent with love, he had risen to the window to open it wider, hoping for more air in this harsh but love-filled hotel room. At home, in the country, such a summer night would be thick with the fragrance of grass, of trees, of flowers, of hot earth. But here in New York the summer night lay heavy on the city in the near-total blackout which throttled the city's ground glow. He could imagine all the city gasping for freshness and for air—he could imagine people in apartments with the windows wide, stretched across their bed sheets; he could imagine people sitting on the stoops of their tenements or on their fire escapes, to flee the multiplication of the heat indoors. He could imagine them all fixed in the iron-grip of the devouring city, clutched by its brutal needs with no escape.

Then, as he stood there by the window, he became aware of the soft padding of her feet, and she was beside him, naked and beautiful, and her fingers, cool and firm, held him by the muscle of the forearm, her forefinger caressing the muscle, gently, in quiet tenderness. She asked him what he was thinking about and he had not known himself, being wordlessly moved by the dark, slumbering city and all the people caught in it, locked in it, without air, without being able to move, all locked to each other yet all of them alone. But aloud he had said how much it reminded him of the cities of Germany he had flown over that night, and how they looked when they burned. And she had murmured something about how dangerous it must be to be flying that high and having people shoot at you, too, and he had said, no, it wasn't the danger, it was the being alone that was the worst. Slowly his arm came around her body and she leaned against him, as strong as he, and she had said, don't think about that. They had been silent then, full of the wonder of their bodies; his hand caressed her shoulders, then slowly slipped down the soft skin of the firm back. In the silence, as both of them listened to the night and their bodies, from above the murmuring and hissing of the night traffic, he could suddenly hear far away the wailing of a siren on an ambulance, and, even more distant, the hooting of a fire engine. Then he had said that no one should ever be alone when trouble came, no one should ever be alone. That was the way he had proposed to her. His hand came up and rested on her head, and his fingers twined themselves in her hair which fell over her shoulders, and he turned her lips to his, her face wet with tears, her lips open, losing their firmness in the swollen dissolution of loving. Then they had gone to bed, not in frolic, but deeply, earnestly knowing each other to the edge of emptiness.

They had waited until Christmas to be married. He had journeyed out to Cleveland, and from there to Mary's home at Floss Hill, where they had stayed at the boisterous house full of Mary's three sisters and younger brother. Mary's father was a judge; but instead of being august and forbidding, he presided happily over a home where the telephone never stopped ringing, where animals large and small darted in and out of sofas, where the only moment of silence was for grace, followed by a flood of noise and laughter, stemmed by the Judge's bellowing for quiet when it grew too loud.

They were married at the Presbyterian Church and Warren did not feel happy, truly, until he had Mary away from the bustle of the house and alone to himself on their one-week leave-and-honeymoon at the New Weston.

They had their first clash on the honeymoon, too—at breakfast one morning, as he yawned over the papers and a headline caught his eye, announcing the promotion and transfer of his chief in Target-Analysis. He studied the story for a moment, conscious of the contentment in him as he read the newspaper across the table from his wife, conscious that his base was solid, that he was ready to go. He could not recall now what the headline was but somehow it must have made him feel he *should* go for he announced that they ought to cut this short and get down to the Pentagon and get in on the new operation.

She had said, "No."

When he looked up, he saw a new expression on her face but he could not measure it.

"There's too much happening down there, Mair," he said, "I have to be in on it; I want to get back."

"But this is my honeymoon, too. I won't let you cut it short."

He had said, "But we'll be married now the rest of our lives; I have to be in on what happens next."

Then she had blazed at him in her first show of temper, and the blaze could be extinguished only with effort as he tried to explain what a new operation, a new program was, and the excitement he felt when things began. She pinioned him that morning for the first time, trying to find out what he really wanted, where they were going after the war. He had quenched the questioning only by coming around the table and taking her in his arms until the moment of separation had passed away in the meeting of their bodies. But the same irritation was to grow, returning over the years, tenderness alternating with anger. For he could never make her understand that when opportunity came, one seized it, wherever it was. Tenderness and argument had alternated year after year but changed in proportion to argument and tenderness. Until that final evening in Paris.

No. He would not call that up. He would push it away. Find something that would lead him into sleep—

Far away, slowly, the sound came into the office. A steamer horn there in the river, baying, coming in or going out. On a rainy day in New York, the sound of the horn came across the hoarse anonymous roar of traffic, deep, mournful, musical, blanketing the lesser sounds of the city. On a clear day like this, when the sky was hollow with blue resonance, the horns of the steamer were fainter, higher, more melodic, as if summoning, mocking, calling the people caught in this city to sail away with them.

Paris. He would think of Washington or of Paris. But not of this city nor of Mary. Paris and the good years there after the war when he had felt free, when he had helped assemble the picture of Europe. He would think of the fog and all the shades of gray of Paris, the pewter gray, the rose gray, the wool gray, the sand gray, the grime gray, he would think of, think of—slowly drowsing, he was being carried back to the good years, the lotus years, the lost years—and drowsing now, his eyes closing, his body settled comfortably into the couch.

The telephone was ringing.

He was wide awake before it had rung twice, his mind groping to seek orientation. Then, rising, he answered the ring. It was Laura.

"I didn't want to wake you. But it's ten minutes of three. You have the three-o'clock story conference; and Austin wanted to know if he could talk to you before you met with Schlafman. The other calls are junk. Want them?"

"Fine," said Warren, stretching the muscles of his shoulders, flexing them back and forth. "I think I'll see what's up at the story conference. Tell Austin I can't see him before four. Then we'll go over the whole picture with Schlafman."

4. The Story Conference

"Crapola, crapola, crapola," Foley, the Managing Editor, was saying in his tone of permanent outrage as Warren opened the door on the story conference.

Foley had not seen Warren come in, and his back was to the door. Purcell—square-faced, solid, his crew-cut bristling—sat at the far end of the room, his face a twist of puzzled judgment, his pipe alight and smoking. As Warren entered, Purcell's eyebrows lifted in welcome and a happy smile of shared amusement curved his lips. Six others ringed the table between Foley and Purcell, their clipboards and folders distributed between the table and the floor. These were *Trumpet's* editors.

All the ideas, the vagrant suggestions, the torrent of manuscripts that poured in through the mail, the reports of the magazine's bureaus and correspondents, the proposals of agents—all were winnowed and screened before they reached this conference room for final argument. After such a meeting, where the editors gathered, noisily chattering or moodily contemplating the stretch of the nation they must inform yet entertain, came final decision on choice, space, color and timing which five days, two weeks, six weeks or months later produced five-million-plus copies of the magazine flung across the country, glistening at every newsstand, a mirror of life.

Warren observed that it was a reduced group today. The lesser editors were absent. But he picked out those present immediately, by department—Valerie Drew, Home & Family; Tennyson, Science & Health; Clement, Public Affairs; Duckworth, Entertainment; Vanetta, the Art Director; Eliot, as Senior Writer. Together they were supposedly contemplating Christmas, but Foley was saying, "Crapola, crapola, crapola. *Life* is doing it. *Look* is doing it. So is *Spectacle*. Then we haul in like a caboose three weeks later with the same stupid thing. Crapola!"

"Why, hello, Ridge!" boomed Purcell as Foley finished, and everyone turned to look at Warren as he stood in the door.

"Sit still, everyone," said Warren, as they shuffled to make room for him, and then, turning to Foley, continued, "Tom, I took up your invitation."

Foley grunted, clearing his throat to answer, when Purcell leaped in, rising. "Ridge," he said, "take my chair."

"No," said Warren, circling and reaching for a chair in the middle of the table, "let me sit here. I just want to listen. All right, Tom, let's have the crapola."

The table laughed and Foley's scowl broke to a grin.

"This is a second look at the Christmas issue," he said. "As it looks now, it's a dog and we're trying to beef it up. Valerie's Home & Family section has tacked up a layout on Presents-for-Father-for-Christmas and we were discussing it."

"We've been trying to increase the helpful, useful article in every issue, Ridge; the service features," broke in Purcell smoothly, "and Valerie's people have this Christmas-Gift-for-Father layout. You know, everybody buys the old man's presents last."

Purcell paused. Warren was not sure who was running the meeting, Foley or Purcell.

"Now, Tom," continued Purcell, "I agree with you there's no real honest-to-goodness 'sell' in the story now. But if we can noodle up a good title for the cover, we could milk real sales out of newsstand—it's only a cover-line that's bothering us."

"Oh, grand," said Foley sarcastically, "so we all agree the story is a dog and there's no point running it without a good cover-line. Also, we agree we have no cover-line. So what are we arguing about?"

"To Father, with Love, from Father Christmas," suggested Valerie Drew cheerily, turning to Purcell. "Would that make a good cover-line, Ray?"

"Something shorter, something snappy," said Purcell, unruffled, thinking out loud, "something to make the reader buy after the cover picture stops them at the stands. Something like, 'Does Your Husband Enjoy Christmas?' I'm just bouncing that one, you understand, but how does it sound?"

Warren noticed that Clement put his hand over his mouth as if to throw up, and someone snickered. Eliot spoke up. "With a reverse twist, Ray, we could make it even better. Like 'How To Enjoy Your Husband.' That would sell the men and women, too."

A chuckle followed, and Clement followed Eliot's lead. " 'A New Husband Every Christmas—Mama's Secret Wish.' How's that?"

A nervous laugh, then Vanetta, the Art Director, said, "Naw, I got a better one—'Is Your Husband Wearing Out This Year?' How's that?"

"With a second deck under it," added Eliot sarcastically, " 'New Glands for Old Husbands.' "

Now the snicker at the table was general, as Foley scowled, Valerie Drew pouted, and Purcell, pained, wrinkled his brow in thought.

"Well," said Tennyson, the Science & Health editor, taking off his glasses and polishing them with a piece of tissue, "I don't want to interrupt this flow of wit, but since we've gotten to 'New Glands for Old Husbands,' I shall now proceed as I have each month for the past year to insist the best story I have is just that. Why can't we run it?"

"Oh God," said Foley, "not that one again, Ten, not today."

"Yes," said Tennyson, firmly, "if we're looking for 'sell,' there it is, the best story in my inventory—'The Male Menopause.' No general magazine has touched the male menopause yet and millions of men worry about it. When a man comes to the age of fifty or fifty-five, he goes through as complete a change of physiology and personality as a woman. I say every man *and* every woman will read it. And we don't have to sweat out a cover-line. Just 'The Male Menopause.' Very dignified."

"Excellent!" boomed Purcell. "A real firecracker! I think we ought to consider—"

"No!" exploded Foley. "Damn it, you're making a Midway out of this magazine. We're having a conference on the Christmas issue that has to start closing next week, and we have nothing but junk between the covers now. Let's stick to business."

He brought his fist down on the table with a thwack, and in the quiet Warren broke in. He was confused. He had not expected the story conference to be like this.

"Tom," he said, "clue me in. Give me the shape of this issue."

"O.K.," said Foley, gruffly, "that gets us back to where we want to be. Christmas issue goes on sale December twenty-third. Which means we have to lock up the late forms by December eighth, Friday, not even a month from now. Today we have Ray with us to plan something special for Christmas, on a crash basis—"

"A creative push," broke in Purcell from his end of the table.

"A creative push," repeated Foley with an edge on his voice, "and we're late, Christmas is almost here."

Christmas was seven weeks away. All across the country, the fall was still in its prime—the leaves scarlet and gold in New England, the underbrush in Minnesota crackling to the tread of the hunter, the pumpkins in Pennsylvania swelling gold to bursting but not yet harvested, mothers still too relieved getting the children off to school to think either of

Thanksgiving or Christmas, the thud of toe against football fresh in a thousand ears—but in this room, Christmas pressed hard. Somehow, here, together, these men must distill the rhythm of the holiday.

"We're cutting down to twelve pieces in this issue because advertising is so thin," continued Foley. "Four of those are fiction which are all copy-read and set. Two are Christmas grinders, but the third one's actually pretty good. The fourth fiction piece is the third part of the new Western serial."

"That's four," said Warren, "leaves eight to go." He wanted to find out what *Trumpet* would carol for Christmas, and was impatient.

"Two of the eight we've closed already," continued Foley. "We fit one serial onto another so as to get a readership carryover, and after the Western serial, we start a series on Larry Ledyard, in four parts. The Christmas issue will carry the second installment of Ledyard—"

"Why Ledyard?" asked Warren.

"Because he's the hottest thing on TV since Godfrey," answered Purcell. "You have to grab a TV personality while he's hot—they burn out in two or three years and Ledyard's there right this minute. You remember what the Godfrey series did for the *Post?* Goosed their newsstand sales by almost half a million for about a month. We figure Ledyard can give us the same kind of push—"

"Why?" asked Warren, puzzled. "What's his story?"

"A real ball of wax," continued Purcell. "He's a poor, mixed-up rich boy, comes from a Long Island home, they send him to Yale, he quits. Goes to a psychiatrist. Disappears. Turns up in Harlem singing at Negro nightclubs. Catches on about eighteen months ago, can have anything he wants, but he still lives in Harlem. He claims Zen Buddhism did it all for him; he sings with peace in his heart. He's got everything. Middle-aged mothers love him, little girls sigh for him. This is his first big magazine spread, the usual story of his life, but Duckworth got a good ghost-job written and Ledyard is signing it—"

"Not only will he sign it," said Duckworth, "he's plugging it on his show. He'll hold the magazine up on camera each of the four weeks it runs and forty-five million fans will see it. We should add a couple of hundred thousand sales at newsstands just out of the exposure on his show. His agent—"

"O.K., Alan," growled Foley, cutting the Entertainment editor short, "it's bad enough we have to print this kind of story, without wasting time talking about him. Today he means circulation whether we like it or not. Two years from now, we'll give him the works. When he starts slipping, we'll run the story of 'How Success Spoiled Larry Ledyard.' Now let's cut to the next item, or we'll be here all afternoon."

"That's five," said Warren, helping Foley get his story conference back on the tracks, "four fiction, one Ledyard, what else?" He was conscious of a growing irritation.

"One sports piece, locked up," said Foley. " 'Hockey, The Most Dangerous Game in America.' And that makes six out of twelve in the early form, and we have to save with something good. We still need a service feature, which gets us back to Valerie's Gifts-For-Father. I still say no. Not that it's a bad idea, Val," he said, turning with surprising kindness to Valerie Drew, "but everybody else is doing it already, so it means nothing. We'll hold on to your layouts until Father's Day. Now, has anyone else got a service feature? Come on, someone, give."

After a minute-long silence, Tennyson spoke.

"Well," he said, "there's this." He lifted his folder from the floor beside him, pulled out a manuscript, riffled through it, shaking his head, and continued, "I've been hanging on to this job about Overeating and Hangovers for about six weeks. The writer's agent is pestering me for an answer. Maybe we could give it a Christmas twist. Everybody overeats on Christmas, overdrinks and winds up with the year's great hangover. It's not what you might call a positive, cheerful, holiday approach. But it touches where the belt squeezes. Slug it something like, 'That Christmas Hangover,' and the title may carry it."

"Have they got a cure for hangover, Ten?" asked Duckworth.

"Alan," said Tennyson, "for your information there is no cure for hangover. There never will be. But every year there's a new theory that makes a story. The new theory is that hangover is a state of bodily dehydration. When you're hung, you lack water. The only way of curing a hangover, it says here, is before it begins by balancing the alcohol intake with lots of water. Eat salted peanuts, potato chips, smoked salmon while you're tanking up, wash them down with quarts of water, and you won't have much fun drinking, but you won't wind up stoned, either. So this writer says."

"How many words does he need to say it in?" asked Foley, his pencil raised.

"Twenty-five-hundred words and with a good layout she'll fit on two pages," said Tennyson. "How do you want it slugged—'No Cure For Hangover,' or, 'That Christmas Hangover?' "

"A moment," said Purcell, removing his pipe with a professorial air, "with a twist, we can make that an upbeat story. Why don't we call it, 'New Cure For Hangover?' "

Purcell paused, an expression of contentment on his face. "Yes," he said, " 'New Cure For Hangover'—I think that has more jump in it, don't you?"

He had addressed the table, but was looking at Warren. Warren turned to look at Foley, who flushed, ran his hand over his face, opened his mouth to speak, thought better of it. With an effort Foley picked up his notes, then, speaking to the group, said, "Let's call it seven pieces. But nothing that says *Trumpet*. There has to be something important in this issue to chew on. What have you guys got to suggest?"

No one answered. It was as if they had toyed with a menu, chosen the wines, the cheeses, the soup, the dessert, the fruits, but still waited to choose the main course.

"An old-time *Trumpet* job," said someone, "that's what we need."

"All right," said Foley, "Clement, you run Public Affairs. What have you got?"

Clement opened his folder of suggestions and said, slowly, as his eyes scanned his lists, "You know Public Affairs doesn't come with sleighbells. I haven't got a single thing that says Christmas."

"The hell with Christmas," exploded Foley in a sudden burst, "Vanetta and I will decorate the book in green and red, gold and blue, holly and berries and bells so that it shrieks Christmas, but what have you got that *means* anything?"

Clement began to read from his list.

"A solid story from our West Coast bureau on missiles—"

"Nah," said Foley, "we've had too much on missiles, I'm beginning to think we invented them."

"Highways," went on Clement. "If they'd only hold still to read this story here, a good job. The chief thing this administration will be remembered for is the new Federal Highway Program—"

"For spring," said Foley, "with big picture layouts, when they start taking the cars out of the garage, and think about driving places, not now—"

"Population boom. Crisis ahead. Where will we all put ourselves—"

"Is that one ready to go?"

"No. But we could slap together some statistics and text in a rush—"

"If it's that way, I don't want it. What else?"

"Inflation. I've got a good story here, and I can put a Christmas twist on it—'The Hole in Your Christmas Pocketbook'—but it's not exactly upbeat."

Foley ran his hand over his face in complete frustration.

"Something new, something new! I've heard all those before, what's new this week?"

"Current Suggestions here," said Clement, opening another folder, "I haven't screened them yet, but this one is marked Christmas, and the title is 'How Goes the Battle for Peace?'"

For the first time in the conference, Warren noted, here was an interesting suggestion. With that title it could be important, or could be incredibly dull. You could not tell.

"What's it about?" asked Warren.

"A suggestion from Mr. Purcell's office," said Clement neutrally.

"What's it say, Ray?" asked Warren, turning to Purcell.

"I don't know yet," said Purcell, "it's just a good title that came to me. I see us opening the magazine on this piece set in Gothic type, with illuminated lettering. We can square off a box on the same page, with one of the psalms set in gold. Then we do this thing in about two thousand words on Christmas as the season of Peace and Goodwill. We'll need a good by-line, of course, to sell the story on the cover, an author whose name guarantees sales, and I was hoping today's conference would suggest a writer—"

Purcell was passing the problem to the table, and Eliot caught it— "What kind of writer, Ray?"

"Well, since nobody really wants to read about peace and disarmament, the name of the author should have built-in 'sell' for the newsstands. Like Churchill."

"Churchill?" said Warren, enthusiastic. "Doesn't *Life* have him locked up?"

"Yes," said Purcell gravely, "you're right there, Ridge. We can't get him, but I'm just giving an idea of the kind of name that sells. I'm trying to provoke thinking. This is a creative push."

"How about Harry Truman?" suggested a languid, bored voice, and as Warren turned to see who had spoken, the other end of the table switched on.

"Too political for Christmas. How about Eleanor Roosevelt?"

"She's slipping, controversial, too," came a reply, followed by, "How about Cardinal Spellman?"

"He doesn't sell west of the Rockies," said another voice, which slowed ruminatively to, "We need someone with a few ideas about peace, and a name like a brand-label of authority, like, say, Lippman?"

"Or like Toynbee?"

"Toynbee's fake, poison on the stands, Lippman doesn't pull a mass audience either—"

"You're wrong, Lippman *would* sell."

"Hey!" It was Eliot snapping his fingers, smiling mischievously. "I've got it! Lippman ghosts the piece and Frankie Sinatra sings it. How's that? Certified Grade A ideas plus certified sell?"

A laugh ran around the table, and Duckworth followed, "No, I've got a better one than that—Toynbee writes it and Marilyn Monroe signs it."

Another laugh—cut off by Foley's hand slamming hard on the table.

"We haven't got very far with that one, Ray," said Foley slowly, "I'd appreciate it if you found the writer who could say anything important enough to live up to that title and still sell copies."

"What did you have in mind, Ray?" asked Warren. "I like the title but I can't figure out where the story will go. What's it going to say— why not approach it that way?"

"It's just an idea," said Purcell, perplexedly, as if he had been misunderstood by everyone, "I'm not frozen on it. I try to keep circulation moving. Christmas is the biggest promotion of the year, Peace and Goodwill and all that, and it seems to me a dignified opening article on Peace ties in with the promotion. What I'm after now is circulation, promotion—not any particular solution to world problems—"

"Oh for Christ's sake!" burst out Foley in a tone of total disgust. Foley slammed his folder shut, angrily scratched a match to light his cigarette and Warren could see that Foley's hands were shaking as if a control had just snapped. Foley puffed his cigarette furiously, and glared down the table at Purcell. To his surprise, Warren found he wanted Foley to say more—he was on Foley's side.

"What's the matter, Tom?" asked Warren.

"Ah, the hell with it," snapped Foley irritably, "I ought to learn to keep my mouth shut."

Foley was silent, red-faced, and Purcell spoke.

"I just can't understand you, Tom. You're too subjective about things. An editor has to be objective—"

"Objective, balls!" snorted Foley, as if glad to have Purcell there to receive an anger intended for someone else. "I'll be objective with you. That story is a phony, and you know it, and I know it, and every reader of this magazine will know it as soon as they read the first paragraph. You shove it in just for a cover-line to sell to the bluejays at newsstands. Christ, I can jazz a newsstand cover anytime I want by putting on a TV star, or a babe in a bathing suit. But if you keep on hitting them with this tears-tit-and-hope formula of yours, and then patch it over with a figleaf of something that sounds important—they just walk away from you—"

"Foley, Foley," said Purcell, as if humoring a child in distemper, "let me put you in the picture and explain why we're hunting bluejays, and where this magazine is. People are moving out of the cities into the suburbs, and the only smart way of reaching them is by direct mail. We poured two million into mailings for new subscribers this year, and we'd need three million to match the competition next year. But we haven't got it, Foley. So we have to engineer our way out of the trap by getting the most we can out of newsstand sales, grabbing people where they stop—by cover and cover-line. We have to engineer an audience out of their appetites, until we get an audience big enough to rent to the advertisers at a profit, and that means socking them," here he swung a pudgy fist pugilistically through the air, "socking them in every issue with enough 'sell'—"

"Ray," said Foley, in dead quiet control of his voice, "will you quit using that word engineering at me? This is a magazine. It used to mean something. When I think of how it used to read—Ray, listen, a magazine has to have 'pull' as well as 'sell,' and they aren't the same thing. You have to 'pull' them back for the next issue and the next issue after that because they want to hear what you're going to say next. We spent two million bucks this year buying new subscribers. Just tell me this, how many of them will stay with us next spring when their trial subscriptions run out? And what's happening to the millions of readers who've stuck with us over the years because this magazine used to be important, because it made them feel important—"

"Now, Foley," said Purcell triumphantly, "we're talking about an article called 'How Goes the Battle for Peace?' If that isn't important—"

"Of course it's important," said Foley in a rising voice, "if you had the ghost of an idea of what you wanted to say in it, it might be important. But I'm tired of these upstairs memos ordering pieces on desegregation, or union racketeering, or urban sprawl, or population boom, as if we could get them out of a Sears, Roebuck catalogue of window curtains and carpeting, pasting the goddamn stories together like clips in a TV documentary without knowing what we think about them. There was a time we talked about these things from the gut, because a reporter came in with a belly of fire, and because, goddamnit, that was the way we looked at the world. Not because it looked cuter one way or the other, or made the best show, or milked a headline or a promotion. What good does it do to fill the pages of this magazine with a lot of shiny, cheap newsstand merchandise—"

As if unable to keep his hands still, Foley had begun to tear his sheaf of notes into bits and pieces, tearing savagely as his voice mounted.

"'How Goes the Battle for Peace?'" he continued rhetorically. "Do you know? Do you care? All you've got there is a cover-line, you don't even know who might have an idea—just a cover-line, like every other magazine on a hundred thousand newsstands. When you sell that story just for a cover-line to hook bluejays, you're selling out this magazine—"

Here, Foley's hand coming down on the table, released some torn scraps of paper. Reaching to retrieve them, Foley upset his clipboard, which clattered against an ashtray, which spilled to the floor. As Foley grabbed for his ashtray, his papers cascaded to the floor after him and Purcell said, smugly, "Get a grip on yourself, Tom—remember it's what they buy that pays your salary and mine."

Foley's face popped up, cherry-red in anger, from the edge of the table, and yelled, "My salary, Purcell, I earn right at this desk, working. I work from my gut. By what I want to know. I don't earn my salary upstairs in a Valhalla of story-engineers who do it by percentage ratings. I'm fighting to keep this magazine important and you—"

"I'll tell you what you're fighting for, Foley," said Purcell, "every single week, every single issue—to catch their attention and sell it. They've all got TV sets now, they've all got cars, radios, boats, houses and gardens to dig in. They haven't got time to think or read. We're not even fighting for their dollars any more, they've all got change jingling in their pockets. We're fighting for their time—half an hour, quarter of an hour, five minutes of their attention. One picture of a mother cooing at her baby in the sun while the baby grabs her finger is worth three articles on the Sweet Mystery of Life by Huxley, Oppenheimer and Einstein. If you want to make this a magazine for world-savers, don't bitch when circulation goes off—"

"Nobody's talking about world-savers; you were the one who brought up this phony Peace story as a hunk of promotion," snorted Foley. "I learned this business by the seat of my pants, wearing them out on benches in police stations, police courts and Tammany clubhouses all over town. I'll tell you what I know: they all want to feel important, every goddamn one of them. And this is a middle-class magazine. It's got to have fun and games and pictures for kicks, but it's also got to make them feel they're getting something out of it. That's the one thing you can't fake. Whether you really give them something or not. It comes from the gut, Ray, and you can't sit there, sucking your pipe and—"

"Foley," said Purcell sharply, removing his pipe, in a voice no longer tolerant, "wake up! This country is too big for the seat of your pants! There isn't any middle class any more. There's one big homogenized America, and it shops in the same supermarket—the broker and plumber, the engineer's wife and the steamfitter's wife. They buy the same Kleenex, the same Scotch tape, their kids want the same cornflakes. There aren't any retailers or salesmen any more—they have warehouses with checkout counters. And we serve them. We've got to offer the big producers the biggest *Trumpet* possible to round up the crowd. The way TV does. TV moves goods off the supermarket shelves like a wind blowing leaves down the street. And we have to match them. If we're going to stay big, we've got to get bigger. We're a marketing instrument. We have to measure it, survey it, analyze it. There's only one big market with the same set of appetites—the only thing they have in common is violence, hope, fear and a few simple sex curiosities. If they want to see the tears glisten on the cheeks of a girl crying, our photographers have got to shove the camera in close enough to get the tears glistening. This is becoming a science, Foley, this is engineering—"

"Oh, Christ, Ray," said Foley, in a tone of disgust more complete than anger, "if that's what you really think, then make that speech upstairs. I'm running a story conference, and I'm sick and tired of sitting here while you flip banana peels through the cage at me. Let's get down to cases. I think this story on Peace stinks for just one reason—you don't give a damn what it says. How's that? Now, do we go with it or not?"

With an abrupt silence, Foley stopped. An unbroken silence followed and slowly, Warren became aware that Purcell was staring at him, Eliot was staring at him, the others were staring at him. Whether by accident or design, this conference had been delivered to him. Warren knew that only he could decide between Foley and Purcell. He knew this storm had been invited by his presence. Yet he could not, would not decide between them in public.

Groping desperately for a compromise he said, turning first to Purcell, "Ray, I think it's a first-class story idea. But I think you and I have to decide first what *Trumpet* wants to say about Peace. You see—"

He saw the door opening and it was Foley's secretary, who said, "Excuse me, it's for you, Mr. Warren," handing him a slip of paper. He opened it as they watched and it was a message from Laura that Schlafman was upstairs, waiting. It was an out from this meeting, but as he looked up, he realized he had broken in mid-sentence and he had to finish.

"Let's have Tom put this issue together the way he wants, and—"

He wished he could go. But both Foley and Purcell were staring at him, as litigants do at a judge pronouncing judgment, and he knew he could not stop there.

"Shall I tell you what I think is the trouble?" he said, rising, thrusting his hands into his pockets.

"Ridge," said Eliot, "we certainly wish you would."

He turned his back on them, to gaze out the window, the words curling around a thought still unformed in his mind.

"Have any of you ever been in Rome?" he asked, turning back to examine them.

Several nodded, and Warren went on, "If you have, you've seen the Forum there, or what's left of it. Those ruins were a fair once. The Forum was a fair. It set the mold for two thousand years of fairs that followed. And that's just what we are. A fair. A fair brought together two different kinds of people—merchants and peasants. The merchants came there once a week to peddle cloth-and-needles, spices-and-silk, cheese-and-sausages. When the merchants started selling forks at fairs, peasants stopped eating with their fingers. When the peasants' wives finished selling their vegetables, they looked at what the other women were wearing—and fashions changed. A really good fair had jugglers, magicians, storytellers, dancing bears, herb doctors, and preachers. The peasants came to have a good time. But what brought them back was something they never recognized. They came to find out what was going on. Because when they rubbed against other people and talked with each other, they heard news and gossip—and sometimes they heard a speech."

Warren studied them, saw they were puzzled, wondered whether they were listening because they had to, or because he was diverting them from the problems of the issue. He continued.

"Caesar took over Rome by talking at the Forum. Peter the Hermit preached the Crusades at the fair. The French Revolution grew out of gossip at village fairs. The people argued about roads and taxes, and the new king, and heard about the next war. They remembered that longer than the last juggler. That's what we have to remember. That any magazine is a fair where the merchants show their wares and the peasants meet once a week. Larry Ledyard belongs in this, and jugglers, and dancing bears, and herb medicines. And virility cures for the male in menopause. But that's not enough. We need ideas, and a speech or two they'll remember—and every now and then something that illuminates the world they live in. The trouble right now is you're getting the ideas and the dancing bears mixed up. There has to be a line drawn between the entertainment for show and the ideas for remembering. I don't care much what we do to build circulation so long as you people down here recognize what we do because it's expedient and what we do because we have something to say. Tom," he said, knowing he had to go, that he had to come down one way or another on this particular issue, "shelve the Peace story for the time being until we decide what we ought to say about Peace. For this issue—either make it all Christmas, with or without holly-berries, or make it all good like an old-time *Trumpet* issue, with or without Christmas."

He was almost at the door. He hoped he had patched the conference together so they could continue putting out the magazine until he got around to their problems. They needed him but he was too busy. As he closed the door, he heard Foley's voice, saying emotionlessly, "Any other suggestions?"

He knew whatever patch he might have placed on this conference was only temporary. He had to be here every week, making them see the country as he did. That was the job, to make of the suggestions and the dancing bears and the ideas a pattern of what he saw, he alone. But Schlafman was waiting upstairs. With other problems. He needed to solve those before he could get back to this. If the figures and the book-keeping and the law really left him time, he would.

5. Rendezvous with a Balance Sheet

When and how the phrase "balance sheet" came to measure so much of western man's activity, no record tells precisely.

But somewhere in the silent wastes of the Middle Ages, even before the Arabs brought the new decimal figures to Europe, Italians had begun to sum up their affairs, in cumbersome Roman numerals, by a method the Florentines first called a "bilanzio." The "bilanzio," when later coupled with the new Asian decimals, became a marvelously supple device, striking clarity from even the most complicated transactions of Venetian, Lombard, or Genoese merchants, quickly weighing obligations against possessions, to measure a man's net worth. From Italy, this strange new way of measuring things spread over the trade routes to the Low Countries, to Germany, then to the English-speaking people. As men passed it on, it acquired a lore of its own; subtleties of accounting developed to mirror each new volcanic outburst of western man's activity, until, finally, it became, as it is today, not only a tool of measurement but more—the supreme judgment of arithmetic on achievements of stone and flesh, of mind and spirit.

Which is how it appeared to John Ridgely Warren as he watched his Treasurer and attorney examining in his office the balance sheets of the corporation he directed to measure its worth and thus, inferentially, him.

As Schlafman questioned Austin, it was as if Warren were observing Austin for the first time in the two years they had worked together. William Bartlett Austin was of the Old Team, a thirty-year man. When Warren had first joined General American Publishing two years ago and first watched Austin at meetings, he had been amused by Austin's doodlings. Across any scratch pad of blank paper, large or small, Austin's pencil would slowly draw a line down the center, then another line across the middle, then another line quartering and subdividing the blocks into columns. Then Austin would endlessly fill the columns with thin neat files of zeros—zero zero zero decimal point zero zero—as if he were drawing an imaginary trial balance. But now, as Austin sat stiffly, prim, lean, white-haired, his pince-nez glistening on his thin nose, a huge black book of accounts awkwardly held on his knees, Austin was not doodling. He was making the figures dance.

Austin clutched the book with the balance sheets almost tenderly. He would have cradled the account books of any corporation with the same tenderness whether the figures reflected the marketing and making of shoes, steel, toilet tissue, rolled oats, or crutches. The figures themselves excited him. Here, in this flat book, acres of ledgers, bills, postings, accounts payable and receivable, payroll cards, Social Security cards, tax cards, came to final mobilization in the beautiful symmetry of addition and subtraction that rendered ultimate judgment of profit and loss. To Austin, Treasurer and Comptroller of General American Publishing Company, the yellow sheets of his big book were a mirror of life itself.

Now Austin was talking to Schlafman in a voice as animated as Warren had ever heard it, while Schlafman sat easily on the office couch with a lawyer's pad on his knees, occasionally taking a note, more often leaning back against the wall, his hands locked behind his head, his dark face intense in concentration. It was as if Austin were cutting a way through a jungle of arithmetic so that Schlafman could follow. Schlafman followed willingly, occasionally asking Austin to slow down when the figures were unclear, occasionally inviting him to hurry when the figures told their own story. As precise answer locked on to quick question, and response led to yet another question, the minds of the two men seemed to nourish each other.

First, Austin described the family members of the corporation, the dramatis personae—except that the family members in Austin's tale were not people but the component operating divisions of the corporation. Austin had taken up the four divisions one by one, as if separating the sound from the sick with complete detachment. There were the three sound divisions. First was the radio division and here Austin's dry voice reached a maximum yet still sterile level of enthusiasm discussing the six radio stations that General American Publishing owned. Warren was sure that Austin had never listened to any of the six radio stations with their never-ending waterfall of thumping music, but the profit they were making, related to initial corporate investment, made Austin breathe over the figures as if he were reciting a prayer. Then came the textbook division, riding on the school boom, a solid, sturdy profit-maker. Then followed the division of trade magazines, published for various industries, job-printed and edited in Cleveland, dull little magazines unknown to anybody—but nevertheless profitable. Altogether these three divisions, these final worthwhile enterprises, were throwing off a net operating profit of four million dollars a year before their offerings were harvested by the corporation where they were absorbed—and lost, by the magazine division.

Though it was the magazines that had given birth to General American Publishing Company, and for a generation had endowed its executives with their importance in affairs, Austin examined the magazines now as if their red-stained figures were diseased tissue. Between them, by December thirty-first of this year, according to Austin's calculations, the two magazines would have lost some seven million dollars! And thus the profit of the good little divisions had been gobbled up by the seven millions the big bad magazines were losing—to make a net corporate loss of three million.

And so Austin came to the cash position. A magisterial disapproval chilled his voice as he lifted his attention from the books to stare at both the men. As the result of this morning's action of Mr. Silverman, the day's cash balance was down to approximately 150,000 dollars and Austin wanted Mr. Schlafman to grasp what that meant. Each month, every single month, the corporation was losing approximately 250,000 dollars. And even though Mr. Warren had cut the paper order today down to one thousand tons a week and thus had choked down the outgo temporarily, it meant they were printing the magazine out of inventory stocks. Even though they were very thin issues, not using much paper, nonetheless by Christmas they would lack sufficient paper even to print the thinnest of issues and still meet circulation guarantees.

Beyond that, glowered the year-end obligations. Five hundred thousand to Silverman on the first of January, promised this morning; another 250,000 dollars due as an installment on the color presses they had bought a year ago; Campbell would certainly press for his overdue 150,000-dollar ink bill when he learned Silverman had received part payment; then there must be another 100,000 dollars of nuisance bills for general services like window-washing, insurance, cleaning service, telephone bills, typewriter repair. To say nothing of the Christmas bonus that everyone expected. Well, there'd be no Christmas bonus this year, he could tell you, said Austin. Oh, there was money coming in all right, said Austin; but more was due out than was due in. It was like a pump, still drawing water, but sucking dry, too. By the first of the year, they needed a minimum, an absolute minimum of one million new dollars just to meet what he could see ahead; and they would still be losing; they would have to borrow, but the bank—

Here, abruptly, Austin paused, detached a paperclip from one of his sheaf of papers and began to twist the clip back and forth in his thin, blue-veined hands.

"Mr. Warren," said Austin as he began to scratch the back of his neck with the paperclip, "I wonder whether I can take up one matter privately with you. I realize I'm being rude to Mr. Schlafman, but—"

"Sure," broke in Schlafman, "why don't I leave the room for a couple of minutes and then come back? I don't mind at all," he said, as he rose.

"No, Nat," said Warren, "one thing at a time—sit down."

Then, to Austin, "Let's finish up with our ledger position, then we can take a break and you and I will talk. You were at the cash position, Mr. Austin—we need, you say, another one million dollars by January first or fifteenth."

"Yes," said Austin, "I had about finished the cash position," and was silent again.

"I suppose," said Schlafman, "that means you'll have to borrow it on short notice, and that means they'll squeeze you for it. What's the general worth of the firm, the general assets you can borrow on—?"

Austin resumed talking, but this time to Schlafman, not to Warren, and a subtle change was now sounding in his voice, as if he were making a plea with his figures.

Austin began slowly on the new tack. He understood Mr. Schlafman was here to give them a preliminary opinion on various legal dangers they might be entering in a tight period like this. Therefore, he wanted to point out to Mr. Schlafman that the picture was not necessarily as bleak as the bare figures showed it. No, not at all. For if the seven million annual loss of the magazines could be suppressed, then the situation would be entirely different. Then General American Publishing could go looking for a loan with a new face. It could show a corporate basket of three divisions throwing off four million dollars of profit a year. Not only that—not a dollar of taxes need be paid on that profit, for the tax-loss carryover of the bad years was great enough to free them from taxes for at least three years into the future. Besides, continued Austin —if one suppressed the loss there would be the empty plant in Anderbury, plus the presses in Anderbury—which might fetch six to ten million dollars in cash if sold carefully. So that, all in all, if the annual seven-million-dollar magazine loss were wiped out, what was now a corporation tottering on the edge of danger would become a prize, a prime candidate for everyone's credit.

"Ah-hah," said Schlafman slowly, for the first time giving up his role of auditor and questioner, "ah-hah, I see what you mean. If you fold the magazines, you've got a sweet operation here—"

"Nat," broke in Warren, coming alive now, angry. "Nat, I didn't ask you over here to talk about liquidating these magazines. We have three divisions running at a profit, and one big deficit-maker. But that deficit-maker could be the most promising thing in the magazine industry six months or a year from now—if we've got the wind to stay with it. That's my job: to whistle up the wind. We need another million this month. Well, we're carrying an open credit of three million from Security National Bank right now and I'll call them in the morning and see if they won't open another million for ninety days. If they won't—"

"Mr. Warren," said Austin sharply, breaking in, "I *must* ask Mr. Schlafman to excuse us. I *must* speak to you, this afternoon or evening, *before* you call the bank."

The normally dry voice carried an intensity of emergency. Austin stared at Warren as if compelling him to yield.

"Do you want me out of the room, Ridge?" said Schlafman, rising again.

"No, Nat," said Warren, "you stay here. I want to talk to you about a few more things. Mr. Austin has finished, I think, and we'll go outside and talk there. Will this be long, Mr. Austin?"

Assured that it wasn't, Warren motioned Schlafman back to the couch, accompanied Austin through the anteroom, to the corridor, then turned to him and said, "What's up?"

"Mr. Warren," said Austin, "this is serious."

"I know it is," said Warren.

"No. What I'm going to tell you. The bank is calling a million of our credit."

Warren moved into the light to see Austin's face better.

"The bank is what?"

"I've been trying to reach you since lunch, Mr. Warren. I had lunch with Tegengren of National Security. Tegengren and I have been friends ever since the days when I first became a certified accountant, and he was assistant cashier over there. He handles our portfolio; he's on their loans committee. He told me to tell you, and no one else but you, that's why I couldn't speak to Mr. Schlafman, he wants this in absolute confidence. In any case, Tegengren wants us to know right away—he's convinced the loans committee at Security National is going to reduce our current line of credit by one million dollars on January first. I asked him why. He said it was partly because they were tightening generally, partly because they didn't like the look of our last three balance sheets."

"They can't do that," said Warren.

"They can. They will," said Austin flatly, "but the important thing is this," he continued, as if trying to drill one thought into Warren's mind, "the important thing is this: if Security National calls in one million dollars of our notes on January first, that's less than two months from now. Instead of having cash obligations of one million dollars to meet, we have obligations of two million dollars. And we simply can't meet them. If our bank cuts our credit, no bank in New York will touch us. We have to find outside money. But where?"

Suddenly, Austin clutched Warren by the elbow as if to press home the facts; the fingers squeezed, as Austin shook the forearm. The voice was no longer Austin's normal, bloodless tone; it quivered as the fingers quivered.

"I felt you ought to know as soon as possible," Austin whispered, as if to keep from being overheard even in the empty corridor. "We have a Board meeting coming up the first week in December, remember that, Mr. Warren, we have to face the Board. We have to pay for paper C.O.D. as of this morning. As of this afternoon we haven't enough cash to meet one half our current bills, one quarter of our current bills, a fraction of our current bills. We're down to $149,687 in the cash account and Security National will know that tomorrow. How are we going to pay everyone? What are we going to do?"

The grip of Austin's fingers tightened on Warren's arm and Warren could sense more than fear, he could sense panic. Instinctively, Warren put his arm around the old man's shoulders as if to steady him, then, feeling the quivering shoulders, he gave them a friendly squeeze.

"Hey, there, Will," he said firmly, "slow down! We have to think about that, but not here in the corridor."

"But we have to *do* something, do something about it *right away*," said Austin.

"Will," said Warren, realizing he had never called Austin by his first name before, "I know this is serious, but we can't do anything about it at the end of the day. You've had a rough time. I tell you what. Just try not to think about it until ten o'clock tomorrow, when you and I will think about it together. Give it to me to worry for the night."

He gave Austin's shoulders another squeeze and let go.

"I've got to go back to Schlafman now, Will. Don't say anything to anyone. Go home now and get a good night's sleep because tomorrow we have to face it head-on," he said, dismissing the Treasurer.

He turned back to Laura's anteroom, the sight of his Treasurer's pale face still printed on his mind; there, as the meaning of Austin's fear came to him, he paused, his hand on the doorknob of his office.

Austin's near-hysteria had forced a discipline on his own emotions. Now, in this moment, it slipped. It was not just another detail that Austin had given him in the corridor. It was not simply a big account chipped away from advertising. It was the clicking of the safety-latch being slipped off the stalker's trigger. If, in addition to the one million dollars in cash he had to have by January first, he needed another million to repay the bank, too, then he was trapped. One million, two million, stabbed through his head. One million, two million—and only 149,000 in cash in the current account this evening. One million, two million.

He saw Laura studying him, absorbed, as he waited.

"Any calls for me?" he asked, covering his emotion.

"No calls. Some late mail. Not important. A personal letter delivered at the reception desk downstairs by hand. I didn't open it."

He took the letter from her. It was in Mary's handwriting. He had not seen the handwriting for four years. He started to open it, automatically; then the shock of Austin's message rose again and swallowed him. He stuffed the letter in his pocket, leaned on the door of his office and turned to speak to Laura.

"Don't wait for me, Laura. This is a long conference. Quit at five. Get some rest and buy yourself some vitamins. We have a couple of mean weeks ahead."

Schlafman was stretched out full length on the couch as Warren reentered his office. Schlafman turned as Warren came in, let his feet drop to the floor and his elbows slowly pushed his body up as if he, too, were tired.

"Nat," said Warren, "don't get up for me."

As Schlafman hesitated, he insisted, "Go ahead, lie down again and I'll get us a drink. What'll you have? Bourbon? Scotch?"

"Bourbon," said Schlafman, lying down again.

Warren realized he was thirsty, that his mouth was dry, that he wanted this drink badly. With an effort he managed not to hurry as he went to the cabinet that held his liquor. As he poured, he noticed that one of his hands shook. He stopped, waited until the hand was steady and began again. When he returned, holding the bottle of bourbon and the two glasses, he carefully deposited the bottle on the floor, gave Schlafman his drink and put his own down. Then, still saying nothing, he pulled around an armchair, loosened his necktie, took a preliminary sip of his bourbon, sat down in the chair, raising his feet to the end of the couch beside Schlafman's, and took a longer pull of the good liquid.

"How are you, Nat?" said Warren finally.

"Tired, Ridge. Rough day in a rough town. But not as rough as yours by the looks of this—" and he tapped the sheets of notes that lay on his chest.

They both paused and Warren said, "Well—what do you think?"

"Think about what?" asked Schlafman.

"About the whole thing," said Warren. "I need some personal advice, Nat. I'm President, Chairman of the Board, Chief Executive Officer—I have as many titles here as the Czar of Russia. But I run a corporation on the edge of insolvency. I have a Board of Directors I no longer trust. I have a basket of problems on my desk this high, each one baited with a hidden hook. And I have to raise a hell of a lot of money in a hurry to keep going."

Warren took a heavy drink of the bourbon in his hand and heard Schlafman say in the silence, not unkindly, "Yup. I see that. Where do I come in?"

"Here. I know there are certain legal rules that bind my conduct, mine, personally, over and above what binds me as an officer of the corporation. What do the rules say? What do I have to be careful of?"

Schlafman let his hand drop to the floor beside the couch where his glass rested and drew it to his lips. He sipped, then put it down and twirled it ruminatively on the floor.

"O.K. . . . . Depends on what you want to do. When you called me this morning you mentioned Chapter Ten in Bankruptcy. I was hoping I'd have time to check the books on bankruptcy in the library before I came here, so I could be precise. I didn't. I came here direct from another conference. So I'm talking now from memory, just the landmarks of the law as I remember them. I'll check details specifically tomorrow morning, now—"

Schlafman came erect, sat on the edge of the couch, and, stooping forward to Warren, cupped his hands as if he were trying to cup a great many odd facts. Then he began to speak, deliberately and carefully.

"Nobody is suing you yet. According to Austin, the creditors are grumbling but passive. There's pressure. But no one's used the word receivership yet. Right?"

"Right."

"O.K. So what we're talking about isn't bankruptcy yet. Now, as for the laws on insolvency and bankruptcy—every individual case differs and there's a cuckoo's nest of law. Federal, State, Common Law, Equity, Fraud all involved here. SEC regulations, too. But most of those are matters of corporate law, stuff for your downtown lawyers to handle. You asked me here to advise you, personally, right?"

"Right," said Warren.

"O.K. Now the important thing you've got to carry in mind as Chief Executive Officer of a publicly chartered corporation is this: Do you believe that this outfit you're running is solvent? Or don't you? Whatever happens later, if you can establish that you presently *believe* this corporation to be solvent, I can prove that all your actions flowed from that reasonable faith and you're safe, personally, from either criminal or civil indictment, get it?"

"Why?" asked Warren, not following.

"Look at it backwards," said Schlafman, "it's easier that way. Let's make believe you're a crook. If you, as Chief Executive Officer of this corporation are convinced that the corporation is now insolvent, broke, can't ever meet its bills—then the law holds you responsible for conserving the assets of the corporation for the first legal claim against them. Which, in this case, are the creditors. If you don't preserve those assets, but keep on spending money, you're a crook. See? If you know that this corporation owes more than it can pay, then whatever is left at this moment belongs, by law, to the creditors and you have to save it for them. You try any tricks with what's left, and that's called diversion of assets and we—well, do you get the picture?"

"I do," said Warren, "but I am convinced that this is a going, solid operation."

"You mean that?" asked Schlafman. "Are you saying that for the record to me as your lawyer, or do you really mean it?"

A silence came over the two men. Schlafman went on, "Look, Ridge, that's not the chief thing I have to say. Let's stop worrying about personal actions against you in bankruptcy. There's something else you have to worry about."

"What's that?"

"Where you have to worry," went on Schlafman, "is when you go out to try to raise more money and make misleading statements to new investors. There you flirt with fraud. They can throw the book at you, then, because the definition of fraud is as broad as Coke's behind—the SEC, the Federal Courts, the State Courts, they've all had a whack at writing laws to put promoters in jail. And the way I see it, Ridge, that's your problem. You're safe personally in that chair from any action at law in bankruptcy against you as an individual. But if you sit still, from what your man Austin says, you're licked. You can't meet your bills without new money, and sooner or later if you haven't got it a couple of creditors are going to court to collect and push you over the edge. So you've got to raise more money fast. But the kind of picture your figures paint won't get you the money unless you color the picture with a lot of hope; and the kind of color you may have to put on those figures can be awfully close to fraud. Well," he concluded, taking another sip of whiskey, "is that what you wanted to know, or shall I make it fancy in longer words?"

"Don't bother with fancy words, I've got it," said Warren, pouring another drink from his bourbon bottle into his glass. "I'll repeat it for you. I'm safe personally if I do nothing. But then we either have to fold the magazines or face bankruptcy. And if I try to raise money, I have to be personally careful of statements with the coloration of fraud."

"That's it," said Schlafman. "Now, if your own bank wanted to advance you another million dollars for thirty or sixty days, which is what you need quick, then that's up to them, they know the situation here, you can't be accused of defrauding them. Have you talked this over with your bank yet?"

"That's what Austin wanted to talk about."

"What?"

"He was told in confidence—the bank is going to cut our credit by one million dollars."

"When?"

"January first. Calling a million cash from us. Which we haven't got. In addition to the other million I haven't got. Makes two million I haven't got that I have to get by January first."

A slow whistle came from the couch. Schlafman put his drink down carefully as if putting it away permanently, picked up his notes from the couch beside him, rose and went to Warren's desk.

"Ridge," said Schlafman, "let's look at these balance sheets Austin left."

Carrying his drink, Warren walked to the desk to join Schlafman. Both of them bent over the big sheets stretched on the desk, their heads close, studying the figures.

"I'm trying to remember what I ought to remember about balance sheets, Ridge," said Schlafman, "now, for example, look at that."

Schlafman's finger waggled at the bottom of the sheet on a line marked, "Fulfillment."

"Look at that—" he continued "—you owe fourteen million dollars, it says here for Fulfillment, biggest single obligation you have, what is it?"

"Magazines we owe to subscribers," snapped Warren. "Subscription fulfillment. Eight million people get these two magazines by mail. They've paid anywhere from one to six dollars for subscriptions running from twenty-nine weeks to three years, and we owe them magazines. But it's not really a debt, it's an asset, it cost us a fortune to get those people to subscribe—"

"Uh-uh, uh-uh," dissented Schlafman, "you made a contract to deliver magazines to those people. You owe them a buck or two apiece. No one of them is going to hire a lawyer to collect that money if you run out on them—but on the books it has to read as an obligation. That may be an asset to you, but downtown at the banks, Ridge, where they read this stuff the way my wife reads poetry, it's a debt, a prior obligation and can choke you."

"Now, look," said Warren, persisting, "it *is* an asset. Those are people all across the country waiting for my magazines. There's years, decades, of loyalty in those names; there's at least a couple of million dollars spent in the last year getting more names on those lists. Nat, that's an audience, the biggest thing we have. They're us. Why I could walk across the street right now to three other magazines, say I'm folding *Trumpet,* ask them if they want to buy circulation, and get two million dollars for the *Trumpet* names alone—I could wipe out *Trumpet's* nine-million-dollar share of that fourteen-million-dollar obligation like that."

Warren snapped his fingers.

Schlafman did not answer. He had been stooped over the sheets on the desk but now he straightened, circled the desk, and sat down in the chair opposite Warren's desk.

"You mean," he said, thinking out loud, "you mean if you folded the magazines, you could wipe that fourteen-million-dollar obligation off your sheets, and sell the *Trumpet* names for two million dollars cash to boot?"

"Yes," said Warren, "of course I could. If I were folding. But I'm not."

"I'm beginning to see what Austin was talking about," said Schlafman, as if he had not heard Warren. "Also, if you wipe out the magazines, you have a plant you can sell for at least six million dollars and that would give you eight million dollars in cash—more than enough to pay all the bills. Then you're left with the other three divisions in the firm all making money. What a property! I'm thinking out loud now, Ridge, but what if somebody makes that pitch to the Board? There's money to be made out of it. That stock of yours is selling for about eight now. It could double, triple, quadruple in value if you killed those magazines. Have you thought about it?"

Warren had thought about nothing else for weeks except that. Yet to have Schlafman say it out loud, so soon after Austin had said it, after all the conversations of the morning, irritated him. The whole world was pushing him, even his lawyer.

"Nat," said Warren quietly, "I hold fifty thousand options and warrants to buy that stock at ten. If it went to twenty, I'd have made five hundred thousand dollars for myself subject only to capital gains. I've thought of it, and I'm not ready to do it—"

"Hit me again," said Schlafman interrupting, "hit me again. I didn't hear it right. Did you say you had options on fifty thousand shares and it can go to twenty if you dump the magazines? Did I hear you right?"

"Yes," said Warren. He enjoyed the surprise in Schlafman's voice, the expression of disbelief in his face.

"Well, I'll be damned," said Schlafman. "I'll be double-damned. Listen, Ridge, this is big money, too big to fool around with. This is a perfect setup for a raid. Anybody downtown who knows the story could move in, buy up this stock at cut-rate right now, liquidate the magazines and come out with a fortune. Have you thought of that? Even if you raised two or three million dollars from the banks, what's to stop a stockholder's committee from forcing your hand?"

"Relax, Nat, the raiders are on board already."

"What do you mean, on board?"

"That's why I called you this morning, they sit on the Board and they're twisting my arm."

"Go on, tell me."

"It's this Board of Directors, Nat, it's so complicated," said Warren, and, as a wave of irritation swept over him, he walked back to the room to pour himself another drink, took an angry taste, and came back to the desk. He was angry, he realized, not so much at Morrissey as the trap.

"Go on," said Schlafman, "I've been here this long, I might as well hear it out. Just give me the headlines, not the detail. And, listen, Ridge, why don't you put that drink away? You've been belting it since you came back in."

Ignoring the last remark, Warren took another drink as he considered how tightly he could summarize the problem, then resumed.

"There's a Board of seven men. Theoretically, it's my Board. I put it together last year, the others had sat there for years—"

"Which others? Who?"

"The old crowd. Lawyers of the Pepper estate. Twenty or thirty years ago this was a family stock. During the war they started selling it to the public, and family ownership is down now to about ten per cent. But the family lawyers and trustees still controlled it until they brought me in two years ago. For a year, I thought they were Daddy—that they'd raise the money for the magazines, the way Congress raises money for the government, and I'd be President—I'd run things. That's what I came here for, to run the magazines. And then I discovered they'd trapped me. They didn't have any money; they didn't give a damn about the magazines—but they didn't have the guts to face the world and fold two household institutions of the country. That's what I was there for. Either to raise money to make them a property worth keeping—or fold them. So I tried to raise the dough."

"Where? When?"

"Lots of ways. First I had to learn about finance. Then I dug up a man called Morrissey who heads up a little clutch of operators downtown. They invest in special situations. They put up four and a half million dollars—in five-year debentures, convertible to stock at the price of ten per share. When Morrissey put up the money, he wanted a place on the Board. And the old crowd couldn't object because the alternative was to fold the magazines; they were afraid to do that, Morrissey and I had them over a barrel. So we reorganized the Board down from twelve to seven—two of the old trustees, plus Morrissey and a pilot-fish of his named Berger who goes in with him on the kill; and me; plus two management men—Austin, whom you just met, and Hopkins of Production. And Mr. Morrissey has decided he wants to fold."

"Why? How do you know?"

"Because of the reasons Austin just gave you. Morrissey doesn't give a damn about the magazines one way or another. He put up four and a half million dollars gambling that I could make the magazines show a profit in a year. Then the stock would jump, he'd convert for a killing, and I could do what I wanted. But we're still in a jam, the stock hasn't jumped, and the only way he can make his conversion on a rising stock is to fold the magazines. How do I know? Because he called me this morning. That's when I called you. He's afraid we're too close to the edge. He was the one who mentioned bankruptcy. He wants us to put together a plan for folding before the full Board meets in December."

"O.K. I get it. But look, Ridge—what the hell happened to the four and a half million dollars he put in last year? Where did it go?"

"Right here into the magazines. I spent it."

"Spent it?"

"All right—I gambled it. Listen, Nat, this whole business is a gamble."

Warren strode to the wall switch and cut the lights, so that darkness blotted out the desks, chairs, sofa, walls. Slowly the windows grew out of the black in a luminous velvet gray, and Warren walked toward them.

"Come over here, Nat," said Warren, and he could hear Schlafman rise to join him.

From the window they could see New York as darkness took it.

"Daylight-saving time ended last week," murmured Schlafman, almost as if he were seeing it for the first time in the year. "They chop an hour off the afternoon, and all of a sudden it's dark when you go home and winter is coming. It's as if they were darkening a theater just before the last act. One week you're still bouncing on your summer tan, and the next week you're getting ready for Christmas."

They gazed from the window. Far away south and off to the mouth of the river, they could see the fading light of day, still washing the underside of the evening clouds with the colors of sunset—lavender, and deep purple, rose, and red. Far, far off beyond the colors and almost beyond the rim of sight there stretched the faintest blue sliver of clear horizon left by the day that now rushed west across the country in swift retreat. But directly beneath them it was already dark and the city gleamed and glistened. Each building broke the darkness with a different pattern of light—some hollow with golden glow; others pricked out by a lattice of windows, each a tiny rectangle, or dot in the distance, of white and yellow; in others entire floors were slashed horizontally by gashes of green-blue fluorescent light; occasionally, shafts of perpendicular light streaked the dark black of a tower from peak to street where the elevators rose and fell. All together now at night, the great dark hulks of buildings seemed like magic mountains folded in ridges and ranges, climbing and aspiring one above the other, forced up out of the ground by an eternal energy, hollowed by mysterious glowing light within. As they watched, somewhere in a hidden place a switch was thrown and a cone of green light carved the huge shape of an entire structure, radiant and resplendent, from the gathering night. It was matched in a few moments, as their eyes rested on the city, by another switch floodlighting a wafer of dark bronze in golden-yellow and it, too, stood suddenly austere and splendid against the night.

"What was it you were going to say?" asked Schlafman quietly by his side, and Warren, with a start, realized he had meant to say something. He wrenched his mind from the hypnosis of the spectacle and said, "See, Nat. There's *Time* and *Life*. The other way you can see *Look*. Down there somewhere is *Newsweek*. There's *Spectacle*. And all the others. Those are their lights. They're all working on new issues of magazines that won't be on the stands for weeks or months—and they're all gambling. They're gambling on what they can dream up this evening that's going to make an echo in the country ten days, or two weeks, or two months from now. Week after week, a bet on every issue that somehow you can reach out from here and touch them beyond the Hudson. And every minute of the time you're gambling—on how to mix hootchie-kootch dancers with TV stars, with girls in pink bathing suits, with disasters, with diaper-rash advice. How to put them all together with presidents, and peace, and war and politics. You're gambling on what's going to suck them in, and what you're going to tell them when they're there; you have to guess for the whole country, all the way off beyond there."

Warren waved his hand toward the fast-vanishing patch of light to the west, which was almost gone. But the further edge of the light, he knew, reached all the way across to the Pacific. He was talking to himself.

"Right here, Nat, you put the point of a compass down where this building is and swing a mile around it. All the radio nets and all the TV nets are in the circle. All the syndicates and all the press agencies. Every advertising agency and word packager is here. The Cardinal sits here. They decide what movies Hollywood is going to make from here. They publish ninety per cent of the books in the country here. The magazines are all here, or almost all of us. And we're all guessing, guessing what makes them angry, what makes them cry, what makes them laugh. We sell them dreams, and ideas, and news. They couldn't live without the stuff, but they don't know it themselves. In Russia, the Kremlin decides what they need to know and dream, but here, we do it—by guessing and gambling and instinct. And all it makes is an echo. People start to listen without knowing, and they stop listening without knowing. And I have to sell this echo to soap merchants and cranberry growers to make a profit on the echo."

He turned now on Schlafman, remembering the question that had launched him.

"You asked me where the money went? That's where it went, into making an echo. People stopped listening to these magazines ten years ago and they kept on buying them only out of habit. That's the way it was when I came in; I had to bring them back. That's where I spent Morrissey's money, building circulation. That's why that list is worth more than two million dollars to me. Those names are my gamble; if I can make them listen to me, I can pull this thing through, I know I can."

"But, Ridge, for Christ's sake, this is Hollywood talk. You can't raise the millions you need on an echo here. This is the town where they count. Dreams have got to balance out on a cash basis like fish-cakes and ladies' wear—"

"To hell with the balance sheet; there's got to be a way."

"Like what?"

"Like a dozen things—sell the radio division and put the money in the magazines. Or spin off the radio stations as a subsidiary corporation and let the stations borrow the money for us and bring the money back up-stream for the magazines, or—"

"If your Board of Directors went along with that, they'd be crazy. If any of them were my clients I'd tell them they were mad to suck up the hard assets and sell them off to feed into the magazines. That's like digging out your guts and eating them because you're hungry—"

"Nat, I can think of a million reasons for this to go under, and I can't think of a single good one to keep them alive except that I *want* them to survive."

Warren found himself pounding his fist on the sill, like Foley, but he did not care.

"Because I want them to," he repeated, "I've gambled this far, and I'm going on with it. What I need now is cash, just cash. If the Board won't help me raise the money, they either have to get rid of me, or let me decide for them. And if that means taking the whole thing to the edge of receivership, they'll *have* to follow me. Somewhere in this town, there's money. All I have to do is find it."

"Hey, Ridge," said Schlafman, still in the dark, his voice puzzled, "let me ask you a personal question now, not a lawyer's question. If you sit still and let the magazines fold, your options could bring you half a million bucks in a year. It's not smart to throw that away. Tell me this— what in hell is making you do it?"

"Why Nat," said Warren, as if he were explaining the sun to a child, "you can't fold these magazines. They're institutions. They're America. It's a matter of conscience. This is my base, Nat—"

"But, Ridge," said Schlafman, "America goes on anyway. And this shop is a better base without the magazines. Supposing you raise the dough, and get through this winter—you've still got a headache on your hands, with a good chance the Board will kick you out the next time it hits the fan, or a receivership will. And if a court moves a receiver in here, he not only wipes out your options, but you lose your reputation, too. In this town, a man who puts a firm in bankruptcy is a leper for the rest of his life. Get rid of the magazines, and you've got a better base and half a million bucks, too. Ridge, can't you see it?"

"Oh the hell with it!" burst out Warren. "Of course I want that half-million bucks, Nat," he yelled, his anger growing because he could explain to neither himself nor Schlafman why he wanted to go on. "But Nat, I've got to be free. And the half a million can't help. Only the magazines can. Without the magazines, this outfit is nothing. I'm not free to torpedo them, Nat. They've got to go on. I'm only free to keep them alive, and then when the echo is back, then I can do what I want. There's something about the way this country is changing that makes me want to keep them alive. The country's getting bigger and bigger, swollen with people, and fewer and fewer people get to have a say about what goes on— Nat, look, do you know anything about the man who founded this company?"

"Not much," said Schlafman, "one of those old families, name of Pepper, got into it through the printing business. What's that got to do with my question?"

"Nat—let me take it from Pepper. He came into this town from upstate New York about eighteen-ninety, knowing nothing except the printing business, and went into magazines. Try to make believe you were back then. They'd just finished building the railways across the country; it was one platform. Now any factory anywhere can ship its goods from coast to coast for the first time. The whole country is one market, you can make one brand image for the whole nation and deliver—but only if you can find a way of talking to the whole country at once. They need a big horn, Nat, a big horn that will reach everybody.

"And Pepper comes along just then—with a magazine he calls *Trumpet*. Not only that. Everything was beginning to fit together then. They were developing high-speed rotary presses that could throw off a couple of million copies of a magazine in a few days, enough to supply the whole country, with the railways finished, ready to deliver. And something else, too—someone develops half-tone photo-engraving so magazines can use pictures, cheap. Pictures for millions of immigrants just beginning to read English, or can't be sucked into reading unless there's a picture with it. All of it right there, coming together, with industry screaming for a way to sell pianos, baby carriages, kerosene lamps, stoves from coast to coast. They want a horn to talk to the market—and there's Pepper with his first magazine, *Trumpet*—"

Warren paused, out of breath, and Schlafman broke in, "Now I know you're drunk. I asked you a simple question, and I'm getting a history of American business."

"It's not a simple question," said Warren, "you asked it, now listen. Do you know what happened when national magazines started to develop?"

"No," said Schlafman, "go ahead, Professor."

"—They had to invent a new kind of person to run them! It was the first time anybody except the President of the United States had to sit in an office and think about this whole damned country all at once. Some editor had to think not just what the local people in Chicago, or New York, or Charleston, or San Francisco wanted to read, but what would hold an audience together across the whole land, from coast to coast. The first time somebody sat in this kind of office in New York and started to play with the mind of the country, things started to happen. Nat, for the past fifty years anything this country has done, the magazines kicked them into doing—the magazines closed up the trusts, cleaned up the cities, put through the food-and-drug acts, amended the Constitution, closed off immigration, with this magazine leading the way! Do you know what I'm saying, Nat? Pepper invented the first talking horn, and anybody who sits in this office has a hold on the biggest talking horn ever built."

He whirled on Schlafman in the dark, trying to drive his point home. "Think of it! The whole country racing and changing all around us, everybody being pushed along into tomorrow or wherever the hell it is we're going. But when you sit here in this office, you're not being swept along—you're making the changes happen. You can take a punk in a local racket and make him a national villain; you can take an ordinary senator and make him a presidential candidate. You can pick anything you want out of the darkness, put the light on it—and the country looks and begins to imitate it. It's more than influence, Nat; it's even more than power—goddamnit, you're free, Nat, and there's no way the balance sheet can count it. I've got the little end of the big horn in my hand, right here, Nat. When I talk, they'll listen. That's why I'm in it!"

There was a long silence, and Warren was afraid he had lost Schlafman, bored him.

"But, Ridge," said Schlafman finally, softly, and Warren realized he had not lost him, "but Ridge, what do you want to say?"

"I don't know yet, Nat," he said. "How does anyone know what he's going to see until he gets to the top of the mountain? We're just getting there, Nat, I've engineered the audience, now all I need is another four or five million dollars just for twelve months to find out what I can see from the top; I'm not free yet, I need that money to find out—"

"Hey, Ridge," said Schlafman, breaking in, "I'll tell you something, it just came to me."

"What?" asked Warren.

"Why don't you run those magazines yourself? You ought to be the editor, the one who sees the way it looks from up top. You ought to hire some jerk as the publisher and let him sweat with the bookkeeping and the Board."

A seventh instinct told Warren to be quiet. When somebody touched you close, the thing was not to give it away by talking. What the magazines needed was an editor, someone who said how it looks. That was what had been wrong at the story conference. If the magazines were to mean anything, he would have to give it to them. It could not be engineered.

Then he shook his head. Somebody still had to raise the money. That was the responsibility he had taken when he became publisher. In this town, unless you had the base and the money, nobody listened to you. The base came first. Then you needed the money to protect the base. Then, after that, you were free to say what you wanted to say. In terms of money, Schlafman was right—he was a fool. He ought to fold. But he could not fold.

His eyes, now accustomed to the dark outside, picked out a flight of birds swooping by his window. You never saw a bird in Manhattan, at ground level, he realized, except for sparrows and pigeons. The free-flying ones stayed high over Manhattan and rarely came as low as this, the level of his fortieth-story window. But these birds he was watching had strayed. Here they were now, swirling late on their autumn flight from north to south, pursued by gathering winter. One of the flight stopped for a moment on the parapet outside Warren's window. It was joined instantly by several others, passengers all, without baggage. They must not stay here, thought Warren, they ought to be moving on. Not knowing whether it was because he wanted to warn the birds or because it was time to go, he abruptly walked away from the window to the side-wall switch, pressed it, and flooded the room with light.

In the light, Schlafman's face was thoughtful. Warren saw the light had warned the birds away.

"It's late," said Schlafman, "I've got to get home. I tell you what, Ridge, I can't bill General American Publishing for this kind of talk, and I don't want to bill you. But I want to see how you work it out. Why don't you call me, personally, in the next month whenever you want to talk?"

"Fine, Nat," said Warren, "and thanks. Let me clear my desk and I'll go with you."

He had to be at Wyman Potter's tonight, and it was a black-tie dinner. He did not want to meet important people, but he knew he could not skip. He shuffled the papers on his desk quickly together, then, patting the pockets of his jacket in the routine gesture of parting, he felt the crumple of paper folded there. It was the letter from Mary which he had forgotten in the turbulence of the long conference.

"Got a second, Nat," he asked, "while I read this? It may change my plans for tonight."

But it did not. It was in Mair's familiar handwriting—round-scrawled, the tops of the *u*'s and *n*'s rounded so he could not tell them apart.

"Johnny," it said in salutation, and then as if a second salutation were necessary, "Johnny dear—! I didn't want to break in on you in conference. And you might not have wanted me to do so, either. I got in late last night from Paris. And I'm staying here at the New Weston until six this evening. You can reach me there. I have a plane ticket leaving La Guardia field for Cleveland at 7:15. I have to be home the first four or five days at Floss Hill. I'll be back in New York Saturday afternoon and be here until about December 10th, staying at Sara Hubbard's apartment on East 63rd Street, TEmpleton 1-9970. I'm not busy when I come back Saturday evening. Don't feel you have to call me then. Or at all. But I knew you'd want to know I'm in town. So I am, and due back in Paris, as I say, on December 10th. Love, Mary."

Warren looked at his watch. It was six o'clock. Too late. He wondered if he could reach her at La Guardia and persuade her, still, to take the morning plane. He really did not want to go to the Potters' tonight. He looked at his watch again. No, it was too late.

He turned to Schlafman, stifling his thoughts.

"I guess we'd better go, Nat. It *is* late."

6. Interlude—6:00 P.M.

1. DUCKWORTH'S OFFICE

Alan Duckworth sat in his office, his long gold cigarette-holder cocked at an angle, and enjoyed the strain on Teddy Wharton's face. Teddy Wharton, he was sure, drew down twice his own salary from Mid-Century Pictures, whom Wharton served as East Coast Publicity Chief. Yet it was Wharton who squirmed; Wharton squirmed not because of Duckworth, but because this was the office of the Entertainment Editor of *Trumpet*.

"Why should I?" Duckworth was saying.

"Because I tell you," said Wharton, "she's great. This isn't just a body I'm peddling, this is a woman who's going to be the greatest actress of her time. All she needs now is space to launch her. A four-page layout, imagine, on her first visit to New York, even a two-page layout. She needs exposure, and *Trumpet* is the place for her—"

"Who else have you tried to peddle her to?"

"No one, Duck, no one. I swear. You're the first. If *Trumpet* gives her space it means more for this kid than any other magazine."

"Nuts. I'll bet you offered her to *Life* and *Look* and *Post* and *Spectacle* before you came here—"

"No. I swear, you're the first, this girl is talent, exciting talent, your kind—"

"Nuts. I bought that line from you last time, and look where it got me. You promised me the first still photos on 'Extravaganza in Blue,' and then they show up in *Life* while we're on press, and we come out three weeks later. We look pretty silly, and Foley chews *me* out. How do I know there isn't already a four-page layout on her on press somewhere else?"

Wharton clapped his hands to his forehead, then took his temples in his two hands and rocked back and forth as if he were mourning.

"I've explained that 'Extravaganza in Blue' thing to you a million times. I got screwed by the Hollywood office. They promised *Life* an exclusive first out of the West Coast bureau, while I was promising you an exclusive first here in New York. I swear to God, this time no one will have her but you. It's not just a pitch I'm making. This kid has class, you can give her a break."

"Why don't you introduce her on one of those TV shows, get her interviewed, get her to do her little dance, or her imitation, or sing 'Miss Bo-Peep,' or whatever it is she does; why come to me?"

Wharton rocked back and forth, his simulated agony accented by his stooped shoulders and rhythmic swaying.

"No, not TV. This isn't a singer, she doesn't do imitations—she's an actress. An actress happens in Hollywood once every five years. I'm trying to do you a favor because of how you got screwed on 'Extravaganza in Blue' and you don't believe me."

"Nuts—! You're doing me a favor? All you want is free space."

"Look, O.K., have it your way and I'm pleading with *you* for a favor. Just look at some of these pictures of her, the new stills, you'll see her quality, see what I mean. For Christ's sake, look at the merchandise first, then give me a hard time if you don't like her."

Without waiting for a reply, Wharton opened his briefcase, pulled out a folder, and spread a sheaf of glossy photographs under Duckworth's eyes. It was a strange face Duckworth looked at: there was depth to the eyes, and the bones of the head were magnificent. He looked at the close-ups, and shuffled through the glossies to the full-view shots. The body was splendid—lithe, not too bosomy, good hips. You couldn't tell in black-and-white, but in full color she might dress up a two-page spread, even a four-page spread magnificently.

But could she act? Did she have a story? Conflicting loyalties clashed in Duckworth. He'd have to see her in color because the magazine had gone hog-wild for color the past few months. He'd have to know the story because there had to be a story for the people who still read. But could she act? That was it. Above all, was she genuine? He could not waste his entertainment space on anyone unless they were already established enough to pull in readership, like Larry Ledyard—or else were discoveries of such genuine talent that someday someone would vaguely remember that *Trumpet* had done the first story, which was more important. Space on the crowded stage of American attention was too precious to waste.

None of this did Duckworth say. But he knew Wharton was squirming because he, Duckworth, controlled one of the few spotlights that could, for a moment, pick one personality out of the jostling crowd and hold her there, briefly, for all the world to see.

Out loud, as he finished flipping the glossies, Duckworth said, "Lousy hairdo."

"I knew it, I knew it, the one thing wrong. I told them so; you put your finger on it right away. That's why I want you to do her with your own photographers, we'll fix her hairdo any way you want; you'll make the first image."

"When's she coming to town?"

"In two weeks. But she'll come any time you want, anytime. I'll fix up a date, dinner for the two of you, then spend the evening with her, bill me for it, she's not only class but she's friendly—very friendly."

"I've got a rule, Teddy—I never make a pass at anybody who gets her picture in *Trumpet*, either before *or* after the story."

"Who's talking about that? She's a virgin, or practically a virgin, at least nobody who's laid her yet has talked, so that makes her a virgin. This is class. All I want to do is arrange for you to meet her. Let me do it."

"I suppose so."

"Just one more thing. I'm not rushing you but suppose you think she is worth a spread in *Trumpet*, when do you think it could run?"

"No promise, Teddy, but let's see."

Duckworth consulted the advance schedule sheets of future issues and ruminated, "I've got all the entertainment stuff they're going to give me space for through Christmas. Got to clear out this Ledyard series first. Then a take-out on the Broadway hits. I'd say the earliest we can run a two-page spread is mid-January."

"Great! Wonderful, perfect timing for us! Listen, right now—let me put a call through to the Coast and talk to them, I'll tell them we're sitting together and—"

"No," said Duckworth, "for two reasons. Let Mid-Century pay for its own West Coast calls. And, second, I haven't said yes or no yet. All I said is I'd like to meet her and make up my mind."

"O.K., fair enough," said Wharton, then suddenly relaxed, the strain going off his face. "Mind if I finish a butt with you?"

"Go ahead," said Duckworth. They were through business now.

If that face could actually act, then the girl might someday be a famous name. If Duckworth chose to pick her out of the darkness and if all the other "ifs" worked—if they agreed to cut her hair differently in return for the pages he offered; if the hairdo clung to her personality; if Mid-Century really let her act; if she really had talent—if all the "ifs" worked, then, he, Duckworth would have introduced an image in the pantheon of the gods and goddesses by which the crowds lived. Some day hundreds of thousands of young women might be doing their hair the way she did, wearing the dresses she picked, aping their manners after hers. More than that—she would become not only an image and a personality, but a property, inflated by the magic value of public notice into a bankable asset for Mid-Century, for her agents, for her lawyers, for her exhibitors, for herself.

Wharton puffed his cigarette slowly.

"Sometimes you must feel like God," he said in a tone as grave and somber as earlier his sales voice had been metallic and wheedling.

"Why?" asked Duckworth.

"You can say yes or no. You say yes and this girl is off. She's a nice kid, Duck, I'm not selling you a pig. But you'll have helped make her. I get paid for making her. I don't say yes or no. They decide, then I go forth. Sometimes I wish I were back on your side of the desk again. I suppose it's money that makes the difference and I'm used to it now. Say, Duck?"

"What?"

"Say, about *Trumpet*—there's all this talk going around. Our advertising people say the magazine is shaky. I'm not nosing but—"

"People have been talking about us for years. I get paid every two weeks, I draw my bonus every year. Circulation is way up. We've got this new wizard who's been here for two years learning the magazine business, and I think now he's beginning to learn. Saw him today at the story conference and—"

Duckworth stopped. There was no sense in feeding the gossip mills of New York.

"I'm glad it's not true," said Wharton, "but if anything should go sour here, I like you. Give me a yell across the alley if you want to shift to the other side of the desk. There's a lot of money in being a flak. We might even have room at my place."

For a moment, Duckworth toyed with the thought of telling Wharton he would rather be dead than sit across a desk like this and promote a story. He was an editor, not a flak. He would live by his own taste, or else . . . he would . . . would what?

"Nice of you to say that, Teddy-boy. We're O.K. now but it's a nice thought."

"Ah, the hell with it," said Wharton, embarrassed, "do what you can for this babe, will you? Not that what I just said to you is tied up with this story about her. Shout at me if you need help, whether you give her space or not. Well, so long now. I got to get back to the horn and give Hollywood the bit about how I beat the brains out of the toughest entertainment editor in New York. The meaner I paint you, the better I look myself. That's life. Bye, kid."

Duckworth watched Wharton leave the office uneasily, reflecting that he ought to be friendlier to the flaks who called around in the next few months.

Not that they would help him. He had been too sharp an editor not to know how many enemies he had made, especially in Hollywood. Elsewhere, too. If they ever caught him in the open without cover. . . . He looked at his watch.

Almost six.

He would be late for that cocktail party. He had not planned on going —a typical Hollywood road show. But now—if he were not Entertainment Editor, to how many more such parties would he be invited?

As he emerged from the elevator to the street, Duckworth noticed the glossy black Cadillac by the door, and Warren's chauffeur waiting beside it. Warren was late tonight, too. Aloud, to himself, Duckworth said, "I hope to God he is learning something."

2 . AT THE BILTMORE

Joe Costello hurried from the office as fast as he could go, down the Avenue to the Biltmore, knowing a taxi would save him no time. He had told Merrill he'd meet him at five forty-five. It was already six. In those fifteen minutes, Merrill might already have hoisted two, for Merrill had begun to drink compulsively. And Costello wanted to put Merrill on the six thirty-five, on the way home to Stamford before he got really loaded.

Damn, if he could only do something to hold Merrill together long enough to last until the turnaround came. One good new account and Merrill would be O.K. A hell of a business this was, where two big new sales a year made you a hero; and without a new sale in a year you went to pieces. Which was why Janey Merrill had called him asking him to keep an eye on Charlie. He had to take care of Charlie Merrill—they'd been friends since they both came into *Trumpet* Advertising Sales together twenty years ago.

Costello burst into the bar, flung his coat at the checkroom girl, and spotted Merrill in a corner table by the platform. He could not tell whether it was the first or second drink, but Merrill appeared alert. Tired. But no more tired than all the others in the crowded room, sipping their strength for the commute home.

"Hi, Charlie," he said as he slid into the seat, "sorry I'm late, but we can still catch the six thirty-five."

Merrill was silent.

"How did it go," asked Costello, "sell any space? Get any knocks?"

"Can't tell," said Merrill slowly. "I gave Foods the college try again today. I used this morning's circulation report, blew on it till it made a flame. I think they're interested. But, you know how they are—they won't believe us until the Audit Bureau certifies the circulation uptown for the spring check. And we need to sell them now."

"Have they made up the placement schedule for next year yet?"

"Some. They've got their TV time lined up. They've got their programs for the women's books lined up, too. I see they've got *Gentlewoman* down for eight pages, which is good. Then, hell, there's an optional list and *Trumpet's* on the optional list. You know them, it's all done with computers—depends on the crop year, the spring plantings, the marketing surveys, what percentage of their budget they allot to advertising. It means I just have to keep calling every couple of weeks so they won't forget us until the time they get their estimates set. Nothing lost today, nothing gained. What happened at the office this afernoon?"

"Saw Russell. That's why I'm late."

"You did? What did he say?"

"Funny. I was just winding up, when he sort of leaned against the door and began to chew the rag. I figure that he must have wanted to spread the word. About the Christmas bonus."

Merrill picked up his glass and gulped. "What about the Christmas bonus?"

"He said he was sure there was going to be a bonus this year, same as last year. He'd been upstairs talking to Warren and Warren is full of jazz. Things look real hot upstairs, a new promotion campaign based on a new Carnahan survey coming out after January first, a new personality profile, a couple of big slugs of full-page advertising in the daily bladders—"

"No kidding!"

"Well, he didn't say bonus outright, but when I asked him, he laughed and told me to relax. He knew I'd spread the word."

"Boy, do I need that bonus," Merrill's eyes glowed. "Janey needs an operation, Lenny's got a new girl he wants to invite to the senior dance—I've got that bonus spent three times already."

"Who hasn't? Say, Charlie, there's Page over there, shall I wave him over?"

"No, I'm sick of him. He's ratting on us to *Spectacle*."

"He's coming anyway; he spotted us."

Page approached, pulled out the third chair of the table, and sat down. "How have our senior space-peddlers done today?" he asked.

"Not bad," said Merrill stiffly, "I got a knock over at Foods today. How's Flash Page been doing?"

"I haven't been trying today," said Page. "No, today I'm in my reflective mood."

"And what have you been reflecting on, chum?" asked Costello. He did not want Merrill upset. He wanted Merrill safely out, relaxed, on the six thirty-five.

"On the stock market," said Page. "Today I arrived at a basic decision. I just sold my stock."

"You mean General American Publishing stock?"

"Got my little five hundred shares out at seven and seven-eighths. Lucky at that. A year ago they were worth ten. When I bought them they were worth eighteen. My broker said it was a brand saved from burning."

"You mean you did it through your own broker, Page? He must have asked you why."

"I told him why."

"But, Page, the word will get around in no time that insiders at General American Publishing are selling out; Jeezus, that's not going to do us any good."

"Nothing's going to do us any good," said Page curtly.

"Oh for God's sake," said Costello bitterly.

"Why not?" snarled Page. "What do I owe this firm? I have a wife, two kids, a mortgage, and over the years I must have spent seven thousand buying those five hundred shares. Now I get thirty-eight hundred out. We know what's happening."

"Well, maybe you've made a mistake," said Costello.

"Tell him about Russell," said Merrill eagerly.

"What about Russell?"

"Russell says this talk about no Christmas bonus this year is just crap. Warren told Russell this morning the whole thing is coming through on the nose. Warren is full of jazz, a whole new promotion campaign, maybe a million bucks of ad promotion to back us up after the first of—"

"Russell told you that?" said Page to Costello, chopping off Merrill. "Yup."

"Why didn't he tell me?"

"Maybe he figured you didn't need it, or didn't care."

Page frowned, then, "I wish I'd known this morning before I sold. Well, the stock isn't going anywhere until advertising shows in the pages and we'll know before anyone. Guess I ought to stick around for that bonus, though."

"Planning to go somewhere, Page?"

"Ain't saying, been thinking."

"Don't let us keep you if you're in a hurry," said Merrill tartly and Page rose.

"Nice sitting here talking with old friends at the end of day. You'll excuse me if I take off now."

"Good-by," said Costello; Merrill was silent.

"Joe," said Merrill when Page was gone, "you've got some of this stock too, haven't you?"

"We all have."

"You think he's right, selling now, I mean?"

"I think he's crazy. A lot of talk and a brain the size of a gold ball, that's Page. If they do fold the magazines the stock is bound to go *up* not *down*. I'm holding."

"You mean you think they could fold, is that why you're holding, Joe?"

"Charlie, I didn't say that. I said Page was a fool, that's all."

"Let's have another drink, Joe."

"We can't, we'll miss the six thirty-five."

"Just one more, Joe, we'll catch the seven-five."

It was either leave him to drink alone until the seven-five, or the seven thirty-five, or the eight-five—or bind him to just this one and get him safely on the seven-five and home. Costello decided quickly.

"O.K. It's a deal. We catch the seven-five. Tell me about this talk you had with the Foods people. Maybe we can put together a special presentation for them and clinch a place on this alternate list before they know about the spring plantings and the crop years, and the computers measure us out—"

"Yeah, let's talk about it now . . . they got these computers over there, they're crazy about computing the market . . . say, Joe, they use this word 'parameter' when they talk about computers, what the hell does 'parameter' mean? . . . Hey, waiter, two more bourbons on the rocks."

3. CIRCULATION FLOOR

When the receptionist called to say Mrs. Logan was in the lobby, Harry Logan's first impulse was to tell her he would be right down. But he checked himself.

"Tell her to come up to my office," he said instead, and heard her instructing Janet how to get to his twenty-eighth floor office as he hung up.

Janet ought to come up and see his new office, Harry Logan thought. He wanted her to feel it the way he did, now that he had made it out of Minneapolis to the New York office of General American Publishing. Big time now. He hastily shuffled the papers on his desk into one big wad and stuffed the wad into his desk. "Clean desk," he muttered to himself, "got to keep a clean desk in the big city."

He could tell by Janet's eyes, as she came in, that she was impressed.

"Welcome to New York, honey, this is where I work." He made a mock bow.

"Oooh!" she said, "Harry, is this really your office?"

"No," he said, "Mr. Warren, my friend, the President, just moved out of these quarters for a few days. Harry, he said, Harry, my friend, I want you to feel you're one of the family. You just take my office for a few days, he said, until we find something a little bit better for you—"

"Oh, Harry, quit kidding. I'm not that much of a country girl. Have you really seen him yet, Mr. Warren, I mean?"

"I haven't been within five floors of where he works, honey, but Corbett says I'll be introduced to him any day now."

"It isn't like Minneapolis, is it?" she said, looking around, "I mean with Morrison and Morrison, Real Estate and Insurance, just down the hall, and Judge Pike on the floor above—"

"And our friend, Geronimo the Indian Elevator Boy, and his ready bottle. No, honey, this is New York. This whole building, all the top seventeen floors, is nothing but General American Publishing. Say, did you call Minneapolis today? Did you speak to the kids? How are they?"

"Oh, Harry, I don't know whether we were right in coming here or not. They miss us terribly. Sally cried over the telephone and Doc tried to make believe he was grown up, but he was so sad. Harry, the kids don't *want* to come to New York. All their friends are in Minneapolis, and Doc said he might make captain on the football team next year if we weren't moving away. He made two touchdowns Saturday. Harry, what are we doing yanking them out like this? There's nothing for kids in New York."

"Look, Janet, we talked this over a hundred times before we decided to come here. There are fifteen million people in and around New York, and they all have kids and they grow up. As soon as you find a house and make some friends, we'll be all right. They'll love it here."

"I know, I know—but—"

"Look, honey, I'm tired of going over this. I could either sit in that three-room office in Minneapolis and be Northwest Regional Director of Newsstand Sales—or take this offer. They don't offer you a jump more than once in a lifetime in this outfit. I could see me tagged as good old Harry Logan, the Minneapolis Stick-in-the-Mud, safe, dependable and never going anywhere. I *had* to take this move. I pioneered the whole distribution of the magazines in supermarkets all by myself from that Minneapolis office when New York laughed at me. Now I'm Supermarket Chief for the whole country. For the first time in our lives we know where we're going. I'm on the track now. Maybe I'll never be Warren but I'm not stuck on my butt in Minneapolis—"

"But, Harry—"

"But, honey, we went through it all last month. I promise you'll feel better as soon as we find a house. Did you see any today?"

"Harry, Mother said over the phone that someone wants to buy our house back home. It's only fifteen thousand dollars they're offering, though. It's barely enough to make a down payment on a good house here. I was up in Briarcliff today, Harry, looking at houses but everything is so expensive. They have good schools there, and it's only half an hour for you by train to town. But . . . oh, Harry, I hate to sell the house back home."

"So do I," he said morosely, perching on his desk.

"Harry, do we have to sell the house back home? If anything went wrong here in New York, we'd always have that to go back to. Couldn't we just rent something here?"

He rose from the desk, took her by the arms, propelled her to a chair and then, reperched on his desk, said, "Honey, let's go over it all again. We can't afford to rent a house here. Right? So we have to buy one. Right? To buy one here, we have to sell the one in Minneapolis. Right? It's the only way that makes sense, so we just have to face it and do it."

"Harry, what if we rented a cheap house, here, and then rented the house back home to pay for it; it wouldn't hurt us for a year, then if anything went wrong—"

"What can go wrong here?" he snapped, exasperated. "Nothing's going wrong here. You're nervous, that's all. New York is tough the first few days. I've been here three weeks and I'm beginning to like it. You've only been here a week and it scares you."

"But if anything did go wrong here, we have friends back home in Minneapolis, lots of friends, everybody likes us there, we know everybody."

"Now, look, honey, I just know if you get a house and get the kids here you'll feel better. You're lonesome. Let's settle on a house by the end of the month and get the kids here and be all set for Christmas."

"But what about Thanksgiving? I want them here for Thanksgiving!"

"Oh for God's sake, Janet, stop crying." His irritation carried him further as he saw her shoulders shake and he added, "How the hell can we move in by Thanksgiving when you can't stop crying long enough to even look at a house?"

Her shoulders stopped heaving and, as she looked up, saying indignantly, "What?" he could see her nostrils begin to grow white. He had planned to have a good time tonight. Quickly he walked over and took her in his arms.

"Aw, honey, I'm sorry, I didn't mean that, I guess I'm tired, too. I love you, honey."

She sniffled and he moved her to arm's length.

"I tell you what, honey," he said hurriedly, "let's say the hell with it all and paint the town. We're away from the kids first time since we were married, all expenses paid. And what's more I've got a beautiful babe if she powders her nose. Come on, let's kiss and make up and paint the town."

He gave her a shake.

"A good steak, and a bottle of red wine, how about it?"

"I'm not in the mood for fun," she said doubtfully.

"You will be," he said firmly and turning her around gave her a spank.

As she fumbled in her purse, he continued, "Supposing Mr. Warren happened in here and I had to introduce you? Mr. Warren I'd say, I'd like you to meet my wife. She just slipped in the mail chute—smeared her makeup and shifted her wig a little, but she's a nice gal. That's all, Mr. Warren."

Janet smiled tentatively and said, "Harry, do we have to eat steak? We can have steak at the Hotel Nicolette in Minneapolis any Saturday."

"Anything you want, honey," he said, as they walked down the corridor, "this is New York. French, Italian, Chinese, Japanese, Armenian, Hindu food—you name it and General American Publishing will pay for it."

She had just finished repowdering her nose when the elevator door opened. Harry Logan saw Warren in deep conversation with a man he had never seen before. There was just time for him to let Janet in first and whisper out of the corner of his mouth, "That's him. Glad you fixed your wig?" She smiled brightly as they stood together and Logan stood very tall and erect. But Warren was busy talking to the other man.

". . . that's all it takes, Nat, is money, that's all."

Then Warren was silent and had left the elevator with his companion.

There's no question, thought Harry Logan, as he strolled out into the streets of New York, his wife on his arm, that New York is a great place to be. This is where the money is. . . . If only Janet can pull herself together and find a house, nothing can go wrong. That's the only problem. We're on the way now, nothing can go wrong.

4. AUSTIN'S OFFICE

Austin listened to Hopkins and tried not to scratch the itch on the back of his neck. It was the nervous itch again. Austin was nervous because of what had happened today, nervous because he had already missed the six-seventeen train home to Summit, New Jersey, and was sure he would miss the six-fifty, too. But Hopkins deserved a hearing. Hopkins had come all the way down from Anderbury and the plant just to talk to Warren; Hopkins was Vice President of Production and a member of the Board, as Austin was himself. Yet Hopkins had waited all day and not been able to get in to Warren.

Hopkins was talking too much. The usually taciturn Hopkins became a talking machine when he arrived in New York. New York upset him.

Now, Hopkins' enormous girth overflowed the chair and the big cigar was smoking like a New England mill; Austin hated the cigars that Hopkins smoked, had hated them for however many of their forty years in joint service to General American Publishing they had known each other. But Hopkins was in full voice.

". . . been here all day, came in on the Owl, caught it out of Boston, got in here at eight thirty, and right to the office. Not a bit tired, though, it must be the air that makes people go like this here. I wouldn't want to live here though, no sir, that's a fact, but I do enjoy a visit here now and then. Makes me glad to get back to Anderbury when I do get home, real friendly town, Anderbury, homey town, wouldn't want a nicer bunch of people to live with, even the foreign element there are fine people. . . ."

Austin wished Hopkins would get to the point of this visit. It was not like Hopkins to come down from Massachusetts except for Board meetings. Peering at his contemporary, irritated by the cigar, noting Hopkins' faded blue eyes, the hair still bristling yet halfway between gray and white, the flushed rubicund face that age brings a man who has always eaten well, Austin wondered if the decades had changed him as much as Hopkins, and wished again that Hopkins would come to the point.

"Well," said Hopkins, as if he had finally been called to order by Austin's tense attitude of expectancy, "both good news and trouble today. Wish I could have seen Warren today but I reckon he's busy. But good news first, like the fellow said when he wrote the soldier his wife was having a baby, and I just wanted Warren to take a look at this package here—"

With this, Hopkins' heavy frame stirred nimbly, his hand slipped a brown Manila envelope out from under his bottom, and he pushed himself up, opening the envelope and spreading its pages before Austin.

"Did you ever see anything like that?" asked Hopkins, as he unfolded several double-page spreads of color printing before Austin. "Did you ever see any color work half as good as that in this country? Why, that's as good as the best color printing they do in Switzerland or France. And this isn't Swiss stuff, either, for a little printing of ten thousand. By God, this is American color work, and we can run off six million five impressions for either magazine on a four-day run. Just look at that gravy!"

Hopkins' finger had stopped at an illustration of a meat loaf. The brown of the meat loaf was a deep, velvet brown, with buds of cream-white onion peeping through the various shades of brown—blood-brown, russet-brown, gray-brown. The colors of the meat loaf had texture, while the gravy shimmered and shone so that as Hopkins ran his finger caressingly over the work, Austin felt the finger might wipe away some of the gravy to lick and taste.

"Good now, isn't it?" said Hopkins. "But look at this Jello ad," and Austin realized he was now looking at the page-proofs of a Jello advertisement in *Gentlewoman*. "This deep green stuff," said Hopkins, continuing, "is the trickiest thing of all, real handwork in the engraving, and the registry's got to be right within a baby's hair to give it depth. Else that green is liable to come out flat as a pancake. Got to know what you're doing with that new color press. But these are just right. . . ."

The colors *were* just right. The green of the lime Jello glistened in every shade from the faintest sheen of emerald, to deeper apple green, to the prickling viridian green of the lime itself. The Jello jiggled on the page-proof. Austin could never understand Hopkins' talk of printing, registry, heat-drying, engraving, rectifications except when they were translated into figures. The colors were beautiful, Austin's untrained eye could admit. But Austin knew the figures were wrong. Warren's investment in the new color press, this toy for Hopkins' plant, was still unpaid for. And another installment due in January.

It was as if Hopkins followed the meaning of Austin's silence.

"Only thing is we ain't getting enough use of that press. Those salesmen fellows ought to sell more ads in the magazine to use that color. Well, if you can't boost, don't knock, like the fellow says. They have their troubles, too, I guess. I just came up here to tell Warren, finally, that our new color press is adjusted, it's rolling, we're proud of it, and we own and operate the best color printing operation in the whole United States of America. What was the matter with Warren, today? Couldn't get to see him anyhow."

"He asked me to tell you he was terribly sorry, he was just tied up in knots."

"All right with me. Just wanted to thank him personally, give credit where credit's due, I say. I'd been screaming for new color presses ever since the end of the war and nobody on that penny-pinching Board even gave me a listening-to until he came along, and saw we needed color just the same as the competition had. That color press and the new Babcock, a million-dollar baby that Babcock, but—"

"A million-dollar monster, that's what the new Babcock press is," said Austin sourly, suddenly scratching the back of his neck, as the thought of all the money tied up in the new plant equipment suddenly came to him. "Very good work, Bert," said Austin, recovering, knowing how much Hopkins loved the machinery, "but that's the good news you said you had. What's the bad news?"

Hopkins folded the page-proofs, deflated, and sat down again in his chair. He lit his cigar, then began again.

"It's the union," said Hopkins, shooting out a jet of smoke, "I think we ought to get ready for them. Contract runs out on January thirtieth, and I've been talking to some of the men at the plant. Informally, you know, no negotiations, you know, just holding my finger to the wind, like the fellow says."

"Yes?"

"Well, they're going to ask another fourteen per cent jump and a whole passel of fringe benefits. I want to be tough this time. Not a nickel more than a six per cent raise. I start by offering them four per cent, then, later, I'll close at six per cent, maybe seven per cent raise, see? But I want to be sure you people in New York back me up."

"Out of the question," snapped Austin with an anger that surprised Hopkins. "You tell them any raise at all now will put us out of business and them out of work."

Hopkins threw back his head and laughed.

"You don't mind my saying so, Will, no offense intended, you sit here with figures, but I handle men. That's the first thing anybody says in union negotiation. I've been saying that to them for eighteen years now. They don't believe it any more than I do. Got to give them *something*. The only question is how little we can get away with without getting them hung on a strike. Stitch in time saves nine, I always say. Once these unions get hooked in a negotiating position, they sometimes have to go out on strike without wanting to themselves. You better leave the union to me, I know them."

"No raise," repeated Austin, white-lipped, tense, "not a penny."

"You mean that, Will?" asked Hopkins, some of the geniality draining from him. "But look, I'm in a terrible position to tell them that. They think we're fat. With these new presses installed and operating like a Swiss watch, the boys have their tail up . . . they—"

But Austin broke in, "Bert—the old presses. What are we doing with them?"

"Why they're right there. We moved some out into the warehouse, some still on the line. Perfect condition. All greased and tuned, spin them once a month to make sure they're all right—"

"How much are they worth?"

"Depends, Will, whether you're buying or selling. Couldn't buy equipment like that for less than a million. Selling? If we handle it right, well—"

"Right now, what could we sell them for?"

"You have to dicker on that sort of thing, Will. With a little country trading, lots of time, I might fetch half a million, six hundred thousand for them. If we peddle it like a fire sale, we'll get scrap-iron men bidding, won't get more than one hundred, two hundred thousand for them. Anyway—it's out of the question, I won't hear of selling them."

"We have to."

"Not unless Warren says so. I'm in charge of Production. Won't hear of anything so foolish. Penny wise, pound foolish, that's what it is. We may not be using them now because the magazines are so thin. But what happens when the turnaround comes? When we have to print one hundred thirty-six or one hundred fifty-eight page editions again? Hey, how about that? Can't do it without the old equipment on standby—"

"We have to," whispered Austin, "now. Right now. Bert, how fast can you move?"

Hopkins stared at Austin, the cigar slowly drooping in his lips. He leaned forward and the ash dropped over his vest. Hopkins did not bother to wipe it off.

"Will," he said, "Will, you mean this talk going around, you mean, this talk, there's something to it? Will, what's happening around here?"

Austin was silent.

"Will," said Hopkins, "I'm on the Board of Directors, too, I'm Vice President of Production, don't hold out on me like a little boy cat got his tongue. Why couldn't Warren see me today?"

Austin was silent.

"You don't want to believe this talk, Will, everybody's nervous in New York," said Hopkins. "It's always darkest just before the dawn. Why I remember when Old Man Pepper put me on the Board back in nineteen thirty-two, we were running *seventy-six*-page issues then, it looked worse than it did now. Say, Will, why that was the year he put you on the Board, too, wasn't it? Both of us in the same year, remember he introduced us and said the firm needed young blood on the Board, hah?"

Hopkins slapped his knees, guffawing. "Young blood, that was us, remember?"

Slowly, a thin smile stretched across Austin's face, and the hand which had been scratching his neck dropped.

"Say," said Hopkins, "Will, do you suppose Mrs. Austin would let you stay in town until nine o'clock and have dinner with me? I catch the night-special at Grand Central at ten o'clock to go back; maybe we could have dinner together and talk about this, and, you know, it isn't often we get to see each other out of the office, now, is it, Will?"

Suddenly Austin *did* want to talk to Hopkins. He had to talk to someone. Not about the bank, and the pressure and the conference with Mr. Schlafman. But about Mr. Pepper and the magazines and what was happening, only not tell Hopkins anything.

They were on the street five minutes later and it was dark and Hopkins was still talking.

". . . hope she didn't mind, Mrs. Austin, I mean. Fine woman you have there, Will. Mine always says bring them home for supper, but it would be different if we lived in New Jersey, too. Nice of her to let you eat with me, I hate to eat alone, anywhere, but I hate most to eat alone in this town. Say, Will . . . I'll be jiggered, what's that?"

Hopkins had stopped to look back at the huge building they had just left and now he was frozen, staring.

"What's what?"

"That!" Hopkins pointed with his finger back to the tower of General American Publishing and there on the top of the tower a huge sign in giant neon letters winked in red *Trumpet* and winked off and was replaced in green by *Gentlewoman*, which winked off and *Trumpet* replaced it.

"Oh," said Austin, his voice frosty, "one of Warren's ideas. He ordered it this summer. A neon sign for our roof. Thirty-six thousand dollars. They finished it last week. If you're high enough you can see it twenty miles away. He thought it was a good idea for us to be conspicuous."

"You've got to hand it to him," said Hopkins. "Not bad. I like the red and then the green. He's got real pep, hasn't he? Just right for the Christmas colors, too, isn't it?"

7. Meeting at a Bar—6:15 P.M.

David Eliot knew that Mary Warren was coming to the end of this conversation; they had not yet mentioned Ridge, and he wondered whether she would. He watched her drawing on her black gloves, the strong slender fingers disappearing in their suede sheathing and decided that New York lit her special qualities differently than had Paris.

In Paris, when Eliot had first known the Warrens, Mary Warren had appeared tall among European women; her black hair drawn back from well-molded cheeks and piled onto the back of her head had given her height, while the black, full eyebrows above the round direct eyes, the wide mouth with its perfect teeth, had given her a quality of directness and simplicity which Eliot had considered particularly American among the tense and brittle European women. When Eliot remembered enjoying the Warren home, it was because of that quality in Mary Warren which he used to think made the Warren apartment in Paris uniquely American.

But here in New York, he could see, the same qualities read differently. In the babble of this cocktail bar her directness was clothed with elegance. She had changed in the years since he had seen her. It was not so much the carriage of her body as she walked, nor its gracefully erect posture as she sat in the chair, nor the coolness of her voice and the hush she made between them as they talked in the noisy room. But rather the composure with which she had been telling him her story, and accepting him so easily back into the confidence of friendship, assuming he would not abuse the confidence. There was always a mystery about a person who held herself with such calm, so easily summing up the emotion of years.

They had only twenty minutes now before she must leave to catch the plane for Cleveland and in the past hour she had brought him to the point where he almost understood. She had spanned the lonely years after the separation from Ridge, gaily yet still seriously mocked her own work at the Cultural Attaché's office in Paris ("we call ourselves the missionaries of discontent"), then come to her meeting with this French engineer, Claude de la Taille, whom she wanted to marry. She had not yet even asked about Ridge.

Eliot did not like the story, at least not the ending of it. He could not say why except that it seemed odd to him that she should be coming back to New York and America to make up her mind whether or not to marry a man.

Now, for the first time, he registered his doubt. "Of course," he said, "if you were mine, I'd never let you get far enough away from me to have second thoughts. Certainly, I'd never let you go home. I'd prefer to force you to make up your mind in my arms."

"Why, thank you, David," she replied, smiling, "that's the American way of doing things. But the French take marriage seriously. Romance is one thing, marriage another. And besides I don't force easily. I think basically it's because becoming French isn't easy for me even though I feel half-French now. Do you know how long I've been away?"

"No," said Eliot, "how long?"

"Since nineteen forty-six," she said, "and it seems like a good idea to come home and touch base, to see my mother and father again, to see what America is like really, and—you can see, there are lots of things to think about."

"Like what?"

"Like, on the one hand, how completely easy I am with Claude when we're alone together, a complete sense of his being interested in me, and I in him. But you never live your life alone with a man, you live it in the midst of all the other people who make the setting of your life. Little things—like when we go to visit his parents and I have to remember to sit with my knees uncrossed. Well-bred Frenchwomen never cross their legs, or didn't used to, and Claude's parents are very proper and old-school—"

"You can learn to keep your knees stiff, while you visit—"

"Or whether I really want to spend the rest of my life in Paris, because it's lotus-land and I love it. Paris is like a feather bed for an American woman—so deliciously comfortable. But if you stay there long enough it begins to smother you. When you come back to New York after being away for so long, the way I did today, America slaps you—like a blast or a storm. There's a wildness and rush about it, as if everyone were hurrying to get something done that had to be done today, this minute. It catches you, you want to *do* things here. It's the drive you feel as soon as the first taxi-driver steps on the gas."

She stopped as if reflecting on her first day back home and Eliot said, "If it was drive you wanted—" Then he, too, stopped.

"Yes," she said, "if it was drive I wanted, why did I leave Ridge?"

Then, almost casually, "How is he?"

"I don't really know," said Eliot, not wanting to say too much, not knowing how to measure her interest. "I saw him today, but I don't see him often. I used to think we were close; I know I did when I was reporting the Marshall Plan out of Paris when I used to come to your house and we used to sit around and talk. Sometimes I think that's part of the coolness between us now: I think he still has me fixed in that Paris picture, the three of us having a good time. But then he was in government and I was reporting him, and now I work for him and I disagree with what he's doing to the magazines. Either reason is good enough for him to draw away from me."

"Probably both," she said quietly, and looked at her watch. "Is there time for one more drink?"

Did she want to talk about Ridge after all? Eliot hailed a waiter, ordered two more drinks and remained carefully silent. Eliot's profession and temperament had made him a watcher—if someone wanted to talk about something, it was best not to interfere by questioning.

"Probably both," she repeated as they waited, "there's always that in Ridge, two reasons for everything—one personal, and the other official, and he can never untangle them. You might think you were terribly close to him and you would suddenly find he was a million miles away, watching something you couldn't know, or thinking something to himself, as cold as ice, even in the singing and music— He used to love to sing, you know. . . ."

She paused, obviously remembering something far away.

"The singing and the music?"—Eliot invited her gently.

"You weren't there at our last Christmas party in Paris. I guess it was in 'fifty-three. No, you weren't there—"

"I came home in 'fifty-two," said Eliot, "to report the campaign."

"That's right," she said, "we had a truly wonderful Christmas party that year. That was the year Ridge was given Ambassadorial Rank and everyone was at our house, close and warm. Office people mostly, but the office people in the Plan were the last romantics left in the government and they were so glad that Ridge had finally made Ambassadorial Rank. They trusted him. Oh, David, more than that—they admired him, and liked him, and respected him, and they were all worried about the noises out of Washington about cutting down the foreign aid programs; they felt that with Ridge there he'd take care of them. They knew that Ridge really believed in things, he believed in what we were trying to do, and would protect it."

"He did, too," said Eliot. "A real ball of fire he was when they were putting Europe together. He used to care. He's still a ball of fire, but in a different way. What happened that Christmas?"

"He is?" she said. "He has that talent, you know, of taking anything and making it seem big and important without understanding even himself what's at the bottom of it. Well, that Christmas—"

She sipped her drink, which had finally come, and looked around at the green leather chairs, and the mirrors on the wall, and the babbling, chattering crowd in the bar and shook her head at them as if measuring and deciding against them, and went on. "Well, after everyone had gone home, there was still a fire in the fireplace and Ridge wanted just one more brandy. He always wants one more brandy. He hadn't been singing that night, and I'd noticed it. Well, we were drinking by the fireplace, just the two of us, and he was staring into the fire; there were only embers left and he said very simply that this was the last Christmas they would probably want to come here. They were all going to hate him when they learned about the firings—"

"Firings?"

"Yes. But he didn't use the word firings. He said he was convinced the new administration was going to cut the heart out of the overseas programs, and he'd been preparing something he called a master plan for reduction of personnel in the Paris office and the aid missions. Those were the same people who'd been with us all evening. Why, we'd spent Christmas together with the Flahertys for six years ever since the first aid mission to Greece in 'forty-seven. The de Kruyns were going to have their baby in June. They were all people who still believed. Ridge said he had to have some plan to offer Congress when they called him up for the hearings on foreign aid appropriations in February. I couldn't believe what he was saying. I asked why *he* should be the one to suggest the cuttings—"

She paused. "—and then that strange, unfathomable thing in him came out—"

"What thing?"

"You know—the hard thing in him. Ridge is all over the place, he can do absolutely anything. But he gets so interested in making things work, that he stops thinking about the people involved or even the principles. He said something had to be saved out of the overseas programs and if Washington sent someone over with a meat cleaver to chop across the board there'd be chaos. But if he planned the firing it would be done neatly, and something would be saved, the core of it, the machinery would be intact."

"Sometimes you have to do that," said Eliot mildly.

"Yes, I know," she said, "but this was something new in him. You see, David, he didn't think they ought to cut the foreign aid programs at all. A few years earlier he would have fought for the people who depended on him. At least he would have let himself be forced to plan firings. But now—no. If the cuts were going to come anyway, if firings were inevitable—he wanted to share the credit for it. If Washington was going to slash anyway, he wanted to slash for them—and testify in public at the Congressional hearings so he would be noticed. That was new."

"Oh," said Eliot, not wanting to show her how suddenly chilled he felt.

"I'm only beginning to see him clearly now," Mary went on. "You've seen him pace. You've seen him cut people short. He's restless. It pushes him from one thing to a bigger thing. In the beginning we kept moving because Ridge was always excited by what came next—and he believed in what came next. Then somewhere in Europe he stopped believing in anything, in what he was doing, in the Plan, even in friendship. It was as if he felt cheated, as if he'd been a fool because he'd been a believer. He wanted to move on to the next thing now, and he no longer cared what it was or how—"

"He did move on, too, didn't he?" said Eliot.

"Oh, yes," said Mary, "Ridge usually gets what he goes after. And he doesn't mean to do it at the expense of other people. It's not nearly that simple."

"Is that why you broke up—over the firings?"

"Oh no, not just that," she said. "It was an awful night. We said things we shouldn't ever have said. I told him he was a hypocrite, I told him he'd sell out his mother and father just to get ahead, oh, yes, I did. I told him he wouldn't have a friend in the world—I made a real bitch of myself that evening."

She shook her head with a sad smile.

"But it wasn't that night that broke it up. It's never just one night or one argument, I think. We'd loved each other. That was the night I suddenly saw I didn't any more. It used to be fun being with him, moving with him, seeing what came next. But the moving produced a kind of aimless drift. For me, mostly. I wasn't allowed to work because of his position, and somehow the moment was never right to have children. Next post, next move, when we were established, we kept telling each other. All we had together was the excitement, and the friends we made, and each other. Then when Ridge no longer cared about friends, and no longer had excitement because he believed in what he was doing—what was there? And those last few years in Europe, it changed between us, too. When we slept together, it wasn't love moving him any longer. There was a hardness, a coldness in his love-making, something savage, as if affection and warmness weren't involved in it, only some strange drive using me. His needs and preoccupations were somewhere else, his mind was away from me. Except in bed, I couldn't get his attention except by hurting him, or screaming at him. I screamed that night."

"I can't imagine you screaming," said Eliot, interrupting.

"Thank you, David," she acknowledged and went on. "But yes, I can. Any woman can scream. A woman who doesn't nag saves it up for a big scream, and I hate to nag. We saved it all up for that Christmas night. I suppose the people who were fired the next year would have been fired anyway by the program, but I couldn't see Ridge making a profit out of firing those same people who'd just left our house full of Christmas love. When he was transferred back in the spring, I stayed. Paris was more home than any place else and I got a job in the Embassy. Silly, isn't it?"

"Not so silly," said Eliot, liking her, "our Ridge is a tough boy."

"He always seems so strong to strangers. But deep down at heart, he's as frightened as he is reckless and he doesn't know what he wants—that's what makes him a gambler."

"He's gambling now, all right," said Eliot, the morning's conversation with Warren coming back at him.

"Oh?" she said, turning her thoughts with the turn of Eliot's remarks. "What's happening? I thought he was all safe and important now with this *Trumpet* and that woman's magazine, what's-its-name, *Gentlewoman*—a big publisher, an adviser to statesmen, friend of the mighty? What's the matter?"

"Damned if I know, Mary. You know how he is. The magazines are shaky. The whole town knows it. But Ridge sits there in his office, confident, easy, and denies there's anything wrong at all. Short-tempered. Always busy. Does it bother you if he's in trouble?"

She was quiet for a long while.

"You know, I thought it wouldn't make any difference to me. But it does. I don't want him to be in trouble."

"I understand that," said Eliot, "neither do I. If I had any sense I'd quit this job while I still have it. You might as well climb the Empire State Building as try to find a good job once you're out in the street. I wanted to tell him I was there for him this morning, that I'd be on deck to help until the sheriff came, but he chopped me off right in the middle."

"No one can help him," said Mary. "Don't try."

She began to make the preliminary moves of a woman preparing to go. She placed her purse on the table, opened it, pulled out her air ticket and stuffed it back. She took out her mirror, looked at herself, put it back, felt the back of her hair. Then, decisively, as if wiping out the conversation, she drew on her gloves again and snapped shut the catch of her purse.

"Let me check the desk for telephone messages," she said, "my bags are in the lobby."

"I'll meet you in the lobby as soon as I've paid the check," said Eliot and watched her go. She walked well, he thought, she neither waddled, nor flounced, nor swung her hips. She simply held her body high and let it carry her. She belonged here, not in Paris marrying into France. He was still wondering when they met in the lobby where she was claiming her bags.

"Any messages?" asked Eliot.

"No," she said, "he didn't call. I was half-expecting him to. David, I want to take back that last thing."

"What thing?"

"About not trying to help him. If you can—try."

Eliot was arranging for the bags to be carried to the street and she said as they walked, "Does he see anyone much in New York?"

"Men or women, what do you mean?"

"Don't tease me now, I'm simply curious—women, of course, or a woman."

"Damned if I know," said Eliot. "He wouldn't talk to me about it anyway, because I knew you. He's too busy going to important dinner parties and meetings to have much private life. Ridge isn't a nightclub boy. No, I'll be damned if I know what Ridge does at night—"

8. Fortieth Floor:
The View at Close of Day

If he knew what had brought him back to the office at this hour, it would be all clear. But Warren did not know and here he was, alone on the night-desolate fortieth floor, pacing the office when he should be home in bed, recharging for tomorrow.

It was not quite so alone, here in the office, as it would be alone at home in bed.

Perhaps that was it.

Warren had left Wyman Potter's party at eleven o'clock, dropped the Frys off at their apartment, then the Clarences, watched the Clarences swallowed by the bronze doors of their building, then heard Michael, his chauffeur, say, "Yes, sir?" then, again, "Home, sir?" before he recognized he could not go home.

Going back to the apartment was not going home. There was no one there—only furniture, and clothes, and bed, objects for a family. There was no one to speak to; or be angry with; or laugh with; or review the day; or discuss, with drowsy malice, Wyman Potter's party—and why, this evening, dinner at Wyman's had disturbed him.

Wyman lived, not in an apartment, but in a five-story brownstone house which spoke of security so deep it needed no decoration. The new rich, when they bought a brownstone on the East Side, did it over with brass, silver, gloss and flamboyant paintings. But Wyman Potter's brownstone was so dark-brown with age, so hung with somber tapestries that the elder J. P. Morgan would have felt at home. The people who came to Wyman Potter's came not so much for friendship or dinner, as to meet other important people.

It was the first time Warren had not been pleased to dine at Wyman Potter's. As he had studied the room of robust men stained with New York pallor, their heads neatly-barbered, their black suits skin-fit, Warren knew that for most of them, as previously for him, mere presence in Wyman Potter's house was, in itself, achievement. The autographed pictures on the sideboard of Wyman Potter's library—"To Wyman, with all best, Franklin Roosevelt"; "To Wyman, affectionately, D.D.E."; or "To Wyman, loyally, Van"; or "To Wyman, a good companion, Lucius," were all trophies of membership in the invisible club of men who decided things. They were not on display; they were there, naturally, because Wyman belonged; being at Wyman's for dinner meant that the guests belonged, too—or almost did.

After the men had finished their cigars in the library, and joined the ladies in the drawing room, Wyman Potter had cleared his throat on the bench before his fireplace and announced, as he always did, that now they would have general conversation. Minister Sharantan wanted to hear everything they had to say. Wyman Potter always built his parties about a guest of honor, occasionally a general or a scientist, more often a visiting foreign dignitary who wanted to meet important Americans. Tonight the visiting dignitary was Minister Sharantan, a squat, brown Indonesian, tongued with a British accent. And Minister Sharantan had wanted to discuss the problems of peace, and of little neutral nations, with these Americans. Minister Sharantan had droned on, and Wyman Potter had droned on, and in a few minutes Warren had realized they had no more ideas about peace than had Purcell at the story conference, and Warren had drowsed, nagged by the thought that someone ought to have some ideas about peace, and that Foley was responsible for getting the ideas into the magazines, but Foley couldn't, and. . . .

He had drowsed through the discussion, relieved that no one called on him to speak, and taken the Frys home, then the Clarences. But then he had not gone home himself. He had come here.

The party at Wyman Potter's had closed the day that Morrissey's telephone conversation had opened, and in the parenthesis they made were the questions. Somehow the walls of this office echoed with questions. Somewhere things had gone wrong.

But where?

Save the magazines. But how? Could you still? Pace. And pace. Pace from window to wall to desk to window to wall. Call in Morrissey and have it over with. Dodge Morrissey and play it to the end. Pace. And pace.

When had it gone wrong? If you could find the beginning of a question, you could find the answer. It had gone wrong before he came here. There never had been enough money from the day he arrived in this office to save these magazines. Then why had he come here? Why had he taken this offer, not the other offers? It had been a mistake to come here. But it was a mistake now to walk out on it. Either way, it was a mistake. But why?

Like Europe. Somewhere there had been a mistake in Europe, too. Had it been a mistake to go there; or a mistake to leave? It was like taking apart a series of Chinese boxes, one inside the other. There was always one more to open.

Start at Europe. Why was that a mistake?

It had seemed in the beginning so natural for the Warrens to go to Europe. The war was over and the Air Force had decided to survey the ruins of Germany. The Strategic Bombing Survey of Germany had held him in Europe in 1945 no more than four months; but then there had been the UNRRA program in Yugoslavia. Mary had joined him there in 1946; and from the first of the aid programs they had gone to the next, to Greece. And then there had been the Marshall Plan, and the lateral transfer to the Occupation in Germany, as Germany had come alive. And then all the other transfers, each one notch higher than the last until two years before the end, when they had finally reached Paris. And there, at the heart and center of the Plan, he had finally won the rank of Ambassador. The last thing I thoroughly believed, reflected Warren, was that it was better to have won the war than to have lost it. And since you had to keep it won, I stayed in Europe.

Was that the mistake, to have believed? Or to have believed too long?

It was in Paris that he had begun to wonder about that, when the rank of Ambassador had come to him because all the early important chieftains of the great Plan had already gone back to their waiting bases, because the impulse of the Plan, the last impulse of the huge war, had spent itself in them, as in the country. Sitting there in the office at the Hotel Talleyrand, where they had made Europe come alive, Warren had wondered how long the office would be there for him. For the more exciting a new government agency, the more bold its missions, then the less security it carried, the more dangerous its beguilement—unless you could go back to a base in the army, or in a university, or in a great industry which temporarily released you for high government service. You needed a base.

There he was, so thinking, when Amos Gurley came through shortly after the new administration had been elected—there was Warren, sitting with the title of Ambassador and the office, recognizing that his friends in Paris, who still remained with the Plan, were, like him, the last of the believers. They, like him, were spending the wrong years of their life in faith—the years of their bursting thirties. For only in the decade of his thirties does a successful man first sense collision with the rocketing thrust of his contemporaries as they all prepare to clash in the tight and crowded passages of their forties where men strike for the levers of command.

Gurley had pointed it out to him, made him see the mistake. Gurley had once been Warren's chief on the early aid mission in Germany in 1948 during the Occupation; but Gurley had returned to his safe base as head of the Caldwell Fund in New York and was passing through Paris to do a quick survey of the aid programs for the new administration. And because Gurley liked Warren, Gurley had told him the whole aid program was going to be cut, slashed to the bone.

Warren had winced. Gurley had seen the wince and remarked, "When there's a big pressure building, the only job an executive has is to translate it in terms of policy for his organization. Other people work out the details. Of course it means firings, Ridge—but being able to fire people is what separates the men from the boys. It's like getting into your first fist fight when you're a kid. After you've learned to fire people, you're a man. It's got to be done. Only a romantic thinks he can run with the hares and hunt with the hounds, Ridge. Don't be a romantic. You have to decide what you're responsible for."

Well, he had not been a romantic. He had suddenly seen them all in Europe, all the remaining staff of the Marshall Plan as it died, as Gurley must see them—parts and pieces of a problem that men like Gurley and Wyman Potter and people who gathered at Wyman Potter's house disposed of. You either disposed of the parts and pieces—or were disposed of, yourself, among them. Thus, he had acted.

But what was the mistake? Staying too long in Europe? Or leaving in the way he did? Either way, he had been flanked by mistake. As now. Either way he would make a mistake.

He had made no mistakes in Washington when he came back after the Plan, however. He had left the service rank of Ambassador for the political appointment of Assistant Secretary at the sub-Cabinet level in the new administration, knowing exactly what he was doing as he did it. The new post was to be a staging base, a scouting platform—for at the sub-Cabinet level one met the most important people and worked with them. It was too late in life to believe in anything any longer—it was time to come in for a landing.

His own scouting was educated by the experience of the many friends who had left government service over the years for the inner circle of executive power and decision outside Washington. Now, in his early forties, Warren could see that in the eyes of the older, important men he was still young. From Washington, the strange clan of Deciders radiated across the country in a thin and shifting net of persons who wove in-and-out of the Pentagon, in-and-out of State, in-and-out of the Treasury, in-and-out of the White House, then returned to bases in New York, or Chicago, or San Diego, or Seattle, or Dallas, or Detroit, or Boston. Together they held the keys to the invisible club of the high places whose rules were never written, and whose abode was never defined. Together, they formed the Establishment. They recruited their own successors by instinct and fellowship, calling on generals, ambassadors, senior officials to join their own younger executives in the deciding group of each succeeding generation. If you did not catch their eye when leaving government, you found yourself in the ten to fifteen thousand dollar basket, pushing brass fittings for an export agency, practicing law in a small town, teaching at a small university—or dropping completely from the sight-range of those who made and acted in great decision.

There had been three ways to go after the two years of scouting in Washington.

Star Airlines had felt him out for a Vice Presidency of Overseas Operations. The salary was good; and even more generous in terms of expense account, stock options, and retirement benefits. But there had been no lure but money in Star Airlines' offer—the real push in air transport came from the engineers, designing new jets with ever greater speed and capacity. The front office merely filled the seats and brought the passengers through customs. You were not really free if you went with Star.

He might have responded to the feelers from the Mid-West Foundation. But the Mid-West sat in Chicago—safe, dignified, goodwilled and sterile. It was not like the Ford Foundation with its odd mixture of brilliance, goodwill, madness and power which awkwardly broke its way into all important decisions. Nor was it a Rockefeller enterprise with its quiet prestige and hereditary pew in the Establishment. It was too early in life to join something like the Mid-West Foundation; it was like settling for the Civil Service, twenty years before; you did not decide, or shape things.

Which left General American Publishing.

It was Gurley who opened the way for him, Gurley whose membership in the Establishment was certified both by family name and the power of the Caldwell Fund that he headed in New York. On one of his visits to Washington, at lunch, Gurley had asked Warren whether he had ever heard of General American Publishing.

Warren had. He knew the two big magazines, *Trumpet*, and, what was it?—*Gentlewoman*.

Well, continued Gurley, they were looking for fresh blood, the properties were being managed badly, they had shown a loss for three years running.

"The art of investment," Gurley had said at that lunch, "is the art of choosing management. You need the right situation, of course, there's no sense choosing the most brilliant management of all in the buggy-whip industry. Buggy whips aren't going anywhere. But even in the most promising situation, you have to find the right man to manage things. The Board over there wants a new man who'll shake up the whole team. Want to talk to them?"

That was the way it began.

Then had followed the screenings he and General American Publishing had made of each other.

Their situation was bad, he knew, as soon as he first studied their statements. They were losing money. Circulation was down. Advertising was down. Production was obsolete. Deadwood crowned the magazines. Deadwood encumbered the Board. He remembered the first lunch which Gurley had arranged with two members of the old Board—talk-stuffed with the names of important people, full of the jargon and chatter of the expanding American market, the fair share of the market. It did not seem to matter to them that he did not know the magazine business. Gurley's authority were his credentials, the famous people of the Establishment whom he knew were his guarantors of managerial ability. Then, after much conversation, came the first hard invitation, the first hard offer. Not much of a salary—forty thousand dollars. Options, of course, on twenty-five thousand shares to begin with, increased by another twenty-five thousand after he had brought in Morrissey.

But the gamble! Oh, the gamble! If you could pull *this* together, then the very rot would serve as pumice to polish the glow he could make of it. And they really did not care whether the magazines survived or died, just so long as the property and the stock survived and made money. So he would be free, free to do what he wanted with them, free to hold the horn in his hand and blow it as he wished—if only he could make the sound of *Trumpet* bear a profit again.

So he had come to it, on the gamble. Except that it was different from all past gambles. There was no Congress to go to for a deficiency appropriation, as in government. Even Gurley was different as soon as Warren approached him, on business, in New York. As soon as Warren had dug into the balance sheets and found there was no cash to gamble with, he had approached Gurley, as President of the Caldwell Fund, for new financing. But Gurley had said the Caldwell Fund never entered speculative situations. Gurley had warmly repeated that he, Gurley, was terribly interested in how Warren would work it out, but that he was sure Warren could find commercial money.

Warren was never sure whether he, or the old members of the Board, were more upset when they found Gurley's patronage did not bring with it the money of Gurley's Caldwell Fund. And thus for the first two months after his arrival as President, Warren frantically pursued money to meet the daily emergencies, finally selling off the lease of the towers here in Manhattan to raise immediate turnaround cash. Then exorbitantly leased the same space back because there was no other way. Then the unending months of exertion that followed until he found Morrissey who bore money, and liked to gamble, too. Then month after month watching the Morrissey money ooze away. Until now, again, there was no money left.

And the logic said, as Schlafman insisted: Quit. Cut. Liquidate the magazines. He was responsible to the Board and the balance sheet.

That was the logic. Just as the logic there at the end in Paris, as the Plan died, as Gurley had explained it to him, had said: Quit. Cut. Liquidate. He was responsible to Congress and the Budget.

Except that no one had understood in Paris. Not even Mary. He remembered exactly the night he had told her what he must do. The wrong night. Christmas Eve. The snow had been coming down on the Seine, ghost-white against the gray of the river as it wound under the grayer bridges, and the singing of carols was still in his ears after everyone had left—and then that fight, that argument, her screaming. They had never slept together again after that, never touched each other again.

Nobody had come to the airport to say good-by when he left Paris. They could not understand; they hated him. Only his secretary came to Orly airport, and a junior embassy attaché, and the minimal farewell delegation of the French Foreign Office to see him leave Europe to return to Washington. Then the empty hotel room in Washington. The empty apartment in Washington. The empty apartment in New York. And he was here, alone.

That was where the logic had led after the decision in Paris. Where did logic lead now?

A different logic worked now in this office than had worked in the office in Paris. In any government office you were *their* instrument. Government had a Congress and a President who made policy; when you read their will, you *had* to do as they insisted. That was responsibility in government.

But when you occupied an office like this in New York? When other people were *your* instruments? When you had sought out a gamble, taken a gamble, accepted the responsibility with it—even if you did not know what the responsibility was, it was different.

Then you were God. Judged only by the balance sheet. And there was no one to pass the responsibility to. You had to decide alone. There was no easy logic to such decisions. Save the property? Save himself? Save the stock? Save the magazines?

He could not see it. The magazines did not want to die any more than the Plan had wanted to die. But Congress and the budget had wanted the Plan to die. There could have been no appeal from that. Here the final appeal came to him. Appeal from Foley and Eliot and tradition and the yesterdays against the balance sheet to him. Appeal from the old crowd and from Morrissey to save the property. But the property would be safe—even in receivership, in liquidation, they would all be covered for their property. Morrissey was appealing not for security but for the killing he could make when he converted the debentures against a rising stock. Morrissey had gambled. As he himself had gambled—for different purposes.

The pacing stopped. Warren sat down where the pacing had brought him on the couch.

Everybody gambled, and everyone used everyone else. If you came late from the outside to the clan of those who decided, you got only the thin end of the gamble. But you must remember what you were gambling on. Liquidate the magazines and there was a killing for all. But that was not why he, Warren, had come here, for the killing on the options. He had gambled on finding a *Trumpet*, to make them listen, to get free so he could see it clear. The sure things were only for the insiders. He had known it was a long, slim thing when he came here for the gamble. And with the gamble he had taken the responsibility for them all, all who inhabited the floors beneath. And for the past and the future. There was no higher floor to appeal to, no Congress to placate, or public policy to use as excuse.

With a start, Warren realized he was drowsing. He must not. He shook his head. He was responsible and now he had to go home to sleep. He heaved with all his strength against the heaviness of sleep and the half-dream . . . and rose to his feet to go.

PART TWO

9. The First Week: Breakthrough

Warren rose early the next morning from the twisting disturbance of his sleep, compelled by some carryover of the previous night's reverie to find himself as soon as possible back at the office, which was now home and hope. He came not only with the knowledge that he had decided last night, for reasons still obscure, to try again and as long as trying might help, but also with a companion awareness: that the unquiet sleep had, nonetheless, brought its unconscious ordering of the previous day's chaos, and a murky vision of the delicate, preposterous course he now must run.

There were, he could see, rising like hurdles before him, three distinct obstacles. They must be cleared one at a time—yet while he cleared one, already he must be gathering himself for the next.

First things first. Thus, first, to get out of the quick trap, he needed quick money. At least two million dollars—one million to make up for the bank's slash, the other to pay bills he could not escape at year-end. This he must have ready for his use before the Board met on that Wednesday in December, four weeks hence. For if, by then, there was no cash to pay the current bills, the magazines could make no appeal from their sentence of death. But even this quick two million dollars could only postpone crisis from year-end to later in midwinter.

Thus the second hurdle: to find three, four, or five million dollars of investment money to sustain for another year the surge in audience and the loss that bled from it, until he could learn whether the audience truly listened and market-seekers would buy its listening. Warren knew there was little hope of bringing such investment money, in hard commitment, to the Board's table in the time left—but he must at least rouse the sound of new investors willing to examine participation in the magazines' future; even the rustle of money would help. Then, with a little luck, a little arm-twisting, and every trick in the bag, *then* perhaps he might carry three more members of the Board with him against Morrissey to see the gamble through to the end.

Third, beyond that, lay the real problem. The real problem was compounded of the ragged fragments of Russell's pleading yesterday; of Mr. Bronstein's conversation; of Eliot's indictment. Somehow, in the next year, he must recapture that personality and identity which had once made *Trumpet* and *Gentlewoman* great. This was apart from the money he needed, and the audience he had mobilized—he must give them voice, himself. Again, as he reviewed the interlocking problems, trying to sort them out, the responsibilities he juggled confused him. He could not start this morning at the real problem, because he was not free to start until he had faced money.

Thus, first, on Tuesday morning, as his thinking mobilized a course of action, came a conference with Austin, master of the figures.

The evening had aged Austin. Austin's pouched eyes under the golden pince-nez lay in a lace of new wrinkles scored by a sleepless night. Austin had to be cheered and flattered, inspired and urged. Then, as Austin's mind began to function, as Warren's will began to harness Austin's panic, they spread out again on the desk the ledgers, the sheets, the figures that pyramided into the shape of their danger, and they began to improvise.

The tourniquet first to be twisted on the outflow of cash: all purchases possible postponed; all corporate contributions to charities and drives to be delayed, annulled, repudiated if possible; the Carnahan survey to be canceled; housekeeping expenses to be savagely throttled back. ("Yes, Will, absolutely—you have the authority to do it without coming back to me—cancel the order for the air-conditioners—No, no Christmas party—I guess Christmas bonus is out, but let's wait a week or two before we say so—No telephone calls except on company business—anything you want—of course, take off the hold buttons on all phones if that saves fifty cents each instrument—yes, yes.") Astounded, Warren heard of Hopkins' visit the day before, laughed when he heard that the union wanted a raise. ("Squeeze the plant," retorted Warren, "squeeze it dry, Will, sell what you can out there even if you have to sell the old machinery as scrap—squeeze everywhere except in editorial and advertising, we can't afford to slow them down.")

Then next to income: the suction pump to be speeded wherever possible, the squeeze tightened on remittances due the corporation from newsstand dealers, from subscription agencies, from accounts due to the profit-making divisions.

Then, finally, the sorting out of the bills they had to meet, deciding which little creditors should be paid, which babied, which could be safely ignored; the weighing of each major creditor, deciding how or who (Warren or Austin) must cozen, cajole, persuade them to tolerance. "Stall!" said Warren. "Stall, Will! Stretch! Coddle, flatter, explain, ignore, but just don't sound frightened! You're the inside man, holding the fort. I'm going to be on the town finding reserves to bring up."

Then, when all was done, and they knew that by straining, by dancing on the edge of time, they could just wriggle round the corner of the year into January if they found the quick two million dollars, Austin, looking up from the figures, said, "Yes, but Mr. Warren—what then? Then we're still going short a quarter of a million dollars a month and we face the same thing in February or March, what then?"

At this, Warren pushed the sheets away from the table and began to talk of the second phase, of the investment money that he must find to carry them through the next year. Reaching beyond figures into hope and imagination, he talked not only to make Austin bold but for practice. For he knew that in the next few weeks he would have to paint this picture of the future with such a glow as to charm the most reluctant money out of the vaults in which it hid. Warren paced the room, sweeping his arms wide as he talked of the opportunity that lay just ahead which any shrewd investor must see; he twisted his fingers as he wrung down stubborn expenses, inflated hope and prospect until he could see by the relaxation in Austin's face that, wanting to believe, Austin was beginning to believe. Then, Warren could dismiss him and sit down to contemplate the vast and mysterious subject of money anew.

Once long ago, as a reporter, Warren had thought there were only two kinds of money. One was paper money stuffed into the wallet; the other existed only in those endless chains of zeros that filled the thinking of economists, statesmen and bankers. The first kind was a delight to possess, the second kind, an intellectual fantasy. But that had been long ago.

New York had taught him differently—that money had as many faces and families as the variety of human activity. Now, as he contemplated each of his deadlines, he reflected that each deadline required him to appeal to a different family of money.

Deadline One was the quick two million dollars—and quick money was commercial money, bank money.

The face of commercial money of the banks, thought Warren now, was pure and austere, as serene and smooth as the surface of a reservoir which in its latent quiet and pressure mysteriously nourishes through underground mains every energy and action of existence. Such money could be tapped, he knew, only by reaching those men whose pens, scratching on paper, turned valves and let credit flow. Flowing then, in its strange circuits from level to level, from bank to bank, from idea to project to equipment, to inventory, to production, branching down to the ultimate capillary of the individual paycheck to be cashed at the supermarket for groceries which, returning to the bank, found its way into the reservoir again—fluid money of this kind was imprisoned by its use. It never leaked away, never drained off unaccountably as it flowed. This was Commercial Money in the vast reservoir of the banking system—at once the quickest and easiest money to tap when one was strong, but the slowest and most difficult to tap when one was weak.

Nowhere, decided Warren finally, as sober thought buttressed his first instinct, would any bank allow him to tap quick money, if Security National, his own bank, let others know that there was a hemorrhage at General American Publishing through which money sinfully drained away never to return. He must meet the crisis where it had begun—at Security National. Security National must help him—or it must be silenced while he sought help.

And this meant Mr. Cameron, Senior Vice President, Chairman of the Loans Committee at Security National. An urgent telephone call. A quick conversation. The appointment set for the next day.

Thus, Wednesday afternoon, Warren sat in Mr. Cameron's oak-paneled office, a smiling, apparently jaunty visitor. Mr. Cameron had not wanted to accept Warren's invitation to lunch uptown; so Warren had made the trip downtown. And, though Warren had lunched twice in solemn courtesy in the past two years at the chambers of Security National, he had always sent Austin downtown to transact actual business. It was Warren's first visit to the working floor of Security National, and the scenery and climate in the windowless office were unfamiliar. Here, at his working desk, Mr. Cameron was different from the Mr. Cameron Warren had met so easily upstairs as a luncheon host. Gravely, Mr. Cameron asked how he could help Mr. Warren and Warren replied that people always came to banks when they needed money.

Warren smiled at Cameron, but Cameron did not smile back.

Yes, he replied, as Warren continued with the first testing question, yes, they were reviewing all outstanding credit lines as they did each year-end. It seemed advisable to the Loans Committee to tighten here and there. Nothing had been decided yet, but he, Cameron, would advise Mr. Warren that prudence should indeed anticipate a cutting of General American Publishing's credit by one million dollars.

"Why?" asked Warren bluntly.

"It's a matter of figures," said Cameron courteously, lifting the balance sheets from the folder he opened, "it's what they say to us. Your balance was actually down to one-hundred-fifty thousand dollars yesterday, wasn't it? Normally, we could arrange to shift the one-million-dollar credit to some other bank who'd take up the slack for us . . . but, you see . . ." and here Cameron began to quote the figures on the sheet as if he were reading a judgment in court. Watching him, listening to his tone, Warren wondered how he could divert Mr. Cameron from the figures to the problem.

He gave Mr. Cameron all the time Cameron needed to talk and the moment finally came as Cameron said, straying from the balance sheet itself, ". . . you can learn so much about a man just by examining his checks— Who pays the bills in his family? Who pays the mortgage? You can learn his attitude to charity, his attitude to his college, about his family's health from his doctor's bills, about his worries. It's a feel that comes from figures, and a corporation throws off the same feel as an individual. Your balance sheet shows cash assets down each succeeding year for the past five years. You were hit unexpectedly Monday for one and a quarter million dollars you hadn't anticipated, your balance almost vanished . . . and, you know, I'm perplexed, I'm . . . well, without those magazines you would be showing a clear three or four million dollars of profit a year. I just can't measure those magazines as assets, Mr. Warren, they're intangibles. Look here, the balance sheet claims an inventory of almost a million dollars in stories for the two magazines. What's a story worth, Mr. Warren? What's a picture worth? What's an idea worth? Where can I get an outside quotation on such things . . ."

But Warren was moving easily in on the opening, on what intangibles were worth. Listening was intangible, so was circulation. But rising circulation was his only strength, and, trying to explain the strange industry of communications in America where attention was in itself a substance of value, Warren rose and walked about the room. As he talked, groping for a way to draw Cameron's mind from the figures, Warren cited individual movies which might make a greater profit than a famous railroad in an entire year's haulage, of individual television stations, blue chips of wealth, whose value lay not in the mechanical image-orthicon tube that sent pictures through the air but in the government's permission to occupy an intangible wave-band—for the government's precious permission could be sold again for four, five, six million dollars simply because it was a franchise to summon attention.

". . . it's attention I'm selling, Mr. Cameron, and I have a sharper rise in attention from the country, on my figures of circulation, than any other attention-getter that prints on paper."

He paused because he finally had Cameron diverted from the figures and asked, "Are these details boring you, shall I go on?"

"Why no," said Cameron, attentive now and warmer, "I'm not bored at all. I like to listen. I find the more you learn in this business of mine, the more you know. I began life in Memphis, Tennessee—back in Memphis there are people who can pluck a boll of cotton from a field, pull it tight in their fingers, and squint at the fiber. Just by squinting they know whether it's a seven-eighths fiber, a one-and-sixteenth, a one-three-sixteenths. They know exactly what it's worth. I've seen people go into a foundry, crack open a casting, rub it on their palms, and they can tell by the grains of black that come off just what the carbon content is. They'll judge the entire plant by what the casting in their hands tells them. There are builders who come in here and tell us they've got the best hard-rock or the best soft-rock engineer in Manhattan working on their foundations, and they risk ten million on that man's judgment."

"Yes?" said Warren, puzzled, not knowing how this affected him.

"They're risk-takers, Mr. Warren, we're all risk-takers. But every man has to stick to his own kind of risk. My kind of risk is a risk on the man plus his figures. If we don't trust a man, he can't borrow from us. But besides that, if we do like him, his figures have to be good. I can get a quotation on cotton fibers, on foundry iron, on hard-rock engineering to back up my judgment when I like a man. I like you, Mr. Warren—but I can't get any quotation to back up the intangibles you say are your chief asset. And I'm bound by law. The National Banking Act, the State Banking Act, the Securities Exchange are watching over us. I'd have a hard time defending the full line of credit to you with these figures just because I like you and your circulation is rising. I'm caught. It's not my money."

Warren knew he could do nothing with Mr. Cameron. But there was a relationship now. The stern engraving of Mr. Cameron's face had subtly changed as he spoke. It showed concern and disturbance. Warren sensed a moment of opportunity.

"Do you know, Mr. Cameron," he said, as a new thought darted, "I really came down here not to protest the reduction in our credit but to ask for more."

"More what?"

"More credit," said Warren, as if it were the most routine request in the world. "Specifically, I'd been planning to ask you to open an extra million for us for six months—"

He saw Cameron's face frown, and he hurried on.

"But I see your point, and I'm not going to press the matter. Let me put it this way though—if you were in my position how would you go about raising another quick million for a hundred and eighty days?"

It was always a good idea to involve someone on your side by asking for advice. If it was bad, you could ignore it and you lost nothing. If it was good, you had a sponsor in spirit. It was the best way of handling older men, and Warren could see Cameron rising nicely to the bait.

"If it were something tangible like a building," said Cameron slowly, and Warren returned to the seat by Cameron's desk and sat quietly, "but with intangibles like yours. And with your balance sheet. The root of the matter is that you need long-term investment money. We can't give you commercial money; as a bank our hands are tied. Let me see—"

Cameron swiveled his chair around and stared at the paneled wall of oak, his fingers tapping on the arm of his chair, thinking—

"I'd be willing to explore almost any legitimate avenue to raise that next million dollars," said Warren softly. He hoped that Cameron had not noticed he had glided in the assumption that Security National would not cut the threatened million if a second, new million could be raised elsewhere. If an assumption entered a conversation early enough, it took a lot of undoing later.

"This is a far-fetched thought," said Cameron, swiveling back. "If you could get someone in the Street—one of the big investment houses—to underwrite your note for a million dollars, why, anyone would advance you the money guaranteed by a good signature. We would ourselves. But they're a clannish bunch in the Street. They do it very rarely, only exceptionally."

"Which house would satisfy you?"

"I can't suggest any names, Mr. Warren. They're all good. Kuhn Loeb. Dillon Read. Meadows, Smith and Colt. First Boston. Stone and Webster. Charles Allen. If anyone of them guaranteed you with a signature, we could let you have the credit."

"And if I found someone to back us for a new million, I could count on my present credit line being renewed without reduction in January?"

Cameron smiled for the second time.

"I should say no. We can't commit ourselves. But I think I trust you—

you can probably count on our maintaining the present line as well as honoring your new note if you get one of them to back you."

Warren rose as if nothing important had happened.

"I appreciate that, Mr. Cameron. I'll call in the next few days to let you know which house we'll deal with."

All the way uptown, Warren's mind reviewed the conversation and it was obvious, slowly at first, but then insistently, inescapably obvious that what had begun this afternoon only as an attempt to persuade Security National to silence had opened an opportunity, a new avenue of escape.

A tiny ripple of excitement began to rise in him, a crest of elation forming on the ripple. It could not be this easy—yet it might. He could be halfway there over the first hurdle of quick money; no, he could be all the way over if he could find just one signature that Cameron would honor for the extra million. One million gets me two million, he repeated to himself, because if I get the new second million on signature, Cameron has committed himself not to cut, to leave the first million put.

At the Board meeting four weeks hence he would mention the quick new million almost casually, without even saying that Cameron had held him by the throat for a few days—he would refer to it as a matter of routine bookkeeping while he summoned the Board to consider the next phase, the second hurdle—the problem of long-range money.

But first the signature. How? And who?

It was precisely ten the next morning, Thursday, before Warren had figured it out and was calling Lawrence Webster of Meadows, Smith & Colt.

The name Webster had come as he contemplated another family of money. It was the money that lay in the investment houses, the money-of-creation.

The money of the investment houses, Warren knew, was small in sum compared to the huge reservoir pooled in deposit at commercial banks, or coursing in hidden torrents, unseen like blood but quite as important in the veins of great corporations. But the money of investment houses was free money—free to act, free to be lost or multiply. Once the great houses exercised the authority of their money by underwriting a corporation's dream or an individual's fancy, they trumpeted to their leadership millions upon millions from smaller banks, from insurance companies, from investors, from savers, from all those who had filtered off enough money from the necessaries timidly to welcome risk.

Warren had met the men of the investment houses of New York in service in Washington or overseas, but not until he had come to New York had he recognized their function. For, though they did not look like artists, they were—they painted and created with money, causing factories, pipelines, railways, housing, ships, to rise across the face of the country. As they matured from pleasant, hard-working younger men to graver heavy-set seniors, they bore themselves about New York in ever-growing silence and solemnity, like barons of the realm, relaxing with few others but themselves. In Russia, they would have been Commissars; under Napoleon, Marshals. They learned, as they grew in importance, never to betray their feelings. They listened always, alert with inner ear and inner eye, to whatever was proposed, seeing it against a horizon of American life whose swift, rushing changes and opportunities might result in disaster or triumph, depending on whether one understood the electric power of money. Many of these men did not necessarily have money of their own. Nor did they, like Cameron, act as technicians in a circuit they could neither change nor interrupt. They held the keys, that was all. And it was among them that Warren felt himself best connected.

He had not wanted to go to the investment houses for the quick cash he needed—such people were not interested in troubles, but in opportunities. Warren had meant to reserve them for the second hurdle, the long-range money which he might describe to their artists' eyes as opportunity. But now, after the talk with Cameron—it would be easy to leap the first hurdle, it was so close, if only one of the investment houses said yes and consented to help. It was a time to use friends.

Thus, over Wednesday afternoon and evening, revolving in his mind all those men of New York whom he had met at the levels of policy and decision in Washington and Europe, seeking one with whom friendship made a bond, whom age had not yet made too important, Warren came inevitably to Webster.

Ever since the year that Meadows, Smith & Colt had lent Webster to the Pentagon for the International Military Aid Program, Webster had been a friend. Webster had spent that year in Paris, and Webster and Tina had spent evening after evening with Warren and Mary in Paris. They had been close. No better name than Meadows, Smith & Colt, and even though Larry Webster was not yet a full partner in the firm, he soon would be. No better way to start.

And so, as Warren lifted the phone on Thursday morning to hear Webster's warm hello, he said, full of boldness, "Larry, this is Ridge Warren—how are you?"

"Ridge," said Webster, "good to hear your voice. How are you? Where have you been keeping yourself?"

"I'm fine," said Warren, "New York's been keeping me busy. How are things down at Meadows, Smith and Colt? Are you fellows making money?"

"Yup," said Webster jovially, "barrels of it, don't know what to do with it, why?"

"That's good, because that's just what I need—money."

"Oh, God," a cheerful groan came over the telephone, "who are you collecting for now? Heart Fund, Polio Fund, Cancer Fund, Blind Children, Mothers' Aid, Community Service, Asia Fund? No. Don't tell me. Let me guess. We've already contributed to every charity in New York. It's got to be something new this time."

Webster and Warren had both learned that great charities and good works in New York are a campus of display of rising executive talent, where important men whose names crowned the boards of great institutions surveyed younger and aspiring men on the way up. Whenever either Webster or Warren found themselves caught in such a charity campaign they traded the contributions of their own firms to charity drives of the other's sponsorship with minimum fuss. But today Warren did not want money for a charity. Not this morning. . . .

"Nope," said Warren chuckling, "I need the money for me. Or rather the firm. We're in a cash-bind that's cramping badly, Larry. Penalty of success—circulation rising, circulation costing more money all the time, expenses still high, advertising only beginning to respond to the new circulation; I won't bore you with it over the phone. The long and short of it is that we need more cash to take us over the top of the hill in this burst."

He paused. Until you had asked a man for money, no matter how well you thought you knew him, you did not really know him. It was like putting your hand on a woman's knee for the first time—no matter how well you thought you knew her, you could never guess how she would react. Webster's voice came back now, different in tone, but still friendly—yet thoughtful and firm.

"What kind of money? And how much, Ridge?"

"Two bites of it. One quick bite of a million now for six months. Then four or five million of long-term money which we'll have to talk about seriously."

There was a long silence on the telephone, the empty stillness of a man thinking at the other end.

"Mmm . . ." ruminated Webster for a moment, "mmmm . . . let me see. We don't do short-term stuff here, Ridge. It's not in the nature of our machinery. And you're in publishing. We specialize mostly in utility financing, know our way around in that almost by smell. The older partners have never gotten used to anything else—won't even touch the oils. And publishing or movies—it's like suggesting they come to work in Bermuda shorts. I'll ask if you want me to, Ridge, but I don't see a chance."

"Well," said Warren, holding on, "let me explain the quick million. Actually, I don't want the million from you in cash at all. All I want is your signature under ours at our bank, down at Security National. . . ."

"I'm not following you, Ridge, will you do it again?"

"Well, it *is* involved. I'll do it again. Security National is willing to put up their cash. They'll let us have the million if you go bond with your signature. No risk for anyone at all, and won't tie up your working funds. And we'll pay whatever fee, or sweetener, you think fair for the kindness."

"That's rather odd, Ridge, I don't think we've ever done that before."

There was a distinct chill in Webster's voice; they were now two businessmen talking together. But Warren continued easily, baiting the hook, dropping it in carefully.

"Yes, of course, I know it's odd. Sounds unbusinesslike. But the main reason I'm calling *you* rather than someone else is unbusinesslike, too. Almost anyone who does a publisher a favor expects a favor in return. I could borrow the money anywhere from people who'd feel they're buying a piece of national influence in our pages with their money. But I don't want that. I know Meadows, Smith and Colt well enough that I wouldn't have that hazard if I came to you. I want clean money, no strings attached. That's the way I see it—no cash from you, just your signature. And no strings on us—except my gratitude."

He knew damned well that if Meadows, Smith & Colt did him this favor they would expect favors from the magazines or influence in return. Everyone did.

He waited. Then he could tell Webster had bit, by the tone of reply. It began with the same pensive "Mm . . . mmmm . . ." but went on, "Now, Ridge, I'm just thinking . . . when you put it that way . . . and only for one hundred eighty days . . . you've got the usual assets to pledge, I suppose . . . who do you deal with at Security National, Cameron?"

"Right."

"As I get the story, all you want is our signature under yours for the bank. None of our cash. Fee to be worked out later. And you want this fast."

"Just as soon as you can. Then, I have to go to work on the long-range financing. Tell me, Larry, how fast can you move once you've decided?"

"Pretty fast when we want to . . . tell you what . . . today's Thursday. Tomorrow's our regular Friday meeting on new business, but that's too quick to bring this up. I'll put in some work on it before next week, call Cameron, urge it around the floor diplomatically, do some lobbying with the senior partners, take it up next Friday, and get back to you right after that. That suit you?"

Warren hung his reply in the air. One week to next Friday. Could he wait that long?

But if he said no, the alternative was to race about the town looking for the signature that would bring the extra million—and to charge about this town on such a mission would stir talk, would show panic. Could he find the million elsewhere without stirring talk? One week to next Friday would be ten more days gone, then only two and a half weeks to the Board meeting. Could he risk that many days on Larry Webster?

"Suits me fine, Larry, if the answer is going to be yes. If it's going to be no, I ought to know right now. How do you feel about it?"

"Can't guarantee anything, Ridge," said Webster, and Warren could detect a returning note of warmth and heartiness in his voice, "but I think I can control the situation down here. The magazines are damned important and everybody likes you. A million for one hundred eighty days seems small enough . . . rather unorthodox but I think I can persuade the house to do it."

"Fine then, Larry, scratch down a favor I owe you."

"No favor at all, Ridge. I'll claim a lunch from you as soon as I clear the matter at next week's meeting. Gives us an excuse to get together, good-by."

As he hung up the telephone, Warren turned to his calendar and marked the next Friday in red. Eight days out of the twenty-five left risked on what Larry Webster could do for him. Should he protect himself by seeking further? Or ride with Webster?

The telephone rang as he debated the problem, and it was Russell.

"Character just called up from straight out of the blue," bubbled Russell with the long-gone gaiety back in his voice, "from Old Prince John Chewing Tobacco. No solicitation at all. He talked as if he had a mouthful of his product, said they wanted to run five two-column ads through the winter. I asked him why, and he said they've decided to dignify chewing tobacco. He thinks we might be just the right place to do their first advertising of the campaign. How do you like that? I told him I'd call him right back. What's policy? Do we want chewing-tobacco ads in *Trumpet?*"

"Hell, no," Warren laughed into the telephone, "if we let in chewing tobacco, then we open the door to the truss ads, the muscle-builders, the nature tonics and all the rest. No! At least not until we have a book so full of class ads that we can absorb chewing tobacco without having it stick out like a sore thumb."

"Fine with me," replied Russell, "I haven't said no to an advertiser for almost a year—makes me feel like a boy again to tell him to go screw."

Warren replaced the telephone, feeling better. He looked again at the calendar with the red circling Friday a week later. Why panic now? Webster had seemed so confident there at the end. The million he was asking of Webster was not really a million, only a signature. The big problem was the next one, after Webster's signature had bought him time—the big problem would be piping up the three or four million of risk money, investor's money to carry through the next year. That would be hard . . . new money, outside money. Panic now would spread the word, would double the difficulty of getting the new money.

He would wait. He would think it all through over the weekend. He would use next week to plan the search for new risk money.

Wearily he reached for the old balance sheets he kept in his drawer, tired of them, hating them—but he must use the notes of the balance sheet to play a new tune.

It was almost an hour later before the logic led him to David Eliot. For, to seek new investment money, he would have to paint a picture of the future glittering and attractive enough to make the magazines seem like the rarest of opportunities. But though he could project and promise new advertising revenues that sooner or later must follow the new circulation, the investors would also insist on new economies. They always did. Yet paper was fixed by the price of the monopoly; and mail costs were fixed by the government; and printing costs were fixed by the union at the plant. There was no give anywhere except in white-collar salaries. Salaries, then, salaries—the only token of economy he could offer.

Yet it had been years since anyone had cut salaries. Newspapers and magazines always died first, they never cut salaries. There was a gallantry of folly about it all, but it was not only gallantry. Once you started to cut, you lost your best men first and were left with the dull-witted and time-servers. A twenty per cent slash of all non-union, white-collar salaries, what would that be? He doodled, then read the answer. Even a deep twenty per cent slash would shave only half a million a year from the running three-million deficit. Not enough to matter, really. Yet important to show new investors they were tightening. On the other hand . . . it did not matter anywhere but in editorial and advertising departments. Cuts that deep in those departments and he would lose the men he most needed to carry on. Or would he? Would he, if they understood?

What would they do? How could he take a reading on their reaction if he slashed?

And thus the logic led him to Eliot. He would talk to David as a friend, quietly, confidentially; probe and find out.

It was Friday, then, the day after Webster had promised help, that Warren turned to the problem of economy and staff. He invited Eliot to lunch with him in the office. Lunch was good, served up to them in his chamber on trays from the kitchen of *Gentlewoman,* with the Martinis ice-cold. Warren let Eliot ramble in his detached manner about politics; about the election-analysis story Eliot was doing; then, about Purcell and Foley and whether you wrote an election story with drama subordinate to truth, or truth subordinate to drama; thus, finally, about the magazines themselves until Warren felt able to ask, "David, how many of the people downstairs give a damn about the magazines?"

"Uh?" said Eliot slowly. "Give a damn about the magazines? I suppose everyone grouses about his job. People would rather be caught in the act of fornication than show they *like* their jobs. They give a damn about each other, of course, about seeing each other every day. You work in a shop long enough and you find your best friends are the people you work with; they're your family. That way, they care. But about their jobs? Their jobs are their personality for most people, now, aren't they? It's like putting on your priest robes and playing your part when you go to work. People are different when they're working than when they're just husbands or fathers or playing or making love . . . I suppose the workers on the GM assembly line like to feel that the Buick or Pontiac or the Chevy they're tightening bolts on is the best car made; it gives them their personality . . . yes, I suppose the answer to your question is that everyone does care, but if you quote me, I'll deny it. Why?"

Eliot lifted his cup of coffee and sipped it as Warren replied, "Supposing I told you the magazines would be out of business in six months, David. Supposing they knew downstairs—how would they react?"

Eliot swallowed from the cup with a gulp, put a second hand up to steady the cup.

"Ridge—are you serious? Is that Lipsett story true?"

"Yes and no. I'm talking to you now in all secrecy as a friend. If I don't refinance this operation before next spring, we're in deep trouble. But if I do refinance, I'll have to cut salaries all along the line. And ask for more work from everyone—a bigger try, better work at the same time I'm chopping their paycheck. How many people downstairs would put their backs into it if they knew the magazines were in trouble? How many would break for the exits?"

Eliot set down his cup. When he replied he began by questioning. How serious was it really? How much time was there? Was any new capital knocking to come in? Was this talk of a cut just an idea—or was it coming anyway?

"Look, Ridge," said Eliot at one point, "I don't want to contradict myself. They *do* care about the magazines. But if you slap a cut on everyone just before Christmas, you're bound to shake them. Now, on the other hand, if they were handled just right, if you could make them feel a part of it, if they knew why, they might just take the slash and work twice as hard, they might even . . . no . . . that's dreaming. . . ."

"Might what?"

Eliot scratched his head, his gray eyes looking past Warren.

"You just might . . ." he said slowly. "No . . ." he answered himself again, "I just had an idea . . . maybe—say, Ridge, since you've asked me about it, let me take it back downstairs. . . ."

"No! Damnit, David! That's why I called you. You can't take it back downstairs. Any talk at all will scare advertisers, frighten investors; talk can ruin us now—"

"You don't follow me, Ridge. I'm not going to get up on a desk and make a speech downstairs. But, listen, if it was up to them to save the magazines . . . look . . . there are always staff committees being formed to save newspapers and magazines from going under but they're always formed too late, when the thing is gasping its way into bankruptcy. They all volunteer to take cuts then and work without pay but it's too late. I'm not talking about a staff committee right now, nothing like that, but you asked me whether they cared enough to stay even at a cut, and I think they care and if we could somehow bring them into it—"

Gradually, as they talked, Eliot wrapped himself around the idea.

Warren watched him narrowly, wondering how the goodwill Eliot insisted was there downstairs for the magazines could be harnessed to his own deadlines. Eliot kept repeating: Why not? Why not let him talk to a few people under oath of secrecy? He would leave Warren's name out. Give him a few days to scout and then report back.

At the end of the lunch, Warren had given consent—yet not sure whether the consent was wise or foolish. Now not only Schlafman knew. And Austin knew. But Eliot too—and those Eliot might tell.

"Oh," said Eliot at the door, "I meant to tell you. I saw Mary on Monday."

"You did?" said Warren, his mind still perplexed by the problems they were leaving, then realized that Eliot was speaking of his Mary, and repeated sharply, "Mary? Here?"

"Yes," said Eliot, "she asked about you."

"How is she?" asked Warren, coldly, irritated that Mary had seen Eliot, not himself.

"Radiant and happy and—" Eliot checked himself. He did not know whether he should tell Warren all Mary had told him. "As I said, she was asking about you," he went on. "I think she was expecting a call from you that night."

"Thanks," said Warren briskly, then, as if he owed an explanation, "I was tied up on Monday. It was a rough day. I think she's coming back tomorrow, though, isn't she?"

"Yes," said Eliot, "she said for a couple of weeks."

"Uh-huh," said Warren to show that he knew, "that's what she said in her note."

He did not have to tell Eliot the thought that had just come to him. Mary had said she would be free Saturday. If he wanted to, he could see her.

Eliot looked at him as if wanting to hear more, but Warren was silent until the door closed.

Tomorrow was Saturday. Why not see her? Tonight he had to go out to another black-tie dinner. But tomorrow morning he could sleep late. Tomorrow evening Mary would be in New York. Surprised at himself, Warren knew he was excited by the thought that tomorrow evening, he might see Mary.

10. Saturday Night

1. THE PREVIEW

The audience had enthusiastically applauded, as it always does at a Broadway preview when the seats are full of friends of the performers.

But Lawrence Webster and Tina, his wife, had not really liked the first act and were embarrassed to say so until next Tuesday, when, having read the critics, they would know whether they had seen a good play or a bad. Besides they were with the Meadows tonight, and the Meadows were always a strain. Partly it was because Mr. Meadows had made Larry Webster a junior partner only three years before and still treated him as a promising son rather than a partner. At the office, Meadows and Colt, the two senior partners, left more and more of the working decisions to Webster; in a year or two at most the firm would be called Meadows, Colt & Webster. But socially, when the Websters met with the Meadows, the role of junior thrust on him had begun to irk Larry Webster. It was best, thus, for the Websters to invite the Meadows to an evening at the theater, like this, when the stage filled the time, and the glamor of the preview made the evening seem important.

It was only at intermissions, as now, that the burden of conversation fell on them.

And so, as they stood there, jostling and being jostled by the herd in the lobby, Webster was glad to hear Tina say, sharply, "Larry, Larry —isn't that Ridge Warren?"

"Where?" said Webster.

"Who?" said Mrs. Meadows. "What name did you say, dear?"

"Warren? Warren?" said Mr. Meadows gruffly. "The fellow at General American Publishing you were talking about yesterday."

"There, on the far aisle, coming out of the right," said Tina.

"Yes, that's Ridge," said Webster.

"Who?" said Mrs. Meadows. "Speak up, dear, I don't hear very well with all this noise."

"Larry, shall we ask him to join us after the show?" said Tina.

"Why not, I want Mr. Meadows to meet him—no, Tina, look, am I wrong? Isn't that Mary with him?"

"Who's Mary?" asked Mrs. Meadows again. "Speak up, dear, nobody tells me anything."

"It's his wife," said Webster, irritated at her chatter and the need of coddling her in public because she was Meadows' wife.

"But why should you be surprised then?" said Mrs. Meadows. "If she's his wife, of course she's with him."

"They were divorced four years ago," said Tina to Mrs. Meadows. "I thought she lived in Paris now."

"Oh," said Mrs. Meadows, "isn't that odd? Going to the theater together. People do things now they wouldn't have dreamed of doing when William and I were married. And divorced. It's so hard on the children, isn't it?"

"They didn't have any children," said Webster.

"Damn handsome couple," said Meadows, craning to peer at the Warrens who, all unaware of being watched, were talking as if they were alone. "What a strapping woman!" continued Meadows. "I'd have had babies out of her, I can tell you that. Sounds like an odd fellow, if you know what I mean, Lawrence. Taking out his wife after they've been divorced, no babies, now this proposition he puts to us. Say, have you talked to the Security National people yet to see if we can check out his suggestion with them?"

Webster saw that Mrs. Meadows had fixed Tina firmly in conversation and he felt more at ease talking with Meadows alone, as they did at the office, about business.

"Yes," Webster said, "it *is* an odd suggestion. I made a preliminary call to Cameron down at Security National. Cameron likes Warren, but the balance sheets are weak—Cameron's going to send some data over. Cameron says he can't tell whether it's because magazines in general are a dying industry, television hurting them, or because of a temporary crisis. The firm is caught that tight in a cash squeeze. Cameron thinks there's no danger in it, assets more than cover long-range obligations—but if they got stuck, the only way anyone could get at them would be through a receivership."

"I can't see why we're considering it then, Lawrence."

"I know, that's why I say it's such an iffy thing. I mean to talk the whole thing over with you at the office next week."

"I don't like to litigate to get our money back. It shows we've made a mistake."

"Yes, that's what worries me, Mr. Meadows. Actually, as a matter of business there's not too much in it for us. But there's an importance in a friendly connection with a publishing house of that impact. Everything is so responsive to promotion and public relations these days—Washington, investors, the market—that having a friendly connection with big magazines with a big voice is . . . well, I was going to say 'useful,' but it's even more than that; I think it's important."

"Don't know about that. Most publishers are as independent as hogs-on-ice. They behave like King John's barons. Oh I know how pleasant they can be when they need money, just like anyone else who comes to us wanting to use our money. But publishers when they make money are almost impossible to talk to sensibly. Unless you reach them through their advertisers and even that doesn't always work. I remember what a hard time their *Trumpet* gave us on the Street during New Deal days. A new exposure every month for years on end. I was just a young fellow then, never knew that Pepper personally, but he was the worst. Many a man would have put out more than a million then just to keep him friendly. You know, Lawrence, I used to read that magazine, haven't seen it now in years. Nobody could talk any sense to that man Pepper. The Pepper family still controls it, don't they?"

"Not really, I think. I've done a first check on them—the family has two people left on a seven-man board, but they've been liquidating over the years. I doubt whether more than eight or ten per cent of the stock is still in family hands."

"That's bad. I mean I'm delighted you started checking that quickly, that's what we need, information. But if the family's been selling out, it means they don't see it as a sound property any more, do they?"

"It disturbs me, too. That's why I checked. It's one of the things I wanted to talk to you about. All in all, it's an edgy thing. The figures, Cameron's attitude, the stock control are all against it. But that one angle does intrigue me—having a voice we can consider our own in this new area of promotion and public relations. Considering their influence, I didn't want to take the responsibility of rejecting it out of hand before we talked it over thoroughly—"

"Very sound, Lawrence, very sound, and we'll talk about it next week before you call him back. By the way, don't call him back on the telephone. It might embarrass him. I hear he's a friend of Wyman Potter's; he was Gurley's protégé once. Write him. It's always better that way. At the end of the week, as if we'd given it a lot of thought. I'd like to help him, you can say; I would, too. But we'd look foolish, Lawrence, we'd look foolish if we went to court eighteen months from now to get our money back like a plumbing-supply salesman. You know what I mean. It would show we judged badly. Oh I know how old-fashioned I sound, and how the country is changing and public relations is important. But there's nothing more old-fashioned than money. When we take our underwriting fees it may not seem there's much work involved in getting others to subscribe their money—but there is, there is, Lawrence, fifty years of building up a reputation for judgment, judgment that no one's ever lost money on our recommendations. People talk, Lawrence, they talk more about money than anything else in the world except sex."

Meadows' voice was rising to its normal office boom, and Webster was growing uncomfortable because the voice was loud; Webster was seeking an opening to interrupt but Meadows was in good flow. "We wouldn't be risking anything on this, Lawrence, not one thing except talk—say, is that the bell? We ought to go in and sit down, I don't like to push over people—not one cent except talk and talk is the one thing we don't want. You follow me, don't you, Lawrence? I don't care about his long-range assets if we have to get at them through a receiver. I see our ladies are going in, we should too; there he is now. A fine fellow, and a beautiful woman he has there, I can't see why he ever divorced her . . . he's supposed to be very ambitious, very able, isn't he? You can never tell . . . well. . . ."

As they walked to their seats, Webster reflected that Meadows was beginning to talk too much, he was getting old. But still Meadows was right. He'd lay the whole thing before the meeting next Friday, he'd give Ridge every break, but as for sticking his neck out . . . no, he couldn't stick his neck out yet . . . he was three or four years from having his hand on the throttle still.

2 . MARY WARREN COMES TO VISIT

Mary Warren knew she should not have come back to his apartment. And now, lingering in the bathroom, she was reluctant to enter the other room and face him.

She sniffed.

That fragrance—so vaguely home and years ago. Memory teased as she recognized it—it was the soap he used to use for shaving, the faintest lingering after-touch of it on the air. He was still using it, then.

She opened the glass cabinet over the basin and looked. There was the same wooden bowl of shaving soap. There was everything arranged as it used to be: the huge jar of vitamins (she had never known a man who needed vitamins less), the large vial of dental floss (he was never without it), the shaving tools neatly laid out (no woman, she supposed, annoyed him any longer, dulling his blades to shave her legs). And the after-shave lotion. It used to be almost a game—she would discard the lotion and replace it with witch-hazel; he would throw away the witch-hazel and replace it with lotion; and she could not abide men's shaving lotions.

She had already taken the bottle of lotion off the shelf by remembered habit, smiling to herself as she moved to toss it in the wastebasket—then stopped. Just what was your relation to a man who was once your husband? And now must treat as a stranger yet could not think of as a stranger? Well, you could not rearrange his bathroom, for one thing. But you could pry. She opened the cabinet by the bath and peered in. The folded towels were arranged exactly as they used to be at home. Only the colors were different. Instead of the yellow and lavender towels they used to share, these were hard red, hard blue. The whole bathroom had a glittering, tiled, masculine look as if unlived in, or rarely used as home.

It was strange, yet familiar, in a subtle mingling of memories recognized and half-felt—as came from the scent of the shaving soap. As came from the sight of his toothbrush, there, above the washbasin. The bristles of the brush were flat and twisted, as they always used to be; so he must still scrub his teeth with the same ferocious action each morning. He probably still ground his teeth at night as he used to when he worried. She wondered who waked him now when he ground his teeth that way. Without thinking, she dropped the worn toothbrush into the wastebasket and turned, out of habit, to the linen closet where they used to keep new toothbrushes. They were still there. She removed a new toothbrush from its package and placed it in his container. And smiled. He would find it there in the morning. She turned back, dropped the lotion decisively into the basket. And smiled again.

But she was dawdling. Because until now the evening which she had expected to be awkward had been fine. She would not have worn this dress if, somehow, she had not hoped it would turn out fine. The dress —vermilion red velvet—was cut to cling to the body. V-low in front and nearly backless, its narrow skirt slit on one side to permit her to walk. Long after you stopped being with a man, a lot of him was still with you. She would never have picked this particular dress from the Schiaparelli sale if remotely in the back of her mind she had not remembered how much Johnny liked high red, cut tight. She supposed it was why she still wore her hair long, even though she had yearned so often to cut it short.

Looking in the mirror, she saw that her hair needed redoing.

Pleased to have an excuse to linger, she pulled out the combs that held it in place and it dropped over her shoulders. She shook her head once and again to throw it back. Then she took his hairbrush from the shelf, began to brush it, and looked at herself in the mirror. She wondered how she looked to him after these years.

The unlined oval face looked back at her from the mirror, the skin still smooth and utter white, the face grave, the black of the pupils absolutely steady as they stared back at her. Twelve years in Europe, six of them in Paris, she thought, and I still look the same. Some women look naturally dainty. Some women look naturally chic. But I, just naturally, look like the President of the PTA back in Floss Hill, or a League-of-Woman-Voters type.

But she knew she liked her face—the nose an almost-but-not-too-much snub, the mouth large and big, the teeth even and white. And I do like my hair this way, she thought, brushing it. He used to love to watch her take her hair down in the evening in their bedroom in the old days and she would prolong it because she knew his eyes were following her, even in the worst periods, even at the end. She would take her hair down last, knowing he waited for this moment when, from the bed, he would watch her. She could see his face behind her in the mirror as he watched, his eyes on the curve of her back, then following her arms as they reached up to unpin the hair, lifting her bosom with it, and the hair would cascade down her back, before she braided it, ending the day for both of them.

What if she walked now into the other room where he was waiting, with her hair down, her hair braided as it was when they were alone?

Caprice! Just as it had been caprice to call him last week—and then flee New York before he could call her back. And caprice again, after the show was over this evening, to agree to come here because she wanted to see his apartment.

No, she thought, not caprice. There was a purpose in seeing him again —to tell him about Claude. She did not want him to hear about that from anyone else. But the evening did not seem to be working out that way and swiftly her mind telescoped it.

The evening had been awkward and confused, yet strangely charmed by risk, from the moment she opened the door of the apartment Sara had lent her to find him there with flowers in his arms. Not knowing whether to kiss him or not, since everyone kissed everyone else in Europe, she had impulsively offered her cheek. When he kissed her on one cheek, she had almost, by reflex, offered the other. Then, as he bent to kiss it, she had pulled away.

She had not relaxed until they found themselves in the neutral elegance of the restaurant he chose, where the public place protected them from each other; and they could look forward to the theater without talking. They had eaten little while the conversation skated easily over the surface, catching up on where she lived, who was left in Paris of the old crowd, what had happened to old friends. His chauffeur had driven them slowly through the strangle of traffic to the play and on the way he told her how uncomfortable the chauffeur had first made him in New York. It had seemed, he had said, as if he did not belong with a chauffeur. But now he was over that, and he would not be without it. The tribes of New York are divided into sub-tribes, he had said, and in this sub-tribe of mine, a chauffeur is the single most important luxury. "Only," he had added, "I wish he wore a beret, and this were an old-fashioned phaeton. Then we could laugh at the others." Then they both laughed, and he told her of the ritual of play-going, why it was important to see a play early. It was part of the ceremonial of New York—seeing a play several weeks after it opened made you a peasant or a stranger from out of town, he explained.

There was a quiet pleasure being with a tall man again who topped her own height by four inches. They had smiled when, weaving through the lobby between acts, they were trapped by a greeting. They shared a prank; he would introduce her as "Mrs. Warren" and offer no more in explanation. They had always played well to an audience of outsiders. They still did.

When it was over, they had waited outside the theater until his chauffeur had found them; and then as the car moved slowly away from the curb, he had said, "Where should we go? My place or yours?"

She might still have suggested the Plaza, or Sardi's, or any other public place where she might have told him about Claude and herself, but she heard her voice saying, "I haven't a thing to drink where I'm staying," knowing that was only half the reason—and the other half was this caprice, this desire to see how he lived, which had brought her here.

"My apartment then," he said, and she let silence consent for her.

Here they were then, while she lingered, brushing her hair in his mirror, knowing they had run through all the easy things to talk about. Her hands went to her hair and slowly began to bind it up again. She powdered her nose. And, since there was no way now of postponing it any longer, she turned and went out to the other room.

He had poured himself a brandy, a whiskey for her, and was sitting there on the couch, nursing his glass, as she entered. Seeing him, she could not help reflecting that she still liked his face in repose, when it became a boy's again, as it was when she had first seen him—the lean jaw, the dark, deep eyes, the thick black hair with no hint of ever thinning, and the enormous mouth that could grin with capturing conspiracy as it was grinning now as he looked up to see her enter.

He had seemed so important earlier with the chauffeur and at the theater, but now that he was smiling, he was just Johnny. He had smiled so rarely in Paris before they separated, that she had forgotten the enthusiasms that the smile had kindled in the beginning.

"Am I right? It's still rye?" he asked her.

"Yes, Johnny," she said, noticing that he remembered. Then, looking around the room, she chose the deep chair across from the couch on which he sat.

"Nobody calls me Johnny any more," he said, "except you."

There was no way of replying to that. She sipped her rye, waiting for him to say something more. Perhaps she should tell him about Claude, now, and get it over with. She opened her mouth, closed it, sipped again. He broke the stillness finally, saying, "Welcome."

A pause, and she searched her mind for something to start conversation. But there was nothing between complete triviality and the thought of their being in the room together to talk about.

"Well," he challenged, "say something. I like the sound of your voice."

"Anything special that you want me to say?"

"No, I just like the sound of it."

It was the wrong way of getting to the subject of Claude. He made it difficult.

"All right, then," she said, suddenly knowing that the moment was becoming ridiculous, "choose a subject."

"Choose a subject?" He repeated the question aloud, then, as if talking to himself, "We have to be careful, don't we? There are all kinds of things we can't talk about any more—let's be neutral. All right—did you enjoy your visit to Ohio?"

"Yes," she said hesitantly, "or maybe I'd better say, I don't know."

"Family all right?"

"Father is fine, Mother isn't too well. They're both worried, it seems to me—"

He lifted his eyebrows in question, and she knew she was beyond the need of making conversation. Johnny was the only person she had seen in years who knew Father and Mother. In a way, that made Johnny part of home, and she no longer felt awkward.

"It's not only that they're getting old," she said, relieved to be thinking out loud, "the neighborhood is changing at Floss Hill, and they're too old to want to move or live anywhere else. Johnny, do you remember our house?"

She knew he remembered their house—the large, sprawling white house on the knoll, six miles out of Cleveland, with its cool, comfortable rooms and banisters down which the girls used to slide, and the lilacs and apple trees from which neighborhood boys used to steal in spring and summer, and the swing that squeaked on the porch.

"Why, of course," Johnny was saying, "with the big porch. I suppose it's a white elephant now. We say in *Gentlewoman* that homes like that are inefficient in a postwar world of no servants. No one builds them any more. But that was a great house. It lived and breathed all by itself. If I had any kids—"

He stopped abruptly, and she hastened on. She did not want to explore that memory.

"Well," she said, "there's a Howard Johnson restaurant on the corner lot facing us now. The old Varney house on the other corner has been torn down and bulldozers are clearing it for a development, and Daddy is furious. He doesn't want to move, Mother doesn't, yet neither of them want to live in the last big house on Floss Hill. The old corner grocery store doesn't deliver any more, so Mother has to do her own shopping at the supermarket and she can't carry the big bundles. Johnny, I feel almost as if I were a stranger here. I guess I am. We left—when did we leave?"

"I left in 'forty-five, you came in 'forty-six."

"I've been away then since 'forty-six, and I'm a stranger here, not only in Floss Hill, but here in New York, too. It's rushing along so fast, nothing stands still, the buildings change, the suburbs change, the cities change. I can go back to Paris twenty years from now and it will still be the same. Doesn't it frighten you sometimes how fast this country is changing, Johnny?"

Instead of answering her directly, he drained his drink, rose abruptly, poured himself another brandy and sat down. What she asked must have touched a nerve. That was his second brandy. She would start again. "Do you drink a lot now?" she asked, then caught herself.

For a moment he frowned, then smiled.

"Does Your Husband Drink Too Much?" he asked of the room rhetorically. "Read this month's issue of *Gentlewoman* for 'The Hidden Cost in Your Husband's Budget of Life.' "

"What's that mean?"

"I'm just quoting a title in *Gentlewoman*. All middle-class wives worry either about their husband's drinking, or smoking, or dressing habits, or table manners. There's 'sell' in any one of them. We publish *Gentlewoman*, you know."

"Of course you do," she whooped in laughter, "I'd forgotten."

She caught herself immediately, for his face frowned again, and she wondered whether he was too important now to be laughed at. Then, as she watched, his face dissolved into the big broad grin, the stiffness went out of him, and he pulled his feet up on the couch and leaned back.

"All right," he said, "tell me, what's so funny about my publishing *Gentlewoman?*"

"Johnny," she said, "you know you don't know anything about women; you never did."

"Want to bet?" he said. "Bet you I know more about American women than you do. I know what they buy, what they read, what colors they like best in automobiles, milk cartons, fabrics. I know what they buy by income groups, geographical distribution, age groups. I know how much they spend on movies, on magazines, on clothes, on food, on doctors, on cosmetics. I know how many mothers are worried by kids who wet their beds, kids who suck their thumbs, kids who have temper tantrums—"

"That's what I mean," she broke in, "you don't know a single thing about women if that's all you know. That's just market-survey stuff. We have all sorts of Frenchmen coming into the Embassy offices in Paris asking about it as if it were a new kind of American voodoo. I tell them it's nonsense."

"It's not nonsense," said Warren. "It's a big country, getting bigger all the time, busting out all over the place. If you're selling an audience to advertisers, you have to know what per cent of your readers are young-marrieds, established marrieds, single women, mothers. You have to be able to measure them. I know what per cent of American girls marry at eighteen, what per cent at twenty-five, what per cent at thirty. I know how many of each read my magazines. I know what per cent of the women of twenty-five will never get married. I can find out how many of the eighteen-year-olds will lose their virginity in the next year—"

"You can, can you?" she said, mocking him. "How many?"

"Four point three per cent," he said, plucking a figure out of the air, "and if that isn't right, I can always buy a survey to prove I'm right."

"But you still don't understand women," she said, "and the magazine shows it."

"What's wrong with *Gentlewoman?*" he shot back, dropping his feet from the couch, rising to take a copy from the rack in the corner of the room, then returning to the couch.

He slapped the magazine down on the coffee table before him and said, sternly, "Come over here."

She did, and sat beside him as he flattened the magazine out and asked, "Five and a half million women buy it every single month and you don't like it. Tell me why."

He was not angry, she could tell; and she began to leaf through it. As she began to talk, turning the pages slowly, feeling unsure of herself, he moved so that they were shoulder to shoulder and she was conscious both of his physical nearness and of his attention to what she was saying. She turned the pages carefully, seeing the colors of the illustrations in all their flamboyance, trying to pinpoint why the words never lived up to the colors and the beautiful pictures.

She stopped at a title that annoyed her, trying to decide why she was annoyed. "YOUR Role in YOUR Husband's Success," read the headline and underneath a question, "What makes one man succeed and another fail?" Then, in red capitals, above a chart, "SCORE YOURSELF ON THIS CHART. How much do you help or hinder your husband's career?"

"There," she said, "that's what I mean. We get these American magazines in the Embassy in Paris and sometimes I can't even explain them."

"Why can't you explain it?" asked Warren. "That's damn near a perfect title for a magazine story. It says 'you' to five million women, it talks to them. They all want to know where they fit in, and we tell them."

"But that's what I mean," she said, "it's the anonymous 'you.' They read this, figure out their score, add it up—and then what? It's like putting children's examinations through a scoring machine, and the machine gives back answers in numbers without ever seeing the child. I don't know, Johnny—the pictures are wonderful, the recipes are great, but the words don't talk to anybody."

He took a pencil and jotted a note.

"What are you writing down?" she asked.

"I'm going to get the percentage of readership on that article. We'll see how many people it talked to when the next survey comes in—"

"Johnny," she said, "have you read this yourself, honestly?"

"No," he replied.

She laughed, for the humor of it suddenly struck her. She rose quickly from the couch, went back to her chair, looked at him.

"What's the matter now?" asked Warren, seeing her smiling at him. "I don't see why that's funny, as if it proved something, honestly I don't. I can't possibly read everything myself. Now, look, Mair, it may seem funny to you, because you're traveled and you think you're sophisticated, but there are certain things you can identify, policy-wise, as being what fundamentally interest women—children, food, clothes, cancer of the breast, body odors, sex, of course, and money—and we have to give people what they want in the magazines—"

"Do you?" she said, finding this talk fun now. He made everything seem important. "Do you?" she continued. "Or do you have to give them more than what they want, and make them reach? Do you remember my sister Beth?"

"The one with the kids?" said Warren.

"Yes," said Mary, "only she'd hate to think you remember her that way. She was a *magna* at Smith. She still lives in Floss Hill, and I saw her on this trip, and I love her, Johnny—but she's tied to the washing machine, the deep freeze, and the station wagon. She was *embarrassed* when I found her reading *Gentlewoman*. But she said nobody could change diapers with one hand and read about missiles, inflation, and negotiation with the Russians on the other. She said she read *Gentlewoman* for the recipes. But I know she wanted something more. Only she doesn't want to know how to push her husband around. She wants to know something for herself, all women do, so men can talk to them and want them, and other women will like them—Johnny?"

"Yes?" he said as she broke with the question.

"Johnny," she continued, "did we for one minute ever discuss my role in your success, so long as we knew where we were going? Ever once?"

Without thinking, she slipped off her shoes and tucked her feet under her. She saw his eyes following her movement and that the tight skirt could not be stretched to cover her knees. Why did Claude's eyes never follow the movement of her body in quite the same obviously hungry way? She knew the skirt showed too much of her knee, and yet she was comfortable, almost at home.

"No," he said, taking his eyes from her knees. "We never did. Maybe that story is too mechanical. I might have had something to say about it if it came across my desk before it went to press, but, Mary, I'm not responsible for every individual story, I can't be, I—"

"Oh let's not talk about that piece, Johnny, I'm not an editor. It's just that living in France where manners are important, and everyone knows exactly what they are, who they are, in every circumstance—it changes your point of view. Here, everyone is always moving, aren't they? I suppose some women do want to know how to help their husbands get ahead, everyone wants to go ahead so badly. I suppose I'm all wrong and you know exactly what you're doing and where you're going now—don't you?"

He had become somber as she spoke, and now he rose and began to pace, as he used to. She watched him as he walked and it occurred to her that his face was pale and drawn. She had noticed he was pale earlier, but then everyone in New York was pale. She noticed as the light caught his hair that it was still jet-black, but at the temples a faint flecking of silver had set in. If she was going to talk about Claude, now was the time, and if he asked her what she was trying to find out, she would tell him.

He had paused at the window and was peering out and when she spoke he did not ask her to go on, but said, "Come over here. Everybody's asking me that question these days. I'll show it to you from the window."

She padded to the window beside him, in her stockinged feet, and was aware, when she put her hand on the sill, that his hand slipped over it.

"You have to see it from on top," he said, "from way up high. Look at those cars moving up the drive."

"Yes," she said, her eyes slowly adjusting to the glittering sight below, picking from the chains of light that festooned the bridges and highways a moving train of luminescence which rolled continuously north along the river's edge. A scatter of winking automobile headlights sparkled in strands in the sidestreets. The strands disappeared, reappeared, halted, moved again as buildings obscured them, but the strands all wove together, finally, into a ribbon which coursed the edge of the island to its northern end where the lights marked the Triborough Bridge. When they reached the bridge, the headlights were no longer individual lights but a river of illumination that forked into tributaries and branches and disappeared into the night as parallel streamers of light.

"What about those cars?" she asked.

"When you stand down there in the street," he continued, "you never know where any individual car is going. You can't tell one from the other. But from up here you can see it's after-theater traffic, Saturday night. No matter what they think they're doing down there, or why they came into town tonight, or where their homes are, you can see from up here that half of them are going to go north at the bridge and home through the Bronx to Westchester and Connecticut. The other half are going to take the other fork back home to Long Island. They all think they're making up their own minds, but they aren't. They're statistics. Any good traffic engineer can tell me exactly how heavy this traffic will be in summer, in spring, in winter, in fall and how much less Sunday night than Saturday night. They can tell me within five per cent how many are going to turn north at the fork in the bridge and how many are going to turn south. You can't guess what any single one of those cars is going to do, but take them all together and you can guess what they're all going to do."

"Isn't it beautiful?" she whispered, looking at the moving garlands of light borne about the city as if carried in some vast tribal procession in seasonal ritual. "They're all going home now."

"They've had their night in town," he confirmed, "they've had their drink, now they're going home. The engineers have figured them out for every day in the year except for the thirty peak hours of holiday traffic when they just boil up so you can't predict their movement. Everything in this town is figured. We move them in by subway at peak hour at the rate of twenty-two hundred a minute through the trunk bottlenecks, and on Saturday nights we let them drive in. That's why they move out to the suburbs to escape from the figuring. But then the engineers catch them there, too. They're individuals only to themselves: we can even find out what stations they're listening to on the radios in their cars at this hour, what per cent listen to one program, what per cent to another and we can sell what they're listening to. You put them all together down there and they become something that isn't a mass and isn't an individual—it's a statistical beast. You can deal with the statistical beast only from one place in this country: here in New York. But then only if you're high enough. Listen Mary—that's it. You're either way up high looking down on them as one big beast you have to outguess; or you're down there in the street walking around like a statistic in somebody else's engineering."

"I'm not a statistic," she said.

"That's it," he said, "you don't want to be a statistic, I don't want to be a statistic, nobody wants to be a statistic. But unless you're on top in this town, that's *just* what you are. A lot of people here at the top wanted to get there only to make money. But a lot more want to be there just to escape from the statistics."

"It's all so different from France," she murmured, "and that isn't at all what I tell them when we explain America."

"You can't explain it yet in France," said Warren, "they'll get this way as soon as they get machinery complicated enough to need this kind of engineering. In France it takes two or three generations to jump from peasant to prince. In this country, you can do it all yourself if you're smart. That's the way they run this town. And only the men at the top are free. Some people get to the top because they were on the right escalator when they started. A lot more people, like me, gamble on making it. I started late, so I'm gambling more. But the men at the top if they're making free decisions look differently, talk differently, walk differently from the lance-bearers who are trying to please them. Their women look different, too. They talk differently, and they wear different clothes."

"What kind of clothes?" she asked, partly curious, partly trying to bring him back to frivolity, for he was disturbed now by something she could not guess. She could recognize the disturbance and the restlessness out of the years she had thought forgotten. She must either share it with him and ask him more, or abandon it. "What kind of clothes?" she asked again. "Not the kind of clothes you have in *Gentlewoman* fashion pages."

"In a way, yes," he said more quietly, "the same clothes—except they'll wear them differently, the same clothes will look different on the wife of a free man than on the wife of a man who's frightened."

"Like the women we saw at the theater tonight?"

"Like some of them. That's what a new show is all about, not just to see the show but for important people to see each other and flatter each other by making a setting of handsome women."

"Did I stack up, tonight?" she asked. "Is that why you took me to the theater?"

"You look wonderful," he said, "you always do. You look the way you did ten years ago, only better. But that's not why I took you."

They were facing each other in the window and he had withdrawn his hand from hers. He was looking at her as she looked back. He looked the same, no older for the years, and they had come down through the same bubble of time together, though apart, and she wondered how she looked to him.

"I'd forgotten how beautiful you are," he said, half-surprised.

From far-off came the warble of a siren, long and drawn-out, rising above the noises of the night which were stopped by the windowpane, penetrating with its thin sobbing rise-and-fall the stillness of the room.

"Remember that?" he said and she could feel him peering at her. She felt his hand gently lift her chin and turn it to him, and she trembled, knowing that the evening could be spoiled in another moment. She could feel his fingers resting light as a twig might rest on grass, touching the ridge of her comb, and she knew that if he undid the comb the whole evening would come apart.

She slipped back from the window in her stockinged feet, trying not to appear in haste, not to appear to be scrambling back from something. She negotiated the furniture in the room quickly and found her shoes. She would have to tell him about Claude some other evening. At a restaurant or a public place.

"Let's just talk," he said, following her back to the middle of the room. "You haven't told me why you came back to the States, or how long you're going to be in New York, or anything."

She was scanning the room, trying to remember the closet in which he had hung her coat. Still standing, she said, "I want to, Johnny—yes, but not tonight. All of a sudden, I'm just tired: too much travel, too much Ohio, too much excitement. I'll be in New York all of this week," she said. "I'm not busy tomorrow, or Monday night—I have a lot of free time. If you want to, I'd like to talk some more, but some other time."

"Tomorrow?" he said. "Tomorrow is Sunday. I'll call you then. All right?"

"Yes, if you want."

3 . DINNER AT TOM FOLEY'S

"I didn't mean to break into a family Saturday night, Tom," said Eliot, as Maud Foley cleared the table, "but that's the way it is, and I didn't think I ought to wait."

"You didn't spoil anything, David," said Maud Foley, "he usually sits around in his shirtsleeves on Saturday night so all tired out he won't even talk." She stopped behind her husband and lifted the now-empty bottle of wine that Eliot had brought and peered at the label. "That was a wonderful bottle of wine. I wish you could teach him to like wine, too," she continued, running her fingers through her husband's hair. "I thought I was marrying a slick newspaperman when I took him to bed twenty years ago, and he's straight corn all the way through."

"Ah, shut up," said Foley fondly to his wife. "The trouble with her is that she believes what she reads in magazines. I can always hire somebody to write that piece on what wine goes with what kind of meal, but myself, I like beer. I wish we'd had more than steak and potatoes for you tonight, Dave. Do you know this is the first time you've been in our house—in how long?"

"Too long," said Eliot, "it takes disaster to get me invited to the Foleys. That was a damned good steak, a bachelor doesn't get fed like this very often."

Maud Foley paused with the tray full of dishes.

"I don't want to miss a word," she said. "I never hear what's happening from Tom. David, why don't you come and sit in the kitchen while I wash the dishes?"

"Hell, honey," said Foley, "we've got a lot to talk about; he doesn't want to sit in the kitchen and see the dishes done; that's why he never got married."

"Of course I do," said Eliot, rising, "I miss the wholesome touch."

He took his coffee cup, the percolator and followed Maud, hearing Foley shuffle dishes together and follow him.

Maud Foley began to transfer the dishes from her tray to the sink, as the two men began to argue about whether Eliot really wanted to wipe dishes or not.

"Oh, stop arguing," she said, "and go on talking. All I want to do is listen; this concerns me, too. Go on, David."

"Just let me get a towel first," said Eliot, whipping a towel from the rod over the sink to help with the dishes, enjoying being with them.

The sound of the faucet's running water soothed them for a moment, then Foley broke the silence.

"When did Warren tell you all this, yesterday?"

"We had lunch together yesterday for the first time in nine months. He didn't tell me exactly what I'm telling you—I'm giving you my polished reportorial summary of a two-hour lunch. We're in trouble. He wants to know what the staff would do if the staff knew. And if they had to take a cut. I took it from there."

"Hell, everybody knows we're in trouble," said Foley, "but if he wants to cut salaries, why didn't he call me in? I'm the Managing Editor, goddamnit. I'm not bitching about his talking to you, Dave, you're his friend, but how am I supposed to run his magazine for him if I never know what's going on? All I make of it is that we're in a hell of a jam, which I already knew, and he wants to cut salaries. But instead of laying it on the line, he calls you in and winds you up to volunteer for a cut—he wants us to form a cheering section at our own funeral."

"The operative word there is funeral, Tom," said Eliot. "There's probably going to be a funeral one way or another—and we can all troop out the door some cold week pretty soon, mourning as we go, carrying our medals and awards and clippings in our briefcases. Or we can try to do something about it. Forming a staff committee was my idea—not his. That's why I wanted to see you fast, to see whether we can do something about it or not—provided you care."

Foley finished wiping his dish and reached for another from the stack in the rack.

"Frankly," said Foley, "I don't know. I'm so damned tired of trying to kick this rubber mattress uphill that—"

"Oh don't be an idiot, Tom, of course you care," interrupted Maud Foley, and then, turning to Eliot, continued, "If they gave out sweaters with their jobs, Tom would be wearing a sweater up Fifth Avenue which read T for *Trumpet*. He loves that job of his. He gives it twelve hours a day every day and sometimes weekends. Tom loves that magazine but he'd rather be caught dead than have someone say so."

"It isn't that," said Foley, "but I've hired half the people on the floor personally. I've got an obligation to them. I sit here and think about Maud and the three kids and this paycheck of mine, and then I think about the rest of them on the floor and if I quit, I've run out on them. What the hell do I do? It isn't this talk of a paycut that bothers me— maybe it's a good idea. If you wanted to find out my reaction, well, my reaction is strictly boy scout—I'll stick around. But when you say do I care, and what can we do about it—you have me baffled. What the hell is there to do that will help?"

"All right," said Eliot, "now sit down for this one. Did you ever think that we might be able to raise the money to save the magazines ourselves? And then we could talk to Warren, equal to equal, and shake the thing down into a real going operation?"

"What?" said Foley. "Are you crazy? Do you know what that means— I've got two life insurance policies I can cash for nine thousand bucks, eleven hundred in the bank, and the kids' savings bonds and that's it. And who else has got any money?"

"Let me be crazy, for a moment, Tom, will you?"

"Sure, go ahead."

"You know when Warren called me in yesterday, I was just getting my teeth into this post-election story I was writing. And I was asking myself why it's so much easier to write about Democrats than Republicans. It's because Democrats are bleeders—they brawl easily and they bleed freely. Republicans don't bleed—or if they bleed, it's mostly ice-water—"

"You're losing me there, I thought we were talking about the magazines—"

"Hold on. Democrats always bleed best just this time of the year—about the second or third week of November. Whether they win or lose elections they always bleed about the press. They denounce all magazines and newspapers as Republican, and against them. Every time I talk to them, I have to hold their hands for five minutes and let them tell me what bastards my editors and publishers are—"

"But I'm a Democrat myself," protested Foley.

"Sure," said Eliot, "we all are, even Warren used to be a Democrat. But big magazines are naturally and automatically Republican. You know how it is when it comes time to write that last editorial before election, and the editorial writes itself—"

"I know," said Foley, "we stand above parties, we examine the issues and the personalities and then, fearlessly, we come out not for the party but for the man, the best qualified man, and he's always Eisenhower, or Dewey, or Willkie, or whichever Republican is running; but what's the point, how do the Democrats fit in with what we have to do?"

"The point is this," said Eliot, "the Democrats say they need to break the curtain of silence. They say we have a one-party press. All right—if we could round up some Democratic money and tell them here's their chance to get their candidates on every newsstand in the country and into eight million homes and—"

"Oh, my God," said Foley, "now I know you're crazy. First of all the Democratic party is always broke. Secondly, the people who run political magazines do it as a hobby and run it from their private fortunes. Thirdly, what we've got here is a mass-circulation magazine that has to be run as a business, that has to show a profit—"

"Now, look," said Eliot, "don't think I'm naïve. We'll be just like all the other big national magazines except, instead of coming out automatically every November for the Republican candidates we'll come out for the Democratic candidates. I'm talking business now, Dave. We tell the big advertisers they have a choice of fifty magazines to advertise in now across the country—all Republican, every one. What we'll be offering them is the only voice on the other side of the fence, see?"

"Nope," said Foley, shaking his head, "I think you're a great writer and a great correspondent but as a businessman, you're stupid, you're just as stupid as me."

"Then I have to spell it out for you," said Eliot silkily. "I'm in and out of Washington writing politics every month of the year. And the government lies over the business of this country like a blanket. No airline does business without thinking about the C.A.B. No railway makes a move without thinking about the I.C.C. Congress' committees and the agencies and the Pentagon together can make or break any business in the country. And one half of the Congress, and maybe half the people in the Pentagon and the regulatory agencies are gut-Democrats like us. Do you follow me now? Anybody doing business with government has to figure on that. Just listen. We need airline advertising, don't we? We need missile advertising? We need highway and travel advertising? We need everything. O.K. Then—if we don't get it, we'll scream in Washington that they're boycotting us because we're a Democratic magazine. We'll work up a little Democratic pressure in all the agencies on the advertisers, the airlines, shipping lines, defense contractors. Those guys advertise in magazines either because they approve of the magazine—or because they're afraid. We don't even have to squeeze hard—once advertisers know we can hurt them, they'll jump right through the hoop for us. They've been squeezing us—now let's squeeze back just a little bit—"

"Well, I'll be goddamned," said Foley, "blackmail, that's what you're talking about, blackmail."

"Why, of course," said Eliot, smiling at the change in Foley's voice from scorn to excitement, "why not? Do you think I'd stop at a little thing like blackmail to save the magazines? Would you?"

"You mean it then," said Foley. "I'll be damned, you're serious."

Foley whipped the dishtowel over the rod by the sink and sat down by his kitchen table. He looked at Eliot, who leaned against the window. Foley pulled out a cigarette, lit it, began to puff furiously.

"No," he said finally, shaking his head, "you *are* crazy. I must be crazy, too, because for a minute I almost took you seriously. Listen, it's a great idea, Dave, but damnit, you have to get someone with money, and just Democrats won't do. From what I know of rich Democrats, they're just like rich Republicans. They all have lawyers, accountants, investment counsel six-deep on guard to keep you from their dough. That's why they've got dough—they know how to hold on to it. You need a man, not an idea. What name have you got with dough? Who can you reach?"

"Supposing I threw a name like Paget at you—would it mean anything?"

"Not a damn thing. Is this a real live man, this Paget, with money?"

"Yes. But I haven't even met him yet. I know a couple of Democrats who can get me to him. He pours out campaign money for the Democrats every four years, and political contributions are all non-deductible from taxes, so he must be loaded. Anybody who can hose out as much as he does politically must be able to drop a couple of million, deductible from his taxes, without even feeling it—I can even make his lawyers see it—"

But Foley was not listening. "Oh, Christ, I don't give a goddamn what his name is. Just someone who saw how important this magazine was, what we could do with it—someone who'd give us a year's run without Warren and that crew of engineers upstairs, someone who'd let us find out what was happening, someone who'd let us walk upstairs and tell the Executive Floor to go to hell—"

"No," said Eliot, "you've got it wrong. We couldn't work this thing without Warren. We need him. We need him to make a presentation to Paget or anybody else we can talk to. We have to get a look at the books; we have to find out whether the magazines can be spun off in some way so that lawyers can make the tax loss attractive; we need his cooperation in anything we try to do—"

"O.K.," said Foley, "O.K.! But only until we get it done, then let's give him the works, then we screw him—"

"No!" said Eliot. "Not screw him! I'm not trying to cut his throat, I'm trying to save us—"

"But you can't save us and him, too. There are two ways to run this thing; either somebody runs it with a potful of dough, or somebody runs it who can make it important again. He hasn't got the dough. And he's around only because the magazines make him important, not he makes them important. I've been here longer than he has—I've been here nineteen years, the last twelve as Managing Editor. When I came here, these magazines were taking this country into the war, a goddamned good war, and we were worrying about the country, not the goddamned circulation figures. This thing belongs to me more than it belongs to him. He came in here only two years ago—"

"But he's kept us alive two years, Tom, we would have been down the drain—"

"I don't care. He's doing it for himself, not for us. Let's think of us. Who runs the magazines if you can sweet-talk this Paget into it? Does

Purcell go along with the package? Who sets policy? What about the advertising crowd? Have you spoken to Russell yet to find out what he thinks? What about the circulation floor? What kind of targets are we going to reach for in audience? How about *Gentlewoman*—are you talking about one magazine or two? All I can talk for is the editorial crowd on *Trumpet—*"

"That's why I came," said Eliot, "not just for steak. Supposing you and I decided that we were responsible for saving these magazines, that a staff committee could find refinancing—would you help?"

"I've already told you," said Foley, "I'm as crazy as you. I just want to talk it over with Maud—"

"Don't talk it over with me," said Maud, who had been quiet throughout the long talk. "I was crazy when I married you. And I married you because you were crazy. And I love you. And—"

"Everybody's against me," snarled Foley, "even my own wife. All right. I'm with you. Only I want to get rid of Warren and Purcell so we can find out what we're supposed to say—"

"I deal with you on Purcell," said Eliot, "on Warren, no. Let's argue about him when we have a proposition to put to him. Right now, fast, who do you think we have to talk to on our own floor, and on *Gentlewoman?* I want to go to Paget next week not as a promoter, but as spokesman of a staff committee able to cut salaries, reorganize, replan, do anything that has to be done. Who do we need?"

Foley snubbed out his cigarette in a saucer. He rubbed his paw-like hand over his rubbery face and when the hand came away it was the office-Foley, not the dishwashing-Foley, who spoke.

"We've got to get this down on paper with a pencil. We need names. The first one we need would be old Ben Mitchell. He's in town from Connecticut this month for Christmas and Thanksgiving. We need him to reach the old-timers—he's the only writer left from Pepper's time. Now the *Gentlewoman* crowd—let me see—Leonie Cahill, and her art editor, Faberhorst. And we need—"

Foley was leaving the kitchen; Eliot followed him. Foley's voice had reached its complete office nastiness, and Eliot reflected on how much he liked the sound. Foley was putting together a complicated issue and was enjoying it.

11. A Week of Waiting

For Warren, the next week hung suspended from Friday's decision to wait for Webster, and strung on the thread of Mary's presence in New York.

The office routine moved in a parenthesis of deceptive calm, and a happy chain of little events gathered to pad his anxiety. Austin was cultivating the books now with every art of his experience, drawing money into the cash account of the corporation from all other divisions, pumping and goading the people who owed it bills. As the bills that others owed General American Publishing on the tenth of the month slowly trickled in with their checks, the cash balance at the bank rose to its usual mid-month hump of fat, and Warren coasted, waiting for Webster's signature to sustain him against the end-of-the-month drain.

Russell reported twice on the first two days of the week. The first time, on Monday, was to announce that six new pages of travel advertising for spring and summer had come in over the transom, completely unsolicited. The six new pages could not be converted into cash for six more months, but they were a new account, and more than hope; they were a commitment. The second report came on Tuesday—that over at Foods Inc., Merrill had at last made a solid tick. If the spring plantings in California were big enough, and if Foods Inc. surveys forecast a big canning pack in store for autumn, *then* Foods Inc. would come back in spring with eight pages in *Gentlewoman* and eight pages in *Trumpet* for their first reentry into the magazines in four years!

Tuesday and Wednesday brought more good news. The final report on the previous week's issue had shown newsstand sales three per cent above the preliminary estimate, and the first flash report on the current on-sale issue was even higher. ("Is God Worried?" was the lead coverline on the current issue, and Warren winced, but it had sold.) From the Anderbury plant came the first response to last week's emergency program. Hopkins thought the union there would talk sense about the raise, once he showed them it was serious. And more than that—sourly, Hopkins reported that if New York really meant it, they could sell some of the old standby press equipment for 150,000 dollars cash. Except that if he had a few months to do some real country trading he might get at least three times that amount. Curtly, Warren telephoned the plant and ordered Hopkins to sell. He knew the 150,000 dollars would disappear as quickly as a pat of butter in a blast furnace. But 150,000 now was worth three times that amount three months hence.

Morrissey pressed. Morrissey pressed twice by telephone, on Monday and on Wednesday. Blandly, Warren fed Morrissey straw on Monday and refused to speak to him on Wednesday. Morrissey, too, could wait until he was in the clear with Security National and had the Webster signature on the line.

The surge of confidence carried through, coloring even the short conversation with Cameron at the bank late on Wednesday. Cameron telephoned to ask whether he was to tell Meadows, Smith & Colt everything. Of course, replied Warren, tell them everything, *anything* they want to know. He hung up the telephone when he was through, pensive for a moment at the lack of give in Cameron's voice, then, on reflection, encouraged. Cameron's call meant that Larry Webster was working on the matter for him, that the silence did not mean a brushoff.

By Friday, he would have turned the first corner. It had to be.

Oddly, this second week of crisis seemed to lock him together with Mary. It was not a week for him to expose himself about town—at dinner parties, or meetings, or his clubs. Nor was it a week to brood alone in his apartment. It was a week to withdraw from appearance, yet be with someone, sheltered by companionship and called "Johnny" again, while he waited.

Thus, from the moment he woke, after her visit, on Sunday morning, late but well rested, she filled the week's need. Unwilling to think of the problems he must face on Monday, knowing she was here in New York with an empty day like his, he had gazed out from his bedroom window and marked the unseen wind tossing the waves of the East River into brisk whitecaps. The water, the wind, the islands, the imagined cut of the chill which he could sense from the frost on his panes—all joined to suggest a day outdoors, and he telephoned her.

The afternoon together passed in yawning, pleasant talk on the waterfront and at the ferries. But not until late, as dusk fell, as the ferry butted its way back from Staten Island toward the snout of Manhattan thrusting its first peak to the sky like the horn of a unicorn to scorn the Atlantic, did Warren realize that a contentment had fallen on him. A gust of the ocean-cold wind swept them as they passed the Statue of Liberty; at the same moment, the wake of a large freighter, passing out to the Narrows and the ocean, rocked the boat. He felt her body, then, thrown against his and through the heavy muffling of their coats, her full weight. By reflex, her hand caught his arm to steady herself, yet when she tried to pull away and he held her with a protecting arm, she did not resist but rested there.

The ferry churned and bobbed toward the mountain of buildings that slowly swelled until it filled the entire sky and for the first time in months it did not frighten him.

They went ashore to a restaurant that crouched alight in the dark and empty ravines of the financial district. A Sunday silence folded about the canyons and pinnacles of finance, empty of the men whom he must pursue here next week, and in the restaurant a victrola played. He did not realize that he had fallen peacefully silent until he realized that she was repeating a question.

"What are you thinking about, Johnny? Are you worried about something?"

"No," he said, aware that for the first time in weeks he had been thinking of nothing, inviting his nerves only to be tired. "I'm happy, as a matter of fact. I was wool-gathering. What were you saying?"

"Nothing important," she said, "nothing, it will wait. I was wondering about coming home or staying in Paris. Go ahead and eat something. The food will get cold. You don't have to talk. I'm enjoying this, too."

He ate and was grateful for her silence, knowing the peace of relaxing with no speech or words, and that casually, unexpectedly, she had brought this peace with her.

The calm of her presence stretched on through the week; the evenings salved the days at the office, for the evenings were Mary's and with Mary it was almost as if he were young again, and could talk wildly when he wanted to, or say nothing when he wanted to. They went to a movie on Monday evening and afterward, in a bar, he had rambled on about the trick of the movies—the trick was to get enough people in a large dark room and cut out all other light and sound except the one source on the screen, so that an artificial hypnosis multiplied every moment, each voice, each sound with an exaggerated emotional effect. It was different from the trick of magazines, he said, which was to make them reach for it, participate. But she interrupted to say that he believed there was a hidden trick to everything. He said there was. They had argued about that wildly, meaninglessly, irrelevantly. They could talk about anything, in just this way, he found, with absolute pleasure in each other's voice—

except about themselves, about her, or about him, when they became awkward.

He brought her again to his apartment on Tuesday, the following night, after dinner, to show her television. Television had all happened while she had been abroad, and he explained, bitterly, how each day, day after day, through the years of the middle fifties, ten thousand new homes across the country had been receiving the box, watching it four and five hours a day, subtracting and mesmerizing the mind of the country. He was almost about to tell her what TV had done to his magazines, and tell her all, when she began to laugh with antic delight. But she was laughing at what was happening on the set, and when they turned off the sound, and ad-libbed the appropriate lines, it was even funnier. "Johnny," she said finally, "do people really take this seriously?" He knew then she had been a long time away, and he could not explain his problem.

Wednesday, however, had been best. Wednesday they had picked up a steak, and gone to the apartment Sara Hubbard had lent her. He seared it over the grill, and they devoured it in the kitchen, draining a bottle of red wine with it. Then he sank back in a deep chair to look at the make-ready copy of *Trumpet*, fresh from the press, that he had carried from the office. How much later, he could not say, he heard through his concentration the sound of her playing on the piano. He could remember her playing the piano at parties in Washington during the war; at her father's house on Floss Hill; in the apartment they had lived in overlooking the Piraeus in Athens; in Bonn, on the side of the hill above the Rhine, on those murky evenings when one could almost believe that Siegfried had indeed slain the dragon on Siebengebirge across the river.

He was conscious, too, of something else—a slow, growing insistence that wanted to touch her. He had risen, and walked across the room to where she played, and rested his hands on her shoulders. She played on as his hands rested there and then, almost of themselves, the fingers had passed from the fabric of the dress to the warmth and living softness of the silken flesh. His hands on the smooth nape of her neck, teased by the silken strands of her straying hair, belonged there. But as his fingers slipped down, the playing stopped, abruptly, by her decision.

"No, Johnny . . . please," she said softly.

It was a moment of indecision. But he knew he could not throw away the quiet of this evening for any lesser need than quiet. He took his hand away. She turned to look at him, her face flushed, and said, almost whispering, "Johnny, don't spoil it. Johnny, I have to tell you something. I should have at the very beginning. I will now—"

He interrupted her.

"Not now, Mair, I'm sorry. Don't stop playing. Please don't. I'll go back to reading."

Whether because the touch of his hands had disturbed her, or that she actually was engaged the following night, he could not tell. But when he finally rose to leave, relaxed, yawning, wishing he could spend the night there, she had announced she was busy the next night. Friday, she said, Friday night—we really have to talk about things on Friday.

"Fine," said Warren, unhappy that she could not see him the next night, not wishing to press her, "Friday night I'll have some things to tell you, too." Friday night he would have Webster bagged, and Cameron bagged, and the corner turned, and he could tell her all about it. They could celebrate. And what would come next—they could talk about that, too.

Friday was unbearable.

By mid-morning Warren had called in Laura and ordered her to get that goddamn clock out of there. After she had gone, he realized that it was not the ticking of the clock on the table of the office, minute after minute, louder and louder, that had exasperated him. It was not the clock, nor the noise of the clock, so much as the thought that downtown, at the offices of Meadows, Smith & Colt they were making a decision on him. By late afternoon he knew they had taken their decision and Webster had not yet called to tell him of it.

By evening, as he dined with Mary, the rear lobes of his mind were tugging away at the meaning of Webster's silence, and the frontal lobes were making mechanical conversation.

He insisted that she come back to his apartment, not wanting to talk to her any more, yet not wanting to be alone. His nerves, frayed by the week's waiting, at once demanded and resented company.

As they entered, and he took her coat from her, hanging it in the closet, he smelled the perfume clinging to the cold fur and decided he would sit still for a while, then he would tell her the whole thing. He had to talk to someone.

"I want to powder my nose," she said, as they entered his apartment, and as he listened to the familiar rhythm of her step down the corridor to his bathroom, he was annoyed with her calm and poise. Then, fidgeting, waiting for her, he remembered that the morning mail should be waiting for him.

Nothing important ever came to the apartment. Still . . . He arose, went to the silver platter in the hallway where the cleaning woman always left the mail and brought it back to the light.

Junk-mail, he noted immediately. Circulars. Magazine offers. Teasers. Electricity bill. Everything important went to the office. Then, the senses of his fingertips clamored.

They had stopped at a white parchment envelope. Important.

He looked at it—Meadows, Smith & Colt, read the letterhead. But it bore no postmark, only the notation in the corner, "By Hand."

That was bad. Good news is always borne by word of mouth since each man hastens to bear good tidings and share the gratitude or happiness of the one who receives it. Bad news is delivered slowly, and in writing, as people hesitate to share the discomfort or anger of those they must hurt.

His fingers ripped the envelope open and two sheets came out—one stiff and heavy, written by hand, the other thin and typewritten, obviously a copy of another, original letter. His eyes picked out the first sentence of the handwritten letter which read:

"Dear Ridge—

"The enclosed left our office this afternoon and you will probably have the bad news at your desk Monday, but before then I wanted—"

Warren had stopped reading the handwritten letter. His fingers snapped the flimsy carbon enclosure from underneath it and his eyes gulped the formal paragraphs on Meadows, Smith & Colt stationery:

"Dear Ridge—

"Our partners met this morning to discuss and come to a decision on the proposal you made to me last week. I speak for all of us now when I say how much we regret the negative conclusion at which we arrived.

"It struck us, after a thorough examination of all the information available to us, that you are faced with a problem of long-term financing. We were impressed by the enormous increase in your circulation and by your prospects, which we are told are extraordinary. Yet we have never underwritten any financing in the field of communications and we feel we cannot now plunge into something so alien to our area of competence.

"As for the more specific matter of co-signing your draft at Security National. We discussed that, too. We have come to the conclusion that it is too great a departure from our normal procedures at this office.

"Mr. Meadows, our senior partner, wanted me to make you aware of our continuing high regard for your entire operation. Mr. Meadows says his personal regret is particularly acute because he should like to be able to say that we helped in the great adventure you are leading. He urges me to assure you that if ever our services should seem useful to you in the more old-fashioned branches of finance in which we specialize, to have no hesitation in calling on us.

"Sincerely yours,

"Lawrence Webster."

Warren's fingers flipped back to the handwritten personal letter. His eyes resumed where they had broken off.

". . . probably have the bad news at your desk Monday, but before then I wanted you to know what was coming and so am shooting a copy by hand to your apartment. These things aren't much fun, but the faster you know about them, the better. At least that's my reasoning.

"I still think your proposition—the long-term proposition, not the co-signature, is a fascinating one. Let me keep my antennae spread for venture capital that may be interested in a speculation more interesting than the four or five per cent we normally deal in. I know a man, Jack Raven, an odd character, who might be interested. Call me if you want to meet him. I wish we could have done more ourselves; but that's the nature of our operation.

"Tina and I saw you and Mary at the preview last week. You seemed so wrapped up in each other we didn't want to intrude. But it was wonderful to see you together again. Will she be in New York long? Is there any chance of your joining us for dinner some evening—?

"Larry."

"No," he said aloud. "Why, the yellow, treasonous bastard," he continued as the letter quivered in his hands.

"Who?"

He looked up. It was Mary's voice. He had completely forgotten her. She was watching him. He did not want to talk about it right away. He had to absorb it. He needed a drink.

"Nothing," he said, trying to keep his voice even, though his fingers were crumpling the two sheets of paper in his hand. "Let's have a drink."

He rose from his chair, poured her a rye, himself a brandy.

"Is it an important letter?" she asked quietly.

"Yes," he said, irritated, "but let's not talk about that now. You said you wanted to talk about something tonight, didn't you?"

"But something's upset you just now," she replied, "was it that letter?"

"What difference does it make; what did you want to talk about?"

He would get to the letter in a minute, he had to choke the anger first before he could talk about it reasonably.

"What's your problem?" he said abruptly, as if he were at the office, trying to clear detail from the agenda before getting to more serious business.

"You're pacing like an animal," she said. "What happened just now?"

"Oh, never mind, never *mind*," he snapped, wishing she would sit still while he made up his mind how to tell her about it.

"Do you want me to go?" she asked. "We're both tired and you're about to bite my head off."

"No," he commanded, "stay."

"Then talk to me," she said, "talk to me and stop pacing."

He was silent, still pacing, and Mary Warren looked around the room, wondering where she had left her gloves. It would be better to go, she thought, this is hopeless, this is no night to tell him about Claude and me. It's one of his old moods, come back.

"I guess I had better go after all," she said, rising.

"Stay," he sputtered. "You can't walk out on me, too. You said you had something especially important to tell me this evening. Let's talk about that and get it over with."

"No," she said, "I couldn't possibly tell you now, not when you're in this mood."

"Don't tell me what mood I'm in, go ahead and talk."

Helplessly she sat down, wishing she had the courage to walk out. He had paced out of the cone of the single light in the room. She was talking to the dark. A surge of resentment came to her, the surge that preceded tears. No, above all, she must not cry now. He could not make her cry. She had left him, he could not do this to her. Damnit, she would tell him flat. Firmly, she began.

"I wish you'd sit down. I came home mostly to make up my mind whether to stay here or live in France the rest of my life—"

"You've said that before. What's your problem?" he asked from the darkness. "Why should you want to stay in France? What are you trying to escape from?"

"I'm thinking of getting married again," she said. There it was, out. She might as well finish it, though she wished it did not sound so like a confession. "To a Frenchman, to Claude de la Taille, I don't think you knew him. . . ."

He did not appear to be listening. The silence infuriated her. He was completely wrapped up in himself; she repeated, her voice strained, "I have to make up my mind whether to marry him and live in France, or—"

"I heard you the first time," he said, now coming back into the light. "How long have you known him?"

"Two years," she replied, her anger rising at his cold tone.

"Does he make a living? Are you sleeping with him?" he asked coldly.

"That's none of your business at all," she said, trying to keep her voice under control.

"You asked me for advice. You were my wife."

"I was your wife. I'm not now," she snapped, "I'm glad I'm not your wife. And I'm not asking you for advice. I'm telling you, because I thought you ought to hear it from me directly, not roundabout, by gossip. He's an engineer. *Polytechnicien.* He's forty-four years old. He's one inch shorter than I. I'm happy with him. He lives in Paris and travels back and forth to South America and Africa. I trust him—"

"And you didn't trust me, did you—"

"We're not talking about you. You can't talk about anything in the world without dragging yourself into it. You've got an ego like a leaky sieve. You have to have someone pour ego-juice into it all day long, with attention and importance and flattery, because it all drains away by night-time and you don't know who you are or what you're doing. Claude knows who he is—"

She could see him white-lipped and she could tell by the control in his voice that his anger was complete. She had hit.

"All right, then," he said, "now you've told me. What do you expect me to do? Send flowers to the bride? Give her away?"

"I don't expect anything of you," she said, her voice sharp with an edge she had not heard in it since she parted from him, "not one single thing out of you. I learned that a long time ago. I'm going back to Ohio this weekend for Thanksgiving, and you go back to whatever is bothering you, your magazines, or that letter, and let's stop cutting each other to pieces again. I thought you'd changed, and I had fun this week, but you're still—"

"What do you want me to do?" he cut in. "You come in here and politely announce you've found a new lover. But I'm not supposed to ask you any questions. What do I do? Laugh? Cry? Roll on the floor?"

But she had risen and was walking to the closet to get her coat. He trailed off into silence, then followed her, aware that she was leaving only as he automatically held her coat and she thrust her arms into it. Again the perfume came to him and he realized he would be alone when she left. He did not know how to ask her to stay, but if she would only wait a minute, so he could talk to her. His tongue reached for a way to say the staying word as she straightened into her coat. But all that came was—"Call me when you pass through New York again." Then awkwardly he added, "Don't call me at the office, I may not be there in a few weeks."

He was like a little boy, he knew, trying to tell someone his thumb was bleeding.

"What does that mean?" she asked coolly, turning.

"That letter you were so curious about," he replied, "it means there may not be any magazines left two weeks from now. But don't worry about it."

"Oh?" she said, the coldness mixed now with concern.

"It was from Larry Webster," he said, hoping she would ask him more so he could talk about it.

But she was quiet, neither inquiring of him more—nor moving to the door. He went on, "I need two million dollars, and I thought Larry would have it available for me this afternoon. I counted on it. But he didn't."

"Two million dollars?" she repeated. "That's an awful lot of money—"

"It's not money," he replied, "two million dollars isn't money for spending, it's the power to do things with, it's for making things happen. Unless I find the money in the next two weeks, these magazines could go under—"

He stopped and looked at her. He did not want to whine. If she asked him a question, any question, he could ask her to sit down once more and then begin again.

Instead, he heard her saying quietly, "David said the magazines were in trouble but I never—"

"David who?"

"David Eliot—he said you were in trouble, but you never brought it up all week and I couldn't—"

"What did he tell you?" broke in Warren.

She wished he would not jump down her throat like that. She wished he would ask her to sit down, or say something that would let her sit down and find out what the trouble was.

"He said he was worried about you, but you were so confident, I thought—"

"Has he been going around town saying we're going to fold?" asked Warren, furious. He could not even trust Eliot.

"Of course he's not been talking," she said more sharply than she wanted, "all he said to me was that you were worried and short-tempered and—"

Short-tempered. That did it.

"You tell him for me," said Warren in a voice uglier than anger for its precision, "that I don't want him talking about me to anyone. Not anyone. You tell him that I want him to keep his big mouth shut—"

"All right, then!" she said, her temper flaring to match his. "I'll tell him that. And you'll kick the only friend you have left right out of your life. But remember, I didn't bring this up. You did. If you don't want to talk about it, let's not talk about it. I'm not pushing my way into your life again. We can both get along without ever seeing each other again just the way we have for the past four years. Good night, Johnny."

She had trailed the last words behind her as she walked down the hall to the door, and as she opened the door, he hastily fumbled for his own coat.

"Don't bother to take me home," she called, "I'll find a cab."

He followed her to the elevator doors because to fumble for his coat would let her shut the door in his face, and it would be ridiculous first to find his coat, *then* to chase after her. Yet as they stood there waiting for the elevator, he knew he wanted to go with her—go anywhere rather than back into that room, and reread the letter, and face the weekend alone.

He cleared his throat and said, "I'm sorry about tonight, Mary. I was upset—I—you're in love with this Claude?"

"I think so," she replied, and then, "I'm sorry about tonight, too. We do this to each other. We should have known better."

"When are you getting back here?"

"I promised Mother and Daddy I'd be home with them for Thanksgiving week, so I'll leave tomorrow. Then I have a week in Washington, and I'll fly back to Paris the tenth or twelfth."

"From New York?"

"Yes. I'll be staying in Sara Hubbard's apartment again the last week."

The elevator door suddenly gaped open and she entered. As she stood there, an afterthought came to her and she said softly, "Oh, Johnny, it was a good week, and I hope everything works out all right with the magazines. I really do."

"Don't worry," he said, "I'm still trying. It was my fault tonight, really mine. I wish—"

But the elevator doors, set by automatic timing, had begun to close. He could not see what her lips were forming to say before the doors closed and she was gone.

He turned back to the apartment and realized that even if he wanted to, he could not be with her this weekend. There was now not a moment to be lost, not a day, not a minute, neither weekend nor weekday. Counting tomorrow, there were seventeen days to the Board meeting. How fast did he have to move?

12. Friday Evening

"How fast do we have to move?"

Dorrance of *Gentlewoman* spoke, and Eliot knew the question was put to him, that he was the leader here.

It made Eliot uncomfortable. At all the political meetings, rallies, and conventions which he professionally attended, it was Eliot's attitude to watch, say nothing, and be amused by the performance of the men who must speak or act. Now he must act.

Eliot knew everyone here at Tom Foley's house. But out of the office they appeared quite different—stripped of their office roles and personalities, they seemed like unfrocked priests—quite ordinary people. There were three from *Trumpet*—Clement, because Clement was the strongest of the desk editors; Foley, because Foley had to be in; and old Ben Mitchell. The three from *Gentlewoman* Eliot recognized by face and name as part of the general office clan, but not members of his working family. They were Leonie Cahill, the Editor; Joe Dorrance, her Managing Editor; and Faberhorst, her Art Editor, the oldest hand on *Gentlewoman's* staff.

"I don't know," said Eliot, faltering, "Warren said it might be six months, it might come faster. It's not an emergency. But for us, now is the best time to raise the kind of money I'm talking about. At the year-end. So we have to form a committee right away. I have an appointment with this man Paget at his apartment tomorrow. He's taking off for Europe and he wants to hear about it before he goes."

"Well," said Leonie Cahill, "it gives me a queasy feeling doing all this behind Warren's back. What if he found out—what then?"

"We don't owe him a goddamned thing, Leonie," said Foley, "these are our magazines as much as his, we've been here longer—"

"—And if they go under, what difference does it make if we get fired in the next six weeks or three months from now?" said Clement. "I'm for going ahead and making a real staff committee out of it."

"You think it's really that serious?" asked Faberhorst of *Gentlewoman.*

"I can't see how we wouldn't have heard before; I think it's only a paycut. . . ."

"What do you think, Tom?" broke in Dorrance of *Gentlewoman,* addressing himself directly to his opposite number on *Trumpet.*

"I don't know, I don't know," said Foley with none of his usual vigor. "I don't see how anyone can keep these magazines running for much longer the way things are going," he continued, "the advance makeup of the Christmas issue is down to sixteen pages of ads."

"How many?" asked a voice.

"Sixteen, you heard me."

"I heard you, but I didn't want to," replied the voice.

"Now there's always dough in a corporation like this," went on Foley very slowly, ruminating, "always enough dough for a few more months. They never let themselves get so close to the edge that a shove can push them over. But somehow, somewhere, somebody is going to realize it's pouring money down the drain to keep them going the way they are. No, this is more than paycut. If I thought it were just a paycut and he had any chance of keeping it airborne another year I'd walk upstairs, spit in his eye, and quit. But if there's really no more gas in the tanks and we're going down to a crash-landing, I ought to stick around and see what can be saved. But one thing, goddamn it, Dave," and Foley now turned to Eliot, "why do we have to go back to him? If he wants to cut pay let him cut pay. If we want to form a committee and try to raise money, let's do it on our own. We don't need him. Why go back to him?"

Foley turned to Eliot as he finished speaking and waited for an answer.

"Because we have to," replied Eliot, "because I told him I was going to speak only to a few key people and I gave him my word that nothing would leak out, and that binds everyone here to secrecy."

Eliot took a sip of coffee, liked the sound of firmness in his own voice and, conscious of a new kind of exertion, went on. "But there's a better reason. We need him. We can't go to anybody, not Paget or anyone else, without having access to the books, and Warren's the only one who can give us access. We have to know how much the magazines are losing, whether the Board will spin them off or take a management contract, whether we have to pay anything for title to the magazines—we can't walk into investors in the next two or three months with nothing but editorial dreams. We have to sound like businessmen. We—"

"Poppycock!"

It was old Ben Mitchell exploding, the first time he had spoken all evening. Short, slim, his bushy eyebrows bristling, his little body tense,

Mitchell now leaned forward belligerently from the sofa where he sat. Eliot was annoyed. Mitchell was supposed to be quiet. Mitchell had been invited only because he was so old that his name would count among other old-timers if they had to be recruited. Once Ab Pepper's favorite correspondent, the crusading lance of *Trumpet* when it saucily and impudently exposed Cabinet members, Prohibition, crooked politicians, Mitchell was a man of another generation.

"Nonsense!" said Mitchell angrily, and Eliot felt exasperation rising in him. Now he had to deal with an old man who could not face reality.

"It may sound like nonsense to you, Ben," said Eliot, "but these magazines *are* in trouble. I've got to go back and tell Warren I've talked to you here, that we're going along with any paycut proposal, that we'll be quiet, but that we want the right to talk to investors, too—"

"Don't talk to me as if I were a doddering idiot," said Mitchell, "damned well right you're going back to him and talk. But about what? I'm too old to be a fool—"

Eliot noticed that Mitchell had picked a doll up from the sofa on which he sat, a child's tousled doll that must belong to one of the Foley children, and was stroking the doll with a gentle caress that contradicted the crackle in his voice.

"Sounds to me like a convention of mice trying to bell a cat," continued Mitchell, "that's what you all sound like. Like a little meeting of boy publishers. *Nothing's* going to save these magazines. Nothing. I can tell it by feel, by the heft of the magazine—lay a copy on the doorstep and the wind blows it away. Not that I'm against your trying to save it. Go ahead. It's like someone in your family dying, you have to try to save him. But let's talk sense—"

Mitchell jerked his head, turned from Eliot to Faberhorst, thrust out a skinny forefinger.

"Fab," he demanded, "how long have you been with this outfit?"

"Twenty-seven years," said Faberhorst.

"Twenty-seven years," repeated Mitchell, repeating the words with all solemnity, "all your working life. And you're going to be fired, Fab, fired. Everybody's going to be fired. And what are you planning to do? Nothing! Nobody's planning to do anything. The printers out in Anderbury have their union to protect them. But how about the rest—twelve or thirteen hundred people going to be kicked out on the street, paid to the end of the week's work, and that's the end of it. What are we going to do about that?"

"You're right," said Faberhorst, cocking his head as if to a new sound, "that's what they'll do. What are we going to do?"

"Now, Fab—now, Ben," said Eliot, trying to get his meeting back on the track, but Mitchell exploded again.

"Separation pay! That's what we have to think about right now—"

"Ben," said Eliot desperately, trying to hold him down, "let's take that up later. We're here to organize a committee to save the magazines, not to liquidate them. You've got an important point, but—"

"But nothing," said Mitchell savagely, "that's the whole point. Separation pay! I'm for your committee. There's got to be a committee. We've got to see Warren—but only to pin him down on separation pay for everybody. Before it's too late. While we can bargain. This is the way we get to him. We'll go to the bridge with him, volunteer for a paycut, volunteer to raise money, anything—but he's got to go down the line with us—"

"Mitch," said Foley, "you've sold me. I knew I felt like a boy scout about this committee. Now I've got a good, mean, satisfying reason for being in favor of it—"

"Hundreds of people working here," said Mitchell, rolling over Foley's interruption, chipping every word from an inner indignation, "money-changers coming into their temple, driving them from the holy place. Hit back, I say! If we can gouge two weeks, ten weeks, twenty weeks of separation pay for the old crowd out of Warren, we have to do it. We're all responsible for each other. You tell me—all they've got the right to take away from this shop is friendship and memories? And that they tried to save it? No, sir! Not enough, I say—they need checks, too. Some people I've known all my life are working here still for eighty-five, ninety-five dollars a week. Not do anything about them? We pushed through the child-labor laws, didn't we? This magazine got the railway pension act passed, didn't it? Can't get separation pay for our own people?— Poppycock!"

"Right!" said Clement. "I make a hell of a lot more than ninety-five a week, but I need every cent of it. I have a four hundred dollar hi-fi set ordered for Ellen for Christmas and if we blow I can't pay for that or anything else. I'm in hock right now. If we have trouble I need severance pay—and time to look for another job."

"Time to look for another job is right now," said Dorrance, "when we *know* the thing is going to fold; there'll be hundreds of us on the street looking for a new desk the day we close—all of us cutting each other's throat because there just aren't enough magazine jobs in New York. The thing to do, if we're smart, is to break and run now. Like getting out of the army in 'forty-five, the ones who got out first got the best jobs. The ones who got out in the spring of 'forty-six are still five years behind on the ladder because they lost those six months."

"You there, Dorrance," said Mitchell, thrusting out his skinny finger again, "you listen to me. Nobody in this room is going to cut and run. I'll take it on me personally to call any editor or shop you find a job in and cut your—"

"Hey, Mitch," said Dorrance, not at all upset, "I was just saying that's what I'd do if I were smart. The time to abandon ship is before the torpedo hits, not after. But I'm *not* smart. I'm with you all the way, may God have mercy on my kids and a Merry Christmas to you all!"

"We're not going down, I tell you," said Eliot, trying to exert control. "We didn't get together to plan on going down, we got together to save it; let's get back—"

"I tell you what," said Foley, "let's not argue that now; let's say we have a double-purpose committee. Warren told Dave to sound us out. Fine. He did it. Now Dave goes back and sounds Warren out. We'll go along with anything he wants to save the magazines. But we want a couple of counter-commitments. We want him to make the books available to a couple of us so we can raise money from this Paget character of Dave's. And we want him to guarantee that there'll be severance pay if the time comes we need it. Otherwise, you tell him, Dave, that you sounded us out on a paycut and that everyone will break for the exits unless we have guarantees of severance. Now let's organize this committee; you want to be chairman?"

"All I want," said Eliot, "is to write my stuff on politics on a magazine that's solid; I'm no organizer. I didn't call this meeting to make myself chairman—"

"You want to be chairman or not?" bored Foley insistently. "Do you want us to make two chairmen, you and Mitchell, one for raising money, one for severance pay?"

"Very good idea," said Leonie Cahill, "but there ought to be someone from *Gentlewoman* on this committee, too—"

"All right," said Eliot, feeling a stir in the room, as if a strange new shape were beginning to take form and come alive, "I'll get back to Warren as soon as I see Paget and make a date for all of us. Let's see, Mitch and I and Leonie and you, Tom, you ought to be there, and someone else from *Gentlewoman* to round it out to five."

"I want Dorrance with me," said Leonie Cahill, "he's my Managing Editor."

"O.K.," said Foley, "let's cut it off there; five's enough to see him; now we have to figure out where we go from here."

The room began to talk all at once. Something had happened, voices quickened, broke aloud, then sounded over other voices, as all began to talk.

"Ought to have some people from advertising in this—"

"Ought to get some of the circulation people in too—"

"How about the people at the Anderbury plant?" "Ought to get a paper and pencil and write some of this down." "Who's got a pencil?" "Who's got paper?" "Look, does anybody here know anything about what paper costs for the magazine?" "If we're going to have a plan, we ought to know." "We ought to work out a severance-pay chart for this meeting." "Does anybody know how a union goes about this sort of deal?" "The hell with the unions, they wouldn't even spit on us now, we never were organized here."

"All right," yelled Foley. "All right! Everybody shut up!"

They looked at him and it was Foley of the office again. He rubbed his hand over his face, brought it away, and his voice was surly and angry once more. They welcomed the tone that made them a team.

"We've got work to do tonight and we have to pull it together," said Foley. "Let's take a break now before we settle into it. Maud's got some fresh coffee and I blew a couple of bucks on a cheesecake for everybody. Let's cut up the cheesecake and then get to work."

2. FRIDAY EVENING: ANDERBURY, THE PLANT

Hopkins, the plant manager, knew that Emmy, his wife, would be angry. She had been angry every Friday evening for twenty years when he was late and dinner grew cold. But he could not leave the plant before the big presses rolled. Every Friday, just about now, at eight, this urge rose, to carry him out of the back door of the plant office, down the corridor, to trace with undeviating routine the backward path of the weekly closing.

First, the composing room. Quiet now. The soft, almost noiseless tapping of the impulse machines stuttering out the tape bearing final copy from New York, two hundred miles away, had long since hushed. The semi-transparent spools of yellow paper tape, studded with the dotted hieroglyphs that automatically operated the hissing linotype machines, lay tangled in the baskets beside the linotypes, their purpose spent, their message frozen in metal. Twenty-odd years now that Hopkins had been watching these newfangled machines—and he still could not get used to the thought that someone in a room in New York could punch a tape and thus move his machines here in Anderbury and make them clank out, instantaneously, the words that had just left some editor's desk in Manhattan.

The composing room was silent and empty, its concrete floors echoing to his solitary step, the hunters' moon outside pouring in through the grime-streaked windows, making eldritch shadows. The crest of the excitement of closing had left New York at half past five, had cleared this room by half past six, but Hopkins followed its cold path back. His nostrils could only imagine the smell of the hot linotype metal now all grown cold. But in the plating room, as he passed, no imagination was needed to catch the hot, sweet, caramel smell of the electrotype alloy. The plating room was empty now, too, the plates already gone on down to press; but the smell lingered with the heat and Hopkins breathed deeply. Supposed to be lead fumes in that electrotype metal. But he liked it.

Out along the catwalk now, ranging the river. It was a river, too, by God, not a creek. Not much use for anything these days except for kids to play in, or skate on in winter. But it was a river, and by this river with its power they had made the locks and clocks that first made Anderbury famous. There'd been Hopkinses in Anderbury ever since they first opened the first mill by the river. Good river.

Along the catwalk, down the steps, along the bank, around through the side doors, into the storage sheds. He liked to do it just this way, filing through the huge columns that the paper rolls made—six of those paper rolls, four and a half feet high, one ton each, and they reached to the ceiling just like the pillars of the Egyptian temples they used to show the children in Sunday-school pictures.

Except it was empty. Emptier even than last week. No more than one week's supply on hand, and this week's shipment so slim he had to fairly gut the inventory. What were they doing, letting paper supplies on hand get so low? A two-week railway strike and they'd be out of business. How could he turn out his magazines if he had no paper?

Couldn't make out what they were doing in New York. First letting the paper in stock run so low it was dangerous. Then Austin insisting they sell off the old Goss presses. Couldn't print a 156-page issue any more if they sold the old standby Goss presses. Penny wise, pound foolish. Sell off the old Gosses for 150,000 dollars, then next year when things got better they'd be stuck, have to pay a million dollars to get a new press. Always darkest just before the dawn. They must be scared in New York. Might be, too, with the way advertising was going.

Hopkins had now come into the big hall with the big presses. He had overtaken the crest of the closing. Two of the presses were running with the middle signatures of next week's magazine. Three more were readying up to roll the late form of this week's magazine. He saw the girls, the "backers," out there by the two presses, waiting to carry away the folds, giggling. The backers always giggled, been doing so ever since he first came to the plant. Hopkins' eye swept the wall high above the presses, scanning the Browning instruments—all the dials were on the nose, gas feed correct, water temperature correct, air temperature correct. Must be almost time for the pull. He knew it was. Didn't want the men thinking he was checking up on them; he always came around at this time, they knew it; his magazines.

Hopkins stopped in front of O'Malley's table, set in front of the presses. O'Malley was the foreman.

"Good evening, O'Malley."

"Good evening, Mr. Hopkins."

Just as always.

His eye followed O'Malley's up and around the huge new Babcock press; twice as big as a tugboat, it was. A million-dollar monster, they called it in New York; a million-dollar sweetheart, it was. The Babcock and the new color presses, that's what he had to thank Mr. Warren for; could have gone another ten years without getting new equipment if Mr. Warren hadn't seen how much he needed it.

The hoses quivered, dangled, shook with the waters, gases, inks, and airs, twisting about the machinery like jungle vines, as if nourished by this chrome, green and black chunk of machinery rather than nourishing it. The hoses trembled as if they carried a pulse that would any minute bring the press to life with a purpose. Hopkins knew the Babcock carried the late-closing eight-page signature. He looked at his watch. Eight thirty-five. The copy that had been penciled and O.K.'d by editorial and proofroom initials in New York only three hours before was already here fixed in metal plates, cased, curved and bolted on the impatient cylinders ready to burst into their run. Hopkins' eye saw the giant cylinders turning on their axes imperceptibly, as the web of white paper crawled slowly through the giant rolls.

"Inching," said Hopkins to O'Malley.

"Yup," said O'Malley, not taking his eyes from the press. "Inching. Five minutes late tonight. Not their fault. Copy was late from New York, twenty minutes late coming out of the composing room. We locked up twelve minutes fast tonight once we had it. Roll any minute now."

"Not complaining," said Hopkins. "If you can't boost, don't knock, that's what I say."

He could see Stapleton, the Number One man of the press crew on the Babcock, coming down the catwalk from the second story of the huge press as he spoke, and turn toward the control panel. The red lights were on, so the press must be clear. He could see Stapleton's body covering the panel of controls.

"Making the pull now," said O'Malley, as if talking to himself.

"Yup," said Hopkins, watching. He had watched this, week after week for forty-five years, ever since he had left Anderbury High School and had gone to work in the plant. He knew.

The alarm bells tinkled as Stapleton pressed the "set" button; Hopkins nodded. The bells warned everybody fiddling near the press that it was almost ready to roll.

Time to circle the machine and get back to the front end, just time, thought Hopkins. He loved this moment. And, as he circled the huge press, he could hear suddenly the whisper as the presses began to revolve, speeding out of their slow inching revolution into their high run, all eight mammoth cylinders synchronized to the microsecond to accelerate at the same speed. There was a slight hiss, a slight hum, a louder hum, a full-throated drone—and then the fragrance of hot steaming paper billowed out, scorched almost to burning as the gas flares instantaneously dried the wet inks, then cooled immediately as the ice-cold rollers saved them from combustion. Hopkins loved the smell—printers' ink and hot paper.

Hopkins did not hurry, but he had circled and was back at the front where he wanted to be—to see the virgin paper come streaking down off the high roller in a diagonal sheet so fast that it seemed rigid as a plank. There, now, as he watched, he could see the paper go black, mottled, blur into a spasm of gray, as the ink caught it deep within the press, printing its message in a convulsive moment of climax. Now the paper speeding down was no longer paper—it was alive, slit by the blade-edges into pages, caught by the machine's fingers and folded into signatures that came feeding out in a caterpillar of folds onto the trays. The girls were racking them on the skids, and men were approaching to move the skids with the page folds to the stitching machines that would make magazines of them.

Hopkins picked up one of the signatures and examined it. He knew they were watching him. They always did. He rubbed his finger over the inked impression and looked at his fingers. Scarcely a trace of gray. The pictures were sharp. Even the shadows were clear. He folded the signature and put it in his back pocket. Would read it later. Another issue gone to press. Couldn't ask for a finer printing job, no one could. Maybe those Midwestern plants could do a cheaper cost job, the way he heard Will Austin say it in New York; but nobody could do a better print job than old New England. No, sir.

"O.K.," he said. "Good night, now."

"Good night, Mr. Hopkins," he could hear the girls chorus behind him, and as he walked away he could hear the Number 2 press spin into the hum of its operation, then, almost at the door, he could hear the Number 3 come alive. Sixty hours later, they would be through with six million copies for the week. Maybe it wasn't the smart way of doing things, printing all the magazines right here in their own plant. Austin kept saying there was too much capital tied up in the plant; New England was just too far away from the rest of the country to print a magazine and get it across to California in time. Maybe you ought to job-print a magazine in half-a-dozen plants around the country all at the same time, on someone else's equipment. But that's not the way old Pepper figured it. And you couldn't beat old Pepper. He made those magazines. Best printing in the country.

O'Malley and Stapleton watched Hopkins walk away.

"Hear he went to New York last week," said Stapleton.

"Yup," said O'Malley.

"What's he say?"

"What he always says about New York," said O'Malley. "They don't know whether they're afoot or horseback."

"They can't scare the union by clearing out inventory. I know they're cutting down the paper stock just to scare us. They try a new trick every time it comes to negotiation."

"Economy's the word," said O'Malley. "Cut-backs. Everybody takes a cut. Including the union."

"Can't do that," said Stapleton, "we have a contract. Got to get a new one. They always cry just before it's time to negotiate with us. But they won't scare us that way."

"Scares me," said O'Malley, "I don't belong to the union."

"Well," said Stapleton, "you wanted to be a foreman. You're an executive now."

"Union won't do any good either," said O'Malley, "if they shut this plant down."

"Ain't gonna shut this plant down," said Stapleton, "the best printing plant in Massachusetts, they can't shut it down."

"Wouldn't be so sure," said O'Malley, "they used to make the best harnesswear in America in this town. Don't make it any more and they were the very best harnesses."

"Couldn't shut this plant down," said Stapleton. "What the hell would Anderbury do? Half the town would fold. Couldn't shut it down."

"Might be," said O'Malley. "You going up to Vermont next week to get a deer? Open the season next week."

"Nope," said Stapleton. "Changed my mind. Put me down as being here. My daughter's getting married in January. I'll need every penny I can get between now and then. Can't afford to lose the pay this year."

13. Time of Torment

For Warren, the next two weeks dissolved into strivings so chaotic that on waking he could not tell whether the memories that woke with him had actually happened the day before, or were indeed happening now, or were nightmares of the torment that ran around the clock, day and night.

There were, in some nightmares, all twenty-six hundred people of the magazines whose eyes followed him, haunting, pleading for their jobs. And in others, all twenty-six hundred people jeered at him, leaving him alone with it. There was the ring of the money—$2,000,000, or $3,000,-000, or $4,000,000—at times so small a sum of money for so great a purpose as to be laughable, at times so huge a sum of money as to be beyond the Himalayan dreams of any reasonable hope.

Now, whether at the apartment or at the office, the vistas and stretch of the city drugged his thinking. He could not tell, peering at its mocking scenery, what it said—whether the audience in the arena of the cliffs turned its back to his struggle, indifferent and uncaring, remorselessly, busily, feelinglessly shutting him out. Or whether from each window, in the checkerboard of windows, men watched from the surrounding towers, amused, excited and entertained.

He could identify the moment that the feeling of the city as audience and enemy came to him. It was when he heard the sound of his own voice Sunday afternoon after Webster had deserted him, and Mary had left. He had gone to the office on Saturday and, all alone, plotting for the resumption of work on Monday, had heard nothing but the sound of his own dialing on the telephone, the sound of his own voice reaching for absent men for appointments. But on Sunday, in a moment of hush in the empty office, he had tried to call Morrissey simply to talk to someone who, like him, might be responsible for what was about to happen. Morrissey had not been home, but the person who answered had said he would call back. Warren had been waiting alone for the call back when he heard the sound of his voice.

"Ring," his voice was saying urgently to the telephone. "Ring, you bastard, ring!"

The telephone sat quietly on his desk, all its translucent buttons blank and mute. But it did not ring.

"Ring," he said again, hoarsely. "Say something."

He turned with a nervous twitch as he spoke, half-conscious of someone in the room watching him. But there was no one—only the buildings outside, rising in the distance, making an empty Sunday audience for his strivings.

In the silence, Warren recognized the quality in his voice—it was the sound of the losers. Warren had played poker all through the army, had watched the gamblers at the gaming tables of Deauville and Baden-Baden when he was in Europe, and the sound was familiar. Always it was the same when a gambler found himself in a game that had imperceptibly grown too large for him—he slowed down and spoke in this voice. He placed his chips on the roulette table more and more slowly, with greater and greater hesitation. He squeezed the cards in his hands more tightly, unfolding them with a tremor, then hesitated over cards which at the beginning of the game he would have bet with a casual flourish. It was loser's paralysis, the narcosis of the nerve, that came over all losers as mistrust of their own judgment transfixed them. Others at the table drew away, edged closer to the winners, as if luck, good or bad, were contagious—and the losers were left alone in their waiting. They could not do else, but wait for the next deal—and yet they feared it. "Deal," they would croak, or, "Spin The Wheel"—but they feared it. Just as he waited alone for the telephone to ring with a call back from Morrissey—and feared it.

Warren's imagination raced down the sleek, kinked telephone cord of rubber that ran to the jack in the floor, and then from the jack along the cables that carried the fibrils to the underground conduits where they twined with all the other millions and millions of fibrils that twisted beneath Manhattan's paving before rising and forking out to other desks, other voices, where the power of "yes" or "no" lay congealed. Of the millions of fibrils only a few thousand ran to the desks of executive decision. And of the few thousand, only a few hundred could make any decision that might help. And tomorrow, Monday, he must start to find them. There was no time now to go slowly, to write, or to investigate. Whatever he must do, he must do quickly, with the telephone his only courier, his only lever to pry a saving decision out of the cruel city.

To sit and wait for the telephone to ring would be to wait for disaster. To wait for Morrissey to call would be to wait only to discuss the terms of surrender. Only lesser people waited for the telephone to ring. If you were at the top, then you had to make it ring in other people's offices. But how?

Warren drew his scratch pad to him and began to pencil, as he always did when planning, "One," "Two," "Three." But there was no answer in his pencil, no lines to fill out for steps One, Two, Three.

He began again, writing "A," "B," "C."

Then he tore off the second sheet of paper, balled it, threw it away.

What you needed was names. Names were people; people were clues to decision; he knew many people; some must be able to lead him to the desk where a decision could be taken.

He drew the Wheeldex of his personal telephone numbers close to him and started on a fresh sheet of paper. Any name, any contact, any lead, among the important and near-important men he had met would do to start his telephone on the trails it must follow. And as he listed the random names that came off the index by alphabet, he knew that all the planning of the past two weeks was dissolving, that he was seeking neither short-term, nor long-term money, but only survival—and a few more months of time in which to try again.

It was only because B followed A in the alphabetical order of his index that at the end of the weekend the list stood surmounted by the name of Louis J. Bronstein. Which was where he must begin on Monday.

"Mr. Bronstein?" he asked quietly into the telephone, after Laura had located the old man at home the next morning.

"Yes, sure—this is Bronstein. Is that you, Warren?"

"Yes, this is Ridge Warren, Mr. Bronstein. Am I disturbing you? I'd like to talk to you for a few minutes."

"Bothering me? Nothing of the kind—I was just reading *The New York Times* again. I'm not busy in the mornings these days. A wonderful paper, isn't it?"

"Yes, it is, Mr. Bronstein— Mr. Bronstein, I have a problem here, and I wanted to get your thinking about it."

"Trouble, huh, Warren? I told you you should call me if you had trouble. Why did you wait two weeks?"

"Well, I didn't think I ought to bother you until—"

"Until you got deep, deep in trouble. So now you're really stuck, you have to call Bronstein. But I understand. Only you should learn that old men like me, we get a kick out of it when somebody thinks we're important enough to come to for advice. Or is it only advice you want, Warren? Maybe it's money?"

Taut as he felt, Warren smiled at the quick working of the old man's mind.

"Both," he said into the phone, relieved.

"It's usually both," said the old man slowly. "When you've got money, you don't need advice. Reminds me of a story—once a fellow went into the store and they asked him for a reference—listen, I'm talking too much, you don't want to hear that story. Tell me—what can I do for you? Advice, I mean, not money. Advice is easy—advice I can give you sitting down, standing up, from the bathtub, over the telephone. Money—that's different, that's serious."

"I'll talk about both at the same time, Mr. Bronstein, if you let me—"

"Sure, go ahead, talk—"

There was no time to be polite. He must say it straight.

"Mr. Bronstein . . . I have to find four or five million dollars fast. I have to find one or two million of that in the next two weeks, and the next three million of that three months later or we're in trouble—"

"You mean it, Warren? Like they say—could the magazines go down?"

"Yes."

A pause, then— "Imagine that! You got to do something then. Right away."

"Exactly."

"And you wouldn't be calling me if you could get money from the banks."

"Exactly, Mr. Bronstein."

"So it's something fancy you've got in mind."

"Mr. Bronstein, you've saved me a long explanation."

"So what do you want me to do?"

"To be precise, I want you to do us a great favor. But it won't cost you or Bruno Liquors a penny. After that, I want some advice."

"The favor is the money part of it, tell me that first."

"I need to find a co-signer of our note of one million at our bank, the Security National, right away. If I can persuade you to do it, Security National will carry me for another million at the same time."

"By a co-signer, what do you mean, Warren?"

"This is what I mean—Security National puts up all the money. We pay all the interest charges. Nobody advances another cent. But somebody, you, has to put the signature of your corporation's credit underneath ours to back us up for a million. Naturally, for the favor, we'll make any sort of arrangement the co-signer requires—fee, option on stock, warrants; in the case of Bruno Liquors, preferred advertising rates. You probably know best what you'd want in return."

He was putting the bite on old man Bronstein hard.

"I get you. Security National doesn't trust you any more. But you think they'd trust us. So we're borrowing the money for you. The only hitch is if you can't pay it back, then we have to pay it. That's the law."

"But there's no danger, Mr. Bronstein, our assets are—"

"But Security National doesn't think so."

The telephone was silent and Warren could hear Mr. Bronstein's breathing. He waited to let the silence build its pressure on Mr. Bronstein, not wanting to do it this way, but he had to.

"Must be you've got a lot of bills and obligations, other things that bother the bank. Otherwise, for a big customer like you . . ." came Mr. Bronstein's voice, thinking, and another pause. . . . "You must have a no-good balance sheet there, you know that, Warren." Another pause. "I'm not being tough, mind you, Warren, I'm just thinking out loud; let me think this around a little bit in my head; you aren't in a hurry to get off the telephone, are you? Naturally, you don't expect me to say yes or no, do you, Warren, right like that, like snapping my fingers, huh?"

"I have plenty of time," said Warren. He wondered whether the old man was simply enjoying an interruption of his loneliness or actually entertaining the thought.

"You know," said the old man, finally, "this is a lawyer kind of thing, isn't it?"

"How's that, Mr. Bronstein?"

"I ask you to call me when you're in trouble, so you call me. I like that. Still and all, it's a million dollars and I don't want to get technical, but it's a lawyer kind of thing. You know, Warren, if I still had the money in my own hands, I'd call in my lawyer, say to him, 'Get Harry Vogelson'— that's our accountant—'look over Warren's books, see if we can help him out.' But now these lawyers, they got me tied up in so many ways, Warren, you wouldn't believe. I don't know what's mine any more and what belongs to my sons. We've got a trust now, a Bronstein family trust, how do you like that, Warren? So the money skips from me to my grandchildren, you know how it is, Warren, just a minute, I want to get a drink of water. . . ."

This was going to be long, Warren knew. He put his feet up on his desk, and patiently prepared to let Mr. Bronstein surface up to reality when and where he wanted.

"Where were we, Warren?" came the voice again over the phone.

"At the Bronstein family trust, Mr. Bronstein."

"How did we get there, Warren? I must be talking too much. Oh, yes, this lawyer thing, this business of co-signing is for friends or for peddlers. Well, we're friends. But I don't really know what part of my money is mine any longer, is it in the trust, or do my sons have it already? You understand, money is still important, but what do I need money for, a man of my age?"

"It's good to have though, Mr. Bronstein."

"Aha." Mr. Bronstein chuckled, gave a happy little sigh, then resumed, "You see what I mean, though, Warren?"

For all his concentration on the talk Warren could not tell whether he was hearing yes, no or maybe. He guessed.

"If I read you correctly, Mr. Bronstein, you're saying maybe."

"Exactly. Absolutely. Maybe."

Warren's head spun. He was making progress. But which way?

"What's the name of the bank who'll put up the money, and the name of the fellow you do business with there?" Suddenly the old voice snapped up to vigor.

"Security National, Mr. Bronstein. The man to see is Cameron. I'll call him, if you want, and tell him to make any information you need available."

"Good. We got that settled. I'll call a couple of our lawyers, call an accountant, have them check your books, the banks, everyone, then if we see it's all O.K., and covered—what's a million dollars between friends?"

Warren held the telephone tightly; he could not respond quickly. Did Mr. Bronstein really mean it? Bruno Liquors' signature did not have the cachet of Meadows, Smith & Colt. But it would do, it would do! It was possible, it was reprieve, it was—but Mr. Bronstein was continuing, he was not through yet—

"To me, that is, I don't care so long as it's safe. But to my sons, that's different, that's where we'll have trouble. They're tough, my boys. They think I'm old. Everything I'm for, they're against. This money, I explained to you, I can hardly put my hands on my own money nowadays. So let me figure it out, I got ways of figuring things out, and when I figure it out, I'll talk to my boys. Maybe a week, maybe two weeks. How much of a hurry are you in, Warren?"

"Just about that. I have to know in two weeks. By a week from this Friday."

"All right," said the old man. "So much for the money. Now about that other thing, Warren?"

"Yes," said Warren.

"The other thing you need, the three or four million dollars for springtime, I say no. We wouldn't touch it. It's all right for tomato-juice people to buy magazines, or grocery-store people to buy magazines. But after Prohibition, I know liquor people shouldn't touch magazines. It's not our business. You get it?"

"I do, Mr. Bronstein. On that second matter, I want advice, not money. You said when we had lunch that this was a crazy business, for crazy men. Do you know any crazy men who want to buy a piece or a share in the two best magazines in the country?"

"At my age, Warren, you don't know any crazy men any more. Either they're dead—or if they lived this long, they're not crazy any longer. But this kind of money you're looking for, you can't find regular business money, it's got to be kind of crazy, kind of family money, gambler's money, something like that. You're gonna learn a lot about money before you find it, Warren."

"I know that, Mr. Bronstein, but if you can help me on that signature, I'll have time to look around."

"Say, Warren?" Abruptly.

"Yes?"

"Warren, I'm tired now. I'll tell my people to contact you. I'm going to hang up."

"Good-by, Mr. Bronstein, thank you. Our deadline is a week from Friday, so if—"

"So if I'm gonna help you, I got to help you before then. I get it. Warren, I'm tired. Good-by." And with a quick, but not unfriendly sound, Mr. Bronstein was gone.

That was the beginning of the unconnected time, the beginning of the strange roaming about the city among strange people seeking secret rescue. It was as if he were acting in a kidnaping, desperately concealing his effort to save something which, if brought to the attention of police and public, would doom what he was trying to save. The banks and creditors were police and public. Once Security National and Meadows, Smith & Colt had both frowned on him, he knew every other door of legitimate commercial money had clanged shut, too.

It was as Mr. Bronstein had said—"Family money, gambler's money, crazy money"—to these he must turn. And Warren learned to know them all as he lurched and struggled through the city.

Family money first. Warren had learned to know his way into many of the sedate and quiet homes of New York where old wealth purrs in unrecognized family splendor. Warren had long known that each great family of wealth branched a sport who could be intrigued by talking of the drama; or of horses; or of art; or of movies; or of blooded herds. Still others found their hobby and delight in good works; while others would listen to the tale of new enterprises in Africa, or Sicily, or Bolivia, or anywhere else if far enough away to lend romance and glamor to mere money-making.

Among them were many who dabbled in publishing, for publishing seems to offer not only a hedge against immortality, but a hope of immediate importance in the mob-life which wealth alone cannot command. It was easy to seek such people out, Warren learned, for the very rich were frequently very bored. Yet the early-morning coffees and the late-afternoon cocktails which Warren found so easy to arrange through his friendships among the great rich families proved the most quickly deceiving of his rounds. For great rich families came always surrounded by a palace guard of lawyers and investment counsel who were quick to demonstrate after his departure that publishing was a ruthlessly competitive game in which money could be lost almost as quickly as at a roulette wheel run by a crooked gambling house. And the unfailing courtesy and good manners with which he was received were not meant to deceive—it was honest payment for the pleasure he gave them. One of the few genuine pleasures of the very rich, Warren decided, as he ruefully heard himself chanting his story one afternoon, was just such audiences as this —audiences with men in their parlors projecting ideas and dreams for investment with such fire, enthusiasm and performance as to offer the rich a sub-species of metropolitan entertainment.

Family money would not help. It was interested neither in a *Trumpet*, nor a *Gentlewoman*, loud and powerful enough to be free, eventually, of its support. When great old wealth moved into the creative realms of art, of publishing, of charity, it moved only to create goodwill for the family name by giving where there was no hope of return—and no chance of losing control.

Within days, Warren recognized that none of his friends among the rich would rescue him from his trap. Nowhere among them had Warren found a trace of hope half as substantial as that of his first telephone call to Mr. Bronstein, whose accountants had now begun to probe his books and talk to Mr. Cameron.

And just as Mr. Bronstein's money was the only family money on which he could pin his hope for quick release from the closing trap, so, slowly, did Jack Raven's money grow larger and larger through the fortnight as Warren turned to the adventurers.

Jack Raven had entered the fortnight early, by the apologetic suggestion of Lawrence Webster who had said, cryptically, "You'll find him interesting anyway, Ridge—he plays long shots, and he isn't nervous, and he may help."

Warren had called for the files on Raven from *Trumpet's* morgue before his first morning appointment with Raven. The lead in one of the Sunday supplement stories about Jack Raven had summed up all there was to say and Warren had known it all vaguely before. The lead had begun in the flat prose of all Sunday supplements.

"Everyone who is anyone knows who Jack Raven is—which is because Jack Raven has made it his business that they *should*. Real Estate Entrepreneur, Broadway Angel, Speculator, Baseball Magnate, Art Collector—all these Jack Raven has become. But essentially, Jack Raven is still a truckdriver who butted his way up from Canarsie to Manhattan wanting people to know and feel his muscle. Father now of two sons (one at Yale, one at Columbia) . . ."

And so the story had run, telling Warren little more than he had known before he began to climb the steps from the reception floor to Raven's personal office. He had not expected Raven to inhabit such an office. The main floor of Raven Enterprises, where the elevator stopped, was the standard expanse of desks, cubicles, and partitions that pen the life of men who work in New York. But from the main floor, where Raven's deputies and lieutenants worked, a winding staircase circled to Raven's rooftop working eyrie. Glowing in bronze, the staircase wound its way upwards between bronze railings, bronze banisters, bronze risers all polished to a subdued gloss. Banisters and railings framed purple-tinted glass panels whose hue was repeated in the thicker purple-tinted glass slabs of the treads, so that walking upstairs on glass to Jack Raven's office was like walking on air—an effect heightened by the dangling mobiles that gently revolved in the eddy of the office drafts.

Raven's office itself was flooded with light—glass-walled on all sides, looking out over the East River, it was decorated in pale blues and butter yellows. Its furniture was a glisten of Fiberglas fabrics tense over chrome tubing, its desk a shimmering flat expanse of glass on a blond-wood base. The walls, repeating the spring colors, were decorated with Impressionist paintings which spoke in gay elegance of unrestrained expense. The sound of the city hummed far beyond the thick twin-panes of the glass walls, while above the threshold of the hum, Warren could make out that somewhere in this room was music—the sound of an orchestra and a voice chanting above it, singing *Carmen* perceptibly enough to hear castanets tinkling.

Square in the middle of the room sat Jack Raven, his big body behind the desk displaying the shoulders of a longshoreman, his skull as clean-shaven as a Russian general's, his face mottled with white and red patches, his chin firm and powdered, his jaw slowly masticating gum. For a moment Warren thought the girl bent at the seat on Raven's far side was a secretary and that Raven was finishing a dictation. But as the girl giggled and lifted a linen towel above the level of the desk, then bent again over Raven's hand, Warren realized that Raven was being manicured.

"Good morning, Mr. Warren, how are you?" boomed Jack Raven, as Warren pushed the glass door open. "Good morning, I'm Jack Raven. You don't mind if I don't get up to shake hands? I'd spill Lucille's bowl if I did. How *are* you? Sit down. Get a load off your feet. Call me Jack. Everybody does."

"Thank you, Mr. Raven. Call me Ridge," said Warren, sitting down, not hurrying, trying to orient, finally, as the brilliance of the setting began to impress him. "You have the most impressive offices I've ever seen in New York, Mr. Raven," he announced flatly, and then added, "Magnificent."

"Call me Jack," said Raven conversationally. "You like it? I like it myself. That's a Buffet on the wall. That's a Matisse; the dancers are real Degas. I suppose you know all that classy stuff, but I still get a kick out of it. Say, hell—you don't mind this music, do you? Some people do. I've had this place wired up by the Muzak people, it puts pep into me while I work. I can cut it off, if it bothers you."

"It doesn't bother me at all, Mr. Raven," said Warren, beginning to relax as the tube-spring chair bent beneath his weight.

"Jack! Call me Jack," insisted Raven sternly. "Say, you don't mind Lucille finishing this manicure while we talk? Lucille doesn't understand anything, she's only interested in boys. Aren't you, Lucille? But pretty, though. Stand up, Lucille, and let Ridge see you. Ridge runs a couple of magazines, baby, and he could put your picture on the cover."

Lucille stood up, a figure with hard little breasts, heavy red lips and a common face that would be young for this year and the next in the vitality of its youth and then soon be sodden with work and strain when she married and babied.

"What do you do besides manicuring, Lucille?" asked Warren, trying to range the frequency on which Raven might be reached; and this might be more than a manicurist.

"I dance," said Lucille with the tight, purse-lipped gentility of someone who has modeled herself on the ladies of television. "At night and on Wednesday afternoons, I take dancing lessons and a friend of mine at the Rockettes says—"

But before Lucille could finish her sentence, the telephone on Raven's desk rang, and Raven had lifted it.

"What do you mean four in the balcony?" he roared after a moment. "It's for *me*, goddamnit! I want four in the orchestra. On the aisle! Tonight! I don't give a damn! I want them! Whaddaya mean, you can't? You *can!* Do I have to buy that theater just to get four seats when I want them? What the hell did I put up the dough for? I want those seats if he has to build them by hand. I want his own seats if he hasn't got any more. What's his number?"

Furiously, Raven slammed down the phone, picked it up again, pulled it to him. He whirled the dial savagely, bellowed at the answering voice, listened a moment, his gum-chewing speeding up to a meat-chopping lashing of the jaw muscles, paused, yelled again, slammed down the phone without a good-by, dialed another number, got it wrong, lost his temper, dialed again, got the right number, began to yell again. Then his gum-chewing mouth began to slow down, his voice lowered several octaves to a contented rumble, then finally, "That's why I invest in Broadway hits. I want them when I want them. You tell him I'm sorry to take his seats away, tell him I'll remember it. But that's the way it's got to be. O.K."

He hung the phone up and his gum-chewing slowly tapered off to an occasional flexing of the jaw muscle, as an automobile engine slows to its purr after being raced. He turned and looked at Lucille, who was still standing, and rasped, "What the hell are you doing? Let's get on with this job, baby, I ain't got all day. Ridge and I are talking business. Come on!" He held out his huge, pink hand. Lucille sat down like an obedient marionette, bent over bowl and towel and Warren could not see her face at all.

"O.K., Ridge, sorry," rumbled Raven. "I got this rule. I take all important calls myself—right through to me on a direct line, no stalling.

Those were four seats for Senator Ireton. He's coming up from Washington tonight. He called me, wanted four. I like to keep those senators friendly. You know Ireton, of course, nice guy. Anyway, important. Let's see. Webster called up about your deal. Smart cookie, Webster, smart cookie. You know, a lot of those guys down there in the Street haven't got the brains to melt ice, they just sit there where their old men been sitting and they sign the papers where the lawyers tell them to sign the papers, and the business has been coming in to them for so long it doesn't know where else to go. But Webster is smart. That's one of the things you got to learn—that some of those boys down there have got real moxie. Webster says you got moxie, too. Let's see, now, you want some fast cash, the bank's got you by the short hairs. O.K., now I'm listening, ouch! watch that hangnail, Lucille, let's go!"

Not knowing whether Raven was talking to him or to the manicurist, Warren launched into the exposition. Picking and sharpening his phrases, he beckoned Raven up to the ridge from which *Trumpet* and *Gentlewoman* bestrode the homes of America, let him see the power, the growing circulation, flattered Raven by implying that the slow follow-through of the advertising was something that Raven with his business insight might be able to stimulate and speed. Under the soothing tone of Warren's voice, the caressing of his fingers by the manicurist, the sweet sway of the piped-in music, Raven's near-brutal face began to soften. Warren felt he was making headway, when the telephone rang again and instantly Raven had it in his paw. Then, after a bit:

"What's he doing in Atlanta if he's any good? . . . They can all hit down there, what else can he do? What does Casey say? . . . Hell, yes, of course we got to have an outfielder if Boone's leg won't mend. Why did he have to double-fracture the goddamn leg, when he hit three-forty last year . . . O.K., O.K. . . . But can this new kid hit big-league pitching? . . . That last cornball wonder they sent up to us wasn't worth the railway fare to send him back. . . . Naw, I'm not mad—you did it already, so you did it, but he better be good. . . . I know we need a utility outfielder, I just can't keep my mind on baseball when the winter starts coming on. . . . Yeah, yeah, I know it's an all-year-round job, that's why we got you. . . . Up your throat, skipper, I'm busy now."

Raven swung back in his chair, apologized for the interruption, said, explanatorily, "I got to clear these important things myself. Me and a couple of other guys own this baseball club. Can't give it much attention, but it's sort of a hobby, like those paintings. Now, that's what interests me in this deal of yours. I could get a kick out of fooling with the magazines if I didn't lose any money on it. Let's have the whole story again now, this time with figures, dollars and cents."

Warren now launched on his financing. He was into his exposition for about five minutes, when Raven's phone rang again. This time it was an action at Las Vegas. It was followed a few minutes later by a discussion of a play that was seeking backers on Broadway. It was followed by a tip on the market. With equal gusto and profanity Raven poured himself into every conversation. During one conversation Lucille rose, packed her utensils in a little case, approached the beckoning Raven who, without stopping his telephone conversation, reached in his pocket for a five-dollar bill, gave it to her, slapped her hard little rump, smiled at her and waved her out. With growing exasperation, Warren tried to present his picture in the short bursts of time between telephone calls, with growing fascination watched the calls come from downtown, Los Angeles, the Midwest, marveling at Raven's coarse domination of each conversation.

Only once did Raven lower his voice. It was an inter-office call which he took from the red telephone on the red cradle.

"We have to check it out, you know that, Al," he said slowly, with the voice almost of another man, a new character. "You know I can't make a horseback decision on that one. The tax angle hasn't been checked out, the field survey hasn't been done; can we get local mortgage money to come in, that's important, too. We can't put our money into a piece of real estate in Fresno, where we don't know anybody, and City Hall out there can break our back because we're New York money coming in from the outside"—Raven's voice suddenly boomed in decision—"Look, there's got to be local participation if we do the Fresno thing; it's weeks away from being ready for me to look at, let alone take it to the insurance companies for financing. . . . *You* handle it! . . . I don't want to hear about it until it's ready for the yes-or-no . . . you know that, Al."

Without looking at Warren, Raven then punched a button on his desk, lifted the phone, and said to someone in his outer office, "Hey! From now on block the outside calls. There's a guy here giving me his pitch and these telephone calls are making him nervous. Give us fifteen minutes . . . yeah."

Raven swung back to Warren, extricated the tired wad of chewing gum from his mouth, dropped it in his wastebasket, and said, "I'm sorry, Ridge. Let's talk business now. You've got the picture on me from those telephone calls. Nothing secret about them, but let me put it this way. All this business over the telephone is horse manure. The only business I'm in, solidly, is real estate. I buy and sell buildings, land, apartments, developments. I borrow, build and loan on real estate; I sub-divide, lease back, operate any goddamn thing under the real-estate laws of the United States from California to New York. I know my way around. Anything else—plays, baseball clubs, oil leases—that's horse manure. I do it for fun. I don't want to make money, but I don't intend to lose money.

"So now you've got the picture on me and I've got the picture on you. You're way out over your depth, up the creek without a paddle. In the kind of water I don't know anything about. You need three million in new money as fast as you can get your hooks into it. I've got three million. I always have a little hot-money around this office ready for a good action, not all my own money, but I have a crowd who goes in with me. Maybe we fit, you and me. Maybe. We got to figure out how. The only way into your deal I can see—and, believe me, my boys downstairs will check this out with a fine-tooth comb before they let me in—is on your real estate. On your plant. You print on special printing presses designed for your own magazines, right?"

"The best letter-press and color printing plant in the country, Mr. Raven," said Warren, a tiny excitement stirring in him as he could hear the sound of Raven's money rustling in the distance. "It cost eleven million dollars to put up over the years and no one in this country can duplicate it without putting up at least eighteen million dollars at today's prices."

"Got the picture," grunted Raven, "also it's in Massachusetts. I wish it were in Jersey or Delaware or one of these Southern states where the laws are made of funny putty. Massachusetts is a great place to manufacture things in, they tell. But it's no place for a fast-action operator like me. Well, hell, that's where your plant is. Is it tied up?"

"No. It's clear. No liens. No mortgage. The corporation has clear title to the plant."

"O.K.," said Raven, "we'll check it out. How fast do you need it?"

"I need a fast answer from you to bring to the Board in two weeks. Right now I need a measuring stick on your thinking to see whether we go on talking. You're talking mortgage, I suppose; I need to talk my Board into that—"

"Any way you want it, if we like the deal," interrupted Raven. "We can buy it and lease it back to you or we can slap a mortgage on it. But what I want to toss in right now is that we got to have a little understanding between us."

What was the hook?

"Let's spell out what you mean by a little understanding," said Warren slowly.

"Sure," said Raven amiably, "like for example, I'm not putting three or four million into anything unless I have a say about it. Now, I'm not telling you how to run your business, get me, I just want to be able to watch what's going on from the inside, see—well—"

Raven unfolded a fresh wad of chewing gum and began to chew happily.

"I've got a boy, my son Henry. Two years out of Yale and a nice kid and not one damned bit interested in real estate. Do you know what he majored in at Yale? Romance languages! How do you like that? I have a feeling that your shop is just the place for him."

Relieved, Warren replied affably, "We're constantly hiring in Editorial. I'd be delighted to take him in at Editorial, either in New York on the floor, or in the Washington office legging it, or in one of the field offices—"

"No"—Raven broke in at mid-sentence—"I don't mean anything like that. The place to get his training is at the top. Henry's twenty-three now. He can't spend all his life working his way up—I did that for him. He already put in four years at Yale learning about writing. I think the place for Henry is on the Board, and he ought to be made a vice president or something so he can watch it every day."

"What?" yelped Warren.

"Yeah, on the Board," said Raven confidently, grinning. "Why not? Young blood on the Board. The more I think of it the better I like it. He represents three or four million dollars of new money if he sits on that Board, if my people let me pump it in on this real-estate deal."

Desperately, Warren tread water.

"Now, Jack, let's slow up a bit on this. I can see your point of view, but I can't make any kind of commitment without Board agreement, and I can't quite see one of them resigning to make way for a twenty-three-year-old youngster. There's something almost grotesque about it."

"Grotesque to you," said Raven, unstirred, "not grotesque to me. No more grotesque than having Morrissey on that Board. I'll bet my Henry read more books at Yale than Morrissey read in his whole life."

"You know Morrissey?"

"Sure. We've cut a lot of deals together. Morrissey wants to fold the magazines, everyone knows it."

"Those magazines are not going to be folded, Jack. I'm drilling the last thousand feet before the oil starts coming in."

"You're not offering me an oil field, Ridge. You're offering me a real-estate deal. I got to tie my money up in you for five years when I could be turning it over. So I got to have a little fun for extra. Fun for me is having Henry on that Board, learning how to run a magazine."

"No dice. I'll take you, not Henry."

Warren rose, hoping against hope that Raven would ask him to sit down again.

"Well," said Raven, beginning his gum-chewing again, "no dice is no dice and usually when a fellow says no dice to a proposition I make, that's it. I don't go round looking for business. But I've never had any fun in publishing before. I tell you what—think about it. I'll hold it open for ten days, until your Board meets. But Henry's part of the package."

"No dice," said Warren, but he could tell his own voice was less firm when Raven smiled.

"Yeah, O.K., Ridge, I know you've got to say that. So say it. But think it over, my Henry's a nice boy and he could learn a lot from you."

Warren did not want to slam any doors. Still on his feet, he paused to think: it might be worth seeing the boy anyway.

"Send him around to see me anyway, Jack, we can always use young talent on the magazines and I'd be glad to help him along."

The phone rang and Raven turned and snarled at the phone.

"Ah, shut up!"

The phone continued to ring and Raven lifted it from the cradle a moment and held it at arm's length, smiling at Warren. A distant voice crackled metallically at the mouth of the telephone, then Raven replaced it in its cradle with a flick, breaking the connection.

"Did you ever use that trick?" he asked, smiling. "Best way of getting rid of a phone call without hurting someone's feelings. It always works," he added jovially.

Raven reached in his desk and flicked a switch. Suddenly the Muzak in the room was louder, very loud, playing a waltz. "I like waltzes," said Raven, "do you?"

Raven rose from behind his desk and as he rose, Warren noticed that Raven was a full two inches taller than he, which must make Raven almost six feet four. The burly man put his arm around Warren, and said, "Keep your pecker up, kid, and call me if you want to talk about that deal I offered you."

They were walking to the door together and Warren knew he was being dismissed by a master.

"Well," said Warren, not wanting to snap the string of hope, "call me if ever you want to see our shop and find out how magazines are put together. Bring Henry along with you. He may enjoy it."

"Nope," said Raven, "let's leave it my way. You call me if you're interested in my proposition. Then Henry and I will come over and case the joint."

The music in Raven's office swayed now with the "Blue Danube" waltz. With Raven's big arm around his shoulders, Warren felt he might almost begin to sway to the rhythm himself. He understood why all the stories about Raven were flat; you could not pin this person to paper in a story and expect anyone to believe it.

That was Jack Raven. Out of the turbulence of the blurred fortnight, Raven rose tall, towering and strong. Raven and Bronstein, as preposterous a pair of saviors as Warren could imagine—yet all he could rouse in interest from the calculating city in which his friends of the inner club had withdrawn from him. Bronstein for the quick signature and quick commercial money. Raven for the long-range investment money, by a mortage on the plant, if the Board would go along.

Or else there was Paget, Paget the unknown and the unseen—

14. Paget and Staff

The name Paget had slipped in so quietly, at such a moment of disturbance, that Warren could barely identify the day he first heard it—only that stream of concern which had borne it to his hearing.

For time now was no longer separated normally into days and nights, week, weekend, and week, but into layers that flowed in distinct, separated streams, all parallel, all horizontally proceeding with their burden of worry at the same time.

It was, for example, a time of alcohol. Warren could not decide whether this was the normally alcoholized climax of the executive year in New York, or his own compulsive need of stimulus. As the holidays approach in New York, as old friends realize they have not seen each other for months and must celebrate briefly and sharply the friendship they cannot nourish with time, as new summer friends try to make firm the friendships before the fraying of winter, drinking mounts in New York toward its Christmas climax. Lunches, cocktail parties, dinners, crowd and duplicate one another until the executive level of the city is almost awash in alcohol.

It was only when, late one afternoon, going to the liquor cabinet in his office and finding it empty, he realized the last full quart of bourbon had disappeared in the past two days, down his own gullet—only then did Warren know he was ahead of the city, outpacing it in the annual bacchanalia. Yet he recognized that now he needed alcohol.

It was, also, a time of bills. As the month wore on to its end, and the fat of mid-month cash in the account began to melt under late-month obligations, as Mr. Silverman bit each week for his 250,000 dollars' worth of paper and the reserve stock at the Anderbury plant melted, Warren delayed and postponed, twisted and turned. Some of the creditors he could, by enormous exertion, charm into waiting as he did with Campbell of Intertone Ink by a prodigious lunch. And as Warren soothed and pleaded with the large creditors, so Austin and Austin's staff wheedled and squeezed with the little creditors.

There was one day when Austin had, with panic, reported that they were down again to 32,000 dollars in the cash account and Warren had taken the sheets from him to scan them. How about this? Warren asked, pointing to a 78,000-dollar cash item.

"But Mr. Warren," protested Austin, "that's not our money. Those are the deductions from the payroll for Social Security taxes; we have to pay those deductions in to the government at the end of each quarter. Those aren't ours, that's trust money; it's the government's or it belongs to the staff, but it isn't ours."

"It's still ours," growled Warren, "so long as it's under our signature, it's ours."

"But Mr. Warren," protested Austin once more, "we can go to jail, both of us, you and I, for touching that money; it has to be there, we aren't allowed to use it once it's deducted."

"We're using it," snapped Warren. "It doesn't belong to the government until January first, and we'll have cash to live on by then, or we'll be liquidating and have cash to pay it. Hopkins is selling the old presses up in Anderbury next week for one-hundred-fifty thousand dollars. We'll put it back in ten days."

"But," began Austin again.

"Will," said Warren, "use it! Send me a memo to protect yourself, protesting its use, and then use it anyway and I'll sign."

It was, completely, inexplicably, a time of Mary-in-mind. Working, telephoning, driving around the city, talking to people, scouting at cocktail parties and at dinners, Warren was little alone. But when he was alone, then, puzzlingly, through the greater worries, she returned to his thinking. Where was she, for example, on Thanksgiving, as he munched a sandwich in his office—and then he recalled that she was in Ohio, with a family about her. Late at night was a time of Mary, too, when he could not sleep and tossed, thinking of her, and cursed the fact that she had returned—for the week they had spent together had opened old softness and pleasure. He wanted her to be there, just be there in the room with him. Worst, worst was one night when, alone in bed, he could not sweep hallucination from mind, and the image of Mary came to him, Mary in bed with another man named Claude, and Mary turning her warm body to another man, and the agony stabbed in him.

It was a time of dissimulation, of concealing, of acting, of denying. Of encouraging Russell one pale and shaking day as Russell reported on the activity of competitors—of rival salesmen already negotiating with advertising agencies to use up the allotment of space to *Trumpet* and *Gentlewoman* as soon as they should fold, if they should fold. "Cannibals," stormed Russell, "this is worse than a cannibal industry; at least the cannibals wait until the body is dead before they start to carve it. What the hell are we going to do, Ridge?" And Warren, forced to laugh at it all, and invent, on the spur of the moment, counter-rumors to pour into the acid vat of rumors that was dissolving their effort. It was a time of dodging inquiries from friends, from investment houses in the Street, who were now concerned with the erratic fluctuation of General American Publishing stock, of the first timid inquiries from the newspapers as to whether any major changes were expected soon in General American Publishing's program for next year.

And it was a time, finally, of dissolution—of dissolution in an unraveling of little things. The machinery of the organization still responded, yet not quite as it did before. People hushed as he entered the elevator, and stared at him as if he were an actor on stage. He sensed that though he could not now reach Morrissey, Morrissey was already reaching into the organization for information, and receiving it, and knowing his every move, his every call. It was as if he were on the bridge of a ship which responded, indeed, to his direction when he commanded, but responded sluggishly as if the ship and its crew were developing a will and instinct of their own.

Warren could not be too sure of exactly what was happening. Caution and judgment restrained him from exploring too vigorously what was happening at staff level. From his first meeting with them, he knew he must keep them at arm's length. But it was they who had brought Robert Paget's name into the picture.

They had filed into his office that first Monday afternoon after Webster had denied help, and arranged themselves awkwardly in the chairs, not only out of place, but out of character, too. Eliot, handsomely dressed in his normal gray, was the only one at ease. Dorrance, fat, breaking out a cigarette immediately on sitting down, was the most uncomfortable. Leonie Cahill, editor of *Gentlewoman*, her suit smooth and wrinkleless even at the end of the day, crossed and uncrossed her legs, nervously adjusting her skirt and position. Mitchell, erect on a straight-back chair, yielded nothing in expression. It was Foley who struck the note—surly and suspicious, Foley lounged in his chair as if expecting a blow to be struck, and warily watched to strike a counter-blow.

As he listened to them, Warren's exasperation grew. First, at Eliot, who had let a private conversation ten days earlier be blown up to this full-dress staff committee. Eliot had let him down and Warren was angry —let him down by talking about him to Mary, let him down by talking about their conversation to all these other people—let him down in what other ways, too? If he could not trust Dave Eliot, whom could he trust?

Now they were in his office, Warren knew he had to handle it so as to send them out with their lips sealed, their uneasiness stilled, with nothing new to add to the puckering of gossip about town. The very fact that he had received a committee of the staff could not be concealed for long from the rest of the organization; now he must throttle the comment it would rouse as best he could.

He was annoyed, above all, both by the preposterous idea they had and the impertinence of the demands they linked to it. Some mad fancy made them believe they could raise political money from the Democrats to save the magazines but beyond that they wanted, actually, to look at the books.

If they were supposed to raise money, they said, they had to be able to describe what was in the package they were selling.

Trying to be firm and courteous, Warren said to Eliot, "I just can't let any curiosity-seekers go through the books of the firm, David, Democrat or otherwise. Give me the name of a man, any man or group, with sound investment credentials and I'll receive him."

"You mean," said Foley, "that we're allowed to find a couple of rich Democrats with a few million bucks, bring them to your office, and then you want us to close the door and walk away like good little boys?"

Warren glared at Foley. The books, obligations, prospects, and salary structure of thousands of corporations were examined by hundreds of strangers down in Wall Street every day, who knew more about the inner life of those corporations than the people who worked for them. Investment analysts were like doctors who had the anonymous professional right to gaze on strange people naked. Downtown, a corporation was only a blueprint of a hundred transparent interlocking parts. But from inside a corporation had to be held tightly, its secrets kept secret chiefly from the people inside, because authority to act firmly must not have its wisdom subject to judgment below. Warren was being questioned now, from below. This had never happened in any organization he had directed. It must not happen. If it did, you fired the questioners. Yet he could not fire Foley now, at this moment. Thus he ignored Foley, and returned to Eliot.

"Bring me the name of a man or men interested in putting up three or four million and I'll answer your question right away—"

"Supposing I put in a name you don't know. Would you take my word that he's serious?"

"What name?"

"Robert Paget—a man I met yesterday."

That was the first time Warren heard the name Paget, and in the context of the child's conversation he was having with them, it did not seem important. It was another name to be added to all the lists of names which he had assembled on his pad for the hunt. Conscious of wanting this group out of the office as quickly as possible and of the need of keeping them quiet by a display of control, Warren said, "All right, fine. Let's you and I talk about this tomorrow morning, Dave, and if he sounds right to me, I'll see him myself."

"Wait," said Foley, as if he were running a story conference on his own floor, as if forgetful that he was a visitor in Warren's office, "that's not the way we said it. This whole thing started with Eliot telling us you wanted us to take a paycut in a fancy way. If you want to slap a paycut, you can do it without talking to us at all. You tell me, I'm Managing Editor, and I'll run a grass-cutter over the payroll at any per cent you want. I'm not guaranteeing what will happen next, but I'll do it. But if you want us to help save these magazines, if you want us to bring in some new investment money that David may be able to mobilize—that's something else. Then we want to sit at the table and square a couple of things away with you."

"Like what?" said Warren coldly.

"Like our right to look at the books, like our right to discuss policy with you," said Eliot, in a carefully soft voice. "We talked this out Saturday night and this staff will go down the line with you on anything you want, on cooperation in any reorganization as total as you want to define it, but Point Number One on our agenda that night was that we get some sort of reciprocal cooperation from you—"

"There's another thing on this agenda," suddenly said Mitchell, who had, up to now, been silent since he entered the room. "Before we get bollixed up in high-level discussion, there's one almighty important kitchen item on that agenda that we have to talk about—"

"That's it, Ben," said Dorrance, coming alive as if someone had banged a gavel. "That's it, Ben, let's get it on the floor now."

"And the thing I want to put on this agenda from the very start is severance pay—" continued Mitchell, clipping his words precisely and sharply, with a harsh New England enunciation.

"Wait a second, everyone, wait a second," called Eliot. "We're getting the cart before the horse."

"Cart before the horse nothing," said Mitchell, "that's what the meeting said: if we go along with Warren, will he go along with us?"

"Now, Ben, I just want a clear answer to my question first, we have to do things in orderly fashion."

"And I want an answer to mine before we get into details; we've been sitting here for almost half an hour of doubletalk and—"

"What do you mean, doubletalk?" demanded Warren, angrily.

"Doubletalk, Warren, doubletalk," said Mitchell stubbornly. "I've been interviewing people for this magazine since I interviewed Pershing in nineteen twenty-four, and I know when I'm getting doubletalk. We're not getting anywhere. These magazines are in trouble and you haven't told us a blasted thing we don't know yet. You want us to help and we've told you we'd do any blessed thing to save these magazines. But we haven't got a word out of you. Now I want some straight answers to a straight question—"

"Ben," interrupted Eliot, "let's straighten out one thing at a time, I'm chairman of this committee—"

"Don't try to stop him, Dave"—that was Foley, still in his slouch, still surly—"let Ben talk, we've got to square things away."

"And the very first thing," continued Mitchell, his teeth locked in the jugular of his single purpose, "is severance pay. If these magazines are saved, all well and good, you can fire me as soon as you want to, any day. But if you want us to help, we want your commitment that if they *do* fold, there'll be severance pay arrangements for all the people who work here. So-and-so much pay for every year they've worked."

"These magazines aren't going to fold," retorted Warren. "There's absolutely no emergency. We have a financing problem that will bind us through spring and next summer, but there's no emergency."

He knew he could not possibly discuss severance pay with a group of employees, that formal discussion of severance pay in the event of collapse would be broadcast over all the floors in two hours, over all the city in two days, that even entertaining the idea made panic, and thus disaster, almost inevitable.

"Great," said Mitchell coldly, "now we have your word for it. I used to cover the White House when Mr. Hoover was President; he used to assure us that the depression either wasn't there, or was just about to end. His personal assurance, too. He believed it, too. Now we have your personal assurance we aren't going to fold. But I want you to back it up with another personal guarantee. That if this crashes, the staff gets parachutes. And parachutes means severance pay!"

"David," said Warren, ignoring both Foley and Mitchell, "this is your committee. You told me this entire matter would be kept in confidence. You gave me your word. You broke your word. Now, are you running this or not? There are half-a-dozen questions here for me to answer; which does your committee want me to answer first—?"

"This committee has two heads," said Mitchell. "Eliot is interested in publishing. I'm too old for that. I'm a Connecticut Yankee hell-raiser, and I'm asking questions for a lot of people who've given their lives to this firm and have got to be taken care of."

Warren looked at them. They were transformed. They were no longer his employees, to appoint, promote, dismiss and deploy. They were something else. They were a new organism come to life, a new factor in a situation that already could not reasonably contain the old factors. They were one step from threatening him. The ballooning of gossip from this ill-timed meeting might destroy the last faint chance the desperate days held. He had to throttle the talk, get Eliot alone, force Eliot to silence the rest. Surreptitiously, Warren pressed the buzzer on his desk, hoping they would not notice in the excitement, hoping Laura would be quick enough to realize he wanted a ring back. The bell on his telephone rang within an instant, and Mitchell paused as the phone interrupted.

"Yes," said Warren into the phone, holding up his hand for quiet to the group, then into the phone, "Just a second," then to the group again— "Just let me get this call, I think it's important."

Over the telephone, Warren could hear Laura's voice saying, "Is it time for me to come in and break it up?" In response, Warren said, "He did? On the phone now? Look, I can't talk to him now . . . he said right away? . . . Well, I need five minutes more here. . . . Tell him I'll get back to him in ten minutes, no more . . . yes."

He put the telephone down.

"I'm sorry," he continued, "that's a call that may mean a great deal. I have to handle it right now. Let me go over all these matters with Eliot tomorrow morning; we have a lot more ground to cover. I have Eliot's word that nothing of what we said goes out of this room, and I'm taking that to cover everybody else here, too."

He rose from his chair to invite them to go.

But only Dorrance followed his example, rising. The others sat and Foley leaned forward to speak, not surly or angry now, but serious and slow.

"All right," said Foley, "we're going. But you said you had five more minutes. Let me use one minute. I didn't know this meeting was going to get this rough. I'll put it on the line for me—I'll do any damn thing you want me to do to save these magazines. What the hell else have I ever done with my life but give it to these magazines? Let's skip the bit about looking at the books. Work that out with Eliot. But just one thing: do we have your word that you'll go along with us on severance pay if it comes to the clutch?"

"One minute for me, too," said Mitchell. "I just want to say I'm not talking for me. You wipe my name off any severance-pay list that's made up—I can live on what my investments bring in and what the cutting of Christmas trees brings off the place in Connecticut. But these people on this magazine are part of me, they've been my family for thirty years. If the magazines are going to fold, it's Thanksgiving in a couple of days, Christmas coming next month— Warren, if we know what's coming and don't try to do something about it, what kind of people are we?"

Still standing, Warren pondered the choices. He required their silence; they must not talk. Could he get it best by whip-lashing them now in this room, or by yielding to them? It was Dorrance who swayed him.

"Mr. Warren," said Dorrance. "I've got three kids and Christmas coming up. The dentist said that this is the year that Tish, our eleven-year-old, has to have braces on her teeth and that will be six hundred and fifty dollars. I can't go even four weeks without pay without going flat-pocket. I love this job; I love every day here, Mr. Warren; I don't think I ever realized it until this week; I've never said it to anyone else . . ."

Dorrance paused as if he had said too much but the attention of the group listening to him urged him on.

"If I don't see severance pay ahead, what can I do, Mr. Warren? I can't take a chance of being cold on the street with only two or three weeks' run left in me and having to take any copy-clerk's job they toss me, like a bone, when things blow up. I can't keep my mind on my work when I worry like this. If I'm not going to have severance pay, I've got to start scouting now. I've been here fifteen years. With two weeks of severance pay for each year, I'd have thirty weeks' turnaround time to find a new place like a man. I could sit this thing out and fight. I want to, Mr. Warren, but I'm a family man with Christmas four weeks away— What more can I say?"

But Warren had had enough. The quality in Dorrance's voice echoed the panic that Warren had fought all weekend, the fear he could suppress only because he must suppress it. The frightened, white-faced Dorrance was pleading, as he himself was pleading, for a chance from the anonymous towers.

"All right," said Warren, "the magazines aren't going to fold. But if the magazine is ever in trouble, you have my word for it, I'll see that the Board takes care of everybody."

"O.K.," said Foley, "we'll go with that. Sorry for shooting my big mouth off," and he rose, the others following. As they moved to the door, Warren stopped them.

"One minute," he called; then, as they listened, "You have my word, but I need yours in return. What we said in this room stays here. Talk can ruin all of us. Do I have your pledge of silence—all of you, individually?"

"Yep," said Mitchell, "that's our deal, one promise for another."

"And no more committee meetings in this office to kick up talk," said Warren. "I'll deal with you through Eliot. Dave, we'll get together tomorrow morning and talk about this character of yours—what's his name, now?"

"Paget," said Eliot, "I'll wait for your call."

That was the way Paget's name had entered—trailed in casually by the staff committee. But by the time Warren realized that Paget was, indeed, important, it was the second week of the time of torment, and Paget was gone. Perhaps because he was gone, absent from New York, Paget began to grow slowly almost to a fantasy in Warren's mind.

Who was Paget?

At first, when Warren asked the question of Eliot, Paget appeared in Eliot's answer a one-dimensional buccaneer. Paget had just left for Paris, reported Eliot, and would be back in a week. Then when Warren asked what he was doing there, Eliot explained that Paget was investigating the Sahara oil concessions, and Warren wanted to know more. Paget, Eliot explained, had been an Air Force colonel during the war, but had remained overseas in the war's aftermath, plunging himself into mines—mines in Morocco first, then mines in the Congo, mines in Peru, mines in Bolivia, mines in all the unstable corners of the world where the hunger for metals must be met. It was not so much conviction that made Paget a Democrat, said Eliot, as being unable to fit in any of the categories of wealth of his dimension. Paget's was new money, imagination's money, bold money shorn of the timidity of settled wealth; thus men of settled wealth distrusted Paget and Paget distrusted settled wealth in return. He was like the old man Harriman, reported Eliot, when the

Morgan crowd wouldn't let him into Tuxedo Park—old man Harriman bought thirty-six thousand acres of land just above Tuxedo Park to look down on it and sneer. Paget's support of the Democrats was part of his affront to older wealth.

It was through Paget's lawyers and accountants, as they began to plough through his books and figures, that Paget began to flesh out. In their conversation, Paget was no priest who served money in the temple as did a Cameron, or a Morrissey, or a Webster—but another Raven, writ large and bold across the world. Yet civilized, not possessed by money, but possessing it for pleasure and adventure. Gradually, through the questioning of Paget's people, it became clear that Paget had no interest in bonded securities or documented obligations of General American Publishing. If Paget wanted anything, he wanted the magazines alone and for himself. You know how he is, said one of the lawyers to Warren at a late session—he doesn't like working around a table with other people. He likes to control whatever he goes into; he hates meetings.

Paget took on body as a gambler in their conversation. Once, after another late session with figures, one of Paget's accountants had said reflectively, "I think he may like this," and a second had replied, "Could be. I wouldn't advise anyone in the world to look twice at this thing, but the longer the odds, the more he likes them"—and the two had paused to yarn about a night in a Winnipeg hotel when Paget had overruled them both on a Canadian gas deal, and had been proved right.

Warren warmed to Paget, the unseen. Paget was out of it, free, free to do as he wanted with his money, free to look at the world and choose the shape he wanted for it. Paget had been a colonel in the Air Force, like himself, but had moved faster, quicker, to break out of the traps into the upper world where men were responsible only to themselves. If only Paget were here in New York, Paget the fellow-gambler, and he could put his arm around Paget's shoulder and draw him to the window and show him what they could do together. But could they both be free and both control General American Publishing? How deeply was Paget involved with this staff committee which was no longer Warren's to control? Where was Paget? How could he get to him directly? How could he tell Paget to hurry?

Once, as the last week drew to a close, Warren abruptly took the telephone and dialed Paget's secretary. She told him, "He said he'd be gone five days when he left—two in Paris, two in the Sahara, one in flight. But that was eight days ago. We really never know when he's arriving until we get the call to send his car to the airport. He gets so excited, he can leave for a weekend and come back around the other side of the world."

Warren insisted that he needed a firm expression of Mr. Paget's intent by the earliest possible day of next week, the second week in December. The next day, Friday, the secretary said she had spoken to Mr. Paget in Paris, and, yes, he was terribly interested in the matter. Would Mr. Warren like to fly over to Paris and spend the weekend with Mr. Paget there? If not, Paget would be returning Monday or Tuesday of next week— and how would that do?

Grimly, Warren knew it would have to do. This last weekend before the Board meeting on Wednesday was already hypothecated to long sessions with Raven's experts and Bronstein's accountants. Would Mr. Paget, he replied to the secretary, telephone him directly from Paris or leave a Paris number where he could be reached? The secretary said she would do her best.

15. Tuesday Afternoon

1. BRONSTEIN'S APARTMENT

By Tuesday afternoon, as Warren sat in the overstuffed furniture of the overheated Bronstein apartment on Central Park West, and went through the figures once more, only the knowledge that tomorrow was Wednesday, and that tomorrow afternoon the Board would meet, sustained him. For tomorrow, one way or another, it would be over.

He did not know yet how it would be over, but he knew he could not go on any longer with these incantations of accounting. All weekend and through Monday and today he had been reeling from meeting to meeting, now with Raven and Raven's lawyers, now with Paget's people. Their interest was still unshaped and unspecified in figures, but solid enough to discuss with the Board. It was like juggling three balls in the air. Raven was ready to put up mortgage money on the plant, but only with his son in the picture. Raven, however, could be squeezed harder, Warren knew, if Bronstein came through with the quick signature which must, this week, be at the bank. And if Bronstein came through with the quick signature, then there would be a few more weeks for Warren to decide whether Paget could be brought in seriously to replace Raven, and, if so, whether he preferred partnership with Paget to association with Raven and Raven's son.

The choice of alternatives depended on Bronstein, yet as Warren talked, he could not tell whether the old man, after all his investigations, was any closer to a decision than he had been two weeks before. Only one thing satisfied Warren about the conversation—that two of the Bronstein sons now sat here with him in the room, listening as he talked. He was glad because they were men of his own age, and all through the past two weeks he had been conscious, as he pressed Bronstein, that he was pressing the affection of a person who liked him into the needs of business. He had been taking advantage of kindness in this city without kindness. Yet there was no other way—if the old man's signature could persuade money from the bank, could buy time for the magazines, then the old man's signature must be won from him; there could be no holding back out of kindness. Thus, Warren was glad that Jack and Leo

Bronstein, the oldest and the youngest of the Bronstein sons, were there listening to him, on guard for their father and alert. If he could talk them into it, then it would be fair going.

Yet as Warren mechanically recited the data he knew so well, he kept watching the two younger men. The old man, their father, nursed his tea, with a rind of lemon bobbing on the top, and said nothing. The younger men nursed Scotch-and-sodas, watching him through sharp black eyes out of expressionless countenances, making no response except for monosyllabic grunts or lean, spare questions. Occasionally, one or the other would get up to mix himself a weak Scotch-and-soda, and each time, politely, would offer Warren a refill, too. Warren, each time, held out his glass woodenly and murmured a thank-you. He could not make out from the faces of Jack and Leo Bronstein whether they were interested, or bored, or liked him, or mistrusted him.

Now and then, old Mr. Bronstein would rouse himself with a wandering remark, or oblique question, and, when he lost himself rambling in the middle of a phrase, would be cut off by one of his sons, saying, "O.K., Pa, O.K.—we know what you think. We're trying to get his picture. Let's have it over again, Warren, from where you left off."

Once, as Warren felt he was talking too long about magazine circulation and renewals, and simultaneously was assailed by the warmth of the overheated room and the softness of its too-comfortable furniture, he said, hoping someone else would speak for a moment and take the pressure off him, "I'm going into this in quite some detail because I don't want to leave out anything you might think relevant. But I want you to stop me if you have any questions."

"Keep going," said Jack, the older one, with no inflection in his voice, "I'm listening."

The voice of the young one, Leo, asking him cordially, "Want another drink?" made the voice of the older one seem cold by contrast.

Warren reflected on the coldness of Jack and what it meant as he waited for the drink to be brought to him, but nobody had spoken in the pause and so he resumed with the sense that Jack Bronstein was measuring him as much as listening to him, and Warren did not like the feeling.

After another long unbroken passage of explanation, Warren decided to invite old Mr. Bronstein back into the conversation to reestablish some sense of connection, some transfer of kindliness and interest from the father to the sons.

"Is this tiring you, Mr. Bronstein, shall I shorten it?" he asked, stopping himself, noticing even as he asked the question that Mr. Bronstein's head had been nodding.

"No," said Mr. Bronstein, bringing himself alert slowly. "No. I think I've got to go to the bathroom, though. Why don't I do that right now, then we can get down to business and decide something?"

"Yeah, Pa, how about going in and lying down?" said Jack, the older one. "We'll go on talking with Mr. Warren and tell you how things come out as soon as we get it settled."

"Sure, Pa," added Leo, "these figures are complicated and we want to dig around in them a bit. Give us ten more minutes, fifteen minutes, Pa, and we'll let you know how it shapes up to us."

"You know, Warren," said the old man, with a flash of his old self, dominant among strangers at the Skyline Club, "my boys push me around a lot. But they do it for my sake. Don't be afraid of them, Mr. Warren. I tell you what—supposing I go in the other room and leave you young fellows alone for a few minutes. Then I want to show you my books and my wine glasses; you'll never see such a collection of wine glasses like this anywhere in America, Mr. Warren. You young fellows talk and I'll be back soon. My boys know the way I feel about you. We'll figure out something together."

He rose to go, and Warren was alone with the two younger Bronsteins. Neither of the two stirred as their father left the room, nor did they ask Warren to sit down again after he had risen at their father's departure.

Instead, they turned one to the other and began a short staccato conversation as if Warren, too, were absent from the room.

"I don't see it, do you, Leo?" asked Jack.

"Never did," said Leo.

"It's crazy," said Jack.

"You got to hand it to Pa, though, he doesn't stop trying."

"You want to do the talking? Or should I?"

"You start."

"Mr. Warren," said the older son, Jack, as if Warren had been waiting outside a door and had just been admitted to hear a verdict, "Mr. Warren, this isn't for us."

Warren held several sheets of paper in his hand and he continued shuffling them. You had to ride with the punch. Maybe it had been wrong to stay so long on the figures—they knew the figures. Perhaps he should have concentrated on *Trumpet*, just *Trumpet* and the long echo that rolled from it through the years of these men's lives, and how it had changed their lives, and how it might yet change other lives.

"It's always pretty difficult to explain the figures of one man's business to men of another business," he said after a moment's silence, struggling to find an opening. "I'm sure I've sprayed too many figures on this to absorb in an hour or two. But let me put it this way, there's a quality of imagination involved in the publishing business that's different from other business; it makes you closer to what's happening in the country than any other business, and if you guess it right, if you hear it right, it explodes into profit. Your father caught it so quickly that . . ." Warren shrugged his shoulders, tried to continue. ". . . If you can't imagine what happens when all the country tunes in on what you have to say . . ." He shrugged his shoulders again, hoping he could tempt them to see.

"It's not imagination this needs," said the younger son, Leo. "It's a rescue squad, it's money."

"I'm not asking for money," said Warren, "I'm suggesting an almost riskless chance of using your credit, not your money, and, in return, get—"

"No point in discussing it," said Jack. "It's not for us. This business of co-signing a note is for peddlers and small storekeepers. What made you think we'd be interested?"

Warren's reply came back a beat too quickly.

"Your father invited me here to talk to you. You came. Reason enough."

"We always come when Pa has one of his business schemes," said Jack coldly. "He can pick up more oddballs, charity fund-raisers, con-men than a blotter picks up water. We came to protect him, that's all."

"From what?" said Warren, as irritation began to ignite the drinks he had had.

"From deals like this. Not that he could do anything about it anyway, the money's all tied up in trust and you couldn't take it from him even if he wanted to give it. But he doesn't know what he wants, and—hell, there's nothing to talk about here."

"I don't like what you're saying, Mr. Bronstein," said Warren.

Jack's face froze, the eyes hardened and he replied, "How do you want me to say it? Should I say thank you to someone trying to take my father for a million bucks?"

"Lay off, Jack," Leo Bronstein quickly said to his brother, "this is no time to get tough. Warren here had a proposition. We don't like it. That's all there is to it. No harm done," he added, turning to Warren in a voice more social than businesslike. "Jack loses his temper easily, Warren, he doesn't mean what he says. All he means is we're uninterested. Pa gets lots of ideas like this and we try to humor him. I'm sorry we wasted your time."

Warren glared at Jack across the room. Things were worse now than he had thought possible. There had been a dozen different ways to say no besides this one; and the implication rankled in him, the humiliation mixing with the shame, with the sense of guilt he had brought with him in pursuing a friendship too far. But he was not cheating anybody, he had not lied to any of them; if they did not want to help, they did not have to—

"What the hell, Leo"—Warren heard Jack, unmollified, even nastier, saying to his brother—"this is an open and shut con deal. I never heard anything like it. The only reason we advertise in those magazines is because of Pa and some crazy pal he used to have years ago, that Pepper. We ought to be in television for the wines, I've said it a dozen times, and in the other big magazines for the liquors. What I'm mad about is not this deal, but, goddamnit, his sucking up to Pa, taking advantage of Pa, and getting Pa excited—"

"He wasn't trying to con Pa," said Leo, "for Christ's sake, relax, Jack. He was just making a pitch; there's no law against it. Anybody'd make a pitch if they were in the jam this guy is in."

"I'm not 'this guy,' " said Warren, breaking in on them, realizing he was sounding impossibly stuffy, groping for dignity. "My name is Warren. The name of the magazine is *Trumpet*, the name of the firm is—"

"O.K., buddy," suddenly yelled Jack, "I know your name, I know your firm, what's more, I know the pitch you're pushing—"

And Leo was shouting above Jack's voice.

"Come off it, Jack, it's only business. What are you blowing your top for? He's a guy in a jam, Jack. Listen, he runs a couple of sick magazines—"

But Jack, not to be quieted, was yelling back.

"I know damn well who he is. So do you. Everyone knows who he is. He's been peddling those magazines of his up and down the Street for a month and nobody will touch him with a ten-foot pole. Ask Dun and Bradstreet. Ask the salesmen from *Spectacle*. Ask the ad agencies. Ask Stippler-Leventritt. Don't think I didn't check when I first heard Pa talk about it. He's taken those two magazines and run them into the ground and now he's running around trying to find suckers to pull his chestnuts out of the fire. What's more, the son-of-a-bitch is getting Pa all excited and keeping him up here in New York when he should be in Florida—"

"Don't you call me a son-of-a-bitch!" yelled Warren, his temper bursting at last. Warren rose, advancing on Jack, his hands clenched, remembering he had not slugged anybody since college, and deciding that he might just as well hit Jack square, just to have hit somebody, or something, because there was no other way out of the room now except to sneak out like a beaten dog.

And as Warren yelled, and Jack yelled, and Leo yelled, calling, "Pipe down, you two guys, or Pa'll be back in here in a minute," there was Mr. Bronstein standing in the door of their room, yelling louder than any of them, the veins of his neck ridging out in anger, his face red, shouting, "Jack! Leo! Warren! What is this? What's going on here?"

Abruptly, all three of the younger men stopped as old Mr. Bronstein stalked to the center of the room, stern, powerful, dominant.

"Sit down!" he commanded.

They all sat down.

"Now, Pa . . ." said Jack, and old Bronstein barked, "Shut up!"

"Pa, don't get excited, it's—" began Leo, and Bronstein turned and barked again, "You, too. Shut up!"

Old Mr. Bronstein looked at all three of them as if they were children, the yellowing whites of his old eyes fierce and contemptuous, as finally they fastened on Jack. His hoarse roar muted suddenly into an angry sing-song.

"What kind of people are you? What kind of children did I bring up? What kind of men are you, that you don't know when you see someone in trouble? He came here because I asked him, because he's a friend of mine, because I like him. To my house. Not yours. Not to the offices, but to my house! And what do you do? You behave like a pig, like a thug!"

The old man stalked back and forth, raging at his sons.

"What do you know, both of you? What did college teach you, what did the schools I sent you to teach you if you don't know what a business is, what it's like to be at the beginning of a business or when a business is dying? A business is something living, something you put together with what's in your belly and your heart. It isn't something you put together just with money and brains you hire. Brains like you I can hire anywhere. Business is when you want something to be alive because you had a dream about it. We were triple-A credit rating before you pissers were able to button your own pants! You never had to worry about stretching the receivables to meet the payables, about dealing with banks, about the chances a man has to take. When *you* take a chance nowadays, you do it with consultants where you've covered yourself ten times coming and going, you've got ten guys under you, so you can fire any one of them for the mistakes you make yourself. You don't know anything about business, either of you—"

He lifted his forearm across his chest and swept a backhand blow in the air, as if cuffing a surly child.

"So you're going to protect me? I'm a baby, am I, I got to be protected? I can read a balance sheet better than any of you, even now I can. He isn't going to hurt me, this poor fellow, but maybe we can help him out, stretch a little here, stretch a little there, what's it going to cost us?"

For the first time, Warren knew how a boy feels when protected from bullies by his teacher or his father. This thing was over. The only opening old Bronstein had made was an opening for his departure, and Warren's mind sought desperately under the protection of the old man's presence, for the role, the style, the attitude he must find, right away, to leave this room with a tiny shred of dignity. But Jack was talking.

"O.K. O.K., Pa, I know I lose my temper. But, Pa, you know the doctor says you're not supposed to get excited. You shouldn't be doing business. And every other week you drag in a new proposition like a kid picking up a dog or a cat in the street."

"Shut up!" thundered Mr. Bronstein. "Shut up! All he wants is our signature on a million credit at the bank. Why can't we do it? They got a plant out there in Massachusetts worth five times as much. Worst comes to worse, all we have to do is sue them, our lawyers clip us for enough money anyway, give them a little work to do."

"Pa, Pa—what the hell's the use of tying up a million dollars in a lawsuit. This guy can't even guarantee that he'll be in the magazine business six months from now," said Jack.

"Don't call him 'this guy,'" roared Bronstein. "This is my house. I asked him here. Respect! Respect a man should have when he doesn't take a business ready-made from his father but tries to make one himself, he puts his guts and life into the gamble! That's what makes this country, not people sitting with market surveys, turning the crank on a business somebody else already built! Respect, you—"

And then, in mid-sentence, as if a blow had slammed into his waist, Mr. Bronstein stopped, half-bent, his fingers curling like claws about his stomach, a groan rolled from deep in his chest, and his flushed face drained, as they watched, to a saffron-yellow. He tottered as he stood there, vitality leaving him, and his two sons were almost instantly by their father's side.

"Papa," said Leo, holding him up, an arm beneath his father's shoulders, "what's the matter, Papa? What happened?"

The old man let himself sag on his son's support and squeezed out words in frightened gasps.

"I don't know . . . my stomach . . . like a knife . . . ooh . . . my chest . . . hurts . . . Leo, get me to bed."

"Get him to bed, Leo," snapped Jack, taking command, "I'll call the doctor."

As the old man tottered off on Leo's shoulder, while Jack disappeared to a telephone, Warren was left alone.

The warm room had become an empty chamber full of fragments of dreams. Silently he stooped to the floor where his papers lay strewn, gathered them, slid them into his briefcase. He looked around, trying to remember where he had left his coat. He found it, pulled it on, held the briefcase in his hand, wondering whether it was best to sneak out in silence, not even saying farewell—or whether the worry and concern he felt for the old man was reason enough to stay and offer help.

As he stood wondering, he saw Leo emerge from the bedroom, and Warren was glad it was Leo, not Jack.

"Is he all right?" asked Warren. "Can I do anything to help?"

"No," said Leo. "I think he'll be all right—at least I hope so. He has these attacks whenever he gets excited. The doctor says we have to expect them. Sooner or later one of them will carry him off. That's why we were trying to get him off to Florida, that's why Jack was mad. Do you mind if I say good-by now? I want to get back into the room with him."

"No," said Warren, "I understand. Give him . . . give him my regards. . . . Tell him I appreciate what he tried to do. . . . I'm fond of your father, very fond."

There was nothing more to say. Scratch the Bronsteins, he thought. And if the old man died—scratch more than that. Scratch it on the memory that I have been a swine today.

"Good-by," he said to Leo again. "Don't wait to see me out. I'll find my way to the elevator."

As he turned, he saw Jack enter the farther corner of the room. Jack stared at him with eyes of hate. They looked at each other and neither spoke. Trying to square his shoulders, wishing he had not worn his Chesterfield, Warren could see himself through Jack Bronstein's eyes in the uniform of a con-man. A con-man peddling two magazines whose traditions and meaning stretched back long before either he or Jack was born, two magazines he had debased, degraded and made fake because he had tried for so long to defend them only with numbers. Long before he had come to this room. Nodding curtly at Jack, Warren walked to the anteroom and waited for the elevator to carry him down.

2. SUBPOENA TO ALLEGED BANKRUPT

He sent his chauffeur off for dinner from the door of the Bronstein apartment, then walked south along the park, then down Broadway, then turned east to his office. He wanted to walk.

The offices were empty on the executive floor as Warren knew they would be at six thirty of a Tuesday evening. But only as he sat down at his desk in quiet did the turbulence of the visit to Bronstein's begin to leave. The solid office supported him. It made unreal the almost unbelievable image he had of himself yelling across the Bronstein living room, the moment of helplessness and shame as he saw again Mr. Bronstein's pudgy figure doubling over, and knew he was excluded from offering help or kindness.

He shook his head, trying to concentrate on the thought that tomorrow was Wednesday, the Board meeting, and he was only a few hours away from the end of trying. Mechanically, his hands began the routine cleaning of his desk top.

First, the afternoon in-basket, and he riffled through the long stack of memos, not reading, letting his eye, rather than his judgment, separate those which he must reread from those he could dismiss immediately.

Then, Laura's pad of afternoon calls; the names were none of them urgent.

Then, another memo from Laura, and he paused.

"Paget's secretary called. Paget is in Paris tonight and trying to reach you. Staying at the George V Hotel there; his message is that he is enthusiastic about the whole matter. He asked you to call him back anytime before one o'clock in the morning Paris time at the hotel."

He almost wished he had not read the memo about Paget. It was one more try he had to make this evening when he had tried all day and all week and the month before that. He did not want to reach Paget tonight, did not want to tell Paget that it was now not long-range financing he needed, but immediate financing, cash in the next few days, cash before the fifteenth of the month, before the bank crippled him with its reduction of credit.

Listlessly, he reached for his telephone, gave the instructions to the night switchboard, heard his own operator repeating them to the overseas operator somewhere in a downtown telephone exchange, heard the overseas operator saying, "An hour's delay on all calls to Paris, please, we'll call you when we have your party."

He sat there, then, waiting, and the thought of tomorrow mixed with the thought of Paris and yesterday and all the yesterdays. He did not know what he was going to say to the Board tomorrow. He would have the Raven proposition to present; and perhaps he might have a Paget proposal to present; but he would also have to present them the true picture of urgency, the state of the cash account, the danger of some creditor's rash or precipitate action. He would give it the pro and con and, if he got some sleep tonight, one more real try to convince them to accept either Raven or Paget. There was the question. Raven or Paget. Or neither. Or fold the magazines.

What could he tell Paget now, when he spoke to him in Paris? What was it like, he reflected, in Paris now as the clock, five hours ahead of New York, raced on to midnight on the Seine? What could he say to Paget there, on the banks of the Seine, from here on the banks of the Hudson, to convey his urgency without weakness? It was clear here in New York tonight with the crystalline clearness of early winter and the cold seemed to purge the city of its constant fume of gasoline. Was it foggy in Paris? Did it smell of chestnuts roasting? Was there snow in Paris yet? Was Paget smoking a cigar in some private room at some great restaurant, languidly full of wine and meat, recharging the drive and energy that New York required? What would he say to Paget once he had Paget on the phone? Should he be friendly? Or urgent? Or casual? Or comradely? Should he be detached and unconcerned, or should he breathe emergency?

A knock now.

A knock.

He heard it at the door.

She did not have to knock at the door to come in. Laura knew that. But Laura had gone home. Annoyed, he wondered who it could be—

The knock came again—groping, uncertain, yet more insistent this time. Then louder. Rapping more strongly. Irritated, Warren strode to the door to throw it open. He wanted this hour of waiting alone, to think about Paget.

He pulled the door open.

Against the darkness of the outer office, the lights from Warren's inner chamber silhouetted two figures. One was an older man, dressed in the square-shouldered suit of all little New York businessmen. The other was younger but Warren could not see the face, for the shadow from the hat slanted across eyes and nose, leaving only the tip of the pale, pointed jaw visible in the half-light.

"Yes," said Warren curtly, "what do you want?"

"We're looking for a Mr. Warren," said the younger man in a sharp, yet uncertain tone.

"What do you want?" repeated Warren. He knew he must not identify himself. Crackpots. There were always crackpots wandering the corridors of great magazines with a message for humanity. Why this late? How had they gotten by the receptionist?

"Sorry for bothering you. But you had the only light on the floor. We have a document for this man Warren," said the young man again.

"What kind of document?" asked Warren. "You can leave it on my secretary's desk and I'll see it when—"

"Are you Warren?" asked the older man.

"Yes," said Warren, caught.

"Here," said the younger man and, reaching in his pocket, thrust two folded forms into Warren's hand.

"What is this?" asked Warren.

"A petition—" began the young man as Warren interrupted.

"I never sign any petitions; these offices are closed for the night. If you come back tomorrow morning, the reception desk will route you to whoever you need to see."

Both men began to talk at once.

"I tell you, all we want to do is talk with you before—"

"Look, Max," said the younger man, "let me do the talking," and then, to Warren, "I'm his lawyer. This is an involuntary petition in bankruptcy, a Chapter Ten Petition in Bankruptcy. The other document is the subpoena—"

"What are you talking about?" said Warren.

The older man replied, "Look, if you're Warren, you're the one we want to talk to. You're the boss here. We got to be paid. We aren't gonna be left the only ones holding the bag. I hear you're paying the big creditors. Anything happens to a big corporation, it's always the little fellow gets taken. I can't get to talk to anybody here. Neither can Arwin Typewriter Service, neither can Mid-Town Stationery; we been checking up on you. There's fourteen thousand bucks you owe us, eight thousand you owe the typewriter people, sixty-four hundred you owe the stationery people . . ."

But Warren was not listening.

In his hand, in the dim light from over his shoulder, the first folded paper read:

United States District Court for the Southern District of New York
Bankruptcy File No. XB 10,529
SUBPOENA TO ALLEGED BANKRUPT
In the Matter of General American Publishing Co., Inc.
Alleged Bankrupt

—And the smaller type, over-the-fold, began—

To the Above-named Alleged Bankrupt in said district: A petition in Bankruptcy having been filed on the 9th day of December before the . . .

The 9th day of December was today. As Warren read, thought, listened, all simultaneously, recognizing that this was a document filed and recorded in a court which he must answer, the figures alone floated clear. Twenty-eight thousand and four hundred dollars. Only twenty-eight thousand four hundred dollars! What were they doing bothering him with this detail when what he owed, what he needed, were millions? He had been racing now for weeks, racing and dodging, staggering in pursuit of millions, his eye on some distant dream, his lungs pounding, his brain striving—and as he raced, here was his foot, now, caught in an inch-high trip-wire thrown across his path at random. And he was down.

He snapped on the light in the outer office to read what the detail of the petition specified. As he did so, he looked at the two men. The younger, with his hat still on, lean, cadaverous, hollow-cheeked, could not be more than twenty-six or twenty-seven. The older man, perhaps fifty, was round-faced, clean-shaven, half belligerent, half frightened. They blinked in the light, like animals trapped in the dark, and Warren, pointing to two chairs in the outer office, said sternly, "Sit down. Tell me just what you think you're doing."

"It's from the Federal Court," said the younger, his voice almost a whine as if the lights disconcerted him, as if he were the one caught, not Warren. But the older man broke in, tougher, firmer.

"Don't try to be tough with us, Mr. Warren, or we get tough with you. I didn't come here to make trouble. I've been trying to get through your accounting department for weeks now. And I can't. I have to collect my bills. I have to pay a Christmas bonus to my cleaning women, the cleaning women who clean up these offices every night for you. It's in their union contract. I've got fourteen thousand of my cash tied up in you. I haven't got a nickel on my account from your firm for more than two months. You're pushing me around. There's all this talk from the people who work here about trouble coming. Maybe it doesn't matter to a big creditor to go down with you for a couple of hundred thousand bucks, but I can't afford it, I tell you, I can't afford to go down with you for fourteen thousand dollars. If I've got to meet my bills, then you've got to meet yours, no matter how big you are."

The older man stopped, out of breath, and the younger man, as if he had taken courage from the older, said, "We could have served a Summons and Complaint on you from the State Supreme Court, but we can't wait the twenty days before you answer that. My clients need their money right now and they don't want to go to court at all. I explained to them that if they wanted to talk to you, this was the quickest way to do it. That's all we want—to talk to you, and get paid. Then we go back to court and withdraw the petition. See? Just pay—I can talk to your lawyer and explain."

Warren let the silence run out and hang over them before he began to speak. He had to keep them here; he had to have the petition withdrawn; he needed to turn the clock back to where it was this afternoon; he could not be pushed over the edge this way, by these people.

"Sit down," he said, short of breath as if he had indeed been running and had fallen. "I know exactly how you feel. Even the largest corporations make bookkeeping errors now and then—but I must say this is a most exaggerated reaction. Will you wait for a few minutes while I telephone my lawyer and find out what we can do for you?"

"We'll wait, we've got lots of time," said the young man.

"We don't want to make trouble, all we want to do is get paid," said the older.

They sat gravely in their chairs, two faces out of a crowd, out of a blur of many faces of New York, and almost as soon as Warren had turned away from them to reenter his office he knew he could not keep the image of their faces in his mind. They might be anybody—any one of the millions down there, working, seeking, reaching; they were anonymous; he did not recall their names. But their paper, with force of law, lay in his pocket. Ten stories below his floor, the men and women of *Trumpet* were closing a magazine designed to amuse, excite and tell such people exactly what was happening to them. But these two had escaped the net of statistics and turned on him. All across the nation, this Tuesday evening, trucks and trains and mail pouches were speeding the new All-America issue to a hundred thousand newsstands where, come weekend, these two might spy its glistening cover and be attracted. The market had closed and six thousand stockholders of General American Publishing would, all across the nation, be marking now by what fraction their investment had lost or gained in the course of a day. To them it was still solid, a property, an investment, an insurance against lean times. But here, on the fortieth floor where he bore responsibility for all this, a ferret lay against Warren's throat, its teeth locked on the life of the magazines.

Hastily, Warren dialed Schlafman's office. He needed a lawyer. A personal lawyer, not a corporate lawyer. He was in quicksand.

"Nat," he said, as Schlafman's voice came through over the line, "you're still there. Good."

"What's up?" asked Schlafman.

"Nat. I need you. Right away. Can you get over here?"

"When, Ridge, now? I promised my wife I'd take her to a cocktail party tonight."

"Now. Right now. Please."

"That serious?"

"There's a fellow and his lawyer sitting in the outside office right now. I've never seen either of them before. They just served a subpoena on me, and a petition from the Federal District Court. Chapter Ten Petition. Involuntary bankruptcy."

"Can you keep them there?"

"I think so, Nat. . . . How long will you be?"

"I'm on my way now. Good-by. Call my wife, tell her not to expect me. Don't say a word until I get there. Oh, Christ!"

It could not have been more than half an hour that Schlafman negotiated, darting back and forth between the two rooms, Warren in one, the two men in the other. Warren passed the assurance that he would have checks for 28,400 dollars ready for their collection by noon the following day; he assured Schlafman he could strip petty cash, could strip something, somewhere, to meet the checks, that tomorrow's incoming receipts would certainly cover the payments.

And then, finally, when the men were gone, Warren, stunned, realized that his muscles ached, up and down his neck, in his arms and his legs, his neck, thighs, beneath his eyeballs. He drank heavily and steadily of the whiskey from the cabinet while Schlafman leaned against the desk, talking aloud with a low, bitter intensity. . . .

". . . of all the cockeyed, screwed-up, nonsensical situations that I have ever seen, this is it, Ridge. Ridge—that little kid, do you know the type? A night-school lawyer, scratching his way up from the gutter, the way we all used to, trying to build a practice in the depression, collecting bills for clients, one cut above ambulance chasing, winding up friends or contacts to let him handle their slow-pay accounts. But he's smart. He's not content with just collecting bills. He's got to prove he's a legal genius. The older one was his uncle and the kid hears his uncle is having trouble collecting from you. He could have gone to the State Supreme Court, anywhere. That's the proper procedure for this kind of action, Summons and Complaint. But not him, that genius. He's going to play it like Samuel Untermeyer. He goes to a legal stationery store, buys a Blumberg Form 1050A and fills the stinking form out, taxies downtown to file it, and have it sworn to. He has *no* idea what's really going on here. That's the irony of it. He just figured that a triplicate involuntary petition in bankruptcy is the quickest way of putting a pistol to your head. If only you *were* solvent, if only you really *had* the dough, if you *weren't* in trouble, I could prove that the alleged acts of bankruptcy in the petition were false, were malicious—I could ruin him, Ridge, ruin him! But we can't, Ridge, we can't—that's the irony of it, the little chiseler turns out to be right. So he's not a chiseler. You've gambled too far. If you pay *him* just to keep *him* quiet, then you are performing an act of bankruptcy, you're giving preference to one set of creditors when you know you can't pay off the other creditors. . . ."

Warren pulled himself together just long enough to ask another question.

"If we pay him, though, Nat, pay him in cash tomorrow and he withdraws the petition as he says he will—how many people will know about it? Can it be kept quiet?"

As if talking to a child about the dangers of traffic or of violence, Schlafman's voice softened to sympathetic gentleness.

"No, Ridge, no," he said. "That's the crowning irony. That lawyer-child was only just so smart—but so ignorant, too. He can withdraw a Summons and Complaint. But he can't withdraw a bankruptcy petition except by consent of all the other creditors. I don't know whether he realizes it or not. Ridge, this is the end. This thing was filed downtown this afternoon at the Clerk of the Court. It's public record now. The credit-reporting services will have picked it up tomorrow at the latest. It'll be on the desk of your bank, of every major supplier who serves you tomorrow before noon. Everyone else you owe money is now involved, whether they want to be or not. The machinery is working, he pressed the button—"

"But I can keep it out of the news, Nat, I'll pay him, I'll pay him tomorrow—"

"Even paying him can be dangerous in your situation, Ridge. Pay him or not, I don't care, but don't worry about him. Worry about the avalanche that starts tomorrow. It's not the magazines you've got to save, Ridge, it's the corporation. But fast. You have to be ready to tell your Board tomorrow how you plan to save the entire corporation; you've only got a few days in which to keep this thing quiet, to sweet-talk the big creditors, to keep it out of the papers. The whole town will know about this by weekend."

He paused. "Ridge," he said, "that dinner of mine isn't important. Let's you and I get a bite together somewhere, and then we'll go to your house or mine and talk this out. Sitting here in this office gives me the willies."

Without a word, as if being led, Warren rose from his seat, went to the closet, pulled out his Chesterfield and silk scarf. By instinct and habit, his hands folded the scarf neatly, then adjusted his hat. Then, still dazed, he turned back to Schlafman.

"I want to take a walk, Nat," he said. "I have to figure out what I do tomorrow. I can keep it out of the papers until the weekend. But I've got to plan the rest of it myself. Thanks a lot, just the same."

"O.K.," said Schlafman kindly, "I understand. If you want me, I'll leave the telephone number of the people we're dining with. Try and get some sleep, and call me early tomorrow."

Warren turned out the lights in his office, and joined Schlafman at the door. As they walked down the hall to the elevator, he heard the telephone ringing in his office—long, throbbing, pressing in an off-normal insistence, as it always rang, either here or at home, when a long-distance message was coming in. The telephone rang again, and then again, and dully Warren remembered Paget, and wondered whether the operator had finally located Paget in Paris.

Schlafman asked, "Your phone, Ridge?"

Warren hesitated for a moment, then plodded on to the elevator bank. "Never mind, Nat," he said, "it's too late now."

The daze took him down the elevator, through the lobby, through the revolving doors, to the street, where Michael, the chauffeur, waited.

Through the nightmare fog, Warren saw the door of the car open and he did not want to be trapped in it, to be taken back to the apartment and nowhere and alone.

"Where are you going, Nat?" he asked, and without waiting for a reply turned to Michael, and said, "Take Mr. Schlafman wherever he's going, then put the car up for the night."

3 . MARY'S APARTMENT

Warren turned north, joining the night float of wanderers up Fifth Avenue, and it struck him fancifully how, this evening, it seemed they were all walking in couples, a man and a woman together. Young man, young woman. Old man, old woman. Arthritic man holding on to a white-haired lady's arm. Giggling girl in sports coat holding on to a youth's arm. Two by two, the world was made, how odd that people should always come in couples, in audiences of two. How odd.

The air, the chill, the grip, the feeling of the street as it seemed to undulate under him, were all part of this daze where Mr. Bronstein doubled in pain and a ferret-faced man stabbed him with a folded paper and the exhaustion of weeks of conferences and striving flooded in.

Warren decided he needed a drink, that was it. He turned east on a sidestreet, found a bar, entered, commanded a bourbon, drained it, laid a five-dollar bill on the counter, then asked for another, took the change, and walked out. Yet the odd, unsettled feeling of the evening was now greater as he walked on, an undefinable strangeness of sound and mood. It was not only the strange parade of two-by-twos. It was more. He stopped at another bar, and looked at himself in the mirror as he drank. He could see that his necktie was perfectly knotted, that his shirt was still spotless white, that his face was not old, but still hard and sharp. I still look the same from the outside, he thought. Looking at me, no one could tell. But once on the sidewalk, the disturbance returned.

He was far east now, on Lexington Avenue, and the smell of meat, frying in deep fat, stopped him. He decided he was hungry—that was the root of the strange disturbance. He entered the glassy counter-restaurant, ordered a hamburger and bun, had munched only half of it, when a wave of nausea, compounded of the heat-after-the-cold, the grease, the bad mustard, the coffee slopped on the counter, lifted him from his seat and propelled him back to the fresh air of the street. He blinked at the green traffic light, knowing now that the mood was partly alcohol, but the light invited him to cross the avenue. He crossed, again aware of the rocking quality of the city's sounds, and that the night was odd, and that it was not only the drink in him.

Then he paused, before an open-air florist's stall. And he could identify it. Yes. Filling his lungs with the cold air, he sniffed the fragrance it bore and, softly, yet swiftly, it came over him what it was that made this evening strange.

It was Christmas time. That was it. It was the odor of pine and fir and hemlock and Christmas. The sound floating about him was the sound of mechanical music all up and down the avenue, the faint ringing sound of the little bells tinkling weakly about the traffic as the Salvation Army Santa Clauses plied their trade. It had been the bells in the windows, the fake snowflakes over the displays, the fake Santa Clauses, the holly everywhere, the wreaths of gold and silver, of green and Christmas berry, the red ribbon bows in every store-front that had been crying to him that Christmas was close.

From the open-air florist's stall where he had paused came all the fragrances of Christmas, imported from the hills of New England, of Canada, of upstate, or wherever they cut the Christmas trees these days.

Warren fumbled at the Christmas trees, wired and roped together in front of the stall, wishing he could unfurl them and free the open pine fragrance of the unswept hills, let loose the folded boughs to spread. He could smell the pine trees in the cold, and he turned to stumble over the threshold into the brightly lit counter-space where wreaths and holly boughs, clippings of myrtle and mistletoe were piled for sale.

"Want anything, Mac?" came a voice.

Warren looked at the bald-headed man, in a fur-lined Air Force jacket, who was regarding him.

"Just looking," said Warren loftily. "You're early for Christmas, aren't you, with this stuff?"

"Nah," said the man, "been selling it for a couple of weeks now. Used to be you didn't sell the stuff till a week before Christmas. Nowadays, bango, the day after Thanksgiving—Christmas is here. It's a promotion these days, not a holiday. Everything's promotion. Got a good choice of trees still, though—want one?"

"Nope," said Warren, "no place to put it. I'm just looking."

"Wreaths, holly, mistletoe—get them here for half as much as it costs in one of those Park Avenue places."

"No," said Warren, "no place to put it."

"Too bad," said the man. "Well, I got to lock the place up now. It's getting late—say, mister, how about some flowers? I've got a close-out on some stuff that's good for three or four more days, cost you a couple of bucks and I'll give you an armful."

"What kind of flowers have you got by the armful?" asked Warren.

"Yellow roses. Give you the last three dozen for five bucks. I overbought. Nobody wants roses this season of the year."

Fumbling, feeling obligated somehow by the conversation, Warren pulled out his billfold, slipped off first a five, then a one, and, handing them over, said, "Wrap them up." Tossing in the extra one made him feel better. It bought a little margin.

"I said five, Mac, what's the extra one for?"

"For Merry Christmas, Jack, wrap them up."

"I'll toss in some ferns. You got a buy there, Mac, if she likes yellow roses." Working the flowers into a huge horn, the vendor kept on talking. "I hope she likes them. If you decide you need a Christmas tree, or wreaths, or holly, come back again, if you get a place to put them; you don't want to spend Christmas alone, Mac, well, good-by, now—"

Carrying the huge green paper horn of roses, with the man's puzzled "Merry Christmas" ringing after him, Warren was back on the sidewalk, steady. He sensed now that the drinks were beginning to tell, but the little triumph of the yellow roses was contributing to steady him. And he knew where he was going, and rather glad that he was beginning to be drunk. Mary was back in town now, she had said she would be back this week. He had been to Sara Hubbard's apartment only that once, two weeks ago, when Mair had played the piano. He knew exactly the corner, exactly the floor, exactly the door, although ten minutes earlier, had he planned to visit Mary, he would have had to consult the address in the telephone book.

It was not far. As he went up in the elevator, he knew his breath was heavy with alcohol, but no elevator operator ever questioned a man bearing a horn of flowers. He decided that if she were not home, he would leave the flowers outside the door anyway, where she would find them when she came. Then, later in the week, when the story was public, she would know he had been there to tell her.

He leaned heavily on the buzzer and pressed.

There was no answer. He pressed again.

He pressed once more, and this time through the baffle of the door he heard a sound—not the click of heels, but the heavy padding of slippers approaching.

"Who is it?" came her voice.

"It's me, open up."

There was a silence, then the door opened. Her hair was braided over one shoulder; her face glistened with face cream; she was wearing the old yellow wrapper that Warren would have sworn she had long since thrown away.

"I brought you some roses," he said, as he walked in and put them in her arms.

"Johnny," she said, flustered; then, gathering herself, "Well, hello."

"Hello," he said, knowing this was where he wanted to be, peeling off his coat and scarf and sitting down.

She looked at him as he walked across to the chair and began to smile.

"Your hat," she said, "do you want me to take your hat, Johnny?"

"I want my hat on tonight," he said, lifting it once from his head, tilting it, putting it back on as he sprawled, and said, "How do you do?"

"I'm fine, thank you, how are you?" she replied with an uncertain giggle.

"If you have a vase," he said, flinging out a commanding arm, "those roses should be put in water. Then, if you have a drink, a little dollop would be good for my spirit and our visit. Am I intruding?"

"No," she said; then, smiling, "Johnny, are you drunk?" He could see by the smile that she was amused, not upset, by the way he was behaving.

"Then take care of the flowers first and after that my thirst, then—do you mind if I take my shoes off? My feet hurt, I've been walking all day."

"Take them off," she said, disappearing into the kitchen to look for vases.

There was a bustle of several minutes as she unwrapped the flowers, sorted them, brought him a drink, and then arranged the flowers around the room.

"They're lovely," she said, finally, surveying the arrangement.

"A coup," he said, grandly. "A buy. A bargain. Three dozen yellow roses for five dollars in the heart of New York. No one else could bring that off. You should be impressed. Warren's Last Coup."

He cupped the drink in his hand, knowing that as soon as he continued, the frivolity of the alcohol would wear off and, ridiculous as he must appear sitting with hat on and shoes off, it was better to appear ridiculous than pathetic.

"Johnny," she said, "I can't tell what you're trying to say, but I am glad you've come. If you hadn't, I would have called you. I'm leaving this Friday, and I hate myself for the other night. How did everything work out? . . . Johnny, has something gone wrong?"

"It didn't work out, Mair," he said; then, "Don't leave Friday night." He put his glass down.

"Why?"

"Because I'm bankrupt," he said flatly.

"Oh," she said in a whisper, not understanding, then not believing. "No, you don't mean that."

"Well, no," he corrected, shaking his head, trying to shake away the blur the drink caused as it receded from gaiety to despair, leaving him stranded. "No, not actually bankrupt. But then, yes, in a way you could say I was, too. Yes and no."

"Tell me from the beginning," she cut in simply.

"All right," said Warren. "I'll try to make it simple. It's half past eight now, and about four or five hours ago a little fellow whose name I can't even remember, a little fellow and his lawyer, went downtown to a place called Foley Square. Do you know Foley Square? A lovely place, with a lovely green park, and all the tall buildings around the park where they try people, and put them in jail—one of the handsomest villages in New York. Well, this little fellow went down to Foley Square, into a Roman building called the Federal Building where the Federal Law sits, and he found a man called the Clerk of Bankruptcy, and handed over a collection of papers. Anyone can buy these papers for a dollar and fifty cents at a stationery store, but as soon as you fill them out, file them, pay the Clerk of the Court a ninety-dollar fee to record them, they aren't papers, they're a Petition in Bankruptcy. And when the little fellow had done all that, he came uptown to my office to summon me to judgment as an insolvent, a bankrupt, a waster, and chief executive officer of a firm unable to pay the debts we owe him, or any other of the creditors who joined him in the action."

He paused, and drained the rest of his drink.

"It's known technically as a Chapter Ten Petition, an involuntary petition in bankruptcy—"

"You're not joking, then," she said slowly.

"No," he replied, "this is no joke."

"But can't you pay his bill?"

"I can and I can't," continued Warren. "I can pay his bill, but I can't pay the others. That's why I came here to talk to you. If I stayed here tonight, and you let me sleep on that couch until late tomorrow morning, or until noon, or even later because I'm so tired—then by tomorrow evening, the whole firm would be finally, hopelessly, over the edge into bankruptcy. The bastards!" he finished bitterly.

"Who?"

"All of them, every one of them—the old men with their old smiles, all the people who might have helped—Morrissey and his debenture holders—they might have tried, too. All I needed was two million dollars for sixty days, two lousy million bucks and not one of them would lift a finger. I hate them. Every one of them. They were responsible for this just as much as me, and now I've got them across the barrel, I can ruin them—"

He was furious at them all, his body shaking with anger. Then his voice dropped, softly.

"But they've got me worse."

"How?"

"Again, the law. I can go to jail. Every time any firm deducts a dollar from a paycheck for Social Security, it's supposed to hold that money in trust at the bank and pay the government what it collects at the end of the quarter. If you use Social Security money and then can't pay it over when it's due, you've breached a trust. And I've used that money, too. If we go bankrupt this week, and the money isn't there, I'm guilty of criminal breach of trust. And that's jail. Would you visit me in jail, Mary, when you come back from Paris to show Claude to your family?"

"For God's sake, don't be silly, we're not talking about me— Are you serious about jail?"

"I won't go to jail!" he said loudly. "And I'm not letting this corporation go bankrupt! Get me another drink, and I'll roll up my sleeves like a magician and presto, tell you how I'm going to be rich."

"Not another drink, you just had one."

"Get me another drink while I take off my jacket, unloosen my necktie, and flip out the white rabbit."

He watched her as she returned with the drink, and, as she bent to put his glass on the table, he could smell the clean scent of soap and water, and the face cream that glistened on her cheeks.

"Mary," he said, "don't go back on Friday."

"But I have tickets, Johnny, and I have to."

"Don't you want to see how the story comes out?"

"What story?"

"The story of Johnny Warren. It's interesting, damnit, somebody ought to be interested, you ought to be interested—"

"Johnny, I can't tell from what you're saying whether you're in trouble or not. One minute you say you're bankrupt and you're going to jail, then you say there's a white rabbit up your sleeve and you're rich. Supposing you make it simple for me—"

"It's very serious, Mary," he began again, no dance left in his voice. "I don't want to go to jail, and I don't have to. I haven't done anything wrong the law should punish me for—what I've done wrong is an entirely different story. But if I let them push the firm into bankruptcy tomorrow, the court has to appoint a trustee to go through the books, they have to find I've used Social Security money to keep the magazines going—and I have to face the law. It makes no difference to the law that I used the money not for me but to keep the magazines alive—I used it."

"What are you going to do, then?" she asked quietly.

"So I have to kill the magazines myself first—before a receivership does it. I have to look as if I've brilliantly saved the corporation from the edge of bankruptcy by executive decision—by deciding to butcher two magazines that held a mirror up to this country, and helped make this country, for sixty years. It's easy to look strong, or brave, in executive decisions," he went on as, speaking, there began to clarify in his mind the beautifully simple logic of taking apart the thing he had been trying to save, like taking apart a toy, or an appliance, or a watch. This he knew how to do—it could be engineered, it could be measured in figures, not in dreams. It was going to be easy, easy, once he got over the shame, and it was going to come out all right, all right, except that as he spoke he could see the slow stiffening of her body, a stranger, tighter concern moving across her face. He finished his exposition abruptly.

". . . within two months there'll be cash in the bank, a tax-free profit from the other divisions; the corporation will float. The stock zooms. Morrissey converts his bonds to stock and makes money. The old crowd makes money. Everyone makes money—even me. I get rich."

"How," she asked, "how do you get rich?"

"I have options on fifty thousand shares," he said. "Ten points more on the price in the market and I can probably have half a million of my own within a year. My own. I kill the magazines and I share in the kill, even if I don't want it, it's there for me—what's the matter?"

She was staring at him. Next week everyone would look at him that way, measuring, questioning his intent—some in hate, some in admiration, but none believing that he did not want the money. Scuttled the ship and came away with the treasure chest, they would say.

"Mary," he broke off, "don't you understand? I came here to explain it to you, because that's what everyone is going to say."

"I haven't said anything," she replied coldly.

"But you are, your face is saying it. Don't you see?" he went on, as if she refused to see. "If I could keep the magazines alive by giving up this money—I'd do it, Mary, I've tried, I've done all I could. You've got to see it. There's half a million waiting for me on one side of the spin; on the other side there's bankruptcy, and the end of the magazines and nothing more I can do to save them, and jail to boot—"

"But the magazines die, and you come out rich, that's it, isn't it?"

"Don't say it that way," he said, feeling himself growing angry, trying to hold it down. "What do you want me to do? You tell me what. Let the whole corporation go bankrupt? I've gambled right down to the gates of jail, I'm not free in this, Mary, I'm responsible to the law, to the Board, to the stockholders, to—goddamnit, don't just sit there looking at me as if I were a hangman!"

"All I know, Johnny, is that when you gamble, you shouldn't get paid when you lose."

She stopped, then shifted. "What happens to everyone else?"

"I told you. They all make money. The creditors get paid. The stockholders make money. Morrissey makes money—"

"I don't mean them," she said. "What happens to all the people who work on the magazines? What happens to Dave Eliot, for example? You say you gambled and now look at you, heads-I-win, tails-you-lose."

"All I came here to say was that I didn't want the money. There are things a man has to do, things he's forced to do, and whatever motives other people read into him, he's forced by the job he has to do the things he must. You always thought you could spray rose water and a wish on anything and make it work. You just don't understand."

"No," Mary replied, studying him as if he were an animal specimen, remote as a stranger. "I never have understood you, I guess. There's something about whatever you do that always has two reasons—one reason is logical and inevitable, and the other reason always makes the inevitable show a profit for Johnny Warren. First in Paris, now here. I don't know how to say it, Johnny, but there's something about a captain going down with his ship that never enters your mind. You're a welcoming committee for disaster."

He bent to put on his shoes, shaking with anger. As he bent, he began to talk and he knew that the only thing was to go home and club away the day with sleeping pills. He had come all the way here and told it to her for nothing.

"Oh, what the hell do you want me to do," he stormed, as he laced one shoe, "lash myself to the mast and direct the movements to the lifeboats?"

He laced the other shoe. "This isn't boy-scout stuff, the captain going down with the ship."

He got up, and another gust took him. "I'm not Rhett Butler, who joins up when the enemy enters the city."

He put on his necktie, pulling his voice down to a cutting edge. "The magazines are going to die anyway. They're going to die whether the corporation goes bankrupt or I keep it solvent, whether I go to jail, or whether I cash the options."

He put on his jacket.

"There's no sense talking about it any longer. I came here because you were the only person in this damned town whom I wanted to understand that I tried, and you refuse."

She was silent.

"Where's my coat?" he said curtly.

She made no reply. He strode to the closet, pulled it open, took his coat, looked for his hat, remembered he was still wearing it, jammed it further down on his head, stuffed his scarf in his pocket and strode to the door, then turned for a final fusillade.

"What do you want me to do then?" he demanded, as if he must wring an answer from her. "Say something! Would it be better, come Christmas, two weeks from now, if I were out on my butt, aged forty-seven, two magazines a failure behind me, no job, and just enough money to wait until I'm trapped in an office boy's job? Do you think anyone in this town would cry for me, instead of laughing at me? Can you think of one person who'd cry?"

He could not hear her reply.

"Well," he said at the door, "speak up. What are you saying? I can't hear the parting word."

This time she spoke distinctly, to herself and to him, and with yearning.

"I'd cry, Johnny," she was saying, "I'd cry for you, but you wouldn't be a failure. The way you're doing it, nobody's going to cry. If that's what you want, you're right. But you won't have a friend left: here, or in Paris, or in Washington, or anywhere else in the world. You'll have half a million dollars, and you still won't be free, and you'll be a failure, a cheap, slick, conniving failure who—"

He marched back into the room and approached her. In a burst of anger, he reached down, seized her wrists and yanked her upright. She staggered as he held her and grated harshly, "You don't *want* to understand. You just don't *want* to understand. I can't let myself be trapped, do you understand, do you understand? It's not the money, it's—"

"Johnny," she said, unflinching, "you're hurting me."

He relaxed his grip, and she continued shaking her head, tasting every word as she spoke. "You're a failure, Johnny. Everybody sets the terms of his own failure, of what they started out to be and what they become. You always start with visions high as the sky, and make everyone else reach with you. Then when they explode, you walk out. You settle for what you can save for yourself. You came here tonight to bleed on me because there's nowhere else to go tonight until you think of the next deal you can make—"

"But this wasn't a deal, Mary," he said. "Those were my magazines, I came there to make them mine. I loved them, Mary, I tell you I loved them. But I wasn't responsible, I was trapped from the moment I got there; they put me at that desk because someone had to take the rap—"

"But you were, you *were* responsible. You took it," she said, wrenching her hands free, "you took responsibility in Paris, you took it here, you made people follow you. You took responsibility for their lives. You can't sell the wreckage for what you make out of it yourself. You say you loved them—love is taking responsibility for something outside yourself, and how you measure up to that is success or failure. Once you take a responsibility, you can't walk away from it—"

"You walked away from me," he said. "I loved you. And you walked out on me."

"No, I didn't," she said. "You stopped loving me first. You didn't want children because they would trap you, you didn't want a home because it would trap you— Oh, Johnny, go away, go away. We're not good for each other, we keep hurting each other— Go home, Johnny, go home."

He tried to pick his way through his emotions.

"I can't, Mary," he said, conscious that he had had too much to drink, that what had been clear ten minutes ago was now totally confused. "I can't go home. The apartment isn't home. That's not true about my not loving you, Mary—"

"Johnny, for God's sake, don't mix us into this; this has nothing to do with us; go home and get some sleep."

"Mair," he said, "but Mair, you said you'd cry if I went under, that mixes us into it, doesn't it?" He approached her as he talked, his coat still on, and as he approached she drew back.

"Let me sit here for a little bit and think," he said. "I have to sort it out, I have to find out what to do."

"Johnny," she said, "it won't do any good staying here. I don't know the answers about the law and corporations. All I know is that how you behave in the next few days is important, so that people trust you, so that you save something more than yourself, so you don't come away only with money. Oh, Johnny, Johnny dear, I was married to you, I don't want to think I gave myself to a bastard. Maybe I'm being selfish. I wish I could help you, I just can't, I know I can't—"

"Yes," he said, taking her gently by the elbows, sensing her fright as he grasped her again. "All I want to do is walk away from it proud. You want me to, too—you're proud— Oh, Mary, that's why I love you—"

"No," she said, "please leave us out of this."

"Yes," he said, realizing what he had just said and suddenly lighter. "Yes," he repeated, stroking her hair, and he could tell by the almost imperceptible sway of her body that she was no longer fighting him and he pulled her to him. It was like coming home from a trip in the old days, late at night, and finding her waiting up in the old yellow wrapper. Gently, as he drew her closer, his lips tried to find hers, and his cheek brushed against hers as she turned, and she protested, "Johnny, you'll get cold cream all over you."

"I don't care," he mumbled, trying to hold her closer.

"You have your hat on," she said primly, breaking away, pulling her bathrobe closer.

"There goes the hat," he said, taking it off and sailing it across the room, then coming back to her.

"But Johnny," she said, "I have to go back on Friday. You know it. But you won't accept it. Johnny, this is a game that gets us nowhere. Wherever are we? Where do you think we are?"

"Well," he said, "we have my hat off, now let's get my coat off."

"All right," she said falteringly, "take it off, but that doesn't answer any questions."

"No," he said, taking off his coat and walking across the room to sit on the couch and look at her, "but it's a beginning. And I know I can't answer the questions by myself; I have to be quiet for a while and think, and I have to be *here* to think—Mair?"

"What?"

"Do you have anything to eat?"

"Eggs," she said, "eggs and bacon."

"And a drink?" he asked. "Something to drink?"

"No more drink for you, not tonight."

"Coffee, then?"

"No coffee, either. You have to sleep tonight and work tomorrow. Tea."

He settled down on the couch, slowly took off his shoes again, lifted his feet and stretched out. He heard her padding off in her slippers to the kitchen.

He did not hear her come back, for when she entered with the tray his eyes had closed and he was sleeping. She looked at him for a moment and shook her head. Putting the tray down on the table, she went to the bedroom and came back with a blanket. She spread the blanket over him, and he did not stir. His head, she noticed, drooped awkwardly, and she returned with a pillow. His head was heavy, she had forgotten how like a dead weight he slept. She lifted it and tucked the pillow under, then switched off the light above him. As she went back to her own room, she wondered whether there would be enough eggs left for breakfast. He would want eggs for breakfast.

PART THREE

16. Wednesday, December Tenth

1. MORNING AT THE OFFICE

In war, defeat is recognized weeks and months in advance. No sudden signal tells uncertain troops they now are captive to fate. Food has been short for a long while. While one's own guns have gasped and stuttered, the enemy's artillery has grown to a well-fed roar. The skies, too, have grown hostile so that the sound of planes and whine of bombs is always the sound of the enemy, never of support. Defeat rarely comes abruptly in a war, but grows week by week until the defeated have in spirit accepted disaster as inevitable.

The conflicts of peace differ.

As Warren entered the lobby of his building on Wednesday morning, it struck him how busily tranquil was this scene he now must shatter. Mary had woken him early; they had breakfasted together as if four years had not interrupted the ceremony. He had eaten well, recognizing that a last burst of energy, a last resource of strength had been released by the papers served on him the previous evening. Now, he no longer carried the burden of the magazines—he was responsible today only for his own performance. He would know soon enough what he was. He wondered how the day would end.

As he joined the scatter of entering latecomers in the lobby, it seemed impossible that this was defeat. All the sounds and sights that greeted him were so precisely normal. The clicking of heels across the marble floors beat the familiar tattoo of girls hurrying to punch the clock or race their masters to their desks. Faces glowed with the cold of the morning outside; scarves and coats fluttered as they always did, when the office people began their preliminary unbuttoning in the downstairs lobby of this, their home. Warren strode quickly through them all to the elevator, nodded at the starter's greeting, and was whisked to his own floor.

The hush of the executive floor was completely normal, too. The sun, pouring through the side windows of the hall, was as it always had been.

The sound of typing was normal. The hum of an adding machine far down the corridor was normal. Even the first whiff of cooking that struck him from the air shaft that ventilated *Gentlewoman's* kitchen was normal. So was the appearance of Laura, bent over her desk, her back to the door as he entered, talking on the telephone until she swung around to notice him, and then—all in a rush—she spoke.

"Mr. Warren! The telephone's been ringing for you, ringing and ringing, the whole town is trying to get to you, from the moment I got in this morning—"

The ring interrupted her, and she swiveled to answer it. "No, not yet—who? Mr. Silverman . . . no . . . yes, Mr. Silverman . . . just a minute, please, my other line is ringing."

She held her hand over the mouthpiece of the telephone. "Silverman of East Coast Paper. The second time he's called. Shall I say you're out?"

The wall of the surf was coming in on him; the only way was to dive at the face and go through it—"I'll take it," he said.

In his office he tossed his coat, hat, and scarf on the couch, moved directly to his desk, sat down, seized the phone.

"Yes, Mr. Silverman?"

"Say, what's going on over at your place?" came Silverman's voice with no word of greeting. "Are you trying to put something over on us, Warren?"

"What do you mean?" asked Warren.

"I've had a credit report on my desk for the past forty-five minutes saying that an action in bankruptcy was filed in court against you people yesterday at four thirty-five and I want to know exactly—"

"Oh, that," said Warren, flexibly, "some damn fool mistake that one of our—never mind, disregard it, Mr. Silverman, that will be vacated at noon today, a complete mistake—"

"Warren, don't try to kid me, are you people in the courts or not?"

"Mr. Silverman—"

"Don't try to fool me, Warren, I'm serious, my neck is out a million miles on your word alone! We have two million dollars of unpaid bills in your firm right now. I can't sit here and do nothing."

"Silverman, listen, you're blowing your top over nothing."

"Nothing?" Silverman's voice shrieked. "We've had a request in with Dun and Bradstreet for two weeks for instant reporting on anything connected with your firm, and here I am this morning sitting with a piece of paper saying that you owe twenty-eight thousand four hundred dollars for service and cleaning that you can't pay and there's a Chapter Ten proceeding begun—"

"That's nonsense, Silverman, one of the most bizarre episodes of this whole—"

"Warren, I don't want big words this morning, we're carrying you for two million dollars. I spoke to Campbell of Intertone Ink—"

"Now wait a second, Silverman, why don't you run your own business and let Campbell run his—"

"I'll talk to anyone I want, Warren. Do you think either Campbell or me is going to let you play with us like a couple of kids just out of business school? Warren, I'll make a long story short—I want to look at your books. I'm talking for me and Campbell and as many others as I care to round up on the telephone."

"Silverman, you're getting your money. You'll have it in two weeks—"

"How do I know that? Where are you going to get it?"

"We have a Board meeting this afternoon that's going to settle everything—"

"Are you going to fold the magazines, Warren?"

"That's none of your business—"

"Don't tell me what's my business and what's not—when's that Board meeting?"

"At two, and I'll let you know this afternoon after—"

"Warren, there'll be a letter on your desk by two, and a copy of it for every member of your Board to consider, and if I don't get a real answer out of you in the next twenty-four hours, then, by God, I'll slap a petition on you myself, I'll—"

"Silverman, I've got two things to say. First, you're going to get paid, believe it or not. And, second—if you give me any trouble this week while I'm trying to pay you, everybody in town is going to hear how you behave when you have a man in a corner."

"Warren, don't pull this gentleman act on me. What am I supposed to do? Just sit still and get taken for two million bucks and try to argue out priorities in bankruptcy with a bunch of shoeshine men, orange-juice peddlers, and typewriter repairmen? You should know that once an action like this is slapped on you, everybody's got to protect himself— I've got to know where I stand by this evening. Are you folding those magazines, Warren?"

"Silverman, I can't talk about that with you. You'll get your money— I guarantee that. If there's any other announcement to make, the Board will make it when the meeting's over. I'm busy now, Silverman, I've got to hang up."

Warren had barely hung up the phone when it seemed to ring back by itself. He heard it ring again and lifted it, the after-anger of his talk with Silverman still surging in him.

"What the hell is it now?"

He heard nothing but the soft intake of breath at the other end and realized it was Laura.

"Laura, I wasn't swearing at you, forgive me—I thought I was still talking to Silverman. What is it?"

"It's Bennett," she said. "He says he has to talk to you immediately."

Bennett was Chief of Public Relations for the magazines; it was Bennett's job to handle all inquiries from the press and the outer world.

"I can't talk to him now, find out what he wants."

A pause, then her voice again. "He says he has a reporter from the Wall Street Journal on his other phone; the word is out downtown that the Board is going to close the magazines this afternoon."

"Tell him to deny it."

A pause.

"Bennett says can he please come upstairs and talk to you for five minutes, their story is awfully circumstantial. . . ."

"Tell him to deny it, and keep on denying it, and that I'll see him as soon as I can; I'm busy."

He hung the telephone up with a click.

His eye fell on his coat, hat and scarf strewn across the couch where he had flung them as he entered. He rose to get them but had scarcely crossed the room before the telephone rang again. Furious, he walked back to the desk and said, "Yes?"

"Lord, I'm sorry, Mr. Warren, I just don't know what to do now, Morrissey is on the telephone. . . ."

"Find out what he wants; tell him I'm in conference."

A pause.

"He says don't you think it would be a good idea for the two of you to get together before the meeting at two. If you're not busy for lunch he can make it."

"Tell him I'm busy, that I'll call him back, I'll see him at the meeting. Then come on in here yourself and let's get straightened out."

She was in his presence by the time he had finished hanging his coat in his closet.

"Laura," he began, and he stopped, for the telephone rang again and she rose automatically from her seat to reach the instrument on his desk. Her hand stopped over the telephone and she questioned him with her eyes.

"Go ahead," he snapped, and waited.

"Yes," said Laura to the voice, "yes . . . Mr. Cameron, oh, yes . . . well he's in conference now, I'll poke my head in and see if he can take it. . . ."

She looked at him again, and his lips noiselessly formed the syllables of "Will call back." She waited a moment, then said to the telephone, "Mr. Warren has some people with him now, he'll call Mr. Cameron back as soon as he's free . . . no, I don't know . . . sometime before noon, I think . . . yes, I'll try . . . good-by."

"Now shut the door," said Warren, "and let the damned thing ring its head off."

She sat down obediently, arranged her folders on his desk, took out her memo pad, then waited for him to talk.

"Laura, some fool slapped an action in bankruptcy on us last night," he said, wondering how to tell her.

"Bankruptcy?" she whispered, and her eyes opened in an unbelieving stare.

"We're *not* bankrupt," said Warren hastily, "it was a damn fool mistake, some bills we let wait too long and we'll have it all cleared up by noon. But the news is out. By now a dozen people must have heard about it, and the rumor will be all over town by this evening and—"

He did not know how to go on.

"What does it mean?" she asked.

"It means a lot of things," and his voice softened as he knew he must now say it aloud, "it means the magazines are over, we have to fold them."

She said nothing, her face suddenly dull. Her lips moved and he could barely hear her whisper, ". . . I'm so sorry, Mr. Warren, oh, poor everybody."

A lump rose in his throat and he struggled to discipline it. He turned away from her and went to the window, hoping the film before his eyes would dry. He blew his nose hard. Then he wheeled, knowing he would have to be tough the next few days, because if he broke in here, he would send her, by contagion, broken from the office, too.

"All right, Laura," he said when he felt he could control his voice, "let's not break up now. There's work to do. I'll tell you all about this just as soon as I get a breather. There's a Board meeting at two and I have to clean away a lot of wreckage before then. Open your folder and let me have the traffic first."

It was the routine of the morning, the routine he had taught her ever since she had first come to him.

"The outside calls first," he said flatly, and her voice, now husky, replied, "Silverman twice. You had him. Morrissey. Just now. Cameron twice, that was the second time. Schlafman, just to tell you he's standing by and can be over and work with you here in this office any time you want. Campbell of Intertone Ink. A long-distance call from Detroit, the Advertising Club there wants you to make a speech in February at their annual banquet on 'Communications in America at Mid-Century.'"

Her face came up at that one; he could see a wan smile beginning; then she went on "—There's also an award for us in the mails. From the Society of American Magazine Illustrators, as the best-illustrated magazine in the general circulation field—"

He smiled, too. Someone *had* noticed the good color work.

"A message to call back Overseas Operator Number One Twenty-three, for your call to Paris, and that's the outside stuff. Now, the inside stuff—this is mad—everybody wants to see you today."

He interrupted her. "Foley and Cahill and Purcell and Austin and Bennett and Russell—"

"And," she broke in as if she were responding in a chant, "Hopkins and Eliot and God knows who else. The only hard item on the inside is the Purcell thing—"

"What about Purcell?"

"His resignation. With a note that if you want to talk it over with him, he'd be pleased with any settlement your generosity felt was fair—"

Warren smiled. Purcell was first off the boat. But there would be no settlement for Purcell. Purcell, like him, had come on a gamble, and quit before the gamble ran out. Purcell deserved nothing. It relieved him of the necessity of dismissing Purcell—and then the smile faded. Gamblers played to win or lose it all.

"O.K.," he said, "I have it now. First, you. I'll tell you everything as soon as I get a moment, but I want you desperately to behave yourself in the next few days. It's important to me, Laura—that you look calm. If you feel like crying, you've got to wait until you get home. If they ask you what's happening—you don't know. How am I feeling?—you don't know. What did the Board do?—you don't know. You don't know anything. Are the magazines going to fold?—you don't know."

"I get it, I don't know a single thing."

"Right. Because between now and Friday, the whole corporation can be fed through the meat-grinder by Mr. Silverman, by the U.S. government, by Mr. Campbell, by Mr. Morrissey—by anybody. I need until Friday to save what can be saved my own way. I don't want panic sweeping this shop until I make up my mind how to do it. We have to play it calm, you and I. Now, let's see. I'll see Austin first. Then Hopkins. Then Schlafman. Then I'll call Campbell. Then Cameron. Then Russell. I'll get back to Bennett if there's any time between now and noon. At noon, I want to lie and sweat quietly at the Wagner Baths—make a reservation for me there."

"What? Today?"

"Yes. There's nothing else I can do except think, I'm going to lie on my back in a Turkish bath from noon until the Board meeting starts where nobody can reach me, and think about the past two years, and the next three days, and figure out what I have to do when I sit down at that table."

2. THE BOARD ROOM—2:00 P.M.

The Board Room, Warren had always thought, was out of place in this Manhattan tower, yet he loved it. The Board Room was Abbott Shalom Pepper's Board Room still. When General American Publishing had leased this space in the then-new tower before the war, Abbott Shalom Pepper had insisted that the Board Room be fitted in his style. Pepper had called it "the watchtower"; but Varian, one of the trustees of the Pepper estate, had explained it better. "Ab used to say that an office should be like a home, and the people who worked in it a family." Pepper had never worked in the office Warren now occupied. Pepper had worked in the Board Room and permitted no telephone there. He held his editorial conferences there. Pepper served his lunches, the famous luncheons with the hot buttered popovers and the great wines, in the Board Room. The room was still his—its dark mahogany paneling, its proud, high-backed, carved English walnut chairs, its deep crimson carpeting, all his. Even the fire in the fireplace was his. Eighteen years after Ab Pepper's death, the heat was still turned off and the windows flung open before Board meetings so that the fire in the fireplace would provide the only warmth with its flames.

Warren had changed little about the Board Room since he had come.

Between the two large windows in the window wall still hung the portrait of Abbott Shalom Pepper, himself—a lean, thin-lipped, warm-eyed face in which the artist had managed to capture the qualities of swagger and concern all at once. On the inner wall, as if there for Pepper's scrutiny, facing the windows, was spread a map of the United States which covered the entire surface. One of the side walls was hung with the illustrations of artists who, over the half-century, had illuminated the words of storytellers in the magazines with the color of their paintings. The opposite wall was covered with action photographs that *Trumpet's* photographers had taken during the war. The photographs were Warren's idea; he had felt that if Pepper had lived through the war he had so eloquently advocated, he would have wanted the photographs there. But all the other decorations of the room still echoed the great half-century in which Abbott Shalom Pepper had elected himself steward over America as it changed. Above and about each wall ran the channels of the draperies so that, when anyone desired, the floor-length draperies of red velvet could be unfurled from their corners and drawn about the chamber to make of it a private auditorium. Then, with the draperies spread, the indirect lighting from the ceiling panels adjusted, the fires burning in the fireplace, the room took on a majesty of its own in which Warren shared authority only with Pepper and the past.

But now, as the meeting opened, with the draperies gathered still in the corners, and winter sun coming in through the west windows, the carafes of water full, the yellow pencils at each setting neatly sharpened, the pads of paper squarely aligned before each seat, Warren knew he was sharing authority and leadership not with Pepper, but with these others.

He wanted to share it. That was the purpose of this meeting. But not quite in this manner. For the very seating at the table seemed to cast its procedure into a dialogue between himself and Morrissey.

Seven men sat about the table, grouped by association. At one end of the table sat Warren, flanked by Austin and Hopkins who, with him, made the three management representatives on the Board.

The two directors of the old stockholders, guardians of the remnant interest of the Pepper family, sat side by side—Fleming, a cold dry man, a lawyer unstirred by emotion, surgical in his questioning, and Varian, a round, kindly face, confused and bumbling when he spoke.

At the far end of the table sat Morrissey and his man Berger. Morrissey sat directly opposite Warren and his cheeks, pasty with old man's tissue, were nonetheless pink and cleanshaven in good health. The scarlet bow-tie bobbing above the promontory of Morrissey's Adam's apple contrasted oddly with the texture of his skin, and even more grotesquely with the sharp, square-shoulder, loose-hanging suit of powder blue. Today, Morrissey was all charm, all easy, all cordial.

Not so Berger. Neat and well dressed as Berger was, the stubble of an early-afternoon beard showed black on his skin. Berger had a cigar and the cigar would rise and fall, spin from angle to angle in his mouth as Berger followed the discussion. Whenever Morrissey was interrupted, Berger would grab the cigar from his mouth, hold it tight as if it were a pipe-wrench and scowl. Whenever Morrissey would score a point, Berger would relight his cigar, whether it needed relighting or not, and sit erect.

Morrissey had intervened within five minutes after Warren called the meeting to order. Warren had made a general opening because he had wanted to force the decision from the table, and cast himself as their instrument, not master executioner at his own initiative.

This, he began, was probably the most important meeting since he had joined General American Publishing. The heart of the decision was whether to suspend or continue the magazines. Never had circulation been higher in the sixty-year history of the magazines than this week. But the magazines were underfinanced as they had been underfinanced for the past ten years, underfinanced to meet the new merchandising and promotional necessities of the magazines and the prospects that lay just ahead. The Board, thus, could help him raise new financing; or it could empower him to liquidate certain of the subsidiaries such as the radio stations or the book division to raise new money for the magazines; it could entertain, if it chose, a mortgage offering from Mr. Raven; or, if it failed to agree to these actions, it must face the alternative of suspension.

"No!" blurted Hopkins as Warren came to the point, "no, sir! I won't hear of it. It's always darkest just before the dawn; we're just coming over the top; we're—"

But Warren, who knew he had Hopkins' vote whichever way he chose to cast it, stopped him gently, to say that there were a number of urgent and important details they must consider but first must come a basic expression of desire to continue or suspend, when, suddenly, Morrissey easily and quietly spoke for the first time.

"Now, Ridge," he said, "let's go in simple steps, starting with number one—now, Ridge, what's this all about?"

"This" was a rose-pink slip of paper which Berger slipped into Morrissey's hand as if waiting and prepared for the moment. The pink slip of paper fluttered in Morrissey's fingers as he brandished it.

"What's what?" asked Warren.

"This," said Morrissey. "It says somebody slapped a petition in bankruptcy on us yesterday. That's not a detail, that's important. We ought to start with that."

"Did you say a petition in bankruptcy, Mr. Morrissey?" asked Fleming sharply.

"Yup," said Morrissey, "just that. Goddamned important from the looks of it, that's exactly what it says here."

"What is that?" asked Warren and knew he should have started with the bankruptcy petition.

"This," said Morrissey, fluttering the paper slip, "is a Special Notice from Dun and Bradstreet Credit Service. I've had them put me on Continuing Service for all credit information about this firm, just to see how it looks from the outside, and, what do you know, this morning I get this thing special delivery, plus a telephone call from the service manager—"

"Now, wait a minute—" Warren attempted.

"May I see that, please?" came Fleming's precise voice as his hand reached down the table for the pink slip.

"I'd really like to show it to you," said Morrissey, drawing his hand away, "but these Dun and Bradstreet people are particular. Everything they give you is confidential. Anybody can buy all the information they want from them about anybody's credit for three hundred and fifty bucks a year, but they won't let you give it away. It's the way they run the business. Can't show it to you"—he handed the slip back to Berger—"but what's in it ain't at all confidential. Three jokers went downtown yesterday and slapped a Chapter Ten petition in bankruptcy on all of us; and I sit here now, you sit here now, we all sit here now as directors personally and legally responsible for a petition brought against us at four thirty-five P.M.—"

"Mr. Fleming," said Warren, slicing his voice decisively through Morrissey's, "this must be put in its proper light. Every corporation of our size has dozens of judgments by disgruntled creditors and fake claimants slapped on it every day. General Motors probably receives a hundred court summonses a week. This was the brain child of a little shyster who rounded up three of our small debtors and persuaded them rather than to use a normal bill-collecting agency, to let him be a hero by making a petition in bankruptcy out of it. The total bill was twenty-eight thousand four hundred dollars and as of an hour ago that bill was paid and—"

"I know, I know," said Morrissey, "Austin here told me just as we came in that they were paid this morning—"

"If you knew that, then why did you bring it up?" snapped Warren with more anger than he meant to show.

He saw Berger's cigar come out, the fingers clamp on the cigar, the scowl pucker instantly, and Berger leaned forward, menacing, from where he sat beside Morrissey.

"Now, Ridge—I know the strain you've been under," said Morrissey, dodging. "Gentlemen, Warren has done a wonderful job here. I tell you there's nobody who's done more to keep this whole thing afloat than Warren. He's been carrying it all by himself. If he made a few mistakes here or there it's not the time to go into it now, and I'm not going to lose my temper because we're all under strain. We're here just to help you, Ridge, you call the turn and tell us what you want to do."

Morrissey was being the charming Morrissey today, all synthetic sweetness. Berger leaned back, put a match to his cigar, and relaxed. Morrissey's tongue flicked out, licked his thin lips, then went on.

"Of course, the petition's been vacated; Ridge handled that shyster wonderfully. But you see, now, if I got a special notice today, then other people must be getting these special notices from Dun and Bradstreet today. Why, Ridge, you ought to see the credit report on us, you ought to ask some pal to get you these reports. Brilliant people, these Dun and Bradstreet boys. Why, you know, we look like a Jersey City toy manufacturer the way we're paying our bills—those reports about us say SLOW —thirty days; or SLOW—sixty days; we got some creditors who report SLOW—ninety days. If these three little guys got scared, how about the big guys? Can we hold the big guys off?"

Before Warren could speak, Fleming in an icy, tight voice was saying aloud—"I think this is a major crisis, Mr. Warren. I can't understand your attempt to conceal this—"

Warren brought his fist down on the table with a thwack. He knew he was losing his temper, yet he could not help the thwack, nor the fury as he spoke.

"Mr. Fleming, there has been absolutely no attempt to conceal anything from this Board. This meeting has just begun; I was interrupted in the first two minutes on a detail of bill payment which has been closed and settled. We haven't got time today to discuss details of twenty-eight thousand four hundred dollar bills—"

"Why you're right, there, Ridge, you're right," said Morrissey soothingly, "I wouldn't want anybody here to think that I brought the matter up just to harass you. I just feel we ought to take a look at where we are. How're we going to pay the year-end bills? Where we going to find the cash? Before we make any basic decisions, for example, who else—"

"Morrissey," broke in Warren, "let me finish."

He had been trapped once off-base by the pink slip. In his folder lay the letters that Silverman had rushed over to the office just before the meeting, with the ultimatum of payment or agreement by Friday. He wanted to announce it first, and not be caught again; it spoiled his agenda, but he had to put it on the table now.

"This meeting has to come to order," he continued. "There are a multitude of matters in this tangle more important than a shyster's pin-prick. I have here and will distribute in a few minutes a letter from Mr. Silverman of East Coast Paper to all of you concerning their interest in this meeting—"

"How large is their interest?" asked Varian.

"Two million dollars," said Warren flatly, and hurried on, "overdue from sixty to ninety days. They've been supplying us with paper on a C.O.D. basis for the past month."

"Oh, my," said Varian and clucked his tongue, "oh, my—do we have it to pay?"

Morrissey now could not be denied.

"That's the big question, Mr. Varian, that's the only question, that's why I brought up the pink slip," said Morrissey. "How many other people are there waiting in line to get a crack at us? Do we have it to pay them? Let's get our teeth into some figures and find out exactly what bills we have to meet by the year-end and what we've got to meet them with. Hey, now, Austin, let's get out those sheets of yours so we can all look at the December first balance, and—"

It was Morrissey now who was leading Austin through the maze of figures. Every now and then Varian or Fleming would ask a question, and Morrissey would answer, explaining and elucidating. Morrissey had done his homework; he knew as much about the figures as did Austin or Warren. Like the master coachman of a team of unruly horses, Morrissey would tug the bit, tweak the harness, and the meeting would veer with him. Warren sat silent, realizing it was better to let Morrissey lead them through the worst of it.

It was almost two hours before Morrissey had finished with his examination of the figures and said, "There just isn't enough perfume in the whole city to cover up that stink. We need two million dollars by the end of the year just to satisfy the bank and part of the paper bill, and then there are all the others—"

Morrissey paused and pushed out his tongue, licking his lips as if he were about to enjoy himself.

"And, Ridge," he concluded, "poor Ridge, we've got to think of him, too, of the personal jam we let him get into trying to save this thing for all of us—"

"Let's go back to the original point, Morrissey," cut in Warren, knowing what was coming. "The point is: can this Board find from its own resources or knowledge enough money to meet those bills? Or will it empower me to mortgage the plant or sell the radio stations to meet those bills? Or does it want me to fold the magazines? What does it want to do? Then let's settle the details—that's the point of the meeting, not poor Ridge—"

"Ridge, Ridge," said Morrissey, as if chiding him in sorrow, "I can't let you talk that way. Gentlemen, you don't understand the loyalty Ridge has shown this firm. But you got to think of yourself, too, Ridge. Now, you take for instance, you've dipped into the Social Security Fund deductions to cover this last little bill. Why, that's the second time you've done it this month. Ridge, do you know you could go to jail for that? None of us here knew a thing about it. You should have asked us about it, Ridge, at least we would have been responsible, too. Now, supposing Silverman and the bank really put us into bankruptcy—you know anybody could right this minute—you'd go to jail, Ridge, do you know that, man? We have got to think of that, Ridge, even if you don't want to."

Berger lit his cigar and blew a cloud of smoke out as if it were a plume of victory.

Fleming spoke with frosty intensity. "Legally, in the eyes of the law, all the members of the Board are responsible. This is mismanagement on a scale so vast, Mr. Warren, on a scale so huge as to be almost fraud. Fraud against our creditors, fraud against our stockholders, fraud against me. I can't be put in such a position. None of us can. Warren, we should have been informed of this earlier. I have sat on this Board for seventeen years as representative of the Pepper family interests—"

"You sat on this Board," said Warren, suddenly not caring, "like a wooden Indian, and you never gave a damn until just now when your own neck is on the block. This was a property to you, like a cornflake mill. You milked this firm for twenty years for dividends when there was no money for dividends; you bled it white until—"

"Ridge," said Morrissey, "Ridge, nobody's getting tough here. We're all worried. Let's not get excited."

"I'm not excited!" snapped Warren, knowing he was, knowing he was the only man around the table losing his temper.

"Yes, you are!" retorted Fleming. "I insist that you withdraw what you said just now. You came in here as the wonderboy, with all your new ideas, and took a property that had survived for sixty years and ran it into the ground—"

"I took a corpse that was walking around waiting for someone to pipe the funeral march and tried to breathe life into it."

"I represent—" began Fleming.

"What do you represent?" asked Warren. "I've always wanted to know that, Mr. Fleming."

But then came a bellow, and Berger had spoken for the first time.

"Quiet, everybody," came Berger's voice in the brass command of a policeman, "the chief wants to talk."

Morrissey sat prim and thin at the end of the table, licking his lips again, and spoke. "Gentlemen," he said in his more familiar business voice, with no syrup in his tone, "I think we all recognize that Mr. Warren needs help even if he doesn't. Let's get down to cases. Ridge, your other ideas don't make sense. You know that. Can't work. Selling off the radio stations or the book division is stupid—they're *making* money for the firm, not losing it. Stockholders could file a suit against us for malfeasance. We'd be gambling that way, Ridge, tossing good money after bad, still be stuck with the year-end bills, if not this year, then next year. Makes no sense. You see that. I see that. Everyone sees that. This is a damned good corporation, fat little chicken, if you just got rid of the magazines. But that's your decision, not mine, Ridge, you say what you want to do and we'll back you up. You're risking more than we are, Ridge, jail possibly. Stockholder suit. What people will say. Stuff like that. You tell us, Ridge—how you going to pay those bills, hey? How you going to keep those magazines going? What are you going to tell this Silverman character, hey?"

The table was quiet. Berger was smoking his cigar and the blue-white curl of smoke made Warren conscious that the fire had overheated the room and it was now stuffy with several hours of cigarette-smoking; that the butts in the ashtrays were mounting and ashes were dusting the table about the trays in the little coronas of filth; that the yellow papers of Austin's doodling were piled in a little heap beside him, torn and torn again into scraps; and that everyone else had a little pile of torn paper beside him, too. Someone had wadded a paper water-cup into a messy ball which lay there, belonging to no one, in the center of the table. It was a dirty room now. Through the windows Warren could see the slow darkening of the sky, and the peculiar purple death of a December afternoon as it passed four o'clock. They were all waiting for him to reply to Morrissey.

"I take it, then," said Warren with all the deliberation he could muster, "that the Board has considered the fact that our circulation and audience is greater than ever in history; I take it our Board knows it requires another year of financing before that audience can be sold to advertisers at a rate which could make us the most profitable publishing property in town; I take it further the Board will not risk financing that year by mortgaging the plant, by spinning off either the radio or the book division. I take it, then, that the Board insists the magazines be liquidated immediately. If that's the way the Board feels then I can't pay Silverman, I can't meet the bank note, I can't do anything else but recommend—"

"No, Mr. Warren, don't say it, make them say it."

It was Hopkins, panting, turning to him, and Varian was also speaking. "Oh dear, oh dear, after all these years, it's so sad—"

But Hopkins was lifting his heavy bulk to his feet and waving his arms as he sought words. Nothing came from Hopkins for a moment but a series of grunts as if he were struggling for eloquence and nothing came but disjointed sentences.

"Every road has a turning," he began, then started again, "I mean, every cloud . . . what will we do in Anderbury . . . this is a living thing . . . you've got to see . . . it's try, try again, try, try again . . ."

Hopkins stood there, his mouth opening and closing, his face stunned and flushed. He held the sides of the table and again resumed, with a long empty sorrowful "Ah . . . ah" when Berger broke in. "For Christ's sake, pop, wake up," growled Berger, "this meeting's got a lot of work to do; we've got to plan the funeral today."

"Don't call him pop!" barked Warren, suddenly aware Hopkins was his to protect, but Morrissey broke in.

"Shut up, Berger," said Morrissey, as if shooing a dog back to its kennel. "I told you before to shut up, let me handle this now. Listen, everybody, there's work to be done in the next forty-eight hours, with Silverman breathing down our neck, the bank right behind him, the rest of the creditors right on their tail. We've agreed the magazines have to fold, but that doesn't take care of the creditors unless we work fast, so let's get on to it."

"We're agreed on our side of the table," said Fleming without consulting Varian. "Now what bills have we got, when do they fall due, what do we have on hand?"

"I've been making a list while we've been talking," said Morrissey, "and here's the way it looks to me—"

The fading light of day dissolved to dark. In the room, questions tumbled one on the other. No vote had been taken, no decision put to the table. But the decision had been made. Warren became aware that the smoke was thickening, the voices growing drier, tired. He observed the water in the pitchers descending, the figures swirling on the yellow sheets as the others calculated.

It must have been an hour later, after Warren had risen to empty the ashtrays into the wastepaper basket and turned to the wall panels to increase the ceiling light, that he saw them in the sudden illumination, yellow, pale and small. They were fumbling at the body of the magazines dying as they had fumbled at their purpose while they lived. They understood them as little in death as in life. He knew the magazines deserved cleaner interment than this.

"Gentlemen," he said from where he stood.

His voice was clearer, he recognized. He had not spoken for an hour, since they had made their decision. They were tired, they were groping as he had groped about the problem for weeks. But he knew where it began, he knew the logic both of the disaster and the solution. They looked at him as he stood there.

"Wipe out the magazines," he began, "and the details you're talking about become irrelevant. We can borrow money anywhere in town once the balance sheet is cleaned up, and we won't even need to borrow money to pay Silverman if it's cleaned up properly."

"How's that again?" asked Varian, confused. The others studied him suspiciously.

"What chokes the balance sheet," said Warren, "is the money we owe subscribers for magazines they've already ordered— Fourteen million dollars to eight million people who get them by mail. If we can convert that obligation into cash, then we'd have quick spending money to meet Silverman and a bankable balance sheet to boot—"

"Say that slow," said Morrissey suspiciously.

"All right—slowly," said Warren, correcting Morrissey's grammar maliciously, "slowly. We've spent two million dollars soliciting new subscribers by direct mail this year. That's the essence of what we possess —those names, and their listening. And I can sell them, I can sell that attention wholesale, even though I can't rent it yet to advertisers. Any magazine that wanted a new audience as large as ours would have to pay between ten and fifteen million dollars to get it by new solicitation. At a guess, I can raise two or three million in quick cash for those subscriber lists right now."

"Well, I'll be damned," said Morrissey, "there's the answer. We sell the subscribers to meet current bills. Clean up the balance sheet. That leaves us the plant and machinery to sell or mortgage. Then we're left with an operating profit in the other divisions and a tax-loss carryover that gives us three or four years on smooth, tax-free velvet."

Morrissey chuckled, Fleming's face lightened, Berger spoke.

"Now you're talking. That does it. But I've got a dirty mind, folks, let me put my two cents' worth in, too. The Pinkertons. We ought to call the Pinkertons in right away."

"The Pinkertons?" said Varian mildly. "That's the detective agency, isn't it? We don't need detectives in here. I'm absolutely sure of everyone's honesty. The Pepper family wouldn't like it if we called detectives in. What a scandal, oh, no, I'm sure that Mr. Fleming didn't mean any offense when he used the word fraud a while ago—"

"Naw," said Berger, "I don't mean that. But the chief and I have been through a couple of these liquidations before. You know how workers are—they'll steal you blind. You close down a factory, they steal tools, raw materials, paper, parts, anything they can lay their hands on. Figure it's theirs. If we announce we're closing, everybody in the joint will be taking home anything that isn't nailed down: typewriters, adding machines, paper, paperclips, books, whatever they use to make a magazine. When you call Pinkertons in, they throw a cordon around the place to keep the staff from swiping stuff. They could cart out maybe thirty, forty thousand dollars worth of stuff, if—"

"Berger," snapped Warren, still standing regarding them, "I'm the only man who gives orders around here until the Board fires me. There'll be no Pinkertons on these premises until I say so."

"Now, Ridge," said Morrissey, and his voice was as soothing and conciliatory as it had been at the beginning of the meeting, "just when we're all seeing eye to eye you lose your temper, jumping to conclusions. Nobody's talking about firing you. If you don't want Pinkertons, you don't have to have Pinkertons."

To Berger, Morrissey turned and said out of the corner of his mouth, "Dick, do me a favor, and for the rest of this meeting, shut up."

The meeting turned to look at him again and Warren realized that leadership now, in the adventure of liquidation, was back in his hands. Slowly, he walked back to the table and took his seat opposite Morrissey. He shuffled his papers together and was about to resume his analysis of procedure when Morrissey again interrupted.

"Somebody's knocking there, aren't they?" he said. "What do you say we all take a break for a minute?"

A welcome scuffle of chairs on the carpet told Warren the meeting had gone on too long. He rose to answer the knock. It was Laura, and she whispered, "They asked me to give you this." She was holding a bundle of envelopes in her hand, her body half-in, half-out of the tentatively opened door.

"Who asked you?" said Warren.

"Eliot and Mitchell—they're still out there, they've been out there for an hour, they want to see the Board. There's a copy of this letter for each one of them."

"Pass them around," said Warren and watched as she circulated among the Directors who had risen and were stretching and talking with each other. She wrinkled her nose when she came back to him at the door and he smiled at her.

"Stuffy in here?" he asked.

"It's terrible," she said, "it looks like fog, the smoke is so thick. I'll open a window."

"What's happening outside?"

"Nothing," she said, "except the phone. And that happens without end. I hang up and it rings back at me by itself. We're unevenly matched, that phone and I."

"Tell Eliot and Mitchell to stand by," said Warren. "I'll try to get them a hearing."

It was difficult calling them back to the table again. They had all read the letter that Laura had handed out and were discussing its meaning. Warren himself had read it twice before gathering its full message. It was signed, he noticed, not only by Mitchell, Eliot and Foley, but by names he could identify in Circulation, in Advertising, in Promotion. They must have been busy today. They were a Committee, so the typed signature above the letter said.

"Gentlemen," it opened.

"The staff of *Trumpet* and *Gentlewoman,* aware of the gravity of the problems the Board is now discussing, earnestly requests, before any decisions are made, that they be given an opportunity to be heard.

"Representatives of the staff are already negotiating with interested parties to explore the possibility of continuing publication of these magazines under new financial leadership. These negotiations require at least another two weeks for completion. The staff wishes to show its faith in the magazines by offering its own services for the next two weeks without salary until it can be learned whether the new financing will materialize or not.

"Further, the staff wishes to press on the Board their conviction that any decision to liquidate the magazines can be made only with due regard to the rights and equities of employees who have served these publications in some cases for forty or more years. If the Board believes suspension of the magazines inevitable, this committee insists on a negotiation of recompense to be paid all employees who are or may be affected by termination of employment.

"Two members of this committee, David Eliot and Ben Mitchell, are at present waiting to be heard and discuss these matters with the Board or designees of the Board.

"Sincerely yours"—and after that came the signatures.

The first voice after Warren had quieted the table again was Berger's.

"Crap," spat out Berger, holding the letter as if it were a loaded gun, " 'insist,' do they? Sound like a bunch of Communists to me."

"They are not!" responded Hopkins heatedly. "They've got rights. Never kick a man when he's down, that's what I say, we ought to give them a hearing. Every man should have his day in court."

"I suppose they are disturbed," said Varian slowly, "and I suppose we can't face them without telling them the truth and I don't know whether we want to make the announcement today or not. Two weeks without pay, they offer," he mused aloud. "What's that worth, Mr. Austin?"

"About ninety-six thousand dollars," said Austin, "for editorial and advertising salaries."

"And what would paper cost for two weeks' issues of the magazines while we waited?"

"If we put out two issues of Trumpet, cost of the paper less the revenues of the advertising in them—could cost us three hundred thousand dollars or more."

"Out of the question, then," said Fleming, as if that settled it. "Silverman won't wait for his money beyond Friday, I'm sure. I'm sure he wouldn't finance two weeks' paper for the magazines out of his own pocket and nobody can pay him in advance for it—"

"Oh, my," said Varian, "oh, my, no, he wouldn't."

"This phrase 'rights and equities,' " continued Fleming, "and their use of 'insist.' We have no contract with the white-collar employees, have we, Mr. Warren? As I remember matters, our only union contract is at the printing plant. What does that say?"

"The union at the plant has a severance-pay feature calling for two weeks' dismissal notice, and two weeks' pay for every year worked, up to two thousand dollars a head. It's going to cost close to eight hundred thousand dollars just to shut that plant down," said Hopkins, rather smugly, it seemed to Warren. "Of course, they're nice people, and if we went about it right and kept the place open they might even be willing to work two weeks without pay, just like the white-collar people. Cost you almost as much to close the plant down, as to keep it running."

"What?" snapped Morrissey. "Say, Warren, have you figured this union severance pay into the suspension proceedings?"

"Yes," said Warren, "we have a problem there and perhaps we ought to go on to talk about this letter right now—" Vaguely, Warren could remember at some time in the mists of the past weeks that he had told Eliot and Mitchell that somehow he would try to get them severance pay. Somehow, he remembered, he had made a promise. But it was best not to discuss the promise now with the Board. He had to have authority in his hands for these next three days and he would see. If there was enough money from the sale of circulation, if there was an easy deal on mortgaging the empty plant as real estate, if—the responsibilities he had thought were over, clashed again.

"Well," he heard Fleming putting down the staff letter, "it doesn't seem to me there's much to take up here. I'm not a hard-hearted man. But if we have no legal obligation to these people then we owe them nothing. We owe money to our creditors, and to this printing union legally which is bad enough . . . It's just too bad . . . I wonder if . . ."

There was a silence and the weariness about the table was now heavy. The powder on Berger's jaws had rubbed off and the black heavy stubble was definitely showing through. The two family lawyers had wilted. Only Austin, prim, neat and bespectacled, and Morrissey, his scarlet bow-tie still jaunty, seemed unchanged by the long toll of the conversation. It was Morrissey who spoke.

"Tell you what," he said, "it's almost six o'clock now. We aren't going to get much work done from now on in. What we ought to do is turn the whole thing over to a smaller committee, say, an Executive Committee of, say, three people, to get to work and see what can be settled between now and Friday, then come back and report. How's that?"

"No objection from our side," said Fleming, "so long as we're all clear.

We represent a property interest threatened by bankruptcy. The only way of avoiding it is by liquidating the magazines and meeting the creditors with what we salvage. I can get us some extension of time from the bank, I'm sure. If Mr. Warren can raise two or three million by selling the circulation, and Mr. Morrissey can explore what quick mortgage money can be raised on the plant and equipment, we can cover our pressing creditors. Who would you suggest for the committee, Mr. Morrissey?"

"Well," said Morrissey, "Ridge here ought to be chairman, because he's President and Chief Executive Officer, and knows more about this business than any of us"—a slight smile crossed his lips—"and since it's mainly a financial problem, then Austin, our Treasurer, ought to sit on it, and then one of us."

"Yes," said Fleming, "why don't you represent the other members of the Board, Mr. Morrissey? You seem to be clear on what has to be done."

"Got a lot of other things to do with my time," said Morrissey. "You sure you want me?"

"Yes," said Fleming. "Perhaps we ought to put the matter to a vote. Perhaps we might best summarize our intention to suspend publication in a formal resolution right now and give you authority to do so subject to our meeting again for confirmation of the terms on Friday?"

"No," said Warren. "We have to keep this under cover for the next forty-eight hours. I want to be able to tell everyone that we're still operating, at least until Friday; it makes my bargaining power on the circulation stronger. I want to be able to deny anything and everything to the press. Let's make that a resolution of the full Board empowering the new Executive Committee to take any measures necessary to deal with the crisis. We'll report back to you on Friday."

"How's that again?" asked Morrissey.

"The Board authorizes the Executive Committee of you, Austin and me to take any measures necessary to deal with this crisis between now and Friday, when we meet again."

"So move," said Morrissey.

"Seconded," croaked Berger.

"Motion?" said Warren. "All in favor?"

A ripple came back around the table bearing with it the mumbled yes . . . yes . . . O.K. . . . aye . . . yes. . . .

"Opposed?" asked Warren.

"I vote no," said Hopkins stoutly, "write it down that I vote no. The boy stood on the burning deck whence all but he had fled. That's my stand."

There was a pause, which Warren broke himself.

"Six ayes, one no," he reported. "The Executive Committee has the authority to take emergency action. We'll all meet again on Friday afternoon."

"What time?" said Fleming, beginning to zip up his briefcase.

"At four," said Warren. "I hope nobody leaves town in the next two days. We may need to call on any one of you."

"If there's anything we can do to help," said Varian, "please let us know."

"Well, fine," said Warren, "Mr. Morrissey and I and Austin will try to pick up as many pieces as we can ourselves. Walt," he continued, looking at Morrissey, "would you and Austin care to stay a few minutes so we can plan?"

"Yup," said Morrissey, "that figures. Want to talk to you, anyway."

"Good," said Warren, "but let's call in Eliot and Mitchell for a few minutes first and calm down the staff as much as we can."

"O.K.," said Morrissey, as the others began to rise and pack, "but let's make it snappy."

"Do you want me to stay with you for this staff hearing?" asked Austin.

"Nope," said Morrissey, before Warren could reply. "Ridge and I, we'll be able to handle them. Matter of fact, I want to talk over a few personal things with Ridge; maybe we don't need an Executive Committee meeting until tomorrow morning, anyway. Say about breakfast, eight thirty? O.K. with both of you?"

3. THE COMMITTEE—6:30 P.M.

It was Morrissey who handled Eliot and Mitchell. Warren could not help but be amazed as, when the two walked into the thick, smoke-filled Board Room, Morrissey worked up a smile of ease and charm that made him seem almost attractive. The apologies were thick on Morrissey's lips as they sat down.

". . . Why I've sat in that outer room waiting for a Board meeting to break up so many times, I almost feel what you're feeling. I just can't tell you how sorry we are, all of us, that this took so long and had you people so excited all day."

"Thanks," broke in Mitchell dryly. "Let's not waste any time on apologies, let's get down to business."

"All right," said Morrissey easily, "I understand exactly how you feel. We're at your disposal. Shoot."

"Good," said Mitchell coldly. "To put things straight—are we talking to you as individuals, or as members of the Board? Who are you?"

"Why, we're the Executive Committee," said Morrissey, "there's a new three-man Executive Committee to handle this emergency. Mr. Warren is chairman, and I'm a member, so that makes two out of three of us, a majority. We can do anything we want to, can't we, Ridge?"

"Yes," said Warren quietly.

Two out of three did make a majority. Was that why Morrissey had wanted Austin out of the way?

"Good," replied Mitchell. "And we represent the staff. Everybody. All the non-union people who work for the magazines, and we want—"

"Everybody?" said Morrissey. "You've got power of attorney to speak for them?"

"No," said Mitchell. "We don't need papers, we've known each other all our lives, we have a committee that has questions to ask."

Morrissey smiled, but the silk in his voice was thin.

"All right, let's not bother with credentials. That's for lawyers. Of course, if we did lock horns here you'd have to prove you really represent something before we could talk with you. But I gather from Ridge this is a friendly visit, isn't it?—so let's talk like friends. How can we help you fellows out?"

"Are you sinking the magazines or not?" demanded Mitchell, not yielding to Morrissey's friendship.

"Who, me?" said Morrissey innocently. "Well, look, I'll be frank with you fellows because I want you to trust me. I'll tell you frankly that we did discuss the subject this afternoon, and I'll tell you just as frankly, that absolutely nothing was decided. Isn't that right, Ridge?"

"Yes," said Warren through his teeth.

"And it's all up to Ridge here," continued Morrissey, "we're just trying to help Ridge. The Board will go up or down with the magazines, just the way Ridge wants us to, won't we, Ridge?"

Warren was silent.

"What *did* you decide then?" asked Mitchell, boring in as if he were badgering a reluctant public official at a press conference.

"A couple of things that are pretty confidential still," said Morrissey, blandly. "Both Ridge and I think there may still be a chance to raise some cash in the next few days to meet the creditors. Now, very confidentially, fellows, very, *very*, confidentially, I don't want a word of this to get out of here, we have some bills that are overdue for so long that—well, do you know what bankruptcy means?"

Morrissey's voice dropped to a dramatic whisper as he asked the question.

"Mr. Morrissey," said Eliot, his voice smooth, "how kind of you to tell us that. We appreciate it. We won't tell anybody, except, of course, people who already know that there was a petition in bankruptcy put on us last night. Ridge," he turned to Warren, "we had to organize this committee on a broad basis this morning as soon as the first news reached us from downtown. I felt you would let us off our vow of secrecy since the bad news was now public to any newspaperman who wanted to examine the court records."

"That's been cleaned up as of noon today, David," said Warren.

"Look," broke in Mitchell, "I want to know one thing, that's why I'm here—do we get taken care of or not? Not me, but the staff? You made us a promise, Warren, and I'm not going to let you run out on it. I'm too old to be bamboozled. Are we folding? Is your Board going to take care of the people if they do fold?"

"Now wait, Ben," said Eliot, turning to his partner.

"Wait nothing," said Mitchell, "if we wait, they'll slip one over on us at the weekend."

"Let's get the facts, Ben," said Eliot.

"The hell with the facts, I want the truth," said Mitchell, as Morrissey broke in.

"I'd like to stay here and listen to you, fellows," he said. "I always enjoy talking to people from the writing world. Some of my best friends are writers. But we're pretty tired and I have to be out of here in about ten minutes and I know Ridge is tired, so if we got to the point—I'm not hurrying you, but it's been a long day. Now, as I get the picture from your letter, you said something about new financing to us."

"Let's talk about severance pay first—" said Mitchell, his teeth locked in his fixation.

"Ben, please," said Eliot, the first trace of exasperation showing through his voice, "give me my five minutes first, and then you go with yours."

"Five minutes," said Mitchell sternly.

"Now, Mr. Morrissey," said Eliot, "you say you've made no decision in this crisis, which means that the Board is open to any new offer of financing?"

"Why, of course, young fellow, of course."

"All right, then—will you give us two weeks in which to raise the money it needs to separate the magazines from the firm?"

"Of course, we would, Mr. Eliot, of course, we would if we could. But I don't think you writers understand business if you don't mind my saying so—"

"Will four million dollars be enough?"

Morrissey smiled.

"Young fellow, if you could raise four million dollars in two weeks, you shouldn't be in your business, you should be in mine. As a matter of fact, I'm always looking for bright young men where I am—"

"Never mind that, Mr. Morrissey. All we're asking you to do is to stand by for two weeks while we go out and raise that money. We'll all work for nothing. I'm sure that the union people at the plant will work for nothing. Just don't cut off the pulse of the magazines without giving us a chance to bid on it—if you cut the pulse even for one issue, it's dead, it can't be revived—"

"I know," said Morrissey, soothingly, "and I keep telling you it's all up to Ridge, here, but let me answer you as maybe Ridge would, let me answer you as a businessman—where is the money you're talking about right now?"

"We have a man who'll be in New York tomorrow, a man named Paget, who wants two weeks more to come to a decision. I spoke to him only this morning; Mr. Warren knows who he is. . . ."

"Oh, yes," said Morrissey, "that Paget fellow that Warren was chasing these past two weeks. I know all about him. Fine fellow. He's got the money, all right. But is he serious?"

"Of course he's serious."

"You know, Mr. Eliot, ever since they invented money there's been only one way of testing whether a fellow is serious or not—and that's by how much he's willing to lay on the line."

"How much do you want?"

"Oh . . ." Morrissey reflected, "say two million dollars in a certified check by Friday noon, how's that? Now I think that would be serious, don't you?"

"But that's preposterous, Mr. Morrissey," said Eliot, "that's only thirty-six hours from now; that's ridiculous, that's so unreasonable as to—"

"Eliot, he's gulling you," broke in Mitchell.

"Mitch, for Christ's sake, I want to save these magazines," cried Eliot, "give me a chance."

"And they're gulling us; they don't want to sell; they want to liquidate; they want to draw us off-base before we get severance."

"Why, how can you say that?" said Morrissey to Mitchell, still easy. "Why, just think of how you would feel, responsible to the stockholders and the law with every creditor in town breathing down your neck, and having to face them all by Friday. Why, I'm more than willing to sell off these magazines, why, I'd be delighted, and I'm touched, I'm sure everybody on that Board was touched, by your offer to work two weeks without pay—but who's going to pay for paper? We buy our paper on a C.O.D. basis every single week. Will your Paget pay for the paper next Monday? In cash? Or the Monday after that? In cash? Hey?"

"Then the magazines are through, aren't they?" snapped Mitchell.

"Oh, I keep telling you," said Morrissey, "that that's up to old Ridge. Old Ridge has got some personal problems involved, too. He's the man responsible to the staff, to the Board, to the stockholders, to the creditors —to the law. It's only Ridge who can do this, not me, I'm just here to help."

"That's first-class poppycock," said Mitchell. "I ran a check on you, Morrissey, and you've gutted every corporation you've ever entered. You're going to loot this one and walk away from it just the way you did the rest."

"You ran a check on *me?*" said Morrissey.

"I certainly did," said Mitchell. "We know where every nickel you've got is invested, and if we can't get what we want for the staff out of you—"

"Look," said Morrissey, the equanimity he had maintained all afternoon evaporating in an instant, "don't get tough with me. I've got my business, you've got yours. Don't monkey with me or you'll lose a finger. As for your goddamn staff committee, we don't owe you a nickel. No contract. No terms of employment. Salaried men. No signatures. No legal standing—"

"Warren," said Mitchell, ignoring Morrissey, "are you still boss of this, or is he?" and he motioned with his thumb to Morrissey.

"I am," said Warren.

"We had your word two weeks ago that the staff would be taken care of. We went on that word until it's almost too late to organize anything. Are you going to keep your word or not?"

"I promised," said Warren, feeling the words stick in his throat, "that I would put the matter to the Board and urge—"

"Putting the matter to the Board isn't nearly good enough," broke in Mitchell. "You've got an Executive Committee of three men, you and this vulture and who else do we have to talk to?"

"Who are you calling a vulture, turkey-neck?" snapped Morrissey.

"You," said Mitchell.

"Ben, for Christ's sake," Eliot was placing his hand on Mitchell's elbow, "let's not get into a fight with them. All we're asking for, Mr. Morrissey, is a chance—"

"Chance, balls!" exploded Morrissey, red in the face. "You find us a certified check for two million dollars by Friday and we'll talk business. Otherwise this is kindergarten stuff. I haven't got time to waste on this— Warren, I'm going to wait for you in your office; you finish up with these birds and tell me how it comes out."

Morrissey walked to the door of the Board Room and turned, quivering.

"And listen, Warren, I'm goddamn tired. I haven't got all night. Wind this up with them in five minutes and come talk to me."

He did not wait for Warren to reply. He had snapped the whip. He expected to be obeyed.

"Ridge," said Eliot, when they were alone, "I spoke to Paget last night. He said he couldn't reach you, so he called me. He's still interested. Give us a chance."

"How fast can he act?" asked Warren in a flat, still voice.

"He can't act for another two weeks," replied Eliot. "He gets back to New York tomorrow. Then he needs five more days to make a final check and decide—"

"No time," said Warren mechanically.

"Warren," broke in Mitchell, "my question—are you going to go down the line to get our money from the Board?"

"I don't know," said Warren honestly.

"Warren," said Mitchell, "you've got to decide now. Are you with us or with him? We have to know."

"Give me a few hours. I've got to go in and get him out of the office. Where can I reach you both later this evening?"

"At the New Weston," said Mitchell. "I'm staying there while I'm in town. I'll eat dinner there. Have me paged. If I go out, I'll leave a message where you can reach me."

"We'll be together," said Eliot, "try to get back to us."

4. WARREN'S CHAMBER—7:00 P.M.

As Warren entered his own office, his subdued anger came to flood.

There, sitting behind his desk, his own desk, was Morrissey—a thin, mummified figure, frigidly silent. Morrissey made no move to stir as Warren entered. Morrissey stared as Warren approached the desk, then said, "Sit down."

Warren sat. It was uncomfortable being on the other side of his own desk. Morrissey sat and stared and finally Warren rose again, went to his cabinet, took out a bottle and said, "Let's have a drink. We need it."

He stood there with the bottle in his hand, two glasses ready, and turned to Morrissey.

"I don't drink any more," said Morrissey. Warren paused with the bottle in his hand, then poured his own anyway, and returned to the armchair opposite his desk, aware of Morrissey's measuring eye.

"Who was that guy?" demanded Morrissey.

"Which?" said Warren.

"The old one, the one who said he'd get me."

"Ben Mitchell—he was Pepper's favorite correspondent; you've seen his by-line in the magazine. Wrote the great exposés when *Trumpet* went in for that—"

"Oh, yuh—the Prohibition guy. I used to read his stuff when I used to read *Trumpet*. Long time ago. So that's him. Looks funny. Thought he was a big shot. All writers sound like big shots in print. Then when you meet them, they're nothing."

Warren did not comment, but sipped his drink, still uncomfortable on the wrong side of his own desk.

"Like generals," continued Morrissey acidly. "Once, during the war, our crowd got a contract for building a training camp. Went out there to see the general in charge. Played some golf with him, took a shower. Saw him in the shower, naked. He had a pot-belly, same as my own. Spindle legs. Didn't look like a general. Talked about the contract with him in the shower. I might have thought he was talking sense, but he was naked. Without the army, he was nothing. Could see he was a jerk. So's Mitchell. Could have rooked the army on that contract for a couple of hundred thousand. Didn't. Everybody thinks I'm a son-of-a-bitch. Like that Mitchell. Thinks I'm a son-of-a-bitch. You think so, too, don't you?"

Warren was silent.

"If he asked for it nicely, I might have given them something. He treats me like a son-of-a-bitch, I treat him the same way. You, too."

"That's the second time you said that, Walt," remarked Warren. "Do you want to fight now or later?"

"Not going to fight with you, Warren. Not if you're smart. Sometimes I doubt that. Took a Board meeting and a bankruptcy proceeding to get to talk to you. As if I smelled or something. What the hell were you trying to do? Thought you could pull this thing out all by yourself?"

"Let's cut the talk, Walt, and get to work. What do you want?"

". . . Going around town," continued Morrissey as if Warren had not spoken, "like a beggar with a tin cup. Meadows, Smith and Colt, Security National, Bronstein, Raven, Paget," the faintest flicker of a smile turned up the corners of Morrissey's lips. . . . "I followed you all around town. Every goddamn thing you did. I take it Bronstein didn't come through?"

"No," said Warren.

"Jack Raven gave you the works, I understand," said Morrissey, spinning it out, "wants that kid Henry of his on the Board. He's going soft about those kids. He ought to kick their pants off. That's what I'd do if I had kids. I never got married. Why in hell didn't you come to me? Thought I was a son-of-a-bitch, didn't you?"

"Walt," said Warren, "if I explained it to you, you wouldn't understand. You're safe, you're covered. You aren't losing a nickel. Your debentures will convert in a year or so to double or triple your money. That's what you wanted, that's what you'll get, and I don't owe you anything, no kisses, no explanation. Now what do you want?"

"A little understanding," said Morrissey, "just between you and me. It's not as simple as you think it is. Even if I handle Silverman, and even if I can talk Jack Raven into mortgaging the plant for some quick cash, we're going to be naked to the wind for the next few days. We've got to get rid of that circulation obligation and raise cash out of it before some joker decides to give us a quick shove into bankruptcy. I know my investment's safe, but I don't want to get my four million back with a piker's five per cent plus from a trustee in bankruptcy—I want this stock to triple my money. That's what we're in it for.

"Those others," continued Morrissey, unbending his rigid posture, leaning forward across the desk for the first time, "those lawyers on the Board, Ridge. Jerks. Both of them. That's why I decided to have an Executive Committee. Just three of us. And two out of three makes a decision. That's you and me. I want this thing in my hand for the next two days. I want you to understand that. Understand?"

"Morrissey," said Warren, "what if I told you to go to hell?"

Morrissey looked at him with a cold eye, then said contemptuously, "I changed my mind. Get me a drink."

Warren sat in the chair for a moment, wishing he could refuse, but knowing he could not challenge Morrissey on this level. He was still host in this room. He must not brawl out of injured pride. He rose, brought another glass, and poured Morrissey a drink. Then, unable to sit in the chair where he had placed so many subordinate executives over the year, he turned and walked to the corner window. He reached it, then turned and asked again, "What if I told you to go to hell?"

Morrissey slowly smiled, leaned back in the chair and swiveled it to the corner so that he had a clearer view of Warren sitting on the edge of the window. When he spoke, his voice had changed again, shifting to the charm-key.

"Ah, Ridge," he said in the tone that he had used to the Board, "that's not so easy, you know. I know what you think of me. But we're partners this week, we've got to go a little way further on this road together, hand-in-hand, like a pair of schoolboys in a jam. If somebody presses this bankruptcy thing on us hard, why, I stand to lose seven or eight million in that stock's prospects, and you stand to go to jail for touching the Social Security Funds. So there we are, partners. You can't tell me to go to hell today. But after this week, if you did—what would I do? After that some people would play it dirty. Say, take a look at your personal expense accounts, this barber you've got coming in here shaving you—pay him out of petty cash, don't you? This chauffeur and his car—office pays, doesn't it? Those illustrations in the magazine, some mighty expensive artists we've got illustrating our stuff—gets framed and the originals hang on your walls? This liquor you've been belting—office liquor, isn't it? Would a man like me think of dirty things like that?"

He smiled and folded his hands together as if he were thinking.

"Why, *of course* a man like me would think of things like that, but I wouldn't do it. You know why? It might make you look like a chiseler around town, but it would make me look cheap, too. So what would I do then if you told me to go to hell?"

Morrissey leaned back; Warren observed him; he could not help being amused by Morrissey's flickering moods.

"Why, I'll tell you what I'd do!" said Morrissey, slowly, coming erect in the chair. "I'd turn a couple of screws on you. Yes, that's what I'd do. Yes. For instance. You have options and warrants on fifty thousand shares, haven't you? And you can exercise them six months after the firm shows a profit, can't you? You can pick them up at ten. So if the stock went to twenty next year, you'd be in half a million dollars. If it went higher, you'd make more. That is, if you were still President and Chairman of the Board. If you were still with us when the stockholders get through meeting in April. Now, that's interesting, isn't it? If you told me to go to hell, why, I'd just have to handle those creditors all by myself and keep the thing out of bankruptcy and make sure that you got canned next spring. No half-million bucks, maybe more, for Ridge Warren. Yes, I guess that's what I'd do."

Morrissey smiled as if a warm and beautiful light had just been lit inside him.

"Good whiskey," he said, sipping slowly, "fine whiskey. Now, what do you say to that, Ridge?"

The thought of the money, of the comfort of money that might cushion him against the devouring city, that might free him for another try, had been so far below the threshold of Warren's thinking, that he could make no reply. All he wanted this week was to come out of it clean and proud. But here, in the foreground, at his own desk, sat Morrissey.

Morrissey was continuing. "Ridge," he said, "you just think about that, and then think about something else. You aren't a businessman, Ridge, you get your emotions involved in the balance sheets and that's what screwed you this time. But I like you, Ridge. Yes, I do. And I can use you. I'm getting interested in a lot of things that never interested me before and I can use somebody like you. Somebody I could trust and who understood me. This Dick Berger I've been carrying around the past five years, he's too rough for a situation like this. I don't think he makes a good impression for me, do you? I think you make a fine impression, Ridge, you look like an All-American boy. I guess that's my trouble, I look like a bastard, don't I?"

"Come to think of it, Walt," said Warren casually, "you do."

"So you see why I could use you. There's not only this half-million dollars you'd have if we saved the rest of the outfit from bankruptcy, but a lot of other very nice things that you could have if you and I had this little understanding and did business together. See?"

"I see," said Warren. "I don't know where you're going, Walt, but for the next forty-eight hours we have our necks under the same ax. I suggest we get rid of the ax first, then do some more talking."

"That's fine," said Morrissey. "The trouble with you is you're a loner. You want to do everything by yourself. Why, if you'd called me in earlier, you might even have saved the magazines, but you had to do it all by yourself. Now, we'll try working together for the next forty-eight hours. You and me. Two out of three makes decisions. And we'll see how it goes."

Then, swiftly, almost with a snap, Morrissey shifted tones.

"O.K., Warren. But one last thing. No monkey business in the next forty-eight hours. Don't try any tricks. Or I'll cut your heart out."

Nobody had ever spoken to Warren with a voice that cut so sharply. It had the crack of a lash, the feel of a slap.

Morrissey repeated the phrase.

"Or I'll cut your heart out and feed it to the birds. Don't pull any tricks."

"Like what?" asked Warren, not budging from his perch by the window.

"Like, for example," said Morrissey, "that guy out there, Mitchell, who said he was going to get me. And all the rest of them. If we come out of this O.K., I'm willing to pay off a couple of the old-timers, the sick ones, a few here or there when I feel like it. But I don't want your boy-scout heart bleeding my money away this week on any settlement that puts us in a corner. Get me? When I'm ready, if I'm ready, I talk to them, *me*. But right now we've got the printing union to pay off, Silverman to pay off, ink bills to pay off, and Christ knows what else. Don't play around with that staff. I mean it. Don't you make any commitment. Or I'll cut your heart out. Matter of fact, there isn't a god-damned thing you do in the next forty-eight hours that you don't clear with me first. I'm buying you. Do you get me, buster?"

Morrissey was making it clear. Warren could probably have the half a million with no greater effort than a nod; but he could not have the half a million and be free; he would have to wear Morrissey's dog-collar for a year, two years, or as long as it took to cash the options; and probably after. There was a decision here coming down very sharp and fine after the long afternoon of decisions. There were no magazines now he was responsible for; he was responsible for himself, and what else? There could be a decision one way, and he would have the money he had earned. But not be free. There could be a decision the other way. Only he needed time to find out what lay on the other side—and not in terms of weeks, or months. He needed time now in days, hours, minutes.

He rose from the window where he had been sitting.

"I get you, Walt," he said. "Now, listen, why don't you take that armchair where you'll be comfortable? You're sitting at my desk and I work best from behind that desk. We've got lots of work to do, so let's get started."

Expressionlessly, Morrissey rose from Warren's desk. Warren noticed that Morrissey poured himself another drink as he rose, then circled the desk to the armchair where Warren had sat before. Warren sat down at his own desk and was about to reach for the bottle, too—when he realized he did not need a drink. He felt strong again.

"Let's line up what we have to do," he said to Morrissey, pulling a scratch pad and pencil to him.

5. CONSPIRACY—8:30 P.M.

It was almost an hour later, hungry, that Warren said good-by to Morrissey.

Now he must work fast.

He dismissed Laura, who had stayed late, from the outer office. No one must be a party to this who did not have to know. He pulled his telephone close, to dial his own calls.

First, Schlafman, as in every emergency of the past month. He knew what Schlafman was going to say, and, thus knowing, was armed. Schlafman resisted. Represent the staff? Schlafman insisted he was a libel lawyer, an entertainment lawyer—not a labor lawyer. Schlafman insisted he could not harass two magazines whose fees he had been accepting as counsel in libel. There were ethics and loyalties involved, said Schlafman. Warren overbore him: the magazines would be dead by Monday, no longer clients; the corporation would be only a property. But the people who *made* the magazines needed him, that was where loyalty lay. He must consent.

Schlafman switched to another tack. This had nothing to do with loyalty to the magazines. He could not be loyal to Warren unless he warned him. Did Warren realize that what he was suggesting was a conspiracy against a corporation Warren was employed to defend? There were laws against conspiracies! What if someone found out? This was flirting with half-a-dozen laws, any one of which could make them both guilty.

Warren was surprised that he was laughing at Schlafman. After all the other gambles of the past month, this was so small a gamble. Finally, wearily, Schlafman—overborne—asked who the contact was with the staff people.

"A fellow called Mitchell," said Warren. "He'll be telephoning you in fifteen minutes. You think out the details for all of us of what it takes to get them severance pay while I brief him. When he calls, just tell him what his committee has to do. I won't be seeing you again until I meet you with them—as their lawyer."

"All right," said Schlafman, "you know that you're not only putting your neck in their noose. You're inviting me to open myself to disbarment. I'll do it. But, Ridge, keep your mouth shut. This isn't a matter of morals. This corporation doesn't owe that staff a thing, legally. So you're conspiring, it *is* conspiracy, to give away corporation money where it isn't necessary."

"Nat, thanks," said Warren. "I know it's serious. But I've paid for this already. I'm responsible."

Then, finally, Mitchell.

"Where are you, Ben?" he said when Mitchell answered after being paged.

"At the house phone, lobby of the New Weston," said Mitchell. "Eliot and I just finished dinner. Shall I go upstairs and call you back?"

"No," said Warren. "Don't waste time. Just listen."

"I'm listening."

"You've got work to do, starting now," said Warren, imagining the suspicious face of Mitchell on the other end of the phone, and liking it, and wishing they could be friends. "You're officially a labor leader from now on. I'm the responsible head of this corporation, until Friday afternoon, at least, and I'm negotiating with you."

"How's that again?" said Mitchell. "That's faster than I can swallow it."

"Don't argue," said Warren, feeling a marvelous release. "You have a lawyer now, or at least your committee has a lawyer. His name is Schlafman. Call him back on this number I'm going to give you in a minute, and he'll fill you in on detail. The guts of the matter is this: Schlafman says you need four or five hundred powers of attorney from all the people in the New York office, a majority of all the people who work in the home office here, empowering you and your committee to make a settlement of claims for them. You've got to get those signatures no later than Friday noon, because when the Board meets later in the afternoon, I probably can't make a binding settlement with you. I may be out. If you can get those signatures by tomorrow night, it's even better. Schlafman will explain everything. Just one thing—you mustn't say you've talked to me or even hint I know what you're doing. If people know I'm in this—that makes it conspiracy, and probably jail for me, and trouble for you, too."

"How's that again?" said Mitchell. "You mean we do this on our own?"

"No," said Warren, "I'm with you. But only you must know that—you and David. It's better if you denounce me. You ought to start mobilizing your people tonight, because, fundamentally, tomorrow's the last full day you'll have the whole family together to work with."

"Warren—are the magazines folding, then? Is that a fact, Ridge?"

"Yes, Ben—no time to cry now, we'll cry next week. We've both got work to do."

"How do we contact you tomorrow if there's an emergency, Ridge?"

Warren paused. He had not thought that far ahead. He had to be careful for everyone's sake—not only his own. For Schlafman's, who risked disbarment. For the committee's sake. If he had to trust someone? —Whom could he trust? Whom could he gamble on?

"Reach me at home," he said with instant knowledge. "I'll have my wife monitoring the phone there as liaison between us. I'll be out of the office most of the day tomorrow, but I'll check through home for messages from you."

"O.K.," said Mitchell, "what's your home number? What's this Schlafman number?"

Warren repeated the numbers, then heard Mitchell saying, "You say your wife—didn't know you were—"

"I'm not married, Ben—but she's my wife. You can trust her."

A pause, then Mitchell, with a tart and understanding turn, "Whatever you say. I've seen a lot in my time. Fasten your seat belt, Ridge —here we go."

17. Thursday

Schlafman yawned over the cup of black coffee. It was not because he was sleepy at this hour of the morning. But he was excited. He was summing up for them for the last time—

"Couple of things I want to repeat," he concluded. "First of all, my neck is in a noose. Every lawyer walks a tightrope of ethics. Off and on for the past eight years, General American Publishing has been calling me in to defend them against libel. I couldn't even sit at this table with you if I had a retainer from them, or acted for the corporation. But just the same, here I am preparing to let blood from their veins with one hand, after taking their money for eight years with the other. Do you realize what the Bar Association could say about that? I'm not going to take a nickel out of this case, one way or another. I want that understood. But if I lose the case, nobody will believe I handled it for free and I'll be tagged as a shyster. I can only prove I'm not a shyster if we win and *then* I don't take a nickel out of it. In this town, the prejudice is always against the loser—"

"We're going to win," said Mitchell flatly.

"Don't be so sure," said Schlafman, "there's not a line, a document, a paragraph of legislation that protects the unorganized white-collar worker in this town. If they wore overalls to work, or had dirt under their fingernails, I'd say they had a chance, with or without contract. But these are salaried people, middle class, full of dignity, without a word in writing between them and their employer. I'm not even sure you can get them to sign the power of attorney without every one of them in turn consulting a lawyer—"

"I have a deep feeling," said Eliot, "that you're going to be surprised. There's nothing more violent, or nasty, or rash than a solid middle-class citizen when someone tries to treat him like a man in overalls with dirt under his fingernails."

"All right, all right," said Schlafman, "I still think we're crazy. Let's review the whole thing once more."

"I have it clear now," said Mitchell, "in our trade we learn to get it clear the first time. I'll play it back to you: Number one, you want your name out of this until we have the signatures all set and you're sure our gun is loaded."

"Right. This whole thing is like a multi-stage rocket; I can't fire the last stage publicly until you've done all the rest"—Schlafman liked the way these men grasped the core of a problem quickly—"and I want five hundred signatures at least. You have nine hundred white-collar workers here in New York, another four hundred across the country. I want a majority of all your staff in New York."

"Good," said Eliot, and he picked up the specimen power of attorney.

" 'I, the undersigned,' " Eliot read aloud, "and you want their full legal names there, 'hereby do appoint, empower and designate David Eliot and Ben Mitchell, co-chairmen of the Staff Committee of the General American Publishing Corporation, our full and legally authorized representatives and attorneys to negotiate, arbitrate, adjust, settle and dispose of all my claims'—I wish you'd let me rewrite this into English, Nat—'for services rendered in the past and for current services and claims for settlement of discontinuance of employment and any other claims I may have against said corporation. In witness whereof, I hereby set my name' —and then they sign. Nat, do you lawyers ever realize how you muck up the English language?"

"Never mind the English," said Schlafman, "I don't try to write articles, don't you try to draw up a legal document. Just get that multigraphed, signed and witnessed by five hundred of your people and you've done your part of the job."

"When do you need them?" asked Mitchell.

"Let me have every batch of names you can round up at my office every hour starting with three o'clock. I have to make an appendix of every name involved in the agreement, and Warren wants to be able to act on it late tonight, or early tomorrow."

"Right," said Mitchell, "and you and Warren set the rendezvous. None of us contact Warren directly on this. We make contact with him through his wife, at home, and when we get together, you have the document with you."

"I will have," said Schlafman. "It'll be a Settlement Agreement providing for Entry of Judgment in event of default. Once they sign it, it becomes a debt of this corporation as solid as if you held a bond. Better than that. It's practically a check on them for roughly one million dollars."

"Right," said Mitchell, "two weeks' pay for every year they've worked here for nine hundred people."

"Right," said Schlafman, "but I want you to remember that it's up to Ridge to work out the timing of payment, and nothing goes if he can't sell the circulation names sometime this morning. He's dancing a ballet with the bankruptcy laws today, and if he can't raise cash out of the circulation, I won't let him sign this thing."

"Tell me, Schlafman," said Mitchell, "is his signature good enough? I wouldn't give a subway token for his chance of staying on in the corporation for another six months, or even six weeks, unless he pulls a miracle."

"What goes on in his mind right now," said Schlafman, "not even he knows. He just wants to see this thing signed for whatever reason his gut tells him. His signature is good if he can add one more to it. This new Executive Committee has complete authority to settle any matter connected with liquidation of the magazines. He and Austin make two out of three. Morrissey is the third. If Warren signed it alone as President, a lawyer might make a good case for the Board repudiating it. But if Austin signs it too, the odds are the courts would support us because the Executive Committee has full authority, freshly empowered to act in precisely this situation. Odds are even better that if we get both their signatures and they have the dough to meet the claim, nobody will consider pressing the matter to court. Last thing: Keep Warren's name out of it while you're signing them up."

"That's my chief area of concern," said Eliot reflectively, as he drained the last of his coffee and knew it was time to go into action. "A lot of people over at the shop still admire Warren, they know he's been fighting to keep the thing alive. A lot of people won't sign because they trust him, they don't want to stab him in the back. Why can't we say he knows about it?"

"Because you *can't*," said Schlafman, "any more than you can use my name. If the word leaks out that Warren is with you, or, worse, that this is his idea, the Board can be convened again this afternoon and withdraw his authority. They can do more than that. They can get together later and scream fraud and conspiracy—it is conspiracy right now, as a matter of fact, and they put people in jail for conspiracy. This has got to look as if Warren has been compelled. Say anything you want to your people —say that he looted the corporation, say that he stands to make half a million bucks for himself, say that he ran out on all of you. But don't let on he knows about this, or that he's with you."

They were quiet. It was twenty minutes past nine. Three blocks away the staff was trooping to its desks.

"We've got the rest of the committee waiting for us in the chartroom, Dave," said Mitchell. "They'll be there on time today. We ought to be moving."

Mitchell pulled himself back from the table and rose. His head bobbed and he said, "Come on."

Eliot rose more slowly, reluctantly. Then, as he came erect, a smile slowly flowered on his face and broke into a huge, anticipatory grin.

"Comrade!" said Eliot, swinging his arm in a wide flourish of salute, then clicking his heels. "We're off!"

"Comrade!" said Mitchell, rising and extending his hand. "To horse!"

2. HEADQUARTERS IN THE KITCHEN—11:00 A.M.

Organizing human beings, grouping them under leadership they trust and to whose call they will respond is difficult at best. But when it must be done in haste among people who have never before been organized, its results are entirely unpredictable—as unpredictable as a chain of firecrackers snapping off a main fuse stem.

By eleven o'clock in the morning, all up and down the seventeen floors which General American Publishing occupied, the firecrackers were sputtering. Eliot and Mitchell had established themselves in a base headquarters in the kitchen of *Gentlewoman's* cooking department immediately after they had dismissed their hastily organized inner committee at ten o'clock. Each committee member had carried away instructions to post a bulletin on his floor for a ten-thirty meeting, then to explain at the meeting what was happening, then to stand by until lunch for the distribution of the powers of attorney all must sign.

Some floors acted at once. Others lagged. Others whispered, and huddled in frightened little corner groups.

Eliot and Mitchell had expected trouble in the advertising department, for the space salesmen had appeared to them most volatile, perhaps the most difficult to sign up. But within twenty minutes of the ten-thirty kickoff, Mitchell had received a telephone call from Russell. Russell was bubbling with enthusiasm—he wanted only to suggest that they postpone the meeting of advertising salesmen until four in the afternoon. He had dismissed every salesman from the office early in the morning, said Russell; he had forbidden them to answer the phone, or make any calls until the situation clarified itself. He had told them to go out, get drunk, go to the movies, lose themselves, speak to nobody. When they came back to check in at four o'clock, he'd pull the meeting together himself—would that be O.K.? he asked.

It was, said Mitchell, and beamed.

An anonymous woman's voice, shaking with anger, came from the switchboard to Eliot. Listening, Eliot realized that in all his years at *Trumpet,* the courteous familiar voice of this switchboard operator had been part of the sound of home. Now it was furious—did his committee really think they could get away with it?

Get away with what? asked Eliot.

Get away with this whole plan to leave out the switchboard girls—they'd worked there as long as anybody, why hadn't they been asked to sign up? They had as much right to severance pay as anyone. Soothing the voice, apologizing for the oversight, talking rapidly, Eliot promised he would be down to the switchboard in person, as soon as the papers were ready to sign, that nobody, absolutely nobody, was going to be left out.

Did he know about poor Mary Maclean? continued the voice, suddenly growing sad. Eliot said, no, he didn't, why? And the voice went on to say that Mary, who'd been there on the switchboard for thirty-five years now, was in the hospital with a mastoid ear infection. Mary couldn't sign. Eliot assured her that Mary's name would be on the list and there would be a power of attorney the switchboard girls could rush to the hospital for Mary to sign, too.

The voice, happy and relieved now, asked whether there was anything they could do at the switchboard. Did the committee want them to tap Warren's telephone? Or the Board Room telephone? They could listen in, giggled the voice, to any call and tell the committee anything they wanted to know. Laughing, Eliot said, no, just to keep the lines to the kitchen headquarters always open and reserve two outside trunks at all times for the staff committee if the board jammed up with calls.

The circulation floor, where they expected no trouble at all, turned out to be the most difficult.

The phone rang peremptorily just after the switchboard spokesman had demanded representation on the committee. It was Al Corbett, Vice President of Circulation, on the telephone.

"Eliot," said the voice.

"Yes," said Eliot.

"Got you now," stabbed the voice, "I've been trying for fifteen minutes to find you or Ben Mitchell. What the hell is going on?"

"What do you mean, Al?" asked Eliot.

"What do you mean what do I mean? Do you know what's been going on down here? Why, Eliot, if I believed what they said, I'd—Eliot, do you know what that bunch of Communists said about you?"

"What, Al? What Communists?"

The telephone sputtered; then, "Don't keep saying 'what' to me when I say 'what' to you. They said *you* told them, it was you and Ben Mitchell started this rumor about the magazines folding. They said it was you and Mitchell who organized this union. Why, Eliot, do you know what these unions are like, do you know what they've been doing down here this morning—?"

"What, Al?" said Eliot.

"'What,' 'what,' don't keep saying 'what' to me. Nothing! They didn't get anywhere on my floor, I can tell you that. I broke it up. I'm going upstairs to Warren personally, this minute, just as soon as I find out who's at the bottom of it. And if you and Mitchell are, I don't care how important you think you are, nobody is going to organize my people into a union, I won't—"

Eliot put his hand over the sputtering telephone and said softly, to Mitchell, "Corbett. Circulation. He broke up our meeting on his floor. Says we're a bunch of Communists. Says we're trying to organize a union."

"Give me that phone," said Mitchell. "Let me give that old fool a few home truths."

"No," said Eliot to Mitchell, "let me handle him, you'll blow your top." Then, turning back to the telephone, he broke in on the flow of talk.

"Al," he said, "something must have gotten fouled up. I think there's simply a misunderstanding. Where are you now?"

"I'm right here in my office," said Corbett, "and there's no meeting going on here."

"I'll be right down, Al," said Eliot. "I'll be right down to talk to you."

As Eliot rose, explaining his mission to Mitchell, Mitchell rose, too. "O.K.," said Mitchell, "you handle Corbett and circulation. I'll go back to the editorial floor of *Trumpet*; we haven't heard a word out of them. Everybody else is having all the fun and if I'm organizing a union, I ought to get some fun out of it."

Corbett was puffing on his cigarette viciously as Eliot entered Cor-

bett's office on the thirty-first floor. He was talking before Eliot had comfortably adjusted himself in his chair, and Eliot gave him head and line,
realizing that the thought that his magazines might fold had probably
never entered Corbett's mind until he had heard it just now, from his
staff, on the floor.

"How long have you been with the firm, Al?" asked Eliot in the first
pause, quietly and thoughtfully.

"Thirty-five years," said Corbett, pulling something out of his pocket.
"Look, that's my twenty-five-year gold watch, got it ten years ago. Never
heard of a union in the place."

Eliot leaned across the table, took the watch and dangled it, by its
chain, in the air.

"Thirty-five years, thirty-five years, and younger than any of the rest of
us, too. What a beautiful job you've done, too, Al. People in the trade
are going to remember this year's circulation jump as long as they remember *Trumpet*. You aren't thinking of retirement, I know, but what
kind of retirement program has the firm got for senior executives?"

"I'm a long way from that, sonny," said Corbett, his tone now having
taken on some of the conversational calm of Eliot's. "There's no real
retirement program in the corporation. Every division takes care of its
own people in a different way. The trade books have one plan, the textbook division has another, the radio division is too young to have a plan
yet. The magazines take care of their own, too."

"I see," said Eliot. "But what happens if the magazines aren't around
to take care of their own any more?"

"Huh?" said Corbett, groping. "Huh? How's that now? Oh, they'll
work something out. I think so."

"You haven't got a contract with them, have you, Al?"

"Nobody has a contract, no executive has. I'm a Vice President. Never
needed one."

"So," said Eliot, continuing to dangle the watch, letting the silence
talk for him.

"My brother-in-law," continued Corbett, as if talking to himself,
"worked for those soap-company people up in Boston ten years ago, when
they decided to move their headquarters from Boston to New York. They
worked out a program of retirement and pay-off for anybody over fifty-
five who didn't want to transfer here with the headquarters. Big companies always do something like that."

"Now, that's very interesting, Al, very interesting. Is your brother-in-
law around?"

"Yuh, he lives in Malden now, why?"

"Al, I wonder if you could call him up and find out what kind of settlement they made for the executives at his shop."

"I suppose I could," said Corbett, meditatively. "Why?"

"It would help a lot if you would, Al," said Eliot. "This pay we're trying to work out for the staff is fairly simple, and there'll be a lot of union pressure from the outside behind the staff. But nobody ever thinks of executives. They're people, too. I think we ought to draw up a separate plan to present to the Board for the executive group. If we could get an idea of what some other big firm did for their executives we might be able to shame our Board into it—particularly if they'd already paid off the rest of the staff."

Eliot now lifted his feet up onto Corbett's desk and wriggled them once or twice, still dangling the watch, letting the sun glint on it through the window.

"It seems to me that this firm owes something more than a gold watch to a man who's given his life to it. Let's see, you said you've put in thirty-five years. Times two. Makes seventy weeks' pay that would be coming to you with any sort of decent settlement. I wonder—could you—uh—would you telephone a bit around town and find out what the procedure has been elsewhere? Then the committee could try to do something about it. Damnit, I wish we had a contract covering people like you."

He handed the watch back to Corbett, and watched Corbett pocket it.

"Not a hell of a lot to carry away with you from thirty-five years' work is right," said Corbett, as the watch slid into his vest pocket. He thought for a moment, then, "O.K., Dave—I'll do my best to find out what they do other places around town and let you know in the morning. You really think they're going to fold the magazines then?"

"I'm afraid so, Al," said Eliot, removing his feet from the desk. He rose and, departing, turned. "You don't mind if I explain to the rest of the people out there on your floor just what they have to do to get theirs, if we can get it at all, do you, Al?"

"Well, shut my door behind you, if you've got to do it. I don't want to know about it. And try not to make it too long, will you?"

"Sure thing, Al," said Eliot, and walked out of Corbett's office.

As he looked down the row of desks, of men in shirtsleeves posting figures, of girls typing, of the junior executives in their jackets studiously bent over their papers, it struck Eliot it was like a large schoolroom in which the teacher had just scolded the class for being noisy and now, in fear, everyone was doubly silent and intent on giving the appearance of work. I might as well pull this one myself, thought Eliot, and see how one of these meetings works. He walked down the row of desks until he was at the far end of the hall.

"Do you mind," he asked a shirtsleeved man posting figures, "if I stand up on your desk?"

"Huh?" said the man, but Eliot was already climbing on the desk.

Eliot cleared his throat, then in a large, loud, clear voice which surprised him by its own strength, he heard himself saying to the entire floor. "Hey, listen, everyone . . ."

He saw the heads lift from their work, and turn to him, the sound of chairs scuffing the floor as they scraped back from the desks, the murmuring of surprise, and he said again, calling, ringing, "Hey, everyone—listen!"

3. THE EDITORIAL FLOOR—11:30 A.M.

The rumble slowly sank in. Foley lifted his head and listened. It carried the far-off gurgle of excitement which had been the music of his life in the days when he used to cover sports.

What was happening? Slowly Foley gave himself to the sound. It was here, on this floor.

Why does everything always break on Thursday? thought Foley. Tomorrow was the day all stories had to close and feed over the wires into the plant at Anderbury. For twelve years, Foley had been hammering at them to goof off, if they had to, on Monday or Tuesday or Wednesday —but on Thursday and Friday, story copy had to feed over his desk on time. For seven years he had been trying to get home early on Thursdays; and for seven years, Thursday after Thursday, he had been there until midnight initialing late copy to feed into the tape.

Here it was Thursday, and they were goofing off. And he wanted this issue to be good. If it was going to be the last it *had* to be good.

He poked his head out of his office, around the corner to his secretary's desk, and began, "What's going on out there—?" and stopped.

Sally, too, was gone from her desk.

He marched down the row of cubicles. All the desks were empty, and as he stalked by them, he felt himself growing angrier. He didn't mind the committee organizing on his floor, but they had promised they would do it at lunch. There was a magazine to get out today. He turned the corner, passed the proofroom, and noticed Schulte, one of the proof-readers, alone in the deserted proofroom.

"What's happened to everybody?" he asked of Schulte, the only person in sight.

"They're organizing a union," came the thin reply; then, with a sniff, "I don't believe in unions. Do you, Mr. Foley? I think they're bad for the country, all these union leaders with their Cadillacs—"

But Foley had passed him, trailing the sound.

They were in the library. As he looked through the glass doors, he could see them clumped and close-packed, on chairs, on desks, some squatting on the floor, some with jackets on, some in shirtsleeves. Together, working as a team in harness, they could make the wonder of a magazine. Here, they seemed like a mob listening to a stranger on a chair in the corner. But the stranger talking from the chair was Clement, the Public Affairs Editor, and Clement was waving his arms, pointing, summoning, orating. Every now and then would come that rumble of mixed approval and anger that had disturbed Foley at work.

"You tell them, Jack," someone yelled to Clement as Foley entered, "every one of us is with you."

"Sign up! Sign up!" came another voice and then a chant, "Sign up, sign up, sign up, signup, signup, signup—"

Foley observed that Mitchell was a few feet from him and pushed through to him.

"Mitch," he said, "what's going on here?"

"We're organizing them," said Mitchell, a pink glow on his gnome's face, his eyes twinkling. "I never knew these unions had so much fun."

"But we have to get this magazine out," said Foley. "You promised me you'd call the meeting at lunchtime."

"There's no time to do it at lunch, Tom," said Mitchell. "At lunch we've got to organize all the other floors, too, and start processing signatures."

"I'm all for the committee, Mitch, but you said lunchtime, you made a deal with me." He grabbed Mitchell by the arm, and shook it, because Mitchell didn't understand—

"Mitch," Foley whispered angrily, "it's Thursday, I have to get this magazine out!"

"There won't be any magazine to get out," said Mitchell harshly.

"I would have heard," said Foley, "I would have heard, I tell you! Warren would have *told* me if they'd already made a decision. I've got to get the magazine out."

Clement's voice rose above their conversation.

"So we have to know, right now, exactly where everyone stands. Mancuso," Clement said, "you run the ditto machine, run off a couple of hundred copies, oh, run off a thousand blanks, will you, and make sure that everyone gets one? We want to know your name, your address, your salary, how many years you've worked here, your Social Security number. Nobody leaves for lunch until he takes one of the blanks with him. Then bring it back and give it to the floor chairman to check. I guess that's the next thing; while Mancuso dittos the blanks, we ought to elect a floor chairman. Hey, does anybody know how a union does these things? Hey, Mancuso, you get to work now on that ditto—"

"No!" It was his own voice! Foley was surprised at the hoarseness of the protest. "You leave that ditto machine alone, Mancuso!"

The audience parted, and turned to look at him. He looked at them all, ink on their fingers, typewriter stains all over them, close-packed. Why, he had hired half of them himself.

"Goddamnit!" Foley yelled. "Do you people know what day it is? It's Thursday!"

They looked at him in silence.

"It's Thursday," he stormed. "We've got a magazine to get out! This magazine closes tomorrow. What do you think you're doing here?"

Clement, still standing on the chair, looked at Foley and Foley noted the puzzlement in Clement's face.

"Tom," said Clement, "this is the meeting we told you about. We had to move it up, because we had to move fast—"

"No, you don't," yelled Foley, "not on working time, you don't. We have six stories to close by tomorrow night! None of the features are even written yet! Where's the art? Where are my layouts?"

"But, Tom—" began Clement again.

"I don't want to hear a word from any of you," yelled Foley. "I'm getting the magazine out on time this week if it's the last thing I ever do. You'll all be back at your desks in the next ten minutes or I'll fire the last one to leave this room—"

A girl's voice giggled, and said, "Everybody wants to fire us, but he wants to be first."

Another girl giggled, and a loud voice came to his ears, "He's crazy."

"Who said that?" snapped Foley, and then came the bleat of two lips compressed in the thridding sound of the raspberry, followed by a laugh.

"Mancuso," said Clement, ignoring Foley, "get out of here and start turning the ditto machine. I want a thousand copies of—"

"Mancuso," yelled Foley, "you can run that machine at lunchtime. If you turn a crank on it now, so help me God, I'll fire you out of hand."

"Get going, Mancuso," said Clement from the chair and everybody watched.

"What do I do?" said Mancuso from his corner. "Mr. Mitchell, you're one of the chairmen of this thing, tell me what I do?"

"Do what Mr. Clement told you to do," said Mitchell. "I'll talk to Mr. Foley."

As the crowd turned back to face Clement again, Foley could only see their backs. He had hired them. They were his people. He had taken care of them. He had hired Mancuso as an office boy. And now Mancuso was wriggling through the crowd away from him. Foley could feel Mitchell's hand on his sleeve now, and Mitchell was saying, "Tom, let me explain to you why we have to do this now—"

"You don't *have* to do it now, I tell you, I got to get this magazine out, don't you understand? The wire to the plant is open now and we won't have anything to feed into it in another couple of hours. I've got to get this magazine out—"

"Tom, let me talk to you—"

"Get your hand off my sleeve, you dirty, double-crossing bastard," said Foley and stalked back to his office.

4. LUNCH HOUR IN THE PROOFROOM—12:30 P.M.

"Yes," said Schulte, the proofreader, over the phone, "yes, who is it?"

Normally, Schulte did not answer the phone because it made him nervous. In nineteen years of work here, Schulte had answered the phone perhaps a dozen times, and usually it had been bad news—one of the kids was sick, or Clara's mother was sick, or something. Someone else always answered. Today, munching his luncheon apple, Schulte was alone when the phone rang.

Normally, all three proofreaders—Schulte, Camp, Lipsky—ate their lunches in the office. Theirs was a large sunny room, which they had defended against every office change of space for ten years. They had to have a sunny room to read close proof, they insisted, and their office was their triumph. Over the years, they had had a good time there. It was funny, Schulte often reflected, how well you got to know people if you ate with them every day. The three brought their lunches in brown paper bags and one of the office boys would fetch them milk or coffee and they talked. For Schulte, the luncheon break was the best part of the day. So that now he was very annoyed with the others because today the other two had decided to go out for lunch with everybody else. If it was true what they said about folding—then it might be one of the last times they could ever lunch together.

Schulte knew that if anything happened he would never see Camp again; Camp lived in New Jersey while Schulte himself lived in Long Island. Maybe he would see Lipsky again sometime, because Lipsky lived in Brooklyn. Yet he knew he would not see Lipsky either. They did not visit each other's homes—and besides, who could find a way through Brooklyn? No, if the magazines were going to fold like everyone was saying, then the proofroom people should stick together the way they always had, and have their last lunch together.

Thus, depressed, nervous and betrayed, Schulte was munching his luncheon apple, observing the sacrament ignored, when the phone rang and he answered it.

"Is this the proofroom?" asked the girl.

"Yes. This is Schulte. Who is it?"

"There's somebody on the telephone who wants to speak to anybody in the proofroom."

"What's he want to know? Who is he?" asked Schulte, flustered.

"I'll put him on," said the girl and clicked off before Schulte could duck the call. Another voice, male and brusque, was on the line.

"Hello," he said, "who is this?"

"This is Schulte. Proofroom."

"Oh, yes. Say, my name is Anderson. Anderson. I'm chief of proof at Lion Lithograph and Publishing. Uh . . . say . . . we don't want to seem like grave-robbers over here . . . but . . . look, the talk is all over town that you may have a couple of proofreaders out of work in your shop next week . . ."

"Yes,"—cautiously.

"Well, we don't want to take any of your men away from you, we don't believe in robbing a payroll, but if anything goes wrong over there, we could use an experienced proofroom man. We all feel we should help out if anything happens to you people and one of your men might be interested in a new job over here. You get my point, we're not trying to steal people, but if anybody is job-hunting next week, we can use a man."

"Oh," said Schulte, blankly.

"Say, are you in charge at your shop?"

"Yes," said Schulte, quivering. There was nobody else in the proof-room now. Of course he was in charge. Camp made the most money—Camp made ninety dollars a week to the others eighty-seven fifty each; but Camp wasn't officially in charge. No, he, Schulte, who sat here all by himself, was as much in charge as anybody else.

"Yes," he said, "you said your name was Anderson. What did you say the firm was?"

"I'm Anderson. F. C. Anderson of Lion Lithograph and Publishing, Proofroom Chief. If you'd put the notice on your bulletin board, it might help some poor bugger out if worst came to worst."

"That's very nice of you, Mr. Anderson. What kind of man do you want?"

"Oh, just anybody. Family man. We like settled family men over here but we'll take anybody who has a good record, shows up sober five days a week, seven hours a day. We're an open shop, but we pay union scale."

"What's that, Mr. Anderson?"

"One hundred five a week for anybody with five years' journeyman experience. Cost of living raises after that. One hundred ten a week if the man turns out to be the kind of person we like. Three weeks' vacation. Sick benefits."

Stunned, Schulte held on to the phone.

"You say—you say, anybody with five years' experience, Mr. Anderson, one hundred five a week?"

"Yup," said Anderson. "We have nice working conditions. Well, if you post that on your bulletin board, or pass the word, just say to call me at my extension any time this week or next."

Schulte hung up the telephone.

One hundred five dollars a week! Seventeen-fifty more then he'd been getting here! And just anybody would do. Why . . .

See, he told himself, see, it pays to eat lunch in the office; a new job, right there. Walk out of here tomorrow night if anything happens, call this Anderson Monday, and tell Clara, bang, Honey, I got a raise.

But what if it didn't fold? What if the magazines stayed in business? He ought to quit and go right over to this Lion company anyway. It was worth it for a seventeen-fifty jump a week. But he hated to leave here. He'd miss the boys. But he ought to take it anyway, whether the maga-zines stayed alive or not. Wait till the others heard about it, they'd agree he should take it—they'd—

What would they say?

Should he tell them? This Anderson hadn't said to tell them. He said post it on the bulletin board. Anderson hadn't cared which one, he wanted anybody. Why should he tell them? There was only one job there. First he'd take the job himself, then he'd see if there was room over there for the other two.

Yes.

No.

How could he not tell them? He ought to tell them as soon as they came back from lunch, then they could all talk it over and decide who should take the job. They'd flip a coin. No, three of them couldn't flip a coin, they'd draw straws. No. It was his job. He had answered the telephone. Flip a coin.

O.K., he said to himself, all alone in the room, the apple still unfinished, O.K.! So I'll tell them. Clara will say I was crazy. She'd be right.

He reached in his pocket and drew out a shiny quarter. Heads I tell them, tails I don't. That's fair.

He spun the quarter in the air, slapped it down on the desk and slowly, half-afraid to look, he peeked at it.

Tails!

With a sigh, Schulte put the quarter back in his pocket—that had been fair. He had won the job with a fair toss, no cheating.

But he could feel his fingers sneaking back into his pocket, fingering the quarter again. This was crazy, it was him or them. And he had won the first toss.

Again the quarter spun through the air, again it slapped on the table.

Tails!

See. That was the way it was meant to be. It was his job. Twice now he had won it, both times fair and square. Slowly, reluctantly, Schulte picked up the quarter and pocketed it again. Poor Camp, poor Lipsky. That kid of Lipsky's he was always talking about, that little store Lipsky's boy had opened; if only Lipsky could help for a couple more years it would be all right. And Camp. Well, Camp was all right, always talking about how much he could sell his house for. But Camp's wife, every nickel that came in, she spent. Schulte was glad he was married to Clara. But poor Camp—you had to know Camp very well to know what a nice guy he was.

The quarter was in his hand again, and his fingers were sweating on it. He had already won the job twice, fair toss both times, he didn't have to toss it again. But it was spinning.

Heads!

He stared at the coin in horror. Heads. Heads he had to tell them!

Heads gave them all three a chance to draw straws! Heads. Now he had to tell them. No other way.

Irritated and annoyed, Schulte picked up his apple and resumed munching. This could be the next to the last day they'd all be together. They might never see each other again. And Camp and Lipsky had wanted to go out, and eat outside the office today with the rest of the crowd. Just for that, just for that he'd wait to tell them. He wouldn't tell them until late in the afternoon. He wouldn't tell them until just before quitting time. That's what he'd do. Let them wait.

18. Thursday Mid-day: Warren Makes a Sale

Warren joined Morrissey and Austin at early breakfast Thursday morning, and together they worked out emergency operating plans.

Morrissey would move uptown this morning from his own office and operate from the Board Room on the Executive Floor. The corporate counsel, Meade & Crane, would send one of their staff lawyers to join him there. Morrissey and the lawyer would handle all outside creditors, while Morrissey would, additionally, try to button down Jack Raven for quick mortgage money, if necessary. Austin would serve both Morrissey and Warren as chief of staff. Warren's mission would be the critical one —to clear the balance sheet by liquidating obligations to subscribers, selling their names for quick cash.

As they broke up, and Morrissey promised to be at the offices before noon, Warren knew he must act quickly and be out before Morrissey with his cold eye would arrive and suspect. Once the committee brought the floors to a boil, he would have to take an attitude. And he could not show his hand until he had sold the circulation. He must then, he noted mentally, be out of the offices by noon, himself, to operate from the apartment. Mary had agreed to be there as liaison with everyone else. There could be no waste motion.

It was a pleasure, almost, as he returned from the breakfast conference to the desk, to hear the constant ringing of the telephone in his outer office, which his new decision had freed him from answering. This morning he had his own calls to streak out; all incoming calls must wait. This morning the city must dance to his tune, not he to theirs, if the narrow passage was to be safely threaded. The calls he had to make were few, for there were few men in all the country who could see as a property, or use, the millions and millions of names of his subscribers—who could balance the liability of providing them with magazines against their invisible value as a meshing of names, addresses, and appetites that was commercially profitable. So he began.

Each time Warren spoke to the men who captained those publishing enterprises which until today had been peers or rivals, he prefaced his remarks with an earnest, short statement that what he was about to say to them was a matter of absolute personal confidence.

With each preface, he could sense their hungry ear at the other end of the telephone, waiting for the news they knew was coming; each time they promised him absolute secrecy. Yet each conversation, he knew, was a nail in the coffin of his magazines, for the announcement that he had to make to precede his offer of quick sale of circulation was the announcement of suspension. The sympathy that came with each reaction was spontaneous and unfeigned. But for all the sympathy, two things were sure.

The first was that his own voice made death a fact beyond any miracle of last-minute rescue. Even if a wand-waver bearing five million dollars should stride into his office as he spoke, the fact that he had spoken made a miracle too late. Each man who heard his statement would use it later, if necessary, to choke a last-minute miracle. In death, the magazines were objects of sympathy, a tradition ended. Revived and alive they were dangerous rivals. Thus, even those most sympathetic to him at this moment would have to use the fact that he had announced death to protect themselves, to make sure that death was irrevocable, and the magazines forever useless as an enterprise. They were down. They must be killed.

And of the other thing, he was more sure: that, despite their promises of secrecy, the men he was calling would talk. He could imagine each one, after the telephone had been hung up, thinking: There, but for the grace of God, go I. They would think this for a moment, and then, in the next few minutes or the next hour, or at the next visit from their trusty—the personal vice president, the assistant, or that individual with whom, in every organization, the chief chooses to share his emotion as well as information—they would say, "Do you know what just happened?"

And the trusty would say, "What?"

And the chief would tell the trusty of his telephone conversation. And the trusty would tell his trusty. And a secretary would hear. And others would hear. By lunch, a dozen people would know he had made these calls. By tomorrow a dozen magazines, large and small, would speed their salesmen up and down Madison Avenue to compete for the advertising contracts which he held, to snatch away as much of the booty of the dying magazines as they could. By cocktail time, a hundred people would know. By dinner time, how many more? The death of such magazines was too important a bit of gossip to keep to one's self. It was important to others to use, to show they, too, knew what was happening on the inside. A secret was something to be used. The only ones who, Warren felt, would keep the secret were the people at *Spectacle*. They would keep the secret because by the end of the morning, they were the ones he had managed to involve.

He had expected the others to say no. There were so few organizations who could suddenly buy, absorb, and then service so many new names. One of Warren's rivals offered, in all kindness, to take a million names off his hands for nothing and try to share the other names out among lesser magazines. But no one offered cash, except *Spectacle*. *Spectacle* had been preparing for this day. *Spectacle* had been waiting for his call and without surprise or bitterness Warren accepted their invitation to talk it over. He had balked only once.

"No," he said to Norris, their publisher. "Not at your office."

"I understand," said Norris, sympathetically. "Why don't I come over to you?"

"No," said Warren, "let's make it a hotel. Neutral ground."

While they munched their sandwiches in the hotel room, Warren watched.

They were all in shirtsleeves—he, Norris, Norris' men, all except Austin. Warren did not mind that he and Austin were outnumbered. So long as they stayed with figures, Austin could hold his own against legion. The one figure that Warren cared about—the price of sale—would not arise until the end of the long examination and so, with half attention, he let them pull apart and analyze the audience and circulation of *Trumpet* while he thought of other things.

These men would prepare the ground on which Norris and he, in a short while, would make decision. Meanwhile they were absorbed in their passionate love affair with the numbers. The digits in the long columns on the long sheets they manipulated had life for these men. A circulation column of figures marked "Expires" had one message, another column marked "Agent-Acquired" had another, a column marked "D-M" yet another meaning, and all they were were abstractions—yet the abstractions could be translated in millions of dollars. Munching his tasteless sandwich, quaffing a glass of milk, Warren knew they were more than numbers and that, somehow, it was thinking of them only as numbers that had brought him here to surrender.

Somewhere out in Anderbury, he knew, in the annex to the plant, these numbers became names on little bronze address plates stacked in endless trays. From the address plates, the names were transferred to ribbons of perforated pink paper, ten thousand names to a spool, sorted by cities, districts, counties, post offices. Then the spools were fed into a machine so that each magazine in the cascade proceeding down the long canvas belt from the stitching lines received an individual sticker from the spool in a single electronic impulse—and then moved on, tumbling over the end of the belt like a waterfall to be bundled, sacked, speeded to the ultimate recipient—a real person.

This was what he was selling, he knew—the name-stickers of the spool. Somewhere, Warren mused, maybe there is a boy living on a ranch in Wyoming who goes to his R.F.D. mailbox half a mile from the house every Friday to pick up the latest issue of *Trumpet*. The boy likes to read about rockets and space and *Trumpet* has been stirring the deep of his imagination for a year with stories of space and rockets; and the boy will now get three more issues of *Trumpet* out of the issues already printed and in shipment—and then, no more. Will there be a gap in his life? Will he become a scientist of space when he grows up? Will *Trumpet* receive credit for having first called to his imagination?

Perhaps in some apartment house in San Francisco an old lady would soon open the door of her apartment, look through the mail and call the elevator man to ask, "What happened to my *Trumpet* this week?" He would tell her there was no more *Trumpet*. If she had seen *Trumpet* in her home since she was a little girl, if she could still remember the earthquake pictures in *Trumpet*, then a link would be snapped, she would be cut off from part of her past.

Of the millions of homes he was now selling, how many would realize *Trumpet* had stopped? Of these, how many would care?

It was after the room service had cleared the littered luncheon tables that Austin and the technicians of *Spectacle* fell silent—their minds had computed and recomputed the figures on the columns, had listened and identified every overtone and subtlety in the digits that to them substituted for people.

Warren saw Norris stretch his arms wide and yawn nervously and he knew that now it was between him and Norris to set the price. Norris seemed emotionless, his hair dark blond, his skin tanned by a recent tropical trip, his eye unclouded. But the yawn betrayed his excitement. Warren knew that he and Norris had been stalking each other like cannibals in the jungles of New York for two years and that today's consummation of the rivalry would put *Spectacle* on top. The numbers Norris could add overnight to his circulation from the columns of these sheets would give him the biggest talking horn in America.

"I think we're pretty generally agreed on the bookkeeping totals here," said Norris, "so we have to start guessing now. Your guess and mine as to what these figures say, and that sets the deal. One thing worries me, Warren—"

"What's that?" asked Warren. He knew now they were about to talk price and his stomach tightened with the old panic as he realized he must have solid money when he left this room to be free to act as he wanted.

"We're taking on a liability here, three or four million names we have to service. I'm buying a switch in reader loyalty. If I buy these names and get normal expires, normal renewals, I'm all right. I'll almost balance out the cost of carrying them by what I save in my own direct-mail costs. And by what I can get by jacking up my advertising rates, if I can do it fast enough to meet the extra paper cost. But if your subscribers insist they want their money back, and they have the right to do it—then I've been had. How many subscribers will want their money back? That's it— that's the gamble. Just how much did those people get out of *Trumpet?*"

Warren arranged the pencils on the table before him very slowly, for he wanted to make the sale and yet make it with dignity.

"There's no way of guaranteeing anything, Norris," said Warren, "but one magazine's very much like another—"

He looked up and saw Norris gazing at him, weighing what he was saying. But he must keep on walking the tightrope, balancing between dignity and need.

"You've got a real point there—or rather, it would have been a real point in another year, Norris, there might have been a core loyalty there too strong to switch," continued Warren, "but now—it's pretty clean. We spent this year engineering them into the tent. Only we didn't have a real show to put on, nothing to say that you aren't saying, or the other magazines aren't saying. What we have is a circulation picture full of mobiles, full of switchers, willing to listen to anything. I was getting around to changing it, but that was for next year. Right now, *Trumpet* has no identity you have to worry about seriously in this deal."

Warren knew that he was repeating what the salesmen of *Spectacle* had been saying up and down the encampments of advertisers for over a year, what Norris had been preaching as their combat call for months.

"I don't know," said Norris, musing, "you were beginning to worry us.

Some of those issues lately were too damned good. I can say it to you now, but a lot of our advertisers were getting difficult because of you, a lot of talk about the new identity you were giving the magazines. And that newsstand rush of yours this fall. You were getting a bounceback there . . . I don't know."

Warren ached to have Norris go on, to hear the bitter grudging praise even at this last moment. But too much depended on the sale.

"It's all done with tricks," Warren said, choking on the words. "Your people know the tricks as well as we do. Let's talk big picture. You're guaranteeing an audience of four million to advertisers now. With what you pick up at this table, you can guarantee six and a half, even seven million certified, for the next eighteen months, without moving a muscle. You can sell an audience almost as big as TV. You'll be in one out of every seven homes in the country. Maybe one out of six. I can put you there. Biggest."

"Kind of difficult to say anything with six and a half million circulation," said Norris, half to himself, and Warren, listening, knew Norris was a real publisher, "yet you have to say something. When you stop saying something you lose them. I wish I knew what they wanted. Say, Warren, where are you from?"

"Upstate New York," said Warren. "Why?"

"I'm from Minnesota," said Norris, as if it were directly relevant. "This city is driving me crazy. Trying to guess what they want back home. I keep hiring these corn-fed kids from back home, and two years after they've come to New York they're out of touch, too, cut off at the roots. Six and a half million circulation. Well . . . what the hell . . . I suppose you have a price tag on this. How much do you want? Names. Copyright. Features. Title. The works. How much?"

Norris came to the point abruptly and was silent with the question. His assistants froze. Austin stopped his doodling. Again Warren felt the stab of panic and knew he must suppress it. It was three million he needed, and three million he had planned to ask. His voice now spoke of itself, and he was surprised by its calm.

"Five million dollars. You're getting four million names on a mailing list free. You'd have to pay ten or fifteen million dollars in mailings to buy that many names and even then it would take you years. You have a bargain."

A snort came from one of Norris' assistants, a whistle from another. But neither spoke. It was up to Norris, whose voice, in response, was even and cold.

"I thought you wanted to do business."

"We're doing business. You know that's cheap, it's worth more."

"I came here with the idea of doing you a favor. Of tossing in a million dollars to buy these names and gambling I could break even. I couldn't begin to think about five million—I might buy some of the names for one million, and leave you stuck with the risk of paying the rest or peddling them off, but five million plus the risk—" He shook his head.

"Well," said Warren, "I thought I'd offer it to you first. You people earned it, and we fit into your circulation pattern. If we aren't going to do business with you, we've got a lot of work to do in the next ten days with other people who might want to divide the circulation up between them, and put the squeeze on you . . . you never can tell who gets the squeeze next in this business."

Warren began to shuffle the papers on the table together. He reached across the table to the long white charts with their columns and drew one of them to him, still talking.

"I felt that with competition the way it is, you might want to jump the others and be Number One overnight. You know your business better than I do. . . ."

He went on collecting his papers. He wanted three million; he had to have it.

"Make it a reasonable figure this time, Mr. Warren," said one of Norris' assistants, "that was the first go around. What do you really want?"

"I said what I wanted," said Warren, continuing his packing.

"Supposing I said two million," said Norris, "does that change your mind any?"

Warren paused, suddenly confident, knowing he would make it.

"A little," said Warren, "not much. Supposing I said four to you. Would that change your mind?"

Norris smiled. Warren smiled. Norris had the money. They were gambling now with chips that meant nothing except pride. Let Norris say it first. Warren waited.

"Split it down the middle?" said Norris.

"What do you think, Will?" said Warren.

"It's up to you, Mr. Warren," said Austin, his eyes pleading.

"It's a deal," said Warren, and reached his hand across the table.

Norris reached his hand across the table, too. Norris held on to Warren's hand a moment, then stiffened the grasp, repeating clearly in the presence of all of them.

"Three million dollars. Title. Features. Copyright. Circulation lists.

Trumpet is out of business. We can use its title wherever and however we want. Subject to the approval of my Board, or my Executive Committee. You have the authority to act for your Board?"

"Austin and I are two out of three on the Executive Committee of our Board with full authority"—and still holding on to Norris' hand, he turned to Austin. "It's a deal with you, too, Will?"

"A deal," said Austin in a whisper.

Norris unlocked Warren's hand and leaned back.

"One thing," said Warren, "now that we've done it—how soon can we lay our hands on the cash?"

"When do you want it?" said Norris.

"Right now," said Warren. "I need a certified check for half of it tomorrow afternoon, the other half of it early next week."

Norris looked at Warren with respect, then laughed. Then he rose and walked to the telephone in the corner of the room. He gave a number to the operator, then began to speak.

"Merchants National Bank? I want to speak to Mr. Cawley . . ." a pause, then, "Ivar Norris of *Spectacle* Magazine . . . yes . . ."

Then Mr. Cawley was on the phone and in a wave of envy Warren listened. The money was being turned on. He could feel, even before Norris' voice resumed, that a valve down there in the great reservoir was to be turned.

"Cawley . . . yes . . . the deal went through . . . I need two checks . . . a certified one-million-five tomorrow afternoon, another one-million-five on Wednesday . . . yes, the usual signatures . . . well, thanks, thanks a lot . . . good-by now."

It was that easy when the money was there.

Norris began to stuff papers into his briefcase, then spoke.

"If you could let me use Mr. Austin's time this afternoon and evening and one of your circulation men and some of your lawyers, I'll put them together with my people so we can have some papers to sign by night. Let's set them all a midnight deadline, and you and I get together at midnight for final signature. All right with you?"

"All right with me," said Warren.

"At my office then," said Norris. "Twenty-seventh floor, at midnight."

He saw Warren wince and, more kindly, went on. "There's nobody around at midnight at my office. Everybody's gone and nobody will see us. If we had the signing at your place we'd have newspapermen all over us. I'd appreciate it if you didn't say a word about this until my public relations people are ready to make a simultaneous announcement with you. We'll be ready with something by the time you've had your Board meeting tomorrow afternoon."

Norris rose and his two assistants followed him. As they grouped at the door, Norris turned again and said, "I wonder whether Mr. Austin would like to share the cab with us over to our place. There's a lot of work to do and maybe he'd like to get on with it?"

Austin looked at Warren and Warren said, "You do as you want, Will. Perhaps it's best to go along with them and find out just what kind of data they need. You can telephone our lawyers and anybody you want in circulation to meet you there."

"How about Mr. Morrissey?" said Austin.

"I'll tell Morrissey," said Warren. "You contact me through Laura. Good luck, Will."

He put his hand on Austin's shoulder and squeezed it hard. He watched them all leave, then turned to the telephone, to check the office.

"Laura," he said, when he had her, after a long wait at the switchboard, broken finally by his insistence that they interrupt her line, "what's up?"

"What's up?" she repeated half-hysterically. "This is a madhouse. There are newspapermen all over the place looking for you. One of them says you've flown out of town with the company funds and wants a statement. Bennett threw him out. The staff is going crazy, meetings on every floor, they're organizing a union. Morrissey has been screaming for you ever since the lunch hour. Foley wants to know where you are. It's—I've never known anything like this."

"Laura, listen. I'm going home now. You contact me there when you need to. Don't tell anyone where I am, not anybody, except Austin if Austin really needs to reach me. Tell Morrissey we've closed the *Spectacle* deal for three million cash. Tell him I'm roaming around town this afternoon trying to clean up the *Gentlewoman* circulation picture, and that I'll pick up messages from him through you when I telephone in. Keep me covered; I don't want to be located this afternoon by anyone."

"But there's a million calls for you—from advertising agencies, from friends, from Washington, from people on all the floors, from your wife."

"What did my wife say?"

Laura giggled. "She wanted to know the telephone number of your cleaning woman. She's at your apartment now and says it's filthy and it's got to be cleaned up. She says you haven't got a single clean shirt left and—"

Warren laughed too.

"Tell her I'm on my way over. Give her the telephone number of my cleaning woman—"

"I already did. Mr. Warren, don't hang up. Look—those people want me to sign one of the powers of attorney, too, for my claims against the corporation. They're saying awful things about you; what do I do?"

"Sign," he said. "Don't tell anybody I told you so—but sign, by all means. Good-by, Laura."

19. Thursday Afternoon

1. RUSSELL'S OFFICE—4:00 P.M.

As Russell waited for the salesmen to come back for their four o'clock rendezvous he leafed through the telegrams that had been arriving all morning and afternoon.

Some were threatening.

CAN'T REACH YOU BY PHONE YOUR SWITCHBOARD JAMMED STOP INSIST IMMEDIATELY REPLY WHETHER OUR SIX PAGES FLOUR PROMOTION BOOKED GENTLEWOMAN WILL RUN OR NOT STOP OFFICIALLY INFORMING YOU HEREWITH ANY SUSPENSION MAGAZINES DOES NOT RELEASE YOU FROM OBLIGATION CONTRACT SIGNED TWO WEEKS AGO STOP WE COULD HAVE BOOKED SPACE ELSEWHERE NOW WE HOLDING BAG VISAVIS OUR CLIENTS STOP IF WE CAN'T SWITCH PLACEMENT OUR SIX PAGES WILL CLAIM OUR FIFTEEN PERCENT COMMISSION ON SPACE FROM YOU.

Some were personal.

CAN'T REACH YOU BY PHONE STOP DON'T HESITATE CALL ME IF YOU NEED A LIFELINE YOUR OLD JOB STILL OPEN FOR YOU STOP COME BACK ALL IS FORGIVEN.

There were the helpful.

DON'T WANT TO MAKE LIKE BUZZARDS OVER DYING BODY BUT COULD USE TWO BEST SPACE SALESMEN LIQUOR ACCOUNTS OUR SHOP STOP LET US KNOW SOONEST BEST TWO NAMES YOU'VE GOT IF THEY BECOME AVAILABLE.

Some were greedy.

DON'T SHOW YOUR HAND UNTIL YOU TALK TO US STOP WE WILLING MAKE PERSONAL DEAL EITHER WITH YOU OR THE MAGAZINES FOR COMPLETE LIST YOUR ADVANCE BOOKINGS ADVERTISING AND YOUR HELP SWITCHING THEM INTO OUR PAGES WHEN YOU SUSPEND STOP PLEASE CALL BACK SOONEST.

Some were unbelieving.

DEAR BOY IMPOSSIBLE BELIEVE RUMORS AFLOAT TODAY STOP NEWS BAD FOR INDUSTRY BAD FOR ADVERTISING BAD FOR AMERICA SAY IT ISN'T SO STOP ANY-

THING LENOX FORD MADIGAN CAN DO THIS CRISIS WE WILL DO BELIEVE ME
OUR HEART IS WITH YOU STOP WE WILLING COMMIT OUR CLIENTS IMMEDI-
ATELY FOR TWELVE PAGES TOBACCO SIX PAGES MORE CRANBERRIES EIGHT
PAGES AIRLINES TO RUN SOONEST IF ONLY YOU GUARANTEE PUBLICATION
OVER NEXT SIX MONTHS STOP WHAT CAN WE DO TO HELP.

Russell liked that one, Lenox had signed it himself.

He also liked the telephones from the district offices and the reports
here in New York. He had never known anything like the drive the sales
staff had mounted in the past forty-eight hours, ever since he had warned
them of a possibly important announcement. The Minneapolis advertising office had booked twelve pages of road-equipment advertising, the
Hollywood office had booked sixteen pages of movie spreads, the Detroit
office had wrung out two of the Big Three automobile companies for a
commitment of twenty pages above normal over the next year. Here in
New York, some of the salesmen had been drunk since morning and
done nothing; some had spent the day telephoning for new jobs; but
half a dozen in the desperation of disaster had throttled, choked,
squeezed and stormed their contacts at the agencies for an astounding
one-day total of forty-four pages of new commitment. All in all, over a
million dollars' worth of new advertising had been lined up in the past
two days—and all too late.

Russell looked up.

Page was standing at his open door, a smirk on his face.

"Got a minute?" said Page.

"What's it about?" said Russell. He hated Page. Page had been leaking every secret of the advertising floor to *Spectacle* since early spring.
Page had sold out long before anyone else. His resignation had come in
on Tuesday, his new job at *Spectacle* was set. He had been laughing all
week.

"What do you want to talk about?" asked Russell.

"I was just thinking," said Page, "about that resignation of mine, day
before yesterday. What the hell, Frank, if you haven't processed it with
personnel yet, let's forget about it. If I sign this petition, I may be able
to take severance pay away from here, too—a good eighteen weeks of it
for nine years' work. No skin off your nose. It's not your money. How
about it?"

Page's resignation had not yet been processed. In the turbulence of
the week, Russell had held it on his desk in the hold box. Tomorrow
was the day he had meant to process it, Friday.

"Tell you what, Frank," said Page, "you tear up that resignation and if I get the severance pay, I'll give you a piece of it."

Russell stared at Page and said slowly, "Why, no, Page, no, I haven't sent the resignation in. As a matter of fact, I don't intend to, Page. Do you know what I'm going to do?"

Page looked back quizzically, and Russell hit. "I'm firing you, Page, right now, this afternoon, before the severance-pay thing is settled. I've wanted to fire you for almost a year, Page, I almost thought I wouldn't get the chance. I'm going to fire you without a nickel. *Spectacle* will sweeten your next paycheck with what you've been doing for them, you don't need another penny from us. The records will read that you were fired for disloyalty. Before the general settlement of dismissal. Now, if you'll excuse me, I want to talk to that meeting they're calling."

2. HARRY LOGAN ON THE ROAD—4:15 P.M.

Harry Logan left the car with the parking-lot attendant and checked in with the room clerk.

"Long distance," said the message the room clerk handed him. "Call operator two-twenty-two New York. Mr. Corbett your office. Urgent."

All the way up in the elevator Harry Logan wondered what could be urgent. He hoped there was nothing wrong with the family. That was why he had come to Boston, to look the New England territory over—because the family was all together in Minneapolis, where Janet had gone to sign the papers closing the sale on the house. Since she was going to be in Minneapolis all week and stay with the kids over the weekend, he might just as well be on the road. Might just as well spend the time in a Boston hotel as a New York hotel. By this time next month, maybe by the first of the year they would have put a down payment on the house in Briarcliff and be all moved in.

"Hello," he said to Corbett as the long-distance operator finally connected them after the wait for a busy switchboard, "hello, Al, just got your message, anything important?"

"Harry," said Corbett, "I can't talk now. There's too much going on. I just want to ask you a question—have you sold your house in Minneapolis?"

Corbett must be crazy, thought Harry Logan, to call and ask him about that.

"I think it's sold by now," he said, "Janet is supposed to sign the papers selling it this afternoon; I'm going to call her tonight and see if it went off O.K. Why? Have you got a customer?"

"Harry. Listen. Don't sell that house. Call Janet wherever she is and tell her to stall."

"Why? What's up?"

"Harry. I can't explain why over the telephone. Come on back into New York tonight anyway. I'll explain tomorrow. If there's still time—"

"Al! Al! Listen, you brought me out from Minneapolis! Al, are the magazines in trouble? Is this rumor true? Al, you got to tell me, you've got to. Are we folding, Al? Al! Are you there?"

"Harry, it looks bad here in New York. The advertising department has told every salesman to stay out of the office today. Austin has stopped all purchases. They just canceled the orders for our new trucks. I was the one who brought you out from Minneapolis. You'd never speak to me again if I didn't tell you to be careful, hang on to your house until we know whether we got jobs in New York or not. For Christ's sake, Harry, I'm sticking my neck out talking to you. But don't sell that house until you get back to New York and talk to me. Harry, I got to hang up on you. Good-by."

As the phone snapped, Harry Logan looked at his watch. It was four fifteen. Four fifteen Boston time. What time was that in New York? No, New York and Boston had the same time. That made Chicago time three fifteen, three fifteen in Minneapolis and Janet said they were going to have the closing this afternoon. The lawyer, what was their lawyer's name? he knew him, he knew him, oh God, what was his name, what was his name, Jack, Jack what, oh God, Jack, Jack Hoffman, yes, Jack Hoffman, good old Jack, he had to reach Jack.

"Operator," he said into the phone, "Minneapolis, right away, please hurry, this is urgent, operator."

"One moment, please, I'll connect you with long distance."

"Hurry, please, hurry, this is an emergency."

"Long distance"—a new voice.

"Minneapolis, please, operator, this is an emergency—"

"Your room number, please."

"Operator, put me through to Jack Hoffman right away in Minneapolis, I'll—"

"Your room number, please."

"Room two-oh-six-seven, the Statler Hotel, Boston."

"I know it's the Statler. What party are you calling in Minneapolis, please?"

"Jack Hoffman, please, operator, this is an emergency, he's in the lawyer, no he's a lawyer in the phone book there, you can find his—"

"Don't you have his number?"

"No, goddamnit, I don't, you get me through to Minneapolis as fast as you can or I'll report you—"

"Say, what do you mean talking to me like that?"

"Operator, please, this is an emergency, a matter of life and death, I'm begging you, operator—"

"How do you spell his name, please?"

He spelled it, reached with one hand for a pack of cigarettes, as his shoulder squeezed the phone to his ear, reached with the other hand for a match, dropped the phone as he attempted to light the cigarette, grabbed for the phone, the match dropped on his trousers, burning a hole. Instinctively, he dropped the phone again and slapped out the little spit of flame, burned his hand, yelled, "Ouch," grabbed the telephone again, and said, "Operator."

"Say, mister," came the operator's voice, "are you drunk?"

"No, please, lady, this is terribly important, I've got to reach Jack Hoffman in Minneapolis before it's too late."

"I'm doing the best I can. There's Minneapolis information now."

He could hear the cross-talk between Boston and Minneapolis on the telephone. He could hear the number, Federal 5-2799, and it sounded right. He could hear the ring of the bell on the other end.

And then, abruptly, the connection broke and the telephone went dead except for the interior hotel hum.

"Operator!" he screamed into the phone. No answer.

"Operator!" he screamed again, flicking the lever which held the phone in its cradle. "Operator!" he screamed as he clicked and clicked and clicked, and the tears streamed down his face.

3 . FARRELL TAKES A TRIP—4:30 P.M.

All afternoon, ever since their lunch, the idea had been growing on Farrell. It had been a wonderful lunch and the idea had been born in the perfume of the wine. But only now, as he saw Joyce departing with the typewriter, did he know he had the courage to do it.

Joyce winked at him as he walked by the bullpen, carrying the type-writer.

"I've been writing on this portable for six years now," said Joyce, "it belongs to me; I'm not leaving it to be sold to the second-hand dealers. I just want to get across town to my apartment with it, before they close the exits tomorrow."

Farrell laughed and knew then that he had to do it. He could still taste that meal, and with the meal the dream.

The meal had been Joyce's idea to begin with. When they had signed the power of attorney before lunch for the committee, the reporters had strolled up the avenue looking for a place to eat and talk it over. As they sat down, Joyce had spread his wallet on the table and begun to sort out the cards that stuffed it thick—the police card, the Press Club card, the United Nations card, the Air Travel card, the Diners' Club card, the edi-torial identity card. Joyce fanned them all out and studied them.

"How long do you suppose they're good for?" asked someone, watch-ing, as Joyce spread the credentials of the trade before them.

"I don't know," said Joyce. "When you get fired you have to hand all the cards in the day you get fired."

"Jeezus," said another, "I hate giving up my police card. It makes me feel naked being without one. I've had mine for eleven years."

"Ah, well," said Joyce, "they're good until the curtain falls. I'm not turning mine in. I'll say I lost mine, that's all. Say," he added quickly, "would you gentlemen like to be my guests?"

"Come again?" asked Farrell.

"Gentlemen," said Joyce, "I represent the General American Publish-ing Company and its senior publication, *Trumpet*. I hold here in my hand," he said, lifting the Diners' Club card, "a little invitation from *Trumpet* for a last luncheon for my colleagues. Will you join me in a hearty meal as a farewell to the old shop?"

"You can't get away with it," began one of the others but Joyce boomed happily, "The hell I can't. I have a credit card here that lets me order any meal I need on company business—and the bills aren't rendered to the company until the end of the month. By that time there'll be no more *Trumpet* and they can send someone whistling after me to collect. Waiter!" he called, and turned and grabbed a waiter by the coat-tails. "Waiter, I want a double round of martinis for all my friends, and bring the wine list with you when you bring the menu, my friends are hungry—"

"Make mine a double bourbon—" said Farrell, falling into the spirit of things, and he could hear somebody else calling for a double manhattan.

Farrell had followed his bourbon with *paté de foie gras*, and then had gone on to lobster; the others had gorged on steak. They had had red and white wines, followed by brandy and cigars, and by the time the check for $141.50 had come, they had all been lifted out of their melancholy.

"Waiter," said Joyce, as they rose, "notice that I'm adding twenty dollars as a tip to this check. Note it well. The next time I come in here I want you to recognize me and smile because next time there may be no tip at all."

For hours after the lunch, the strange idea had lingered with Farrell. Only he, Joyce and Eliot as senior writers had full credit cards. They should be used. It was so easy to use them. It was, however, only when he saw Joyce walking out with the typewriter that Farrell knew he had to do it. He might never have an Air Travel card again. The Air Travel card said the world was open and *Trumpet* picked up the tab.

Farrell quivered with anticipation as he left the desk to find his coat and hat.

He was still quivering as he took his place in line at the airlines counter. He wanted to stay here at least until Christmas and celebrate Christmas at home. But there was no telling when the airline might present the bills for Air Travel cards to the corporation once the news was out. So he would have to skip Christmas at home and leave this weekend before they could cancel the tickets. Well . . .

It was his turn now. He laid down the airline credit card on the counter so that the girl might see it easily and then,

"This is going to be complicated and I'll get into detail later but what I want is to leave December fifteenth or sixteenth on a round-the-world trip—"

"Economy or first-class flight?" asked the girl, as if people stopped at her counter to go around the world every day.

"Oh, first class by all means," said Farrell, "it's company business." Theft was never easier. Except, smiling, he told himself this was not theft—this made up for the two thousand dollars a year more he should have been getting, for the vacation he had missed when the flood story broke, for everything.

And if somebody was going to make a couple of million bucks out of the folding of the magazines, he was entitled to one little trip around the world.

"Which way?" she said.

"Which ways have you got?" he said happily.

"I mean, do you want to go through Europe first, or through the Pacific first?"

She frowned at him as if he were making fun of her. Farrell looked out the plate-glass windows and noticed that it had begun to snow. Paris was good any time of the year—why waste Paris on the winter snow, when it was cold, and foggy, and drizzly and no place to go? He should save Paris for the spring.

"I'm sorry," he said, throwing on the smile, "Hawaii first."

She jotted Hawaii down on her pad and pressed a button on the machine that coded advance reservations. As she waited for the little desk machine to respond to her, he dreamed a bit.

"Tahiti after that," he said. He had never seen either Hawaii or Tahiti, they would both be warm and balmy and he could almost certainly rest up on the beaches there and get to feeling brown again. If he didn't do Tahiti now he never would.

"We don't fly Tahiti," she said, "there's an Air France connection through from Hawaii; we can fix that up with no extra charge."

"Why, thank you," he said to her and he noticed that she was pretty. "How would you suggest going on from Tahiti?"

"Where do you want to go?" she said, smiling back.

"Hong Kong eventually," he said, and then feeling as if he needed some explanation for the casual air, "this is a trip around the world for our magazine. An article about what the rest of the world thinks of America."

"Gee," said the girl, her pencil poised, "you writers and newspapermen are so lucky. That's a wonderful trip. I'll be looking for your article; your name is Farrell, it says here. I read an article in one of the other magazines last week that says that nobody likes Americans any more. I don't think that's true. Whenever I go abroad people are very nice to me."

"Why anybody would be nice to you," said Farrell, smiling gallantly.

The girl smiled back, then became formal again.

"Air France has a connection," she said, looking at her chart, "from Tahiti to Samoa, and we can pick you up at Samoa and take you to the Philippines and Hong Kong. I imagine you want to stop off at each place for a week or so?"

"Yes, of course," said Farrell, drawing out one of the cigarillos he had acquired at the lunch and lighting it. He blew a round puff of smoke in the air as the girl made the jottings on her pad, "but let's not fix any dates for flight from one place to the other. Just so long as the connection is available, leave the flight dates open and I'll fill them in as I go along."

"After Hong Kong?" she said.

"After Hong Kong, Rangoon; Burma; then New Delhi; then . . . let me see . . ." His eye fell on a poster on the wall behind her, of a young man and a young woman peering up at the domes of St. Sophia. He had never seen Stamboul. Why not now?

"Stamboul."

"Then after that Cairo, I suppose," said the girl, as if it were a guessing game they were playing.

"No, not Cairo, Athens," said Farrell.

"Not Cairo?" said the girl. "Don't you care what the Arabs think about us?"

"I know what the Arabs think about us," said Farrell loftily. "Oh, I suppose I have to, put down Cairo, but leave the date open."

"I'm always suspicious of people who want to go to Cairo," said the girl, volunteering a thought for the first time, as if he had passed a test, and briefly Farrell began to explore her thoughts about Cairo. This was a very nice girl. He felt the nick of a briefcase being set down behind him and a voice asking over his shoulder, "Hey, I hate to interrupt, but is this where I get a ticket for Boston?"

The girl stared beyond Farrell at the voice and Farrell turned, wrapped in his new toga of foreign correspondent, circling the globe on the magic carpet, and stared disdainfully at the stout, Homburg-hatted businessman behind him. The man was obviously in a hurry. That was the trouble with Americans, they were always hurrying.

"No," said the girl, "you want *American* Airlines office. That's across the street. They fly to Boston. We only ticket for overseas. Yes," she said, turning to Farrell with obvious pleasure, "after Cairo, Italy?"

"Rome," he said, "then Cannes."

"Not Germany?" she said, as if he were trying to play hooky from his tasks.

"I'll do Germany from Paris. Take the train. Or drive. It's lovely driving in France in the springtime."

"I know," she said enviously.

"Let's just stop it short in Paris, with the return flight from there to New York left open. I'll do London from Paris."

"Are you staying long in Paris?" she asked.

"I'll probably write my piece out of Paris," he said, "and hole up there until it's done. May take a few weeks off then."

"You'll need it," she said, "that's some trip."

When he got to Paris he would be just about ready to go. He might stay in Paris for weeks. Might look for a job in Paris. Yes, look for a job in Paris. Never come back here. Turn in the overseas flight ticket home for cash and look for a job.

"When will those tickets be ready?" he asked.

"Oh, in about an hour," she said, "I have to work out the fares and make sure that the connecting flights with the foreign airlines are all right."

"Swell," he said, "I'll be back about five thirty to pick them up. And thanks a lot, you were a big help."

"Gosh," she said, "I envy you newspapermen."

20. Thursday Night: Two Out of Three Makes a Majority

Warren was anxious that the ceremony of capitulation be over quickly. It was the next step that was important.

Warren, Austin, the Meade & Crane lawyers, the General American Publishing experts, sat at one side of the mahogany table in the Board Room of *Spectacle*. Norris, his comptroller, his lawyers and assistants sat at the other. And the papers were in motion. Shifting and fluttering from lawyer to lawyer, as a change was initialed here, a seal pressed down there, the papers seemed animated leaves in a ballet. Warren would sign, and Austin would sign, and Norris would sign and other strange men signed, and only the lawyers, whirling and weaving among the groggy principals, seemed to be sure of exactly what was happening.

Conversation had now died at the table, so that the murmur of the lawyers, talking to each other about their respective principles as puppets, seemed mechanically loud and important. But Warren's eyes were fixed on Austin, for Austin was his next target. He had to bring Austin back with him to the apartment, where Schlafman, Mitchell, and Eliot waited, when this was over. That was the plan. He *must* bring Austin with him when he left.

Warren had first measured Austin again when he arrived at the *Spectacle* Board Room a few minutes before midnight for the final signing. Austin, even then, appeared tired and haggard, and Warren had ordered sandwiches for Austin, pressed a Scotch on him, ministered to him, babied him as much as he could in the business of the final detail about the table. For a moment, just at the end, Warren feared that Austin had been pressed too far by his long day's toil, too far to think, or to agree, or to operate as he must, in Warren's mind, now operate.

The last paper had been signed; the lawyers were counting copies of the documents to make sure each side had the proper number and kind of documents; then, finally, when one of the lawyers had said, stretching, "Well, I guess that's it. I think we can all have a drink now," it was over. It was at this moment, as Norris and his lawyers all began to pour themselves a drink, that Warren noticed Austin's head sag with a jerk, then come upright, then sag again, and he observed that Austin was almost collapsed with exhaustion.

Warren put his arm about Austin, turning to the others at the table and said, "Will and I are pretty tired. It's drinking time for you people, but we still have some loose ends to sew up. Will," he continued, "let's you and I be on our way."

He had Austin by the elbow, and the old Treasurer was resting his weight on him, and for a moment that old familiar sense of shame, which had so overwhelmed him at the Bronstein's two days before, came over him, for he could sense by the sag in Austin that he was with him, that Austin now trusted him. Yet, as he led Austin by the elbow, and the urgency of what he must do came back, he knew this time there was no shame truly in what he was about to do. This issue, at least, was clear.

They were in the elevator, descending, when Austin spoke, suddenly, making it easier.

"I'd have to wait until one thirty," said Austin, "to catch the next train out to Summit. I think I'll stay in town tonight, Mr. Warren. What hotel would you suggest?"

"Will," said Warren, "it's time you stopped calling me Mr. Warren— why not call me Ridge? We're both tired and I don't think you ought to stay at a hotel. You come home with me, have a nightcap, spend the night in my guestroom, and we'll find out what we have to do in the morning."

"But I couldn't do that Mr. Warren, Ridge, I mean. I couldn't think of imposing on you."

"Oh come along, Will. Neither one of us is going to get any sleep tonight if you go to a hotel room and I go back to the apartment. We've got to unwind—come on!"

He took Austin by the arm again as they left the elevator and walked out into the street.

"But I haven't any toothbrush, or a change of shirt, or—"

"We'll buy you a new shirt in the morning, and I have an extra tooth-brush—and, Will, I can't get to sleep after all this unless I have someone to talk to for a little while—so come along."

A taxi was approaching, and Warren hailed it.

"All right, then," said Austin, "if you're sure I'm not imposing. But not too late, Ridge. This rash of mine is bothering me again; it always does when I'm nervous."

It was almost half an hour before Warren felt that Austin had relaxed enough to begin.

Warren had felt Austin pull himself together as they walked into the apartment and saw the others there—Mary and Schlafman, Eliot and Mitchell. But Warren had acted as if their presence here was completely normal, as if only their anxiety had brought them to his apartment to hear of the ending. He knew it was odd to introduce Mary as his wife to Austin, who had never known him to be married, yet so much was bizarre this evening that Austin expressed no surprise at all.

"You must be hungry," Mary said, "poor things. Let me get you something to eat."

"Oh no," said Austin primly, "I don't want to bother you; I didn't know you had company tonight—"

"Now, Will," said Warren, "this isn't company, these are all part of the family. Ben and Dave and Nat Schlafman—Mary, can you make us some scrambled eggs? I don't think either one of us could put down anything more."

"Just a glass of milk for me, Mrs. Warren," said Austin, "just to settle my stomach."

"Would you like a drink, Mr. Austin?" said Mary, moving to the bar table. "Just a touch of Scotch or brandy? You both must be absolutely exhausted."

"Oh, no!" said Austin, "I already had one drink this evening. I never drink more than that. Two drinks will make me reel. No. Just a glass of milk, and my rash is bothering me—it always bothers me when I'm nervous."

"Just a touch of brandy in your milk, then," said Mary, mothering him, "just a drop? I think it would be good for your rash if you're nervous. It's soothing."

"Do you think it would be good for my rash?" asked Austin uncertainly as they all watched him.

"Of course," said Mary, "of course, it's just what you need. Now why don't you take off your jacket and be comfortable the way everyone else is while I bring it?"

As Mary slipped off to the kitchen, Warren squatted on the floor and waved Austin into the armchair. The three other men were already in shirtsleeves and Warren easily slid out of the jacket that bound him. He urged Austin to do so, too, and unbelievably there was Austin, with vivid red-and-blue suspenders and quite a different man—disarmored, frightened, his shirtsleeves cut off above the elbows. As if apologetically he said, "Mrs. Austin always cuts my shirtsleeves off for me; I get the itch at my wrists, too. It helps not to have any cuffs."

"What happened, Ridge?" said Eliot finally as they lowered into the silence that precedes conversation, and Warren began to tell them of the day's events. There were no secrets now except the secret they were about to make with Austin. So Warren told of the day's negotiations, and of his two visits to Norris, artfully moving the conversation again and again to Austin's participation, to Austin's discernment, to Austin's handling of the *Spectacle* people until it seemed as if it were Austin who had outbargained Ivar Norris and *Spectacle* and managed the afternoon's affairs all by himself. Never had Austin been so flattered and so praised and when Mary stooped over the two men with a tray bearing scrambled eggs, toast and milk and said, "I've added just a touch of brandy to your milk, Mr. Austin, just a touch to settle your stomach," Austin, trustingly, turned his face up to her and said, "You just call me Will, Mrs. Warren, I feel we're all friends here."

"I feel we are, too, Will; won't you call me Mary?"

"You're sure this isn't strong now, Mary?" he asked and turned back to the conversation which, now, had been taken over by Mitchell. Mitchell was holding the conversation, as at a wake, about the memory of the departed as if *Trumpet* were a family figure, beloved, who had just died. All of them watched Austin as the dark, brandy-tinted milk began to descend in his glass, and as Mitchell talked of old man Pepper in the days of long ago, and began to reach further back in memory to the days when *Trumpet* had printed the first pictures of the Pancho Villa expedition and of his own first interview with Pershing, Mary poured a straight brandy for Austin, and Austin sipped it and began to talk himself.

They were all working on Austin now, the four of them, talking of old times, and Austin was beginning to lean back in his chair, his speech slightly less precise than usual, repeating his words and phrases, dropping the *t*'s and *d*'s from the ends of words in a slur.

". . . Oh, I know people think I don't care," Austin rambled, "but the situation is this, you see, when you're the Treasurer you have to think about paying the bills. The situation is this kind of situation when it's all outgo and no income that the Treasurer is the first man to see it and no matter what he feels, he feels, no matter what he feels he can see it first, first that is when the situation is the way our situation is, was, I mean you take Hopkins, why when I think of him now I think we ought to take care of him, I mean, the situation is when a man puts in thirty years at the plant and gives his life, you know the situation was several years ago, long before you came in, I was the first one to say, you know, this was years ago, there ought to be a pension fund for the older people now, not a fancy thing but that was when we could have afforded it just after the war, but no, nobody listens to the Treasurer, nobody respects a Treasurer, if people had listened to me—"

And at this point, which was the best point, Warren decided he must move in.

"Will, that brings up one of the last things we still have to talk about."

"How?" said Austin blankly as the others leaned forward from where they sat.

"We've got to do something about the employees, about the staff, before it gets let out tomorrow, about people like old Hopkins."

Dolefully, Austin shook his head. "Don't see what we can do, you know the situation is the kind of situation where with the best will in the world, well, the situation is still money, and it's easy to forget now that we have this arrangement with *Spectacle* that we're still on the edge of bankruptcy."

"But there is money now," interjected Eliot, "you and Warren have just got three million dollars from *Spectacle*—"

"Haven't got it yet," said Austin. "If our Board agrees tomorrow, oh, they'll agree, I know that, that's what they want, then we'll have three million by next week and we have to pay Silverman about two million in the next few months, and the ink, and other obligations and the union with their contract in the printing plant calling for severance pay—"

"Isn't it a shame," said Mary, chiming in, "all those union people because they have a contract will get paid off, and the people here in New York won't."

"Yes," agreed Austin, hissing one word into the next so that it sounded, "Yess-a-shame. I called my secretary this afternoon, she said they're trying to form this union today over at the office, she wanted to know if she could join, too, to get her severance pay—"

"I joined up this afternoon," said Eliot.

"So did I," said Mitchell.

"Will," said Warren, as if the thought had just come to him, "I think you and I ought to do something about it."

"What can we do?" said Austin, staring down at the floor, his head bobbing a little, as if asking a rhetorical, answerless question. Everybody watched him.

"May I say something?" said Schlafman, speaking for the first time.

"Why, hello, Mr. Schlafman," said Austin, recognizing his presence.

"These people have organized a committee, Mr. Austin, and they have almost five hundred powers of attorney they collected today—enough, I think, to let you deal with them legally."

Schlafman proceeded suavely as if what he were discussing were the most routine matter in the world.

"They've also drawn up a rather simple scheme for severance pay for all white-collar employees and members of staff to be dismissed, something like two weeks' pay for every year of service they've worked."

"Do you know what that would cost?" asked Austin, shaking his head confusedly as if to shake off a blur, and then, "Who's got a pencil?" he asked. "I can't think without a pencil."

Eliot presented him with a pencil. Austin took it, then his fingers let it drop.

"I don't need a pencil, I penciled it all out after the Board meeting yesterday; why that'd come to a million dollars alone for severance pay, out of the question, it's a shame, but it's out of the question, isn't it, Ridge?"

Schlafman continued as if there had been no interruption, addressing himself to Warren, as if it were Warren who must be persuaded.

"Now what they've drawn up is an agreement of settlement dated tomorrow—which is today, Friday, because it's past midnight—which acknowledges the corporation's indebtedness for severance pay to all dismissed employees, payments to be spread over a year so as not to embarrass the corporation in the next month when it's short of cash and recovering."

"That's right," said Austin, "couldn't possibly do anything this month, we're so short."

Then he shook away the thought with a toss of his head.

"Funny what those people will do," said Austin, ruminating, "these union people are smart, aren't they, got smart lawyers."

"It's not those people," said Mitchell, tartly, "it's me. I'm chairman of this committee, Eliot and I are chairmen of this committee."

"You?" said Austin. "You, Ben?"

Austin suddenly giggled.

"Ben, you going to be a union leader now?"

He giggled again.

"Ben, what would old Pepper have said if he'd seen you leading a union?"

"We wouldn't have needed a union if old man Pepper'd been around," said Mitchell with surprising mildness. "Wouldn't have needed severance pay, wouldn't have needed pension agreements, magazines wouldn't have folded, that's what, Will," he continued. "But I do wish he were around, don't you—I'd like to have seen him take the switch to this Morrissey, wouldn't you?"

"Would have been different if he were alive all right, Ben," said Austin, "he wouldn't have had any nonsense out of this Morrissey, that's sure, why, Ben . . ." Austin was off again with Mitchell, reminiscing about Pepper.

The minutes dragged. Warren fidgeted. He could see that Schlafman and Eliot were as nervous as he, as Mitchell led the reminiscences back through the corridors of time. He wondered how it would come out, and he heard Austin telling of his first years on the Board with old man Pepper and how Pepper would say that the Board was his cabinet, there to help him, not to vote on him.

". . . Never took a vote once all the while I was on his Board; Pepper would listen to everybody, then he'd make up his mind, move it, second it, pass it, bang the gavel and that was it. . . ."

"Would the Board have to sign this settlement agreement, Nat?" said Warren, knowing the answer, but wanting to have Schlafman and Mitchell press on Austin.

"The Board wouldn't have to sign it," said Schlafman. "The Board set up an Executive Committee of three men with full powers to liquidate the magazines on Wednesday. You and Austin are two of the three. I think if you and Austin signed it, as President and Treasurer of the corporation, and as a majority of the Executive Committee, that would do it. Just the two of you."

"Sign that union thing?" said Austin abruptly. "You mean me sign it?"

Austin reached for the nearly empty glass of brandy and, awkwardly, he tumbled it on the floor. He stooped immediately to mop up the stain, and Mary hurried to the floor beside him to help. The others watched, tense, until the mopping was done and Austin was seated again.

"How does that read, Nat?" continued Warren, trying to sound genuinely perplexed. "Will and I have a real problem. The three million that we get out of *Spectacle* will barely get us around the corner of the year and we can't toy with another bankruptcy possibility in the next few weeks."

"We've considered all that," said Schlafman, as if Warren and Austin were equally innocent of the proposal. "Payments under this agreement start this year, and then they run out in installments so that you don't meet the last big sum until April thirtieth."

"Hmmm," mused Warren, "what do you think, Will?"

"Well," said Austin, feeling his way among the questions in his mind, "in a way yes, in a way, no . . . but . . . well, it's money that belongs to the stockholders, not to us, we just can't give it away . . . and it doesn't seem right to sign without Morrissey."

"That vulture," said Mitchell, coming in on cue, "that carpet-bagger, I just wish old Ab Pepper and he were in one room together for five minutes; he'd pluck Morrissey bald-headed, he'd use his tail feathers for pen quills."

"You and I make two out of three on that Executive Committee," said Warren, as if thinking to himself. "I suppose we could sign it if we wanted to, Will."

"Sneaky," said Austin suddenly.

"Sneaky, sneaky, sneaky," continued Austin, "ought to call him up right now and telephone him straight to his face, if we were going to do it."

Austin's fingers gripped the sides of his chair. An idea had come to him. He pulled at the chair and rose unsteadily.

"Won't do anything sneaky, no, I won't; what do you say we call up Morrissey right now and tell him what we think? If he thinks so, and you think so, Ridge, well, I think so, too, that's what we should do. Where's the telephone?"

Austin peered about the room, located the telephone, began to move toward it, stopped, said, "You talk to him, Ridge. . . ."

Mary spoke. "It's after two o'clock now, do you think you ought to wake him up at this hour, Will?"

"Surely—why not?" asked Austin, his hand on the phone.

"He might not see it our way," said Warren, "waking him up out of a good night's sleep. He might be irritated, might not see the picture as clearly as we can see it."

Austin stood listening, teetering and swaying, and Warren continued.

"We've got to think of the whole corporation, not just this million dollars. Firing all these people before Christmas Eve is the worst kind of publicity for us. Those labor unions might start boycotting us. You know the textbook division is all involved in selling books to school boards, and politicians might crack down on our textbook sales if the unions forced them to—look what they did to that plumbing firm. No, Will—this is complicated, we're responsible, we've got to think of the big picture."

"Would you like another glass of milk, Will?" asked Mary.

"I have this rash again," said Austin as he stood by the telephone, and his hand came away from the instrument.

"Where is it?" asked Mary. "Sit down and let me look at it."

"Back of my neck," said Austin docilely, unbuttoning his tie and sitting down on the sofa. Mary walked to the back of the sofa and began to finger the nape of Austin's neck, soothing and stroking it. Mitchell's face hardened, and Warren wondered how long he could keep Mitchell from losing his temper. Eliot's eyes bugged out in suppressed amusement. Only Schlafman sat controlled and neat as they waited.

"I think a glass of milk and tea is what you need," decided Mary. "Let me give it to you."

As she left, Warren reached to Schlafman for the papers that lay on the floor before the lawyer.

"Let me see how that agreement of settlement reads, Nat."

Schlafman handed it over.

"How many powers of attorney have you got from the staff?" Warren asked of Mitchell.

"Almost five hundred today," said Mitchell. "We'll have another hundred tomorrow. Enough, according to Nat, to give us the appearance of legality."

From the corridor, Warren could hear a radio just turned on. Mary must have turned it on. He winced. It was the sound of a Christmas carol. She was carrying it too far.

"Here, Will," said Warren, trying to distract his attention, "you ought to read this, too," and he handed over a copy.

Austin held the form without looking at it for a moment as if he were listening to something. The music was faint but definitely there in the background.

"Christmas," he mumbled, "it's a shame," and fell to reading, his eyes following the lines automatically.

Schlafman rose and tiptoed to Warren. "The seal," he whispered, "your corporate seal. With the corporate seal on it, and both your names, I think we've got better than an even chance in court. Your seal? Who keeps it in your corporation?"

"Secretary," whispered Warren, "Austin is Treasurer and Secretary. We've been using it to seal the papers at the *Spectacle* office; I think it's in his briefcase now."

"Get it," said Schlafman.

When Warren came back, the seal concealed in the palm of his hand, the room was hushed. Austin had finished reading the agreement, and was leafing through the powers of attorney, shaking his head.

"Now," said Schlafman, taking out his pen, "I think Mitchell and Eliot ought to sign first, for the committee, relieving the corporation of any further claims against it," and briskly handed the pen to Mitchell first.

Austin turned from the powers of attorney to see what was going on. His head sunken, his eyes slowly revolving around the room, his hand clutching the glass of milk to steady him, it was as if he were squinting through a keyhole, trying to make out what was going on.

"Here," said Mitchell to Eliot, "you sign next."

Eliot scratched.

"Mr. Warren," sputtered Austin through his confusion, "what if they don't sell the plant in time for the first January fifteenth payment on this agreement? Then we're in danger of bankruptcy again."

"That's almost settled, Will. Morrissey has been talking to Jack Raven today about mortgage money and the deal is all but set."

"Mr. Morrissey is going to be awfully angry about this, awfully angry."

"I'll explain everything to him in the morning, Will, just let me handle him."

"Are you going to sign this yourself, Mr. Warren?"

"I am, Will, and I think you should, too—if we don't announce a settlement at the same time that we close the magazines, think of all the adverse publicity we'll get. It could cost us a lot more than this in the long run."

"Ridge," said Schlafman, "you sign first, where it says President, Chairman of the Board."

Warren took out his pen and scratched. Schlafman took the first copy and handed it to Austin, with another pen. As Warren signed the second copy, his pen dragged for he was watching Austin out of the corner of his eye, and he could see Austin pause, holding the pen in his hand, and then Austin, baffled and confused, was slowly, waveringly, scratching his signature under Warren's own signature on the first copy. Warren signed the second copy, handed it to Austin, and found Schlafman at his side. "The seal," whispered Schlafman. Warren's hand raised the seal-stamper to his knee from the floor and pressed it as Schlafman indicated. Then he signed the third copy. And sealed it. And sealed another. And Austin had finished signing.

The whole room now peered at Austin—and Austin smiled.

"That Morrissey," said Austin, "that Morrissey is going to be angry tomorrow, isn't he? When are we going to tell him about this, Ridge?"

"At the Board meeting, Will, at the Board meeting tomorrow afternoon, there's no point in telling him, or worrying him before then," replied Warren.

"No," said Schlafman, "or of telling anyone else, either. What's happened here tonight has to stay secret for twelve hours—and, as far as I'm concerned, permanently secret. There's disbarment for lawyers for conspiracies like this."

Schlafman picked up his hat and his briefcase, and as he rose, Eliot and Mitchell followed. Austin had sagged by the time the others had left and, gently, Warren and Mary led him to the guestroom.

"Well," said Warren as they closed the door on Austin. For the first time in months he felt triumphant. He stared around the empty living room and realized that he and Mary were alone.

"Well," he said again, awkwardly, as a smile of happiness came to him and he realized that on top of the triumph here was Mary's presence and he wanted her to stay. A new message was cutting its way to his consciousness as he looked at her and she was very beautiful.

"Well," he said, advancing on her, "that leaves the master bedroom doesn't it?"

"No," she said, her hand on her throat, a nervous smile on her lips. "No," she said again, the smile fading and her lips parting, as she retreated, "Johnny, I have to go home now."

"But what would Austin think," he said, "if you weren't here in the morning? Who'd make breakfast for us?"

"Johnny," she said, "this is ridiculous. You're making a joke of this. I have to go back to Paris tomorrow . . . oh, no . . . oh, go away, Johnny . . . Johnny, this isn't something that should happen by accident."

He had her in his arms, and was holding her to him, and her voice was protesting, yet her body was not and he said, "This isn't any accident, Mair."

"But this isn't fair to anybody, Johnny . . . it doesn't answer anything, Johnny."

"Right now and here it does, Mair. . . ."

And, still talking, he led her away to the master bedroom.

21. Friday, December Twelfth

1. LUNCH WITH UNCLE WALT

The morning would not halt to let Warren examine what had happened.

There had been no moment to speak to Mary when he woke late and found her already preparing breakfast for himself and Austin, not a moment of being alone in the haste to go, except the flustered whisper at the door, as he held her, tried to kiss her, and she turned her head away.

"Will you be here when I come home?" he asked.

"Johnny, hurry, Austin's waiting," she said.

"You haven't answered my question," he insisted.

"Johnny, we can't go into us now. Forget about last night, please—there's such a day ahead for you—"

"All right," he said, "we'll skip 'us' for this morning. But I won't forget about last night. Be here, just be here, where I can reach you."

"Johnny—go to work."

"Where can I reach you?" he insisted.

"At Sara Hubbard's then—anytime this afternoon. Johnny, call me and tell me what happens."

Then he was gone and, with a somersault, caught in the turmoil of the morning at the office. It was suddenly as if complete control were back in his hands. Hurried telephone calls to Norris at *Spectacle*, timing the announcement of suspension for late evening. Hurried telephone calls to publishers to whom he was now willing to give *Gentlewoman* subscribers away to clear his books of obligations. His own calls, quick, sharp, bold, his moves daring, all the skills and confidence returned to him. Conferences with Austin on the day's scheduling of events, the timetable of death. Hasty conferences in the corridor with Morrissey, as Morrissey reported on his dealing with creditors, the banks, Jack Raven. He could face Morrissey, this morning, with pleasure, buoyed by the knowledge of last night's deception. And when Morrissey suggested they have lunch to review the entire situation just before the Board meeting, Warren happily accepted the invitation. In fact, he was looking forward to it.

"You know, kid," said Morrissey at the end of the lunch, "I think we're going to get along. Wednesday night, I thought they were going to cart you off to the glue works and today you don't give a damn."

Morrissey had begun to call him "kid" halfway through the lunch as he waxed expansive.

"It's only a game, Walt," said Warren, "it's only a game; you try until the last man is out and when it's over, it's over."

"That's right, kid," said Morrissey, "that's right, and you stick around with me and you'll be farting through silk. This is as sweet a little operation as I've ever been on—"

"How sweet, Walt, how does it shake down now?" asked Warren, leading him on.

Morrissey rubbed his hands, took out a ball-point pen from his pocket and began to draw on the white linen tablecloth.

"I haven't even figured until now. We aren't out of the woods yet, we've got another ten days or two weeks of short cash, and until you've signed the split-up of *Gentlewoman* circulation, our balance sheet is vulnerable; but look, kid—"

Morrissey drew two parallel columns down the white linen tablecloth.

"By next week we have the three million from *Spectacle*. Then Raven —the way we've worked it out on the phone he'll let us use three million of his for six months secured by the plant, but the son-of-a-bitch wants to twist the thing into a capital gains for himself. He wants a quick transfer of plant title to him, now, then we get an option to buy it back six months later for half a million more than he paid. Neat trick if his lawyers can work it out. Well, what the hell—if we find we can get along without his three million in the next couple of weeks, we'll screw him and won't sign. But he's got it for us if we need it."

Morrissey scrawled a black six, followed by six zeros at the bottom of one column and went on.

"Then, what we owe—all told for paper, for ink, for other bills, for that goddamn union at the printing plant in severance—about three million dollars. We can probably get by the end of the year with the *Spectacle* cash just by a hair, and if we can sweet-talk the bank to hold still we won't even need Raven's cash, and we'll be O.K. by January fifteenth—"

"We ought to be a lot more than O.K.," said Warren.

"Leave it to Uncle Walt, kid," replied Morrissey. "I haven't finished. We'll have three divisions remaining in the firm pumping out four million dollars of profit a year, we'll have a tax-loss carryover big enough to choke a horse so we won't pay a nickel tax on operating profits for another three-four years. We'll take away between six and eight million from selling the Anderbury plant—kid, that stock is going to go up straight as a choirboy's prayer."

"How high do you figure, Walt?" asked Warren.

"It closed at eight and a quarter yesterday," said Morrissey, "by January its physical assets plus cash alone, net after liabilities, should be about seven dollars a share, and earnings could be about three a year. But I can make earnings look like four or five. If we play this stock right, make it fashionable, it'll be twenty by next June, and maybe thirty a year from now, if it catches on."

"And you triple your money," said Warren flatly.

"I could clear as much as eight million dollars out of this, kid," said Morrissey, "not all mine; I've got to whack it up with the crowd. But you make a potful yourself, too—you've got options on fifty thousand shares at ten. If it went to thirty, you could clear a million, too. Pretty good for a young fellow—"

Then, with one of those fluid changes of personality Warren had come to expect of Morrissey, the voice changed from joviality to ice.

"That is," continued Morrissey, "you can have it, if you behave yourself. You play with me and we'll try to make this Executive Committee a permanent thing. You know, two out of three runs that Committee and then the two of us decide what to do. We've straightened that one out now, haven't we?"

"I think we understand each other, Walt," said Warren, smiling.

The waiter came and left a check at the table. It read $12.70. Warren knew he had thirty-odd dollars in cash in his pocket and the $12.70 suddenly seemed substantially large. He wanted to take this check. Morrissey was talking.

"Let's be sure we do," said Morrissey. "These staff people now, Ridge—are you worried about them, can they make us trouble? They've been raising hell up and down the floors yesterday and this morning. Berger went to one of their meetings yesterday and you'll laugh at this one—some of them think you've run out with the dough; they didn't see you in the building yesterday. They're in a dirty mood. Maybe we ought to call in those Pinkertons after all, this afternoon—"

"No," broke in Warren firmly, knowing that with the agreement signed last night Eliot and Mitchell could hold the staff just this side of mob action. "We won't have any trouble. They get through work at five and there'll be no announcement of closing until a few hours later. They were paid their last paycheck this morning—I released the last few dollars at the bank on the strength of the *Spectacle* sale. They'll all have cash in their pockets, so they won't make trouble at the beginning of the weekend—"

"But if they come in on Monday, we owe them for a day's work, Ridge. What the hell—let's get out a telegram to all of them over the weekend telling them the job's over and making the office open on Monday to pick up only their personal stuff. Make the telegram full of regret, Ridge, you know, a lot of malarkey about with what sorrow you announce the closing and the end of their jobs—but get us off the hook legally. Get them out of the shop quietly, fire them at home, that's it."

"There's usually a two-weeks' notice on things like this, Walt—"

"The hell with that. We've got nine hundred magazine people in New York and four hundred across the country. Figure an average of a hundred bucks a week wages, and it's damned near three hundred thousand two weeks' notice would cost us. Not with my money. Every nickel counts."

"O.K., Walt. Have it your way. I want to get back and clear my desk before the meeting at four. I get your message."

The waiter approached, lifted the check, and faced both of them.

"The check, gentlemen?" he said.

Morrissey's hand fumbled slowly and reluctantly in his pocket. The thought came to Warren that this lunch was costing Morrissey a fine packet in severance pay. He smiled, quickly brought out a ten and a five, and gave it to the waiter. Morrissey nodded gratefully.

"So long as you understand me," said Morrissey, his voice softening to friendship as the waiter took Warren's money. "The way I said Wednesday night when I thought you wanted to screw me—I can use you. You get to a certain point in business where the money isn't all. What the hell can you do with it except go to Miami and play the horses? You take a guy like Raven, though, he plays around with Broadway, and this art crap of his, and I know he's making a front for his kid—but he enjoys it, he meets a new class of people. Well, I can raise as much cash on the line as Raven can, but, you know, well, you know—"

This was another shift in Morrissey, his face now very old and sad.

"Nobody gives a damn about me. Nobody can hurt me, you know, but then nobody cares whether I come home or not, you know what I mean. Maybe you and I can do some things together like Jack Raven does. Maybe if you'd trusted me we could have done something about those magazines; they would have helped take the smell off me. If it hadn't been for the money, maybe—"

Morrissey shook his head of the encumbering thought, freed himself of the melancholy, and his face was sharp again.

"—But you can't do what you want with eight million dollars net staring at you, right there to grab. You've got to do what the money says, that's all I know, kid, you aren't free. The hell with it. There are lots of other things we can do together; I've got plans for you. Thanks for lunch."

"Let's go, Walt," said Warren. "We have work to do."

"I know, I know, kid," growled Morrissey. "But aren't you going to get some change out of that money? You ought to get half a buck back out of that check. No sense spoiling these waiters with twenty-five per cent tips. You got a lot to learn from your Uncle Walt."

2. THE BOARD—5:30 P.M.

It was dark now with the deep early dark of December, the remorseless closing of night as the days of the year dwindle under winter's coming, and the fire in Abbott Pepper's Board Room crackled loudly. Outside, Warren knew, guards Austin had summoned patrolled the elevator exits of the Executive Floor, sealing off any intruder from the floors below. Inside, the table was a long untidy clutter of paper and memoranda, and the meeting rested in Warren's hands.

He had dominated this meeting completely, rapping it to order sternly, squeezing its questions to his own timing, marching its business relentlessly to his own agenda.

They had approved the negotiation with *Spectacle* and Austin had telephoned from the Board Room across the square to *Spectacle* to confirm simultaneous release time of the news in a few hours. They approved Morrissey's tentative negotiations with Raven for mortgage money. They approved Warren's tentative morning negotiations to split the circulation of *Gentlewoman*. As each matter came up and Warren briefly reviewed the solutions of the past forty-eight hours, there would be a murmur of approval, and someone would suggest that it be put in motion. Someone else would grunt, "So move," a ripple of "ayes" would follow, and they would so move, and pass on to the next matter—inquiring only of detail, questioning no policy, relieved, all of them, as a family is relieved when an undertaker instructs them in procedure and acts upon it.

Warren watched the hands of his watch creep around. It was five o'clock and they had disposed of the circulation of the two magazines. It was five thirty, and he had finished an exposition of the clean new balance sheet. It was six o'clock when Warren was finally informed by a note from Laura, as he had directed her to, that the staff had departed quietly, except for a few last drunks and the committee waiting in the kitchen headquarters to hear from him. And newspapermen and cameramen waiting for whatever announcement the Board might make. It was time now that the ceremonies of death become public and known outside this room.

Making his voice hard, Warren explained that the Christmas issue would begin to roll in a few minutes at the Anderbury plant, that the advertising it carried in no way balanced the four hundred thousand dollars of paper and press time it consumed. Calling for objections and finding none, he proposed that it be suspended on press. That was Hopkins' job.

Hopkins lifted his heavy frame from the chair and surveyed the room, staring at them for a minute that stretched and stretched, and Warren knew that Hopkins was waiting for a word from someone beyond the resolution just passed, and he must give the word.

"You can use the phone from my office to Anderbury, Bert," said Warren deliberately. "Laura will get the plant for you. Tell them it was a decision forced by the Board and that you voted against it."

The door closed behind Hopkins and Warren found that his throat was dry. He let the silence hang for a minute until the choke was gone; then let the silence continue until it filled the room, and the men at the table fidgeted uncomfortably, waiting for him to resume, but no one spoke. Warren wondered how many of them had ever visited the plant they owned at Anderbury, or ever seen the great presses rolling, making words on paper, making meaning of words, whether any of them could even imagine what happened when you pressed the emergency stop on a press and the paper, snapped in its furious run, came bursting out in a great ruffle of torn streamers and ribbons and became waste.

The quiet hung, and the pulse in Anderbury was being cut, and, "That leaves the statement to the press and the telegram of dismissal to the salaried staff," said Warren in the quiet. "Let me read you the statement to the press on the suspension of *Trumpet* and *Gentlewoman.*"

He read the statement to the press, first in its entire context and then, once more, slowly, paragraph by paragraph. There was no objection. He asked Austin whether he would carry the statement away immediately and instruct Bennett on its mimeographing and release, in accord with *Spectacle*, for eight o'clock.

"Now," he said, "there's this last matter of dismissals and I'll read it to you."

Slowly and distinctly, he read the telegram he had drafted in the afternoon.

"It is with deep personal regret that I inform you that your employment at General American Publishing was terminated this afternoon at five o'clock. Circumstances beyond our control have made further publication of the magazines impossible. The offices will be open Monday and all the rest of the week for you to occupy and dispose of your personal effects. A staff committee headed by David Eliot and Ben Mitchell has made arrangements with management for severance pay and a full settlement of all your claims. You are advised to take up any personal details for presentation to management through them. With deep personal affection and my thanks for a gallant effort."

He paused.

"And I sign it," he said, "John Ridgely Warren, President and Chairman of the Board."

He scrutinized their faces. Who would react first? At the end of the table, facing him, Warren could see the contentment slowly fade from Morrissey's countenance. The thin eyebrows tautened, and a wrinkle overlined them; the thin tongue darted out, wiped its lips, a scowl settled. Morrissey leaned across the table, searched Warren with his hard blue eyes, then puckered his lips to speak.

But Fleming questioned first.

"I didn't quite follow that. Will you read the last sentence again?"

"The last sentence?" Warren repeated the question. "It reads, 'With deep personal affection and my—'"

"No," said Morrissey, breaking in, "not that one. Not that crap. The one before about the arrangement with management. What arrangement?"

Warren read again slowly. "A staff committee headed by David Eliot and Ben Mitchell has made arrangements with management for a full settlement of all your claims, and you are advised to take up any personal details of your claim for presentation to management through them."

"What arrangement?" repeated Fleming. "What claims? We paid them for their work today, didn't we?"

"Warren," grated Morrissey, over the silence, "are you monkeying around with me again?"

"Why, no," said Warren, completely relaxed. "Why, no, Walt," he continued, "there are only two things left on the agenda and the next thing is this arrangement for severance pay with the white-collar staff."

"What arrangement?" rasped Morrissey. "Warren, if you've pulled a fast one on me and this Board, I'm going to cut—"

Warren gave Morrissey a big, happy smile. It was amazing how easy it was to handle him if you knew what you wanted. If you did not want money, he could not hurt you.

"You're out of order, Walt," said Warren blandly. "I want to explain the severance arrangements," he went on, taking the edge off his voice but holding control of the meeting, "which are very simple. Every employee of this firm will receive next week a two-weeks' paycheck in lieu of notice. There will be an extra week for each six months worked over one year here, an extra two weeks for every full year worked. The arrangement will cost us something like one million, one hundred thousand dollars, the first installment to consist of two-hundred-fifty thousand dollars paid this year, the subsequent two installments on January fifteenth and April thirtieth of next year. That's the arrangement, Mr. Fleming, any questions?"

Fleming opened his mouth to ask a question of Warren, then turned to Morrissey instead.

"Are you aware of this, Mr. Morrissey, is anybody else here aware of this? When did it happen?"

"I can answer that," said Warren. "It happened last night shortly after the sale of the circulation to *Spectacle* was consummated. Mr. Morrissey has been completely unaware of this until now—"

"It's preposterous," snapped Fleming. "I'm not a hardhearted man, but this makes our edge against bankruptcy in the next two or three weeks just paper-thin. I refuse to go along. We have no legal obligation to white-collar employees. You're making a gift of our money. The matter has to be brought to a vote here and now, and I, for one—"

"Yes," said Warren, "you've registered your opinion, Mr. Fleming. The fact of the matter is that we have already entered into a settlement agreement with the staff committee as of this morning. They can put the firm in bankruptcy anytime in the next ten days if we refuse to honor this debt."

"Let me see that agreement," said Fleming. "I'm not too sure of my commercial law, but if I know my corporate law, the whole thing is illegal."

"Here it is," said Warren, pulling out the agreement. "It's entirely legal. On Wednesday, this Board, including you, gave the Executive Committee power to dispose of matters and report. We've disposed and here is our report, and here is the document."

"Let me see it," called Morrissey, and Warren passed the paper down the table.

"Why, you double-crossed me," said Morrissey, after he examined the signatures. "Why, you flannel-mouthed, Ivy-League crook, you double-crossed me. You and Austin. Warren, I'm going to get you for this. . . ."

He sputtered in rage and Warren noticed that Hopkins had returned to the room. He was pleased to have Hopkins at the scene.

"Mr. Morrissey's interpretation of our resolution," said Warren explanatorily to the Board, "was that two out of three members of the Executive Committee had authority to act for the whole. Mr. Austin and I as two out of the three, as President and Treasurer, so interpreted the resolution last night when we signed this agreement."

"Mr. Warren," said Fleming, "do you realize that you've deceived us again? Deceived me. Deceived Mr. Morrissey."

"Mr. Fleming," said Warren, completely free at last, "I was acting for the interest of the corporation. In the coldest business terms, one million dollars payment to severed employees is the cheapest possible cover for the stench and publicity this closing will make."

A clucking noise came from Mr. Varian, who had not spoken during the afternoon.

"Well, now that you put it in a business light, Mr. Warren, you may have a good point there—I felt so badly myself about the way we were treating them, but we had to have a business reason and now—"

Warren's mind recorded instantly that Varian's voice added to his, Austin's and Hopkins' made a majority of four at today's meeting.

"I was sure *you* would understand, Mr. Varian," said Warren, "even in business terms it makes sense. But for Mr. Fleming and Mr. Morrissey I want to add a few other reasons. No, don't interrupt me, Mr. Fleming. The staff committee will be releasing the text of this agreement to the press in a few minutes. The morning papers will carry it as part of the settlement. You have to think of several things. Whether you want to contest the agreement in court and reap the publicity that could eventually ruin the other divisions. Next, whether you want to chance a court suit in the next ten days of vulnerability—Mr. Silverman and Mr. Campbell are pacified now and will wait until January for the money they know is coming to them. But if they hear of a court suit, they could move immediately. And the subscriber obligation of *Gentlewoman* circulation still has to be disposed of—all agreements on its disposal up to now are entirely oral and in my hands at the moment. You might upset this agreement in court and you might not, for the legal question is moot. After all, you appointed an Executive Committee with full powers for three days—and I am President and Austin is Treasurer—"

"Not for long, Warren, not for longer than the next ten minutes," snapped Morrissey.

"That's another interesting legal question, Walt," said Warren, "but I won't argue that one now. I concede this Board has full power to fire me any time it wants—but getting back to this agreement, I want to point out that no judge, subject to politics and normally ambitious, is going to rule in Christmas season against employees dismissed after a lifetime of service in favor of questionable repudiation of a legal obligation by a group of stock-market raiders and plush-bottomed trustees—"

"Watch your language there," said Fleming icily.

"—who milked two great magazines dry," continued Warren, "and beyond that, if the committee wins in court, then you're up the creek so deep without a paddle, you're right back where you were last week. Plus the adverse publicity, that can so hurt the sales of every other division of the corporation as to cost you more than one million, one hundred thousand dollars—"

"It's not the dough," said Morrissey, "but you screwed me; nobody screws Walt Morrissey."

"Ah, Walt," said Warren, completely enjoying himself, "in this town everybody has to get screwed sooner or later. Everyone does. You have that big fat eight million dollars in the market you can take a year from now. Maybe you can even start backing Broadway plays like Jack Raven with what you make—"

"You know, Warren," said Morrissey, "I never thought you had it in you. So help me, I did trust you on this. If only I could see some way of putting you in jail for using the Social Security money to pay current bills, I'd—"

"But there isn't, Walt, and you're greedy," said Warren, as if admonishing a child. "You want your killing and satisfaction too. You have to choose, you know. You can't have both. Anyway, as soon as we deposit the *Spectacle* check in the bank, Social Security is covered—"

"Warren," said Morrissey, "do you know you're still responsible here? Do you know this goddamn settlement gives us just a paper edge in the next two weeks? I don't want to operate the next two or three weeks with a pistol in my back—"

"Why, Walt, I've been operating that way for six months," said Warren, "it's exciting that way. Compared to what I've been through, the next few weeks are nothing. And Jack Raven will bail you out for a fee. This is a property now, everyone's got the right to cut himself a slice of what he can get—"

"Not you, Warren, not you. You know those options you've got? I don't think you've got them any more. You can't exercise them unless you're working for us and you aren't going to be—you thought of that yet?"

"I've thought of that, Walt, and I don't really care—as you said at lunch, what can you buy with money?"

"I'm glad," said Morrissey, "I'm glad, because you just tossed half a million dollars out the window. I'm glad you don't need money. You and that Austin, both, you aren't going to be here long."

"Glad you brought that up, Walt, very glad. Lay off Austin. I did it. He was scared. I told him you'd be delighted. I painted you as a gentleman, as a man of large vision. Austin's loyal, Walt—loyal to anybody he works for and what's more, he's prepared to like you. Not many people like you, Walt."

"My grievance, Warren," said Fleming, interrupting, "is not against Mr. Austin, but against you—I've known Mr. Austin for years and I trust him. But you—"

"Mr. Fleming," said Warren. "I'm turning over to you a property far more valuable than the one you gave me. I was hired to be executioner of two magazines you didn't have the courage to destroy yourself. You still need me. And you need Austin, too. Silverman would be happy to file bankruptcy on Monday against you—all I have to do is telephone him. I still have to sew up the distribution of *Gentlewoman* circulation in the next few days. You won't be safe until that's done. This whole thing can still come down around your neck and without my going to jail, either—"

"Now, I presume, you're blackmailing us," said Fleming.

"What a nasty word that is, Mr. Fleming," said Warren. "Blackmail looks different from where you stand. But the only thing I want at the moment is to see a contract signed in the next few days by this corporation protecting Mr. Austin, say a three-year, or five-year contract. Or I bring this thing down when I come to work on Monday—"

"You've got everything figured out, haven't you?" said Morrissey.

"Not quite," said Warren, "but I can learn this sort of thing fast. Where I went wrong you wouldn't understand, Walt, not at all. Nor you, Mr. Fleming. You even less than Mr. Morrissey. Walt—I make a deal with you. Austin is in and I'll promise to behave."

"All right," said Morrissey. "Austin is in, but you're out—"

The door opened and Austin returned to the room.

"Did the press statement go out, Will?" asked Warren.

"Yes," said Austin, "they're rolling it off the mimeograph now. The staff committee is holding its statement to the press announcing the settlement of severance. I hope that's all right with everyone—"

"Perfectly fine, Will," said Warren. "I've just been explaining the settlement to the Board and I think we're all in agreement. Isn't that so?" he asked of the Board.

There was no answer, then Varian, "Well, yes, I suppose so."

"I'll read the telegram to the staff again," said Warren, "and see if it's all right now."

He read the statement and paused at the end of his reading.

"If there are no objections," he said, his voice rising, "I'll get it off now. Any objections?"

There was a silence.

"No objections, so ordered," said Warren, "and now there's only one thing left on my agenda."

"Just a minute," said Morrissey, "it comes to me we ought to fire you at this meeting, too. No telling what you're gonna do next. You see it our way, don't you, Ridge?"

"Why, Walt," said Warren, "why, Walt, our minds are working together at last. That's the last point on my agenda, too. Only I call it my resignation."

"I prefer Mr. Morrissey's phrasing," said Fleming, stiffly. "Dismissal. I feel we ought to express ourselves. I take a very unhappy view of your attitude to all of us, to the corporation, to this last week's transactions."

"It's just a matter of phrasing, I know," said Warren, "but, of course, dismissal takes effect immediately, and my resignation takes effect on January first. If you want to clean up the mess yourself, starting on Monday, you can fire me. But I felt I ought to be around to bury the bodies and mop the blood off the floor for you until—"

"I prefer dismissal without severance pay," said Fleming, firmly, "immediately."

"Me, too," said Morrissey, "but he's got us across a barrel there, Mr. Fleming. When's your resignation dated?"

"January first," said Warren, "no severance pay."

"Well," said Morrissey, "let's just reorganize the Executive Committee, first. Mr. Fleming to replace Mr. Warren. Executive Committee of Morrissey, Fleming, Austin with no power to act without the full Board. Mr. Warren to report to us in the next three weeks on any matter of substance before making decision."

"A fine resolution, Walt," said Warren. "If you let me make my resignation an amendment to that resolution, I'll vote for it myself. As a matter of fact, I so move—any objections?"

"Yes," said Fleming, "I do."

"Vote," said Warren, "by a show of hands."

They raised their hands. First the ayes. Morrissey, Berger, Warren, all at once. Then Austin, seeing Warren's hand in the air, followed suit. Then Varian, shaking his head sadly.

"Five ayes," said Warren. "Nays?"

Fleming raised his hand.

"One objection. Five ayes, one nay—there must be one abstention."

"That's me," said Hopkins, "the way I feel, if we can't all sit at the table together, let's knock the legs out from under the table and we'll all sit on the floor, like the fellow says. But you can't put that in a resolution."

"No," said Warren appreciatively, "but I like the thought. That makes five ayes, one nay, one abstention. And I think this meeting is over."

It was over. It was all over.

"This meeting is over, gentlemen," he repeated, rising to his feet, "and if I hear no objection, I now adjourn it, holding myself ready to meet the new Executive Committee any time after Monday."

There was complete silence at the table.

He stood very tall, feeling very much himself, and strong, and sad, and free, and said, "I hear no objection. Meeting adjourned. Gentlemen —A Merry Christmas and a Happy New Year to you all."

3. ELIOT'S FRIDAY

All through the hours of Friday from early morning, as he wandered from floor to floor, goading his committee members for last-minute signatures, Eliot had mused on how he would write such a story if he were reporting it from the outside—for acting on the inside of a story, as he was now, was entirely different from observing it from the outside.

From the outside, this was an office building, on the top seventeen stories of which were scattered hundreds of people bound together over the years by the companionship of purpose, and tomorrow when the purpose dissolved, their lives and friendships would dissolve too. Each floor was a fragment of a confusion that could be explained as a story only if one knew what was happening elsewhere. In the vault of *Spectacle*, Eliot knew, there reposed one agreement signing away the life of *Trumpet*; in another vault at Nat Schlafman's office reposed the staff agreement he himself had signed last night with Warren buying for each employee a little time to start again. But Eliot could say nothing to anyone of either agreement until the Board met and the committee learned whether the agreement had been confirmed by the Board—or must be fought out and established in court.

So, all day, floating among the people who drifted from floor to floor, confused and baffled, who gathered in random knots that formed about the water-coolers, about the elevator exits, at any chance desk where three other people had already stopped to talk, Eliot moved and listened.

The early-morning rumor on the advertising floor was that Warren had absconded— "He's gone, I tell you, he's gone," Eliot heard one voice rising from a knot of troubled men, and then, "How do you know he's gone?" "They saw him at the airport last night, going to Bermuda." "You're crazy, why should he run away?" "Because he's running off with the dough, I tell you, he took it, he milked it dry." "Yeah, didn't you hear about this bankruptcy petition, they can put him in jail?" "Not for bankruptcy, it's a civil offense." "Who cares about him—are we bankrupt?" "Sure, we're bankrupt, for God's sake, it's all over town."

When that rumor had spent its vigor and was killed by Warren's late arrival at the office, there came the optimistic rumor which flourished at *Gentlewoman*. "Did you hear, did you hear?" "What?" "*Spectacle's* buying *Gentlewoman*. Did you hear, they're gonna keep on publishing; we're in, goddamn it, we're in." "No, you got it wrong, they bought

Trumpet, they're going to publish *Trumpet,* make it an all-text magazine." "Do you suppose they bought both?" "Why not?"

There were the timid rumors: "Don't sign that petition, don't sign it!" "Why?" "I just heard that they're going to blacklist everybody who signed the thing, nobody'll ever get a job in the magazine business who signed it—get your power of attorney back. . . ."

"Did you hear? Did you hear?" . . . "No, What?" . . . "They've got a rich Democrat going to buy *Trumpet,* it's going to be the Democratic Party magazine . . . starting next week."

"They aren't going to fold it . . . the Board is meeting this afternoon to toss Warren out, we're going to have a new editor. . . ."

"Jack Raven is buying it, did you hear? . . . yeah . . . the word is all over town . . . my bookie called me and told me about it. . . ."

Then, as the morning moved past noon, and Eliot found himself on the circulation floor, with the circulation men he had organized, he found it was today's paycheck that made the rumors spin.

"That severance-pay thing that we signed, Dave, if they go bankrupt how can they pay that, Dave?"

And before he could answer, another voice breaking in, "The hell with the severance pay, how about today's paycheck, is that coming through? There's two weeks tied up in that, it ought to be here by now, it always comes by noon, are we going to get paid today?"

And another voice, "They paid the advertising department at ten thirty this morning. They paid editorial. The ghost always walks last down here in circulation, she should be here any minute now—"

"But will the checks be any good if they're bankrupt, and today's Friday—?"

"Tell you what, fellows, as soon as I get my hand on it, I walk downstairs to the bank, change it into cash, Uncle Sam's promise to pay, the only one I trust—"

"I've got a lunch date, I can't get to the bank that fast—"

"Banks close at three. Be smart. Keep your lunch date waiting and cash the check first."

"But it's about a new job—"

"Don't be a dope, cash the check first."

There was a burst of noise and a cheer from a knot of people at the far end of the floor. They turned and looked.

"There she is now," said someone, "she's got the envelopes in her hand. Take one last look fellows, as the money-wagon goes by."

Eliot watched them huddle and crowd like a group of schoolboys about the girl bearing the paychecks, then watched them dissolve almost immediately toward the elevators that would carry them downstairs to the bank.

A laggard suddenly burst by Eliot on the empty circulation floor, his coat buttoned, his muffler wrapped about him.

"Say," he called, "did Mike go, too?"

"I don't know Mike," said Eliot. "What's the matter?"

"He owes me ten bucks on the pool we had for the guess of newsstand sales last issue. I won. He said he'd pay me the ten right after he got his paycheck. He'll duck out on me if I don't get him now, this is the last paycheck. 'Bye—I've got to run now—"

Eliot watched him scurry off to the elevators.

By the time Eliot returned from lunch at three o'clock, dissolution was proceeding steadily.

Reporters from newspapers, news agencies and magazines had arrived at committee headquarters in the experimental kitchen. Prevented from penetrating the Executive Floor and the Board meeting by the guards at the elevators, they clustered around the committee's table, pounced on Eliot as he entered, questioned him for the timing of a committee statement. They were relaxed and professional as they questioned him, as he had been relaxed and professional so many times himself on similar occasions. The reporters had piled their hats and coats in one corner of the kitchen, had commandeered several telephones, and when they learned there would be no statement until evening, began to wander about the floors seeking fragments of color and human interest to pad out the statement and the facts when they should be ready.

Eliot sat down by the committee desk which was being monitored by Clement and began to pick out on a typewriter the two alternate statements he must have ready by evening—the one denouncing the corporation for repudiating its obligations and announcing a fight in court, the other to be released if the Board approved—simple, somber and straightforward, announcing amicable agreement on severance pay.

As he typed, he could hear fragments of conversation on Clement's busy telephone.

"Yes," Clement was saying on one call, ". . . we're taking all job offers down right here and we'll post them on the bulletin board on Monday . . . to give everyone here an even break off the mark . . . that's fine . . . I have it now . . . two space salesmen, one a liquor specialist, two newsstand circulation men . . . two secretaries and a posting clerk . . . now, wait a second . . . look, I appreciate what you're doing, but don't make it between twenty-eight and thirty-five . . . half of our people here are over forty years old . . . I know, I don't want to write personnel policy for you . . . but let me post it on the bulletin board as between twenty-eight and forty-five. . . . It's going to be hell on morale here, every job offer that comes in here is limited to people under thirty-five . . . you don't have to take them, you don't even have to see them, but let me post these jobs as open up to age forty-five . . . you're a good man . . . thanks. . . ."

He could hear Clement again, later.

"What? . . . What? . . . Where is he? . . . Did they hurt him? . . . Good . . . listen, he's probably just drunk, he's a good guy . . . I'll be right up myself to bring him down, we'll get him home . . . be easy on him, thanks a lot. . . ."

"What's that?" asked Eliot of Clement, and Clement answered, "That was Warren's secretary. One of our ad salesmen must have come back drunk from lunch. She said he came up to the Executive Floor, burst through the guards there, said he was going to beat the pulp out of Warren for what he'd done. . . . He got into a scuffle with the guards, they ripped his shirt, and now he's crying. . . . I've got to go up and get him and send him home with someone in a cab. . . . Will you take the phone, Dave?"

That was the beginning of the tide of drunks. The drunks began to filter up to the committee headquarters shortly after four, after they had finished drinking whatever was available on their own floors. Eliot could not tell whether they were coming here because they wanted consolation at the committee's desk, or because the committee's desk was in the experimental kitchen of *Gentlewoman* and word had spread that they were cleaning out the iceboxes in the kitchen and having a party, and that the wines *Gentlewoman* had acquired for its special Spring Gourmet issue were being distributed.

Eliot was amused by their disappointment. Mrs. Conover, mistress of the *Gentlewoman* kitchen, had come back to the kitchen after her own lunch with a huge suitcase, and begun to pack it. With an unerring instinct for value, she had chosen the spices of the spice story, the tinned imported delicacies, the shelf full of goose livers she had ordered from the Rhineland, Alsace, and Perigord, the truffles from Italy. She had, at lunchtime, acquired several chunks of steaming dry ice, and she wrapped these in cotton batting, and packed the caviar tins, too. Her assistants watched her without rivalry or apparent jealousy, for Mrs. Conover directed a taut staff, but as soon as she had buckled the suitcase, the rest of the kitchen staff began to wrap skillets, pots, pans, utensils and all the other devices of kitchenry that *Gentlewoman* was constantly testing. A locust horde plucked the kitchen clean and Eliot was sure that on all the floors of General American Publishing, everything movable was similarly being stripped, from paperclips to projectors.

The drunks argued loudly with each other, now abusive, now melancholy and five o'clock came and went and the word passed that there were to be no dismissals this working day, and the drunks argued again, even more loudly, whether this meant salvation or not and slowly, as hunger and home began to call them, they began to thin out.

Now, at six, as Eliot still waited for word from Warren on the Executive Floor as to which statement he might release, and the newspapermen grew impatient as their deadlines approached, and some began to compose leads for their stories, wondering how many words it would take to write, the people in the kitchen had dwindled only to *Gentlewoman* editorial staff—

In one corner Eliot could see two men and two women on the *Gentlewoman* staff sitting on the floor with their arms around each other, harmonizing in the Undertakers' Song . . . ". . . Oh, the worms crawl in," the worms crawl out, they crawl all over your eyes and mouth . . ." they chanted, staring into space. Nearby, a blowsy middle-aged woman, thoroughly unhappy, was crying and nobody was paying her any attention. Eliot wished that someone would see her home safely, but she was *Gentlewoman* staff and he did not even know her name. He could see a boy of perhaps twenty-four or twenty-five sitting on the floor with his arm around a young researcher. The young researcher was very pretty, and the boy was talking very earnestly, and as Eliot watched, the boy put his arm around her protectively. Silently Eliot urged him on. She was such a pretty girl and he was a handsome boy, and Eliot reflected on all the marriages that had been made in this building of such girls and such boys. Eliot hoped the boy would get the girl—when he was interrupted by two men belligerently leaning over his desk.

"Are you Dave Eliot?" asked one.

"Yes," said Eliot.

"The chairman of this committee?" asked the other.

"Yes. What can I do for you—"

"Well, you people better get wise to yourselves. You're all going to be out on the street tomorrow and unless you have public opinion behind you—do you know what just happened?"

And as Eliot listened to the TV men he found out exactly what had happened to them. They had set up their cameras on the editorial floor of *Trumpet*— "Just to get some human interest pictures, you know; TV can't use statements; we wanted a few pictures of them crying, that gets you sympathy; we were trying to help you"—and a man called Foley had come up to them, and he had socked the TV announcer right on the nose. "Bust him one." So bad that he had to go back and change his shirt because the one he was wearing was all bloody. Did this committee want favorable publicity or not? "And the old one, the old one, Mitch something or other, threatened to toss our TV cameras out the windows unless we got the hell off the floor right away, and—"

Eliot soothed the two TV men, concealing his envy of Foley who had been able, actually, to sock someone. Eliot promised the two TV men they could set up their cameras in the downstairs lobby, and that he, personally, would read the staff statement to them for their cameras as soon as it was ready for release.

He mollified them, and denounced Foley, and denounced Mitchell, and hoped that by now things had come out right enough at the Board meeting so that they would not need favorable publicity and as the two TV men turned away, he heard them saying, "Ah, Christ—there won't be anybody crying down there in the lobby, you've got to show the tears on their faces. You'd think they'd understand, they have to cover stories, too—"

Eliot wondered about Foley for a moment and whether he would be all right. He looked at his watch, saw it was seven o'clock, then decided he might as easily wait for Warren's message down on the *Trumpet* floor where he belonged, as here on the floor of *Gentlewoman*.

There could have been no work done here, today, thought Eliot, as he entered the desolate floor of *Trumpet*. Over each office cubicle dangled a hangman's noose of yellow hemp. At Christmas season, year after year, the editorial floor of *Trumpet* was hung with green and red ribboning. Now, Eliot saw that someone this afternoon had stripped away all the holiday decorations and, instead, the entire floor was strung with black ribboning—paper carbon ribbons of electric typewriters, black fabric ribbons of other typewriters, were coiled and twisted and strung over walls, chairs, hanging fixtures. There was a spatter of empty beer cans, of paper cups, of cigarette butts in the ashtrays and on the floor. Over everything hung the haze of smoke, and through the smoke Eliot's eye caught a Santa Claus. As he came nearer, he saw that it was a huge, hastily painted poster of a Santa Claus which hung over the aisle that led to the Art Department, and that Santa Claus had a black beard, and a black tasseled hat, and was grinning with fiendish glee from a green-and-black skull. Underneath, the caption read, "We regret to inform you that Santa Claus died this week."

Beyond, in the far corner where the pulse of the magazine had always beat, was a light, and from the corner came the murmur of voices, and Eliot knew, as he had been certain, that there in Foley's office sat the deathwatch. The deathwatch sat on the couches and easy chairs of Foley's conference room, all there as if at a story conference—Duckworth, and Clement, and Mitchell, and the others he knew so well. Foley sat at the head of the table, as Eliot would always remember him, in shirtsleeves, rubbing his face with his paw as he thought. The crumbs of sandwiches, half-broken slices of bread, morsels of ham covered the table and empty beer cans were stacked raggedly in a row.

"Have a sandwich, Dave," said Foley, as Eliot entered, "no gourmets here. Last meal we get out of *Trumpet*—corned beef, tunafish, ham or cheese?"

Eliot leaned over the table to reach for a sandwich because now, with his own people, he felt suddenly hungry, and he wanted to eat, when the telephone rang.

Foley lifted it, said, "For you, Dave," and handed it over.

It was Laura.

"Mr. Warren said to tell you that the Board has confirmed the severance agreement and you can announce it whenever you want . . . he also said not to go home until you had a word with him. . . ."

They looked at him as he put the telephone down; he put aside the sandwich he had been about to eat. He looked at them all, and they had become with the telephone call only people—what had bound them together over the years, the magic of taking the truth and the dream from the chaos of the world about them, was gone. They were his friends now, and they would always belong to a part of him, but they no longer made home as they had made home until a few minutes ago.

"I have to give the statement to the press, now," he explained. "The Board agreed. The severance settlement is in the bag. And then I've got to face the routine of the TV cameras in the lobby downstairs, and then— then maybe I'll be back, maybe I won't. See you all on Monday."

The rest was routine. The statement, the questions, the quotes. The trip down the elevator to the lobby, and the light of the cameras on him, and the faces peering at them from the dark, and the smooth voice of the TV interviewer, his own face always directly at the camera, now smiling, now gravely sorrowful, his enunciation perfect, his fresh blue shirt clean, trying to explain what this all meant.

Eliot slipped out of the circle of light as the TV announcer turned with a smile to summon another victim to the camera, and, as he turned, there was a touch on his elbow.

"David," said the voice, "can you tell me how to get to Ridge's office? He called for me to meet him."

It was Mary.

"Mary," he said, "why don't I take you there?"

"No," she said, "you have to stay for the end of this, don't you?"

"I don't have to stay for anything," said Eliot. "It's all over now. This is just the burial detail."

4. VIEW FROM THE FORTIETH FLOOR

Warren was watching the night snow as they came in. It must have begun to snow in the afternoon. But from this height, he could not tell whether the snow as it fell was piling deep in drifts in the city streets below, or melting to a slush. It had been that way all the time at this desk—from this height you could not imagine how it truly was down below.

He turned as they entered. He had not expected them to arrive together. He saw that Mary was dressed in a gray worsted suit, and he could not tell whether it was just a suit, or a traveling suit, and the thought passed through his mind how greatly the clothing of a woman changed her personality. In her wrapper, with face cream glistening, with her hair braided, he could approach her softly. Sheathed in this stern suit, she was very beautiful, yet very strong, and he did not know whether she was strong now on leaving, or strong now on staying. He was glad she had come with Eliot. It would be easier to talk to her with Eliot here, than alone.

"Hi," said Eliot, "I brought you a visitor."

"Sit down," said Warren. "I wanted Mary to see this office before I left—or she left. Sit down—Mair."

"No," said Eliot. "You two probably want to be alone. We can talk later."

"I can't make you sit down, David," said Warren, "because I've just put a telegram on the wires firing you along with thirteen hundred other people. So you're not working for me and you don't have to stay—unless you want to."

"Please," said Mary, "stay, David."

They sat all three and Warren asked Eliot what had happened this day downstairs. Eliot tried to describe it, threading together the episodes he had seen, but there was no describing it because the death of the two magazines had been shared by too many people. And no one could say when the spirit left. With curiosity, Eliot asked Warren about the Board meeting and as Warren told what had happened, he could feel Mary's eyes on him.

"And you," asked Eliot, "where do you come out?"

"I'll be out in three weeks. They've given me that much time to bury the bodies and mop up the floor and then it's over."

"Severance?" asked Eliot.

"For the staff, yes, as you know. For me—no. That was part of the package. It got noisy at that point. But I could finally hear myself thinking —and it was worth it."

"That's quite a lot to pay just to hear yourself think."

"Well," Warren shrugged, "you have to pay something if you want to be free. It seemed better to pay it that way than the other way—"

"What did you hear?" asked Mary softly, speaking for the first time.

"It comes and it goes, when you listen to yourself," he said, turning to her. "That's what was wrong the past two years. This afternoon I was listening about responsibility the way you said I must, the other night. I had to get the staff its severance pay, and I did that. And I had to take care of Austin. And I had to get Morrissey the killing I promised him a year ago. And I had to give the Board back a property, safe, and —the only thing I couldn't meet was because *Trumpet* was dead already, and it was too late to listen—"

"I'm not sure I'm following you, Johnny," said Mary.

"You have to listen," he said, stubbornly trying to explain it. "You have to listen to yourself. With an inner ear. This town is full of roar and sound. And we people in magazines, in radio, in TV, in newspapers, live in a bath of noise; it makes a static around us, we drench the country and ourselves in noise. So we have to listen harder than anyone else for what is faint and fragile and really new or really true. You have to strain it out of the air the way the grid of an audion tube picks up the faintest wave-length from the air, and clarifies it, and makes it louder, until every-one else can hear it over all the other frequencies. If you hear it, you can make them hear it, too. And if you don't hear it yourself you can't get away with turning up the volume and making it loud. I gambled on volume and it didn't work— Mair, look, I wanted you to see this the way it looks from my windows."

He got up, knowing he would not long have these windows and this view. Somewhere out there the sweep of the towers, the ranges and reaches of the city had misled him for too long, and he had learned too late.

"You, too, Dave," he said. "You won't be a visitor in this office when I leave."

It was very dark outside, and he let their eyes adjust to the dark before he spoke. He knew what he wanted them to see. The scud of flakes swirled close by his windows in gusts of invisible wind, then vanished, then returned. The snowclouds were indistinct in the night. Yet every now and then a black veil of cloud would drift low between the windows from which they watched and the silhouette of other distant buildings, so that the buildings rose from a pit of darkness without foundations.

"Sometimes," he said to them, "I used to stand here on a hazy morning, when the fog was very low, and then all the buildings, all the towers, seemed to be rising from a bed of fog, as if they had no roots, only reach."

The buildings around twinkled and glittered above the billow of darkness. The streets below and the ground in which the towers were socketed were lost.

"I thought," said Warren, "you could measure everything the way a builder measures buildings. So much for engineering estimates, so much for ground cost, so much for construction costs, so much for mortgage— and then you rented out the space at a profit. If the figures were right, you couldn't miss. But that's not so. That's where I went wrong, that's where the whole gamble went wrong."

"How, Johnny?" asked Mary.

"Because every tower out there was built on someone's dream. The dream first, then they measured it out. You see, this country was built of dreams as well as appetites. And I gambled on the appetites. I thought if I measured and packaged enough appetites in a big enough audience, I could come out with a profit and be free. But you know, even if I'd won that one, I would still have been caught. The way Morrissey is caught. The way the TV boys are caught. The way all the balance-sheet boys are caught. You have to start not with the figures, but with the dream. Chances are you'll lose that way— But if you do win by listening to your inner ear, then you can be really free, it's the only way."

"Free for what?" asked Eliot.

"Free to choose your own responsibilities. That isn't easy even when the dream wins. It gets big, it acquires a body, uses people—and they need housing, organization, roofs, desks, lofts, towers, buildings. When it gets too successful, the organization catches up with it, and the organizers think only in numbers. The life drains out of it. But the highest towers in this city were built by people who had dreams. That was the way the whole country was built. And this business of ours was a business of truth and dreams. That's all we had to sell—a vision of America. That's what they wanted out of *Trumpet*, that's where the responsibility was, that's what Ab Pepper gave them, and I let them down—"

"Who?" said Mary.

"Everybody who ever bought this magazine, or was touched by it, or grew up with an idea he never knew came from it. This country was put together not by blood or kin or tradition but by people of every seed and stock in the world who came because they had dreams about tomorrow. I let them down, everyone who was yearning, without knowing it, to find his place in what's happening now and what's going to happen tomorrow and wanted a real vision of his life and couldn't find it with us. I thought I could measure out their appetites, organize my numbers, make a profit, and then be free to put my dreams into the magazines. It didn't work. I didn't listen first inside. So now I have to start all over again."

"Where?" said Mary.

"I have to think that out later," said Warren slowly, "but I want you with me when I start."

Eliot broke the silence. "Hey," he said, "shouldn't I go now? I'm bushed and this is the time for me to go."

"No," said Warren decisively, "this is a hell of a night to be alone. Snow and slush on the street, and the city occupied by the enemy. Come home with us. Mair?"

He turned to Mary, all three of them at the window, and he could not see her face or her expression, only the outline of the body, the white of her face in the dark, the smooth roundness of her cheeks, and the incredible fact that she was still young, and that together both of them could still be young. He waited, unwilling to press her further. She had to come home on her own.

When she spoke, it was completely matter-of-fact.

"There isn't a thing to eat in the icebox. I looked this morning when I cleaned up. But maybe we can find a delicatessen. That's really what I'd like. There isn't an American delicatessen in all of France. . . ."

They moved from the room to the elevators, and out through the lobby. They kicked their way across the marble floor, strewn with press releases, empty except for two men somberly unraveling a complicated vine-tangle of television cables that carpeted the floor.

The snow had turned to a drizzle, Warren noticed, when they came out of the revolving doors. Across the way, a huge white silhouette of a Christmas tree in electric lights blinked and twinkled in the rain. Christmas music filled the air. Down two blocks, the majestic store-front of a department store offered a glistening Christmas display, the cherubim and angels mechanically swinging their staffs and cradles in the beat of the brassy music.

"Joy to the World, The Lord Is Come," blared a brazen horn, amplified by electronic magic from the cavernous entrance to the store. Up and down the avenue the music washed, laving the naked streets and pavements with the exuberant expression of the merchant's goodwill, offering holiday song around the clock night and day to all men—customers or not.

"Joy to the World, The Lord Is Come!" caroled the music in the rain and Warren turned to Mary and Eliot and said, "Stay here in the lobby and I'll get a cab."

"No, let me get it," said Eliot.

"Stay here," said Warren, commanding, "I'm good at this sort of thing."

Warren ran across the street and they could see him waving furiously at a distant cab, out of their vision, which must be approaching.

"He likes to do it," said Mary. "He really does like to make things happen."

The cab had stopped, and Warren was speaking to the driver. Then they could see Warren loping back across the street to fetch them. It was the lope of a man who likes to run.

They ran through the rain, meeting Warren in mid-street.

"Stop a second and listen," he said, halting them.

They listened, and there was nothing but the mechanical amplification of horns.

"I can hear Christmas through that," he said. "How's that for listening?"